Marketing Management in Practice
2006–2007

KU-470-657

The Chartered
Institute of Marketing

Marketing Management in Practice
2006–2007

John Williams and Tony Curtis

ELSEVIER

AMSTERDAM • BOSTON • HEIDELBERG • LONDON • NEW YORK • OXFORD
PARIS • SAN DIEGO • SAN FRANCISCO • SINGAPORE • SYDNEY • TOKYO

Butterworth-Heinemann is an imprint of Elsevier

Butterworth-Heinemann is an imprint of Elsevier
Linacre House, Jordan Hill, Oxford OX2 8DP, UK
30 Corporate Drive, Suite 400, Burlington, MA 01803, USA

First edition 2006

Copyright © 2006, Elsevier Ltd. All rights reserved

No part of this publication may be reproduced, stored in a retrieval system
or transmitted in any form or by any means electronic, mechanical,
photocopying, recording or otherwise without the prior written permission
of the publisher

Permissions may be sought directly from Elsevier's Science and Technology Rights
Department in Oxford, UK: phone: (+44) (0) 1865 843830; fax: (+44) (0) 1865 853333;
e-mail: permissions@elsevier.com. Alternatively you can submit your request
online via the Elsevier website at http://elsevier.com/locate/permissions, and selecting
Obtaining permission to use Elsevier material

Notice
No responsibility is assumed by the publisher for any injury and/or damage to persons
or property as a matter of products liability, negligence or otherwise, or from any use
or operation of any methods, products, instructions or ideas contained in the material
herein. Because of rapid advances in the medical sciences, in particular, independent
verification of diagnoses and drug dosages should be made

British Library Cataloguing in Publication Data
A catalogue record for this book is available from the British Library

Library of Congress Cataloging-in-Publication Data
A catalogue record for this book is available from the Library of Congress

ISBN-13: 978-0-7506-8011-0
ISBN-10: 0-7506-8011-3

For information on all Butterworth-Heinemann publications
visit our website at books.elsevier.com

Typeset by Integra Software Services Pvt. Ltd, Pondicherry, India
www.integra-india.com
Printed and bound in Italy
06 07 08 09 10   10 9 8 7 6 5 4 3 2 1

Working together to grow
libraries in developing countries

www.elsevier.com | www.bookaid.org | www.sabre.org

ELSEVIER   BOOK AID International   Sabre Foundation

Contents

Preface
welcome to the CIM coursebooks

An introduction from the academic development advisor

The authoring team, Elsevier/Butterworth-Heinemann and I have all aimed to rigorously revise and update the coursebook series to make sure that every title is the best possible study aid and accurately reflects the latest CIM syllabus. This has been further enhanced through independent reviews carried out by CIM.

The revisions to the series this year include continued development at – Certificate in Marketing and Professional Diploma in Marketing, as well as at Professional Postgraduate Diploma in Marketing level. In particular we have aimed to develop the assessment support to include some additional support for the assignment route as well as the examination, so we hope you will find this helpful.

The authors and indeed Senior Examiners in the series are commissioned for their CIM course teaching and examining experience, as well as their research into specific curriculum-related areas and their wide general knowledge of the latest thinking in marketing.

We are certain that you will find these coursebooks highly beneficial in terms of the content and assessment opportunities and a study tool that will prepare you for both CIM examinations and continuous/integrative assessment opportunities. They will guide you in a logical and structured way through the detail of the syllabus, providing you with the required underpinning knowledge, understanding and application of theory.

The editorial team and authors wish you every success as you embark upon your studies.

Karen Beamish
Academic Development Advisor

How to use these coursebooks

Everyone who has contributed to this series has been careful to structure the books with the exams in mind. Each unit, therefore, covers an essential part of the syllabus. You need to work through the complete coursebook systematically to ensure that you have covered everything you need to know.

This coursebook is divided into units each containing a selection of the following standard elements:

- *Learning objectives* – tell you what you will be expected to know, having read the unit.
- *Syllabus references* – outline what part of the syllabus is covered in the module.

o *Study guides* – tell you how long the unit is and how long its activities take to do.
o *Questions* are designed to give you practice – they will be similar to those you get in the exam.
o *Answers* (at the end to the book) – give you a suggested format for answering exam questions. *Remember* there is no such thing as a model answer – you should use these examples only as guidelines.
o *Activities* – give you a chance to put what you have learned into practice.
o *Debriefings* (at the end of the book) – shed light on the methodologies involved in the activities.
o *Hints and tips* – are tips from the senior examiner, examiner or author and are designed to help you avoid common mistakes made by previous candidates and give you guidance on improving your knowledge base.
o *Insights* – encourage you to contextualize your academic knowledge by reference to real-life experience.
o *Key definitions* – highlight and explain the key points relevant to that module.
o *Definitions* – may be used for words you must know to pass the exam.
o *Summaries* – cover what you should have picked up from reading the unit.
o *Further study* – provides details of recommended reading in addition to the coursebook.

While you will find that each section of the syllabus has been covered within this text, you might find that the order of some of the topics has been changed. This is because it sometimes makes more sense to put certain topics together when you are studying, even though they might appear in different sections of the syllabus itself. If you are following the reading and other activities, your coverage of the syllabus will be just fine, but don't forget to follow up with trade press reading!

About MarketingOnline

Elsevier/Butterworth-Heinemann offers purchasers of the coursebooks free access to MarketingOnline (www.marketingonline.co.uk), our premier online support engine for the CIM marketing courses. On this site you can benefit from:

o Fully customizable electronic versions of the coursebooks enabling you to annotate, cut and paste sections of text to create your own tailored learning notes.
o The capacity to search the coursebook online for instant access to definitions and key concepts.
o Useful links to e-marketing articles, provided by Dave Chaffey, Director of Marketing Insights Ltd and a leading UK e-marketing consultant, trainer and author.
o A glossary providing a comprehensive dictionary of marketing terms.
o A Frequently Asked Questions (FAQs) section providing guidance and advice on common problems or queries.

Using MarketingOnline

Logging on

Before you can access MarketingOnline you will first need to get a password. Please go to www.marketingonline.co.uk and click on the registration button where you will then find registration instructions for coursebook purchasers. Once you have got your password, you will need to log on using the onscreen instructions. This will give you access to the various functions of the site.

Focus of the module

This module is assessed by either examination or Integrated Project. The module enables students to practise the development and implemention of marketing plans at an operational level in organizations. A key part of the module is working within a team to develop the plan and managing teams, implementing the plan by undertaking marketing activities and projects. Its aim is to assist students in integrating and applying knowledge from all the modules at Professional Diploma in Marketing, particularly as part of a team. The Marketing Management in Practice syllabus requires a broad and practical demonstration of marketing at an operational level and an awareness of the strategic context. It provides an opportunity for students to develop and implement an operational marketing plan, so applying, as part of a team, the theory of research, planning and marketing communications provided in the previous three modules. This module also provides the final assessment of students' ability to create an operational marketing plan. As such, it forms an important measure of the students' ability to meet organizations' requirements of an operational marketer. Marketing Management in Practice is about developing and managing teams to add value to the organization's activities and deliver effective results. Like members of other functions and disciplines within organizations, marketers work towards departmental and broader organizational objectives. They work in teams, both within the marketing function and, importantly, with people in other functions. The context within which marketers are operating is continually changing as a result of both external and internal influences. No organization is detached from international influences, even if the organization does not have to deal with international customers. Organizations source materials from around the globe, access international markets from a desk, compete with other organizations from around the world, and imitate global behaviour. It is therefore appropriate in this module to cover international issues as part of everyday marketing life in organizations. Marketers and marketing managers must be able to work effectively themselves, for example managing time and problem solving. They must also be able to manage and motivate people and teams to produce results. Using Adair's model of leadership, effective team performance is contingent on a balance between:

o The needs of the task.
o The needs of the individuals within the team.
o The maintenance needs of the team as a whole.

The syllabus for the module uses Adair's concept. It provides underpinning theory on managing teams to help with managing individual needs and team needs to get the most from the team. It also provides basic project management techniques to help with managing the task. These two elements provide the final skills and knowledge for marketers to develop and implement marketing plans at an operational level. The remainder of the syllabus for this module is about the development and implementation of an operational marketing plan, including the management of information, communications and human resources. Students should apply (within a marketing team) the theory of marketing research and information, planning and communications covered in the earlier modules. This should be achieved through the vehicle of a project.

Study note © CIM 2005

unit 1
management and marketing roles

Learning objectives

○ To describe the nature of relationships with other functions in organizations operating in a range of different industries and contexts (1.1).

○ To explain the importance of developing and maintaining effective relationships with people in other functions and disciplines (1.2).

The learning objectives are only partly covered in this unit and they are a theme throughout the book. Other units will also be concerned with these objectives, particularly the units that focus on the use of teams and communications.

Glossary

Accountability – The extent to which individuals and managers are held responsible for the outcome of the decisions they make.

Autonomy – Independence to make decisions within a decentralized working environment, where decision-making is passed down from the top of the organization to the lower levels.

Fads – Fashions that enter quickly, are adopted with great zeal, peak early and decline very fast.

Flat hierarchy – An organizational structure that provides a wide span of control within only a few layers of organizational hierarchy.

Global firm – A firm that by operating in more than one country gains R&D, production, marketing and financial advantages in its costs and reputation that are not available to purely domestic competitors.

Global organization – A form of international organization whereby top corporate management and staff plan worldwide manufacturing or operational facilities, marketing policies, financial flows and logistical systems. The global operating unit reports directly to the chief executive, not to an international divisional head.

1

International division – A form of international marketing organization in which the division handles all of the firm's international activities. Marketing, manufacturing, research, planning and specialist staff are organized into operating units according to geography or product groups, or as an international subsidiary responsible for its own sales and profitability.

Marketing database – An organized set of data about individual customers or prospects that can be used to generate and qualify customer needs, sell products and services and maintain customer relationships.

Market research – The process of (1) analysing marketing opportunities; (2) selecting target markets; (3) developing the marketing mix; (4) managing the marketing effort.

Marketing mix – The set of controllable tactical marketing tools – product, price, place and promotion – that the firm blends to produce the response it wants in the target market.

Market segment – A group of consumers who respond in a similar way to a given set of marketing stimuli.

Market segmentation – Dividing a market into distinct groups of buyers with different needs, characteristics or behaviour, who might require separate products or marketing mixes.

Management

Introduction to the book

The coursebook is targeted at assisting you to pass the Marketing Management in Practice examination. The main focus of the CIM Advanced Certificate Course Marketing Management in Practice is on the development and implementation of marketing plans at an operational level in organizations. The Marketing Management in Practice unit helps students to develop and implement marketing plans at an operational level in organizations. A key part of this unit is working within a team to develop the plan and managing teams implementing the plan by undertaking marketing activities and projects. Its aim is to assist students in integrating and applying knowledge from all the units at Professional Diploma, particularly as part of a team. This unit also forms the summative assessment for the Advanced Certificate.

The syllabus is covered in eight units and these cover the main areas that contribute to effective marketing management. A marketing-oriented company needs to align its distinctive competencies with market opportunities but to do this effectively requires a team effort.

CIM Professional Marketing Standards

These set out a competency framework that can be used as the definition of marketing practice and the requirements of organizations that employ marketers. The framework has been developed in partnership with large organizations including multinationals, and is based on competencies defined through marketing job descriptions. This framework defines what marketers in organizations actually do – identifying the knowledge and understanding skills.

What form do the CIM Professional Marketing Standards take?

The Standards are an easy reference matrix, combining six key marketing roles and four job levels. The marketing roles established through research are:

1. Research and analysis
2. Planning (at an operational marketing level or at a strategic level)
3. Managing brands
4. Implementing marketing programmes (of various types)
5. Measuring marketing effectiveness
6. Managing marketing people.

Marketing orientation

Marketing as a management philosophy and orientation, espoused and practised throughout the organization, is being seen increasingly as critical to the success of any organization. Customer focus needs to be shared by the whole organization and should not be seen as just the responsibility of the marketing department. A marketing orientation involves multiple departments or functions sharing information about customers and engaging in activities designed to meet customers' needs. However, whilst a marketing orientation is seen as increasingly important, marketing as a stand-alone function in the typical organization appears to be more in decline.

A key element of a market orientation is intelligence-gathering about customer needs and preferences and what influences them. This should involve people throughout the organization but channelled for analysis towards a particular part of it. This may be carried out by a marketing department in larger organizations. A business that has a marketing orientation sees the needs of customers and potential customers to drive all strategic decisions. Everyone in an organization needs to be aware of the marketing message, visions and goals of the company. Every contact with customers and potential customers, whether it is through advertising, personal contact or other means, should carry a consistent message about the company and product. In effect, every employee is a sales person, and every employee is a customer service representative. Kohli and Jaworski (1990) define market orientation in terms of three dimensions:

1. The generation of market information about needs of customers and external environmental factors
2. The dissemination of such information among organizational functions
3. The development and implementation of strategies in response to the information.

Different orientations to the market

There are three main alternatives to adopting a marketing orientation. These are:

1. Sales orientation
2. Production orientation
3. Product orientation.

3

Sales orientation

Some businesses see their main problem as selling more of the product or services already available with them. A sales-orientated business may pay little attention to customer needs and wants and does not try particularly hard to create suitable products or services.

Production orientation

A production-orientated business is said to be mainly concerned with making as many units as possible, aimed at maximizing profitability through exploiting economies of scale. The needs of customers are secondary compared with the need to increase output. Such an approach is likely to be most effective when a business operates in very high growth markets or where the potential for economies of scale is significant.

Product orientation

Products may be launched as fully up to date but, by failing to consider changing technological developments or changes in consumer tastes, a product-orientated business may find that its products start to lose ground to competitors.

The structure of an organization can be a barrier to success if it separates one department from another. In some organizations, sales, marketing and customer service are organized as a team but finance, human resource management, research and development, production, purchasing and management all affect the marketing effort. To ensure that everyone is working to the same broad objectives as a team requires good communication and an awareness and respect for each other's contributions. The book looks at these key issues. Unit 1 introduces the broad subject of management in the context of marketing and marketing management. The diverse roles of marketing management and the various ways in which the marketing function is organized are discussed. Guidance on examination preparation will focus on the examination techniques that will maximize your probability of passing.

Managing people and teams

This element provides the underpinning knowledge required for the selection, development and maintenance of effective marketing teams. Marketing teams are operating in an organizational and global context, and how different organizations adopt different approaches to marketing depends on their context and culture. Key Skills – 'Working with others' and 'Improving one's own knowledge and performance'.

Managing marketing projects and activities

Managing the planning and performance of a marketing task by a team requires skills in planning, scheduling, directing, motivating and monitoring. The techniques of project management equip marketing managers to manage marketing activities and projects effectively.

Managing knowledge and delivering market research projects

Knowledge management is about people. People need to be motivated and enthused to share and exchange knowledge. This cannot be done by simply presenting them with a piece of IT equipment. It requires a cultural norm of open communication, informing and sharing knowledge, and motivating and rewarding knowledge-sharing that benefits the business.

Developing and implementing marketing plans

This element requires effective teamwork and a good understanding of the marketing planning process and techniques to produce successful outcomes.

Awareness of similarities and differences

Examples from one sector may not always be appropriate for understanding what happens in other sectors. There are stereotypes about what happens in both the 'private' and the 'public' sectors from within each sector. It is important to go beyond the stereotypes to look for similarities as well as differences. Not all private sector management is good and public sector management bad and vice versa.

Fads and fashions

Writing about management is prone to fads and fashions, with management gurus often very influential in disseminating ideas about what seems to be working. However, not all popular management ideas are effective. Some management ideas have had a negative effect on some organizations. In the early 1990s, the Chief Economist of Morgan Stanley argued strongly in favour of downsizing, saying that it was a cure for companies' problems. By 1997 he had changed his mind and argued, on the contrary, it could be a recipe for disaster. In 1982, Tom Peters wrote *In Search Of Excellence*, a book that identified 43 successful companies and gave reasons for their success over 20 years. However, many of the companies, including the computer company IBM ran into problems not long after the book was published. Peters apologized, saying that 'there are no excellent companies' and now says of his writing 'Some of my stuff is wrong. Some stuff is right, but I hope all of it is provocative.' This shows that case histories of organizations date rapidly as the world changes and old business books often include examples of companies that now don't exist or have experienced major problems and management fads come and go faster than ever.

What is management?

'Management' is an inclusive term that is used in a variety of ways. Generally, it is the process of planning, organizing, leading, co-ordinating and controlling aspects of an organization's resources to achieve organizational goals. It is the organizational process that includes strategic planning, setting objectives, managing resources, deploying the human and financial assets needed to achieve objectives, and measuring results. A manager assesses an organization's goals and resources, formulates a plan of action and implements it.

Management functions are not limited to managers and supervisors. Every member of an organization has some management and reporting functions as part of their job. Different managers have different styles that are formed by their past experience, the nature of the tasks they have to undertake, the context they work in, and the expectations, capabilities and motivation of the people they work with. Studies of management behaviour show that there are wide variations both for the same manager from 1 week to another and between managers in similar jobs. There are also wide differences between managers' jobs in the same country as well as across countries. Individual influences such as gender, age, ethnic background, education, career experience and personality may also have an impact but there is no conclusive evidence about whether and how these factors influence management behaviour. The use of high performance work teams can result in changes to a manager's role. A manager may be required to adapt to change, provide vision and principles and align people towards a purpose, set direction and strategy. As teams take on more and more responsibility, a manager's focus may shift from controlling to motivating and inspiring.

The following case study provides an example of a modern conception of management.

Case study

Premier Travel Inn

Management Culture

Ours is a non-hierarchical culture. So although our managers provide strong direction to our teams, they also listen to each and every person within those teams. Above all, they pay very close attention to the needs of their guests. And that's why they're at the heart of our success.

Practical, analytical and charismatic, they're helping us become an ever more nimble organization, which can move fast to meet customers' changing priorities.

Premier Travel Inn's managers foster a fun atmosphere, where everyone is eager to do better and better. Join us, and you'll encourage a sense of friendly competition, ensuring people have a real incentive to continually improve their performance. Everyone will be proud to be a part of your team. And you'll be proud to lead them.

 ## Activity 1.1

The above case study identifies a number of key themes in modern conceptions of management, for example fostering a non-hierarchical culture, customer focus, team working, listening, being responsive and fast-moving. However, whilst this may be the theory of how management should or could be practised, the issue for all organizations is whether any of the theory is actually translated into practice.

How would you characterize management in your own organization? Is it like this or is there a gap between the theory and the practice? If the latter, why does this happen?

Studying management

Key issues to bear in mind when studying management are: firstly, although it is possible to identify trends that are occurring in some large well-known companies, this does not necessarily mean that they are occurring everywhere in all sizes and types of companies. It is also important to be aware of cultural differences when thinking about management practices.

Culture

What happens in one country may not be easily applied to other countries because it is difficult to transplant all the social and cultural conditions that make a particular initiative or innovation a success. In recent years, there have been many attempts to use Japanese management techniques with varying degrees of success. Much management writing is based on what happens in companies in the USA and the UK, so it is important to be aware of cultural differences and how other countries do things. What works in one context may not work as well in a different context.

When Parker Pen devised advertisements for its ballpoint pen they were meant to say 'It won't leak in your pocket and embarrass you.' However, in Spanish 'embararzar' means pregnant, not embarrassed and the advertisement was translated as 'It won't leak in your pocket and make you pregnant.' In Chinese, the name Coca-Cola was translated as Ke-kou-ke-la to make it sound similar to the original. However, after printing its signs, the company discovered that, in at least one dialect the phrase means 'female horse stuffed with wax'. In Taiwan, the slogan 'Come alive with the Pepsi Generation' was translated as 'Pepsi will bring your ancestors back from the dead.'

The following example demonstrates how careful advertisers need to be when choosing content for advertisements and how important it is to seek advice from sources that can give sound advice about cultural issues.

In a reminder about cultural sensitivity, China's State Administration for Radio, Film and Television pulled a Nike television commercial from the airwaves, citing rules that require commercials to 'protect national honour and traditional Chinese culture'. The advertisement is part of an international marketing campaign for Nike Basketball that uses symbolism from traditional Chinese culture including dragons, stone lions, goddesses, Yin Yang and Buddhas. The lesson: Be sensitive to national pride when picking advertising and media content. The Nike 'Chamber of Fear' advertisement, created by agency Wieden + Kennedy, showed National Basketball Association star LeBron James triumphing over animated, allegorical figures representing 'Hype', 'Temptation', 'Haters', 'Complacency' and 'Self-doubt'. The figures include a martial arts villain, two floating Chinese women throwing money and two dragon-like monsters. The People's Republic of China government said the advertisement offended many Chinese viewers, because it featured a foreigner handily defeating Chinese challengers and blasphemed national practices and cultures.

Source: Adapted from *China Business Review*, January–February 2005.

Language is only one aspect of culture. The term refers to a complete way of life of a people: the shared attitudes, values, goals and practices that characterize a group; their customs, art, literature, religion, philosophy and so on; the pattern of learned and shared behaviour among the members of a group. The following insight provides an example of how attitudes and approaches to management can vary across cultures.

Insight

Comparing management differences

Mexico, Canada and the United States

Doing business in Mexico is very different than in Canada and the US. The values, social practices, managerial methods and belief systems of the Mexican worker and Mexican manager are different. The major aspects of management differences are described in the following comparison table:

Management Comparisons

Aspect	Mexico	Canada/USA
Work/Leisure	Works to live. Leisure considered essential for full life. Money is for enjoying life.	Lives to work. Leisure seen as reward for hard work. Money often end in itself
Direction/Delegation	Traditional manager is autocratic. Younger managers starting to accept and delegate responsibility. Subordinates used to being assigned tasks, not authority.	Managers delegate responsibility and authority. Executive seeks responsibility and accepts accountability.
Theory vs. Practice	Basically theoretical mind. Practical implementation often difficult.	Basically pragmatic mind. Action-oriented problem-solving approach.
Control	Still not fully accepted. Sensitive to being "checked upon." Sensitive to giving and receiving critical feed-back.	Universally accepted and practiced. Critical feed-back expected and discussed.
Loyalty	Mostly loyal to superior (person rather than organization). Beginnings of self-loyalty.	Mainly self-loyalty. Performance motivated by ambition.
Staffing	Family and friends are preferred due to trustworthiness. Promotions based on loyalty to superior.	Relatives usually barred – No nepotism here! Promotion based on performance.
Competition	Avoids personal competition; favours harmony at work.	Enjoys proving self in competitive situations.
Training and Development	Training highly theoretical. Few structured programs.	Training concrete, specific. Usually structured programs.
Time	Relative concept. Deadlines flexible. Mañana can mean 'not today'. What is happening now is more important than the future.	Literal imperative. Deadlines and commitments are firm. What is happening now is only important if it contributes towards the future.
Planning	Mostly short term because of uncertain environment and sense of 'now'.	Mostly long -term in predicted environment.

Source: Adapted from *Management in Two Cultures – Bridging the gap between US and Mexico*, by Eva Kras (1995), Intercultural Press.

However, its is improtant not to fall. into the trap of trying to be aware of cultural differences and ending up peddling stereotypes of similarities and differences between cultures. There may be as many differences within a cultrue as there are between them.

Activity 1.2

With increasing globalization there are more opportunities for working in other countries. The cost of sending employees and their families to foreign countries is high. To be effective, managers need to understand and be sensitive to the cultural values, norms and practices of the host country. Choose a country and identify what you might need to prepare yourself for a successful transition to your new assignment. What sources of information would you use?

Management roles

Henry Mintzberg analysed the nature of managerial work and concluded that management consisted of a mass of fragmented activities, constant interruption, pressure for immediate answers and reliance on word-of-mouth messages. Managers value 'soft' information, often acquired through gossip, hearsay and speculation. Consequently, important information for the organization is held not necessarily in the memory of its computers but in the minds of its managers. Mintzberg offered a view of management based on 'roles'.

INTERPERSONAL	**Figurehead**	Performs ceremonial and symbolic duties such as greeting visitors, signing legal documents.
	Leader	Sets the strategic direction of the organization, motivates managers and other staff.
	Liaison	Maintains information links both inside and outside the organization.
INFORMATIONAL	**Monitor**	Seeks and receives information, scans periodicals and reports, maintains personal contacts.
	Disseminator	Forwards information to other organization members, sends memos and reports.
	Spokesperson	Transmits information to outsiders through speeches, reports and memos.
DECISIONAL	**Entrepreneur**	Initiates improvement projects, identifies new ideas, delegates responsibility to others.
	Disturbance Handler	Takes corrective action during disputes or crises, resolves conflicts among subordinates, adapts to environmental crises.
	Resource Allocator	Decides who gets resources, scheduling, budgeting, sets priorities.
	Negotiator	Represents department during negotiation of contracts, sales, purchases, budgets.

Figure 1.1 Mintzberg's managerial roles
Source: Mintzberg (1973)

Each of the ten roles covers a different aspect of managerial work. The ten roles form an integrated whole but different managers are likely to give greater prominence to different aspects of the job. For example, sales managers tend to spend relatively more time in their interpersonal roles, while production managers tend to give relatively more attention to the decisional roles. Mintzberg found that the amount of time spent in the three sets of roles varied with the level of the manager. For example, first-line supervisory positions are likely to have more decisional roles (at a day-to-day operational level). Senior managers spend more time on interpersonal roles. Middle managers tend to be more occupied with informational roles. Roles will also change with culture and organizational size.

Over the past two decades there has been a change in management practices in many organizations. This shift is based on a greater focus on customers' needs and aspirations, and engaging the commitment of all employees to meet those needs effectively. Typically, the organizational boundaries that used to exist between people are being replaced with internal networks that emphasize team working. Enterprises are being transformed from hierarchical organizations with simple jobs, to less hierarchical, more decentralized and network-oriented organizations with more complex jobs. Charles Handy in his book *The Empty Raincoat* (1990) has written about the future 'Shamrock' organization that would concentrate on fewer full-time people at the core whilst others had to develop 'portfolio' lives, a mix of different bits and pieces of part-time work. However, he felt that people were not being properly prepared for this kind of future.

 ## Activity 1.3

Write some brief notes summarizing what you think 'management' means. What is your experience of management? – As someone who has been managed or when you have managed something or someone. Think of the best manager that you have encountered – what characteristics did they possess? Who was the worst manager you have encountered and what were their characteristics? What conclusions do you draw from this exercise about what makes an effective manager?

Marketing management

CIM's definition of marketing is 'The management process which identifies, anticipates and satisfies customer requirements profitability.' This process varies depending on factors such as the size of the organization, the sector in which it is located, the type of work role performed by the manager and the career experience that the marketing manager brings with them. Generally speaking, the smaller the organization the more multifaceted are the roles of the marketing manager.

Marketing management is the application of marketing techniques and the analysis, planning, implementation and control of programmes to create, build and maintain exchanges with target markets. The marketing manager has the task of influencing the level, timing and make-up of demand in a way that will achieve the objectives of the organization.

The activities that a marketing manager may be involved in are:

- Understanding the economic structure of an industry or sector
- Identifying target markets
- Identifying segments within a target market
- Identifying the marketing strategy which best fits the organization and its goals
- Marketing research to develop profiles (demographic, psychographic and behavioural) of core customers
- Understanding competitors and their products
- Developing new products
- Establishing environmental scanning mechanisms to detect opportunities and threats
- Understanding an organization's strengths and weaknesses
- Auditing customers' experience of a brand

○ Developing marketing strategies using the marketing mix variables of price, product, distribution and promotion

○ Creating a sustainable competitive advantage

○ Understand where brands need to be in the future, and writing marketing plans to achieve goals and targets

○ Establishing management information systems to monitor progress and, if necessary, adjust the process.

One of the main responsibilities of a marketing manager is to identify the target market for products and services, devise strategies and select media that will reach and attract the target market. A marketing manager needs to work with a range of people inside and outside the organization on all aspects of marketing. Inside the company the marketing manager may work with the sales force, promotion manager, product development teams and market research. Outside the company this may involve advertising agencies, consultants and market research organizations. This means that marketing managers need to have good people skills. A marketing manager's responsibilities include large-scale customer relationship management, utilizing skills in customer segmentation, customer loyalty, customer satisfaction, database marketing and direct marketing. These jobs may require market research skills or they may be the responsibility of a market research manager.

Recent changes and future trends in Marketing Management

Across organizations there is more emphasis on developing marketing strategies rather than just using marketing tactics. The focus is on building brands through a coordinated integrated marketing strategy that involves all points of contact between the company and the public.

Other key features of change are:

○ Recognizing the lifetime value of a customer and retaining existing customers are key driving forces rather than just a short-term focus on profit.

○ Analysing how the whole value chain contributes to meeting the end customers' needs.

○ Segmenting markets using a range of variables, such as customer segment and behavioural variables such as usage rate, loyalty or benefit.

○ Measuring performance by financial, strategic and marketing metrics instead of a sole emphasis on financial metrics.

○ An emphasis on satisfying all stakeholders not just shareholders.

○ Everyone in an organization undertakes some marketing, not just a specialist team.

○ Greater use of cross-functional teams rather than functional divisions.

The following case study demonstrates how some organizations are changing to reflect the growing importance of technology in marketing.

Case study

Marketing organization of the future

JetBlue, the low-cost airline, just moved to a new chain-of-command. The technology department now reports to the marketing department. It is not the only one with such a structure. Chemical giant DuPont moved its technology department from the operations and services division to marketing and sales. Toy maker Mattel has long had IT reporting to marketing. Placing the IT department under the auspices of marketing and sales helps ensure that technology will be used to solve customer issues. Additionally, technology is becoming an increasingly important component of marketing. Just look at CRM, campaign management, database marketing and more. On the other hand, such a reporting structure has the technologists up in arms. Technology serves all parts of an organization as well as customers. Many marketing personnel don't understand technology. Infrastructural upgrades may have to compete with advertising for funding. In many ways, this argument misses the point. It reflects the hierarchical, mass-economy view of the past, where companies were organized with command-and-control structures. Today, companies should be organized around customers, not functions, products or regions. IT then becomes a support infrastructure, reporting not to an individual, but, in effect, reporting to a particular customer or set of customers. Funding then becomes not a competition between, say, advertising and new PCs, but rather a reflection of what is required so the company can keep profitable customers.

http://fusionbrand.blogs.com/fusionbrand/2004/06/marketing_organ.html

Marketing titles

Marketing titles and positions vary considerably along with the particular responsibilities that accompany them. They span a range of positions, including marketing director, marketing manager, sales manager, advertising manager, promotion manager and public relations manager. A marketing director is responsible for directing overall marketing policy. Marketing managers work with service or product development, market research and others to develop detailed marketing strategies.

Marketing departments

Some writers argue for the value of the marketing function beyond an organization-wide market orientation, suggesting that the marketing function can and should coexist with a market orientation and that the effectiveness of a market orientation depends on the presence of strong function that includes marketing. In this view the marketing function facilitates the link between the customer and various key processes within the firm. On the basis of an extensive study of managers across a wide range of business types and six different functional affiliations, Moorman and Rust (1999) drew the following conclusions:

1. Marketing is best viewed as the function that manages connections between the organization and the customer. The primary connections may be viewed as the customer–product, the customer–service delivery, and the customer–financial accountability connections.
2. The extent to which the marketing function manages these connections contributes to financial performance, customer relationship performance and new product performance, beyond the impact of an organization-wide marketing orientation.
3. The marketing function can improve its contribution to the firm by expanding its scope beyond the traditional customer–product connection to include more emphasis on service delivery and financial accountability.

Many marketing, sales and services departments still operate in a traditional, fragmented fashion with various advertising agencies, direct-marketing firms, market research companies, data wizards, PR spin doctors, corporate communications people and brand marketing. The traditional marketing structure can be slow moving. Some companies, for example, Starbucks have created fluid marketing organizations to enable them to spot opportunities, allocate resources quickly and move people in and out of teams according to their skills. All members are responsible for identifying opportunities and should receive the tools, the technology and the leadership needed to achieve results.

A marketing department should act as a guide and lead the company's other departments in developing, producing, fulfilling and servicing products or services for their customers. The marketing department should have a better understanding of the market and customer needs, but should not act independently of product development or customer service.

It is important to gather information from many people within the company. Not only does providing input help the rest of the company understand and support the marketing efforts, it also provides some invaluable insights into what customers want and new ideas that may have slipped past the rest of the company.

For example, customer service personnel will have great insights into customer opinions and needs. Marketing is a team effort and whilst individuals may have their own goals and priorities if they don't also consider the goals of the company it may hinder efforts and make carefully planned marketing efforts fail. A marketing department studies the market and the customers, determines the best way to reach those customers and works with the rest of the company to help determine the new product needs of the market and represent the company in a consistent voice.

Working across organizational boundaries

Marketing management has an important role in working across organizational boundaries to help prepare managers to develop strategies for their products and services, and incorporate marketing into the corporate strategy. This means that marketing managers need to work with, for example, colleagues from Human Resources and Finance to deal with recruitment and the reward of staff as well as securing and monitoring budgets and expenditure. If a company has introduced a human resource management approach as opposed to a 'personnel' approach, a manager may find that many of the responsibilities that used to belong to the personnel department have been pushed across to line managers.

Insight

A survey on Marketing in British organizations by McKinsey & Co. found that the role of marketing was at its most sophisticated in the Business-to-Consumer area (B2C) and the lowest in the Business-to-Business area (B2B). The primary role of marketing for a quarter of all sectors' respondents was promoting sales. But B2C gave greater weight to building brands (28 per cent). Many organizations ran a marketing function without a specific department – 47 per cent for either B2C or for B2B operations, where only one type of marketing operation is found in an organization, and 39 per cent where 'Both' operations are carried out within the same organization. A specific marketing department was found in 41 per cent of B2C organizations, but in only 15 per cent of B2B and 29 per cent of 'Both'. Almost a third (31 per cent) of all B2B respondents combined marketing with sales or other functions, compared with 23 per cent of 'Both' and only 6 per cent B2C. Less than 10 per cent of respondents stated that marketing does not really exist as a function within their organizations.

Just over half the respondents showed that the most critical change required in their organizations was the need for enhanced collaboration between marketing and other functions. Nearly half of each sector stated that marketing worked with other functions 'most of the time' (45 per cent B2C, 47 per cent both, 46 per cent B2B), and slightly less specified 'all the time' (32 per cent B2C, 29 per cent both, 29 per cent B2B).

Source: McKinsey *Marketing Practice* (2002).

The extract from the survey shows that there is a lot of work to be done to improve cross-organization working and, in particular, the way that marketing works with other functions in the organization. This is looked at in greater depth in Unit 3.

Are there any particular difficulties in how different functions relate to or communicate with each other in your organization?

Are there any particularly successful strategies deployed for overcoming communication problems?

Argos is one of the UK's largest chain stores owned by GUS plc. In the late 1990s a new boss set out to improve its performance by changing the business culture, that is the values and beliefs shared across the organization. The new culture he wanted to promote was one that was based on:

○ Good customer service
○ Close teamwork
○ Managers being given more responsibility
○ All staff showing respect for each other
○ All staff wanting to better compete and to improve the business.

The sense in which all employees feel that they work for one organization rather than a particular department or function in an organization is a key aspect of organizational success. A feeling that we are 'all in it together' based on good relationships is likely to be a more effective approach than one where there are a lot of internal rivalries and destructive competition.

 ## Activity 1.4

> How is marketing activity organized in your organization? How would you describe collaboration? Is it successful? If so, what factors contribute to its success? If not, how could it be improved? The following extract written by a marketing manager shows some of the diversity that exists in marketing jobs.

Insight

I am a marketing manager in a services company. There is a flat hierarchical structure, with a CEO, a layer of senior management and then the rest of us. We are a small team of self-managers and are encouraged to manage our own career-development. We are not issued with job descriptions to demonstrate that the role is dynamic and evolving. We are also encouraged to develop our roles individually rather than have our workload dictated by the management. Our jobs have 'breadth' rather than 'depth' which makes us less specialized but more able to handle *ad hoc* enquiries across different areas and we are each required to turn our hand to whatever situation arises.

Question 1.1

Do you have a job description? – Is it useful or does it gather dust? – Does it accurately reflect what you do? Is it reviewed regularly? – If you do not have one, are there any problems that arise because of it?

The following insight describes the organizational structure of Tesco.

Tesco

We are a very flat organization in Tesco. There are just six levels from me to the front line, and there are only five rungs, therefore, on the ladder to climb. There are no great hierarchies or job titles to complicate things and to keep people in their place. It is a nice simple structure that is designed to be open and to encourage talent to rise to the top. At any one time, we are preparing one in ten people to come through, and people do come through from the bottom rung right away to the top of the organization. Secondly, we have a very simple management tool that helps keep us on track. If you went backstage in any one of our stores, you would find a big chart on the wall. We call it the Tesco Steering Wheel. Why? It looks like a wheel, and it helps us to steer the business. It is broken down into a number of performance measures which we monitor and review regularly. It is a simple system, so that every time they go in, staff can see at a glance how they and their store are doing, their particular contribution and the difference it is making. It is a very simple idea, but it is one I can tell you helps everybody in the business.

Terry Leahy, Chief Executive of TESCO, Speech to the Institute of Directors (2005).

Another issue that is important for considering working relationships is how the marketing function relates to professionals. Professionals tend to value autonomy and having control over their working life. It is not always easy to incorporate them into marketing activities. Throughout the 1980s and 1990s, there were major changes to public sector organization and management. A key aspect of this change was the emergence of a 'new managerialism', that is the importation of modern private sector management techniques which challenged some established principles and practices within the public sector. It was seen as a threat to the traditional dominance of professionalism and professionals. However, the following case study from Serco – a private sector company with a number of contracts in the public sector – shows that some of the stereotypical views that are held about the differences between the private and the public sector are rather simplistic.

Service managers do not surrender their commitment to public service when they make the transition from the public to the private sector. These people retain their strong sense of vocation when they take up the management of public services under contract. When it came to differences, contract managers mentioned three significant factors:

1. The relative lack of bureaucracy in the private sector. Whether it was in the recruitment and management of people, budgeting and financial accountability, introducing new ideas or responding to service failings, managers reported that they had greater freedom and were able to implement change more quickly.

2. Closer management of staff: One of the consequences of increased autonomy was greater freedom to build their own management teams, tailored to the particular challenges facing them in the service in question.
3. Personal accountability: Service managers feel more accountable in a contractual environment. They are held responsible for outcomes rather than just processes, and this requires them to have an intimate knowledge of the service in question.

Source: The Serco Institute (2005).

Organizational culture

Organizational culture is an amalgamation of the values and beliefs of the people in an organization. It can be felt in the implicit rules and expectations of behaviour in an organization where, even though the rules are not formally written down, employees know what is expected of them. It is usually set by management whose decisions on policy usually set up the culture of the organization. The organizational culture usually has values and beliefs that support the organizational goals.

The culture of the organization, if it is positive and helpful can help to motivate staff or at least prevent them from becoming dissatisfied. If the climate does not satisfy the needs of staff, then it will probably cause dissatisfaction and so people would become less inclined to want to work towards achieving organizational goals. The following case study gives an indication of how one retailer interprets organizational culture.

Homebase is part of the Argos Retail Group, serving 1.5 million customers a year. The culture of an organization is the way that it and its people behave. There are clear guidelines which help to motivate staff. Homebase's values are:

o Good service
o We put the customer first
o We succeed through teamwork
o We make it easy
o I make a difference
o The customer is our No.1 priority
o Look after our customers and they will look after us
o Everything we do must benefit the customer
o Treat customers as you would expect to be treated yourself
o Listen to our customers and go the extra mile.

We never want any customer to have a wasted journey. Empowerment means giving greater responsibility to staff. It is a good motivator. Homebase has a teamwork approach with regular meetings called 'huddles' where team-building activities and two-way communication take place. Empowerment encourages independent thinking and decision-making. Staff should think 'I make a difference' and can be rewarded with Homebase Recognition Awards of bronze – star, silver – hero and gold – legend. Gold is the ultimate award with only 16 awarded across the company.

Interpreting and understanding organizational culture is important for managers because cultural assumptions can both enable and constrain what organizations are able to do.

Charles Handy reporting the work of Harrison suggests that organizations can be classified in terms of four cultures. He felt that every organization was a different mix of the same four basic cultures.

Power culture

Handy describes this as the Zeus Culture, after the head of the gods, where an organization is dominated by the personality and power of one person, often the owner. The visual image is of a spider's web with power residing at the centre controlled by a single owner or a small group. Power and influence spread out from a central figure or group. The organization is dependent on the ability and judgement of the central power base.

Role culture

Handy calls this the Apollo Culture, after the god of harmony and order, and represents a culture dominated by rules and procedures. Work within and between departments is controlled formally by procedures, role descriptions, lines of authority and well-defined systems. Matters for decision have to be taken up the line and co-ordination is at the top by the senior management group. Role cultures tend to develop in relatively stable environments. The civil service and the IBM of the late 1980s are examples of a role culture.

Task culture

This is called the Athena Culture, after the warrior goddess. It is a culture that is suited to project work and is typical of consultancies and advertising agencies. The visual image used by Handy is a net with its vertical and horizontal lines and, not surprisingly, network and matrix organizations are examples of this kind of culture. People with the necessary skills, sometimes from different levels of the organization, are brought together to work on specific projects. The teams can be formed for specific purposes, disbanded, reformed and reconfigured according to the nature of the work that needs to be undertaken.

Person culture

Handy calls this the Dionysius Culture, where the individual has the freedom to develop their own ideas in the way they want such as in an artist's studio or a traditional university. In this type of culture it is difficult to manage individuals since there is very little structure and individuals are relatively autonomous to carry out their work in the way that they want. Some consultants, barristers' chambers and universities are examples of such a culture. Typically, individuals work on their own but they do find administrative support useful.

Every organization is different from each other but they are all a mix of the same four basic cultures. The problem is that some organizations get 'stuck' in one of them instead of mixing all four. Every organization manifests patterns of member behaviours and values which together may be said to form a 'culture'. Organizational leaders may intervene to influence and shape what they perceive to be a less advantageous culture in their organization. The assumption is that organizational effectiveness and decision-making processes are substantially influenced by cultural expression, for example attitudes and responses of employees, styles of management and so on but culture is also a dynamic, evolving process.

Activity 1.5

A Monochronic/Polychronic Self Test

This instrument is designed to assist you in understanding your personal cultural preferences, with respect to both work style and management style. Choose the letter that best describes your preferred opinion or behaviour in an organizational situation. The letters A through E are a scale with C representing the midpoint between the two extremes. As best as you can, determine where your opinion or behaviour would occur most consistently on the scale for each of the situations below.

1. When working on a project, you find it most effective to:

A	B	C	D	E
Work through each part of the project in an orderly fashion				Work on many different parts of the project at the same time

2. You work most effectively in an organization when:

A	B	C	D	E
You are seldom interrupted by and rarely interact with other employees				You are constantly interacting with and interrupted for discussions by other employees

3. When you are assigned a project that is due at a specific time, you:

A	B	C	D	E
Establish a specific plan for achieving the project by the deadline, if not before				Create a flexible plan which may or may not accomplish the project by the exact deadline

4. Organizational information is most efficiently shared and disseminated through:

A	B	C	D	E
Detailed or written memos or internal communication systems				Informal interoffice verbal communication among employees

5. To be successful, an organization must focus most on:

A	B	C	D	E
Reaching projected goals and accomplishing task objectives				Developing each worker and establishing quality relationships among employees

6. The best project results are produced when everyone agrees:

A	B	C	D	E
To a detailed plan which is executed and completed according to the original design				To an informal plan that is adjusted as the project proceeds

7. When you want to discuss something with a co-worker whose office door is closed, you would probably:

A	B	C	D	E
Walk away, assuming he or she does not want to be disturbed				Knock, open the door, and ask for a few minutes to discuss your concern

8. With respect to your valued possessions, you:

A	B	C	D	E
Almost never lend them to anyone				Lend them often and easily

9. When you are late for a scheduled appointment, you feel that:

A	B	C	D	E
You should apologize for being late				You should not apologize, assuming that he/she will understand that something important came up

10. In general, after you no longer serve a valued client, you tend to:

A	B	C	D	E
Lose contact with him/her because of your busy schedule and/or you no longer work with him/her directly				Stay in communication to know how his/her life is progressing

11. A sign of a good manager is his/her ability to:

A	B	C	D	E
Solicit employee input, but use executive decision-making where vital business and policy issues are concerned				Extensively involve employees in deciding vitally important business and policy-making issues

12. Your business presentation style tends to be:

A	B	C	D	E
Orderly, sequential and logical				Flexible, spontaneous and adaptable

13. Businesses run best when job responsibilities are:

A	B	C	D	E
Fixed and uniquely adapted to each employee				Constantly changing and overlapping between employees

14. In a fast-paced, decentralized, information-oriented society, important business matters:

A	B	C	D	E
Require immediate and decisive decision-making				Demand sufficient time for discussion, consensus and deliberation

15. The most successful business ventures are dependent upon:

A	B	C	D	E
An in-depth analysis and thorough discussion of all information relevant to the transaction				The people involved and their ability to work together effectively

16. The most effective way to contribute to an organization is to:

A	B	C	D	E
Specialize in one area and become an expert on a subject				Accumulate cross-disciplinary knowledge in as many areas as possible

Scoring Instructions

For each letter chosen, A, B, C, D or E, write the number of times it was circled next to the appropriate letter in the spaces below, and multiply this number by the figure shown. For example, if B was circled five (5) times, write 5 in the blank space beside B and complete the multiplication, $5 \times 2 = 10$. Finally, add the products in this column to obtain a total numerical score.

A———— × 0 = ————

B———— × 2 = ————

C———— × 5 = ————

D———— × 8 = ————

E———— × 10 = ————

TOTAL

Interpretation of scores

0–40 Highly Monochronic = A to B range on the scale.

These individuals approach work with specific and detailed plans and schedules, to which they are highly committed. The realization of business objectives is their highest priority, and personal relationships are one dimension among many towards this end. These individuals prefer specialized and unique work responsibilities, private working conditions and short-term, formal work relationships. They are inclined to communicate impersonally and in low context. Their decision-making tends to be individualistic, timely and based on their position of influence within the organization. The essence of leadership is the individualistic vision of the future.

41–80 Moderately Monochronic = B to C range on the scale.

These individuals demonstrate an organized approach to projects and are committed to their completion on time. They ultimately prioritize the successful completion of projects, and tend to address tasks in an analytical and information-oriented manner. These individuals tend to prefer an isolated and uninterrupted work environment; social interaction has its appropriate time and place. Their significant communications are usually to the point, logical and written. Though group input is an important element in these individuals' decision-making process, they ultimately rely on personal judgement to make important final decisions.

81–120 Moderately Polychronic = C to D range on the scale.

These individuals tend to assign work projects into a general time frame for completion, flexibly approaching project implementation and readily adjusting its execution when something more important comes along. They prefer performing many activities at the same time and working in teams. These individuals develop many informal, long-term working relationships as their means to realizing goals. Their communication of information tends to be personal and informal, rather than through official channels. They solicit and rely heavily on employee input for most decision-making.

121–160 Highly Polychronic = D to E range on the scale.

These individuals multi dimensionally approach work projects with flexible, adjustable plans and shared responsibilities. They tend to believe success of business transactions is ultimately determined by the individuals involved and their cohesiveness as a team. Work is founded upon quality interpersonal interaction and long-term investment in community, which takes precedence over all forms of activity. Communication tends to be spontaneous and of high context. Decision-making is based on extensive group involvement, discussion and consensus. The essence of leadership is the subtle balance of group consensus and personal vision.

Objectives of an organizational structure

Organizational structure refers to the pattern of relationships among positions in the organization and among members of the organization. The purpose of structure is to divide work among members of the organization and co-ordinate their activities so that they are directed towards achieving the goals and objectives of the organization. Structure defines tasks and responsibilities, work roles and relationships and channels of communication. It should embrace:

- Accountability for the areas of work undertaken by groups and individual members of the organization.
- Co-ordination of different parts of the organization and different areas of work.
- Effective and efficient organizational performance, including resource utilization.
- Monitoring the activities of the organization.
- Flexibility in order to respond to changing environmental factors.
- Job satisfaction of members of the organization.

An organization's structure is said to have two major components, these include formalization and centralization. Formalization is the extent to which rules and regulations are used to regulate behaviour. This is affected by the size of the organization because a small shop will not have as many rules as a hospital or an oil refinery. Centralization refers to where decision-making powers lie within an organization. In highly centralized organizations, most decisions are made at the highest level of management and these are communicated to other members. In a decentralized organization, the authority to make decisions is more widespread at all levels of management. Most organizations use a variety of these forms and may combine aspects of both for different parts of the organization.

Hierarchical models of organizations

○ Responsibilities and duties are clearly laid down – strong on formalization and strong on centralization.
○ Specialized rather than generic roles.
○ Vertical rather than horizontal communication.
○ Decision-making is strongly centralized at senior levels of the organization.
○ Clear lines of accountability between different levels of the hierarchy.
○ Clear rules of procedure written down.

Collegial models of organizations

○ Authority is generally through expertise and knowledge rather than necessarily through position.
○ Weak on decentralization.
○ 'Bottom-heavy' – large numbers with the same pay and conditions.
○ Common goals and purposes – people work together in teams.
○ Formal and informal opportunities to participate in the development of initiatives.
○ Employees are autonomous individuals needing a minimum of rules.

Handy's model of organizational culture can be put together with the formalization and centralization dimensions to form a matrix as shown in Figure 1.2.

Figure 1.2 Models of organizational culture

The following case study identifies what is needed from an organizational structure and culture.

Case study

Coca-Cola: Organizational structure

Coca-Cola is a global company but it also has to meet the needs of regional markets. It needs an organizational structure that is flexible to meet both global and local needs. At the top of the structure is the corporate segment (Head Office) which gives direction and support and makes strategic decisions. The 12-member Executive Committee each has responsibility for a major region or specialism, for example finance.

The Company operates five geographic operating segments – Strategic Business Units (SBUs) – covering each world region. Each is then subdivided into smaller regions. At a local level, management is divided into functions such as marketing and finance. There is central direction but the structure is also flexible and focussed at a local level where it can take account of factors like languages and culture.

Important aspects of the culture at the Coca-Cola Company are an emphasis on teamwork and empowerment. It has built flexible structures which encourage teamwork. The company has developed a strategy and structure that suit its operations globally and locally. People are encouraged to make decisions in response to customer needs and to the changing nature of the Group's activity.

The case of Coca-Cola demonstrates the need to balance a knowledge of local markets and also being able to see the global picture and balance central direction with local discretion to make decisions.

Types of organizational structure

Functional

This type of structure groups major functions, for example information, finance, personnel and marketing. The advantages of this kind of structure are that it increases the utilization and co-ordination of groups of people with technical/specialized expertise. It can encourage sectional interests and conflicts, and make it difficult for an organization to adapt to product/service diversification.

Figure 1.3 Traditional organization of Marketing departments

Product/Service

This is where there is grouping by service/product. For example, in the Health Service, the structure could have groupings around specialisms such as orthopaedic, surgical, psychiatric and so on, rather than medical, nursing and paramedical functions.

The following provides an example of a large marketing-oriented organization chart. In this kind of structure, marketing is represented at board level and a Marketing Manager co-ordinates the marketing activity in the organization.

Figure 1.4

Geographical structures

Geographical structures traditionally developed as companies expanded their offerings across territories. There was usually a need to be close to the customer, and to minimize the costs of travel and distribution. Today, the economics of location is important but information technology is making it less important in certain industries. The use of geographical structure depends on the industry. In service industries where the service is provided on-site, geography continues to be a structural basis for many companies. Sales forces and knowledge services like consulting were traditionally managed out of local offices, based on personal relationships and knowledge of the region. However, industry knowledge and expertise are becoming more important. Geographical structures are occurring in industries where the technology is creating a smaller efficient scale and flexible plants, and where customers demand just-in-time delivery.

Figure 1.5

Division structure

This is where the organization is divided into divisions with devolved responsibility for the conduct of their business and financial performance. The grouping is based on services and/or geography and functionality (but often with functions such as finance, personnel and planning retained at headquarters). This can be suitable for international companies that are highly diversified, working in more than one country, for example a pharmaceutical company with divisions in each country producing and marketing products developed by the parent company. Divisional structures can be tight or loose, that is with varying degrees of central control and common service (finance, personnel, computing, etc.). Examples of this kind of structure are General Motors and GEC (UK).

The divisional structure is often developed in response to the difficulties associated with the functional structure. Divisions or business units are set out, each being regarded as a profit centre. Often the divisions are decided upon according to processes, geographic region, product type or, sometimes, some combination of two of these. There is often diversity within a division which can be combated by subdivisions (e.g. product divisions further divided according to geographic region), or by having a functional structure within the division. The main advantage is that each division can be managed almost as if it were a separate company, which helps to deal effectively with different products or markets. This division of the company can, however, lead to wasteful duplication of services. This structure is suited to companies which are able to very clearly distinguish between different divisions. When there is confusion as to which division should be responsible for something, it can lead to considerable managerial difficulties. Advantages include improved decision-making, accountability for performance and better co-ordination of functions. The disadvantage is that economies of scale can be lost and rivalry among divisions might be fostered.

Figure 1.6

Matrix

To make use of both marketing and product know-how, modern companies establish a matrix organization. It should combine product and marketing know-how in a flat hierarchy that is flexible towards market requirements. The matrix approach involves organizing the management of a task along lines that cross normal departmental boundaries so that the ability of product managers and functional managers to communicate with each other is crucial. For example, a new product development team might be formed with an engineer, a research chemist, a marketing manager and a designer. In the matrix, individuals have two or more 'managers', for example a sales manager will report to the marketing director and the product manager. Once the project has been finished, the team may be disbanded, with the individual members being drafted into other teams or absorbed back into the organizational structure. This kind of structure should ensure that the project is better co-ordinated than with four or five departments contributing occasionally. If many different project teams are organized, it gives more people an opportunity to use their capabilities. It emphasizes that project aims are all-important. The disadvantage is that individuals may suffer if both managers make heavy demands on them and there can be conflict between the project leader and the functional leader. Sometimes there can be a failure to provide clear lines of accountability.

Figure 1.7

Case study

BIC

A company's values should help to determine the way it behaves. BIC's values relate to its products, which are:

o Functional – designed to perform a specific function well, for example to draw a line, produce a flame, shave hair. The key to achieving functionality is to adopt the most appropriate design, engineering and technology.
o Affordable – achieved by using appropriate design, materials production and distribution channels.
o Universal – capable of being used by anyone worldwide, for example the ballpoint pen, the pocket lighter, the one-piece shaver.

BIC has three core categories for products, based on a global range, designed for mass appeal. BIC then helps local retailers to select the products that best suit their own customers' needs from this range. Each of the product categories is managed by a Category General Manager, who has the overall responsibility for the marketing, development and manufacturing worldwide. In recent years manufacturing operations have been simplified and super-factories serve very large geographical markets. Product distribution is then organized by continent, with country managers reporting to their continental manager. The organization is a matrix structure based on two main lines of communication:

1. By product category
2. By geographical region.

It means that an employee working, say, in a pen manufacturing plant in France would be accountable both within the Western European division and the stationery category.

From the BIC case study it can be seen that the matrix structure is aimed at maximizing the benefits of strong product expertise with strong operational structures in each major geographical area.

The problem with all forms of organization structure is how to encourage people to feel that they belong not only to their part of the organization but also to the whole organization. The Singapore Airlines case study provides an example of how managers are encouraged to have a company-wide focus. Do you have any similar policies in your organization? Do they work? Do they cause unanticipated problems, for example loss of expertise?

Key marketing roles and tasks

Marketing titles and positions can vary among different organizations and sectors of the economy along with the responsibilities that accompany them. The marketing function can also be organized in different ways depending on factors such as size, management philosophy and type of business.

A summary of some of the main marketing management roles is shown below.

Advertising

Advertising managers may oversee account services, creative services and media services departments. Planning and managing advertising campaigns and briefing and managing advertising agencies are a key part of the role, particularly in larger organizations. In larger firms, advertising managers oversee in-house accounts, creative and media services departments. An account executive manages the account services department, assesses the need for advertising and, in advertising agencies, maintains the accounts of clients. The creative services department develops the subject-matter and presentation of advertising. A creative director oversees the copy chief, art director and their respective staffs. A media director oversees planning groups that select the communication media – for example, radio, television, newspapers, magazines, Internet or outdoor signs – to disseminate the advertising. Assessing the effectiveness of advertising is often undertaken in conjunction with market researchers. In a small firm, managers may serve as a liaison between the firm and the advertising or promotion agency to which many advertising or promotional functions are contracted out.

Brand management

Brand managers design and enhance the brand image to support the marketing strategy and plans. They identify the issues to explore with consumers about their brand experiences, and they build the research capabilities to gather that intelligence. Then, with help from each of the company's functions, product development, manufacturing, marketing and sales, they translate this learning into specifications for product development and process design. They also fund the development of brand-building capabilities and track the performance of the functions they oversee. The following two extracts show the developments that are occurring in brands and their management. The developments have implications for the kinds of management skills needed to be a successful brand manager and the trend towards interactive and more customized marketing.

Extended knowledge

The New Brand Management – Traditional brand managers are responsible mainly for managing promotions, advertising and relations with the trade. Often, they have neither the authority nor the skills to articulate the strategic, cross-functional, long-term perspective that is required. It takes someone with the power, skills, perspective and access to information necessary to drive the development of new products and the design of new business processes.

Category Brand Management – Category managers patrol the boundaries and relationships among brands ensuring that a company's brands are not competing with each other.

Corporate Brand Management – A manager must have a holistic perspective on the consumer's experience and on the entire business system that defines a brand. The levels of managerial expertise are higher, and the stakes involved in launching, maintaining and evolving a brand are also higher today compared to the past.

The following insight provides an example of the difficulties faced by a global brand.

Labels like Nike are out of favour on Wall Street – and losing their cool on the high street. On both sides of the Atlantic, the story is the same: It's not easy for a global company whose trainers are on every high street to remain fashionable. Young people like brands that are (a bit) rebellious and Nike is perilously close to being the establishment. A decision was taken in the mid-1980s to turn the business into 'a marketing-oriented company'. Nike stopped making anything and became a kind of shell, branding and distributing products. An assumption grew up that all products were the same because technology made goods so easy to copy. Values, though, were different. You couldn't copy 'Just do it'. Brands that are seen to be too big and homogenized need to diversify. McDonald's has bought Prêt a Manger, and Coca-Cola hedges its bets by buying up or creating sub-brands. The future for the big brands is to get customers more involved. Megabrands aren't offering what consumers want. Now the challenge is how to involve the consumer and individualize the product.

Source: Geraldine Bedell (2003) *The Observer, Sunday*, 19 January.

Direct marketing

This develops the direct marketing strategy, ensuring it complements the overall marketing strategy. It requires an understanding of the various channels through which customers can be reached directly. It requires building, developing, maintaining and using large databases. Campaign results and trends need to be analysed and presented to senior management. External agencies need to be briefed and managed.

Market research

Virtually every company in the UK uses market research and it is one way of keeping the company in touch with its customers. It is often commissioned from external agencies. The main purpose of market research is to provide information about actual and potential customers to support marketing decisions. A marketing manager's responsibilities include large-scale customer relationship management, encompassing the key customer approach and utilizing skills in international marketing, customer segmentation, customer loyalty, customer satisfaction, database marketing and direct marketing. These jobs may be very intensive in market research skills or may be the responsibility of a market research manager. Within market research firms or consulting firms, marketing research managers might specialize in market strategy (including new products and markets), customer satisfaction and customer segmentation (customer care in many consulting firms), service marketing, database or direct marketing and emerging technologies such as e-commerce. The following case study provides an example of one major retailer's approach to market research and product development.

Much of Gillette's success comes from its ability to develop the new products that customers want. Gillette's first successful product was the safety razor, introduced by King C Gillette in 1901. The challenge for Gillette is to continue to make shaving easier by producing efficient tools but also to make it as pleasurable an experience as possible. This means coming up with new ideas and then using modern technology to develop the products.

First mover

Over the years, Gillette has continued to be the 'first' to the market with a number of innovations, including the first twin bladed razor, the first pivoting head razor and the first triple blade razor. It also produced the first razor specifically aimed at women. Being first gives Gillette advantages. The innovator, or first mover, in a market can often win, and keep, a major market share before any competition arrives. Gillette is also a leader in many areas of operation which include Duracell batteries, Braun electrical goods, Oral-B dental products and the Right Guard brand.

Researching the market

Market research is used to find out what sort of products consumers la might want. This may be either: (1) Qualitative – such as working with small focus groups; (2) Quantitative – involving large samples and the use of strategies such as questionnaires. After this, Gillette carries out technological research and development, to test the viability of the new product. It will also carefully forecast the possible effect of competition and whether the product can be profitable.

Product development

Gillette's research has shown that it needs to develop shaver products for several distinct markets within the world shaving market – worth over £5 billion a year. It has targeted two main markets: systems and disposables.

- Systems are where the razor is bought to last with the customer by buying replacement blades.
- Disposables are where the razor is bought for limited use and then discarded. Both sectors are then further divided into premium (top price and quality) markets and standard markets. Quality is all important. Whatever market the razor is in, it must produce an efficient, clean shave.

Conclusion

Gillette uses market research to find out what people want and then develops these products. Much of its success comes from being a first mover.

Public relations

Public relations managers conduct publicity programmes and supervise the specialists who implement them. They provide advice about pitfalls to avoid and opportunities to pursue. A key part of the role is to monitor and assess PR activity to ensure that it is effective, for example, evaluating advertising and promotion campaigns to see that they are compatible with public relations efforts. Adverse publicity needs to be managed, and media coverage needs to be archived and distributed to managers so that they are aware of what is being written about the company. Keeping track of competitor activity, as reported in various types of publications, is also an important part of the role. Public relations managers may specialize in a specific area, such as crisis management, or in a specific industry, such as health care. They may produce internal company communications such as newsletters and liaise with financial managers to produce company reports. They can also have a role in drafting speeches, arranging interviews and maintaining other forms of public contact.

Product or service management

The original purpose in creating product or service managers was to have someone who would take full responsibility for an individual product or a portfolio of products or services. This meant that the role was there to ensure that important issues were not overlooked. Product management involves monitoring the performance of a specific product or service group in the marketplace. This makes it possible to avoid having a marketing department that focuses only on a few favoured products or services. The potential benefits of product and service management are:

o Expertise and know-how is acquired about all aspects of a product or service group.
o New product or service development is better oriented towards market requirements.
o A more cost-effective marketing mix for the product group can be developed.
o Changes in the marketplace that are relevant for the product or service group can be identified more quickly and acted upon.
o Someone is responsible and accountable for the profit generated by the service or product group.

The product manager needs to co-ordinate all activities relating to the product and service. One of the problems often associated with the role is the lack of direct authority compared to functional department heads. This cross-departmental role means that a product or service manager often needs to work by persuasion rather than through direct authority to champion the product internally as well as externally. A service marketing manager's role is often parallel to that of a product manager. For example, on the service side of a computer manufacturer's business, the ongoing servicing of the product and customer over several years may be a much larger piece of business compared to the initial sale.

Figure 1.8 The cross-departmental role of the product manager

Promotion management

Promotion managers direct promotional programmes that combine advertising with purchase incentives in order to increase the sales of products and/or services. They direct promotion programmes combining advertising with purchase incentives to increase sales. In an effort to establish closer contact with purchasers, dealers, distributors or consumers, promotion programmes may involve direct mail, telemarketing, television or radio advertising, catalogues, exhibits, inserts in newspapers, Internet advertisements or websites, in-store displays or product endorsements and special events. Purchase incentives may include discounts, samples, gifts, rebates, coupons, sweepstakes and contests.

Not-for-profit marketing

Marketing is often criticized for promoting materialism and unnecessary consumption. However marketing can be good or bad depending on who uses it and to what use it is put. Many not-for-profit organizations routinely use marketing to further their mission and goals. Not-for-profit organizations have more 'key publics' that they need to consider compared to commercial organizations. These can be classified as:

o *Beneficiaries* – People who benefit directly from services.
o *Funders* – Funding may be offered and received from many sources. The people providing the funding may have different motives which may raise ethical issues when deciding whether or not to accept funds.
o *Internal staff* – These may be mostly volunteers who undertake the work for a variety of reasons and motivations. This can alter the manager–employee relationship and, for example, volunteers may not want to undertake certain tasks. The manager may not have much leverage beyond personal influence and persuasion. This may be an issue if levels of customer service are compromised by an unwillingness to undertake certain tasks.

Social marketing

Social marketing involves the application of marketing principles and techniques, developed in the private sector, to social issues. It has been defined as 'the design, implementation and control of programmes calculated to influence the acceptability of social ideas and involving considerations of product planning, pricing, communication, distribution and marketing research' (Kotler and Zaltman, 1971). They argue that every organization performs marketing-like activities and that marketing has evolved from an economic discipline to one concerned with the relationships of organizations in the broadest sense. The effective performance of marketing roles requires good working relationships with a wide range of people inside and often outside the organization. This means that there is also a need to develop a range of other social skills as well as marketing expertise. Marketing managers need skills in the following areas:

o Communication
o Project development
o Team leadership
o Delegation
o Time management
o Working across organizational boundaries
o Negotiation and conflict resolution
o Project planning
o Managing people
o Performance management
o Coaching.

Activity 1.6

You are employed as a Marketing Manager by a service organization that supplies services to hospitals . Your Managing Director has asked you to prepare a presentation for junior marketing recruits explaining the characteristics of services marketing and how they apply to your organization. Draft a document which details the areas you will need to cover in your presentation.

Corporate social responsibility

The values and standards of companies are of interest to a wide variety of stakeholders, for example, consumers and employees, investors and legislators. An MORI poll found that four-fifths of the public believe that large companies have a moral responsibility to society – a view with which many industrialists would probably concur. But the majority of the public also believe that large companies 'don't really care' about the long-term environmental and social impact of their actions.

Reputation And Corporate Responsibility, Stewart Lewis, Director, MORI, January 2003

In recent years companies have taken the offensive in promoting themselves as socially responsible organizations. It is now commonplace for large companies to report on this aspect of their work as a major aspect of how they want to communicate their values to their various stakeholders. For example, Nike has been criticized for some of its practices. On its website it discloses its supply chain as part of a process of moving to common standards and promoting greater collaboration to foster the development of a marketplace where responsibility and competitiveness go hand-in-hand.

http://www.nike.com/nikebiz/nikebiz.jhtml?page=25&cat=activefactories

Starbucks is another example of a company that has gone to great lengths to convince its publics that it operates ethically and follows the principles of Fair Trade.

Insight

Starbucks: The art of creating passionate consumers

There is a fundamental change in the way consumers buy their products and services. In addition to the price, the convenience, and other benefits, consumers are demanding more. They want products or services that create a powerful and enduring emotional connection. At Starbucks there is significant loyalty and value around the trust we have built with our customer. The issue of trust has become and is the most powerful foundation for consumer choice. Consumers now commonly engage in a cultural audit of providers. People want to know your values and ethics demonstrated by how you treat employees, the community in which you operate, and many other things that are important to them. This is not a trend, but a new way of doing business by and with consumers. The implication for marketers is to strike the balance between profitability and social consciousness and sensitivity. Traditional advertising and marketing is not enough to build this relationship; those companies that turn their backs on the balance of short-term business and long-term sensitivity and relationship will lose in the marketplace.

Well, it is not a programme, or a quarterly promotion, but rather a way of life. You have to integrate this level of social responsibility into your operation. It has to be aspirational for your people and for the customers. One of the significant drivers in our success is the trust that our employees and our customers have in our way of doing business.

Howard Schultz, CEO Starbucks, July 2005 http://www.brandautopsy.typepad.com/brandautopsy/ 2005/06/howard_schultz_.html

McDonald's is a company that has suffered from bad publicity but has managed to recover from some very damaging publicity and some high profile court cases. McDonald's invited customers across Europe into its kitchens to see how food is prepared in an effort to combat rising concern about obesity and the quality of its ingredients. The 'Open Doors' scheme, involved 30 countries where sales of McDonald's burgers, fries and salads are lagging behind recovery in the US. The company also mailed millions of nutritional leaflets to households in Britain, where the company has been hardest hit by alarms over obesity. The following insight is taken from the US McDonald's website.

Insight

McDonald's supports new SAFE protections for tomato farm workers

Social responsibility is a priority at McDonald's. We care about the communities we serve and work only with suppliers who share our values. McDonald's established our existing Code of Conduct for Suppliers in 1997. We require our suppliers to fully comply with our Code, and we monitor suppliers' performance against these standards. As part of our continuing efforts to ensure social accountability within McDonald's supply chain, we actively support the newly-established Socially Accountable Farm Employers (SAFE) code of conduct for the tomato industry, created by the Redlands Christian Migrant Association (RCMA) and the Florida Fruit & Vegetable Association (FFVA). SAFE provides verifiable protection for workers and offers assurance that lawful wages and workplace safety protections are provided to workers. Our support of this initiative has resulted from our serious engagement with a number of different parties, including our suppliers, industry groups and advocacy organizations such as the Coalition of Immokalee Workers (CIW). Socially responsible employment has a broader focus than just worker wages, and we believe that the SAFE approach will result in a more comprehensive and long-term benefit to those workers. As a result, McDonald's will purchase from suppliers that buy product from growers that participate in this program.

http://www.mcdonalds.com/corp/values/socialrespons.html

However, there are also sceptics who doubt the real intentions of organizations as outlined in a Report from Christian Aid.

Insight

Report reveals the true face of corporate social responsibility

Christian Aid calls for laws to make multinational companies meet basic social and environmental standards in poor countries.

Christian Aid is calling on the politicians to take responsibility for the ethical operation of companies rather than surrendering it to those from business peddling fine words and lofty sentiments. The image of companies working hard to make the world a better place is too often just that – a carefully manufactured image – says *Behind the mask: the real face of corporate social responsibility*, a new report from Christian Aid. Its target is the burgeoning industry known as corporate social responsibility – or CSR – which is now seen as a vital tool in promoting and improving the public image of some of the world's largest companies and corporations.

Some of those shouting the loudest about their corporate virtues are also among those inflicting continuing damage on communities where they work – particularly poor communities, says Andrew Pendleton, senior policy officer at Christian Aid and author of the report. Legally binding regulation is now needed to lessen the devastating impact that companies can have in an ever-more globalized world. *Behind the mask: the real face of corporate social responsibility* demonstrates how over the past decade companies have used an image of social responsibility to oppose regulation and convince governments in rich countries that business can put its own house in order. The report concludes that the voluntary approach to improving corporate behaviour is wholly inadequate and that international legally binding standards are now needed.

http://www.christian-aid.org.uk/indepth/0401csr/index.htm

January 2004

Sometimes managers make decisions which conflict with their own or society's values because of what they see as the pressures of the business world. Doing the right thing is one of the most crucial questions that managers have to face. Is it a manager's job just to maximize profits? Or should managers be concerned with using their organization to carry out other social responsibilities such as supporting education? The following case study demonstrates that a commitment to social responsibility may be only conditional. It concerns the closure of a much-praised Study Support Centre that had also brought much good publicity for the football club.

Case study

Leeds United Football Club: Learning Centre

The centrepiece of Community United is the Learning Centre, 10 000 sq ft of classrooms beneath the stadium's south stand. Fitted with the latest IT equipment, the centre is used by 5000 primary and secondary schoolchildren each year to improve their reading, maths and IT skills. The Leeds United Learning Centre was the first educational establishment in the country to be awarded Advanced Status as a study support provider under the national Quality Assurance Framework, QiSS (Quality in Study Support). The Club is able to testify to the amount of positive publicity and exposure they have received through the local, regional, national and international media – which, if it were 'bought', would cost, by their estimation, five times their revenue investment level. The Learning Centre has played a major part in influencing key business partners to work with the Club. These have, in recent years, included NIKE, HSBC, IKEA and Leeds City Council. The fact that the Club can demonstrate that they truly are 'a club with a conscience' with an understanding of and commitment to their corporate social responsibility has led to sponsorship support.

However, a change of ownership and a change of policy have led the Football Club to close the Centre.

http://www.qiss.org.uk/assets/Leeds%20United%20March%202005%20revised.pdf

Summary

- Marketing departments can be organized by:

  - Function
  - Geographic area
  - Products or brands
  - Matrix
  - Corporate divisions
  - Global aspects.

- A marketing manager needs to work with a range of people inside and outside the organization on all aspects of marketing.
- The marketing manager is involved in a wide range of activities, particularly in small organizations.
- The marketing function is organized in different ways in different organizations, depending on factors such as size, geographical spread, management philosophy and type of business.
- A matrix structure is suited for collaborative working focused on projects that cross normal departmental boundaries.
- Managing effectively requires knowing yourself. Effective managers understand how their behaviour affects others and are able to adapt their style to the context in which they work. Personal management skills are common to all management jobs at all levels.

Further study

Book

Kolter, P. (2000) *Marketing Management: Analysis, Planning, Implementation, and Control*, 10th edition, Englewood Cliffs, New Jersey: Prentice Hall.

Websites

1. Management Learning website: (http://managementlearning.com/art/culttsoc/index.html)
2. Reports, books, newsletters or websites on permission-based e-mail marketing: (http://www.email-marketing-reports.com/report_imt1.htm)

3. Connected in Marketing – A site dedicated to e-marketing: (http://www.cim.co.uk/ece/cfml/index.cfm)
4. What's New in Marketing Newsletter? (http://www.wnim.com/issue13/pages/index.htm)
5. Free articles: (http://www.marketingprofs.com/intro.asp)
6. Free marketing articles: (http://www.bizweb2000.com/articles.htm)

Hints and tips

- o Where possible, include examples from the marketing press, textbooks, journals and Internet to support your examination answers. This is one way of demonstrating your wider knowledge and understanding to the senior examiner.
- o Marketing is a practical business so examples that illustrate the way that theory relates to practice will demonstrate your broader knowledge and understanding of marketing.
- o Reports from examiners are published regularly and are available to students. These reveal that there are similar concerns and problems occurring frequently across all subject areas. The most common mistakes are caused by a lack of exam technique and examination practice.
- o *Not answering the question set* – Examiners are looking for both relevant content and its application in an appropriate context. You must be able to work flexibly with the material you have studied, answering different questions in different ways, even though the fundamental theory remains the same.
- o *Presentation and style* – These skills are important to a marketing practitioner. The examiners expect work to be presented in a well-written, professional manner. 'Report' style, using sub-headings and indented numbering for points and so on looks much more credible than an essay style. This approach allows you to break the work up, highlight the key points, and structure your answer in a logical way. Take care with your grammar and use of language; small errors can change the sense.
- o *Timing* – The scarce resource in an examination is time. You must control your time carefully. Read the instructions carefully, identify what has to be done and how the marks are allocated. Spread your time proportionately to the mark allocation. Allow a few minutes at the end to read through your work.
- o *Theory without application* – The examiners expect relevant theory to be illustrated with practical examples and illustrations. These can be drawn from your own marketing experience observations, or your reading. A theory paper without evidence of practical appreciation is unlikely to be successful.

Bibliography

Bedell, G (2002) 'The changing face of the brand', *The Observer*, 19 January, <http://www.observer.co.uk/review/story/0 6903 877476 00.html>

Boddy, D. (2002) 'Conventional and critical perspectives and studying management', *Management: An Introduction*, pp. 30–32.

Christopher, M., Payne, M. and Ballantyne, D. (2001) *Relationship Marketing: Creating Shareholder Value*, London: Butterworth-Heinemann.

ESCAP: Guidelines for Development of Railway Marketing Systems and Procedures, www.unescap.org/tctd/pubs/marketingtoc.htm

Gronroos, C. (1994) 'From marketing mix to relationship marketing: Towards a paradigm shift', *Management Decision*, **32**(2), 4–20.

Handy, C. (1976) *Understanding Organizations*, Penguin.

Handy, C. (1991) *The Age of Unreason*, Business Books.

Harrison, R. and Stokes, H. (1992) *Diagnosing Organizational Culture*, San Francisco: Pfeiffer.

Kohli, A.K and Jaworski, B.J (1990) 'Market orientation: The construct, research propositions, and managerial implications', *Journal of Marketing*, 54 (April), 1–18.

Kotler, P. and Zaltman, G. (1971) 'Social marketing: An approach to planned social change', *Journal of Marketing*, **35**, 3–12.

Kumar and Nirmalya (2002) 'The path to change', *Financial Times*, 6 December.

McKinsey Marketing Practice, 'Creating leading-edge marketing organizations', <http://www.mckinsy.com/>

Mintzberg, H. (1973) *The Nature of Managerial Work*, London: Harper & Row.

Paraguayan, A., Zeithaml, V.A. and Berry, L.L. (1988) 'SERVQUAL: A multiple item scale for measuring consumer perceptions of service quality', *Journal of Retailing*, **64**, 13–37.

Moorman, C. and Rust, T. (1999) 'The role of marketing', *Journal of Marketing*, **63**, 180–197.

Peters, T. and Waterman, R.H. (1988) *In Search Of Excellence*, New York: Harper & Row.

Sedloff Orton and Linda (2002) 'Growing your marketing department into a knowledge management team: Aim to hire assets not overheads', <http://www.llrx.com/features/market.htm>

Past examination papers for the Marketing Management in Practice module can be found in Appendix 5.

unit 2
recruiting the team

Learning objectives

o Describe the functions, roles of marketing managers and typical marketing jobs and the nature of relationships with other functions in organizations operating in a range of different industries and contexts (1.1). This objective was also partly covered in the previous unit.

o Identify and explain the key challenges of managing marketing teams in a multinational or multicultural context (1.3).

o Explain how you would use the techniques available for selecting, building, developing and motivating marketing teams to improve performance (1.4).

o This last objective is partly dealt with in this unit and also in the following unit. In this unit, the focus is more upon selecting the team.

Statement of Marketing Practice

Lc.1 Manage a marketing team.
Lc.2 Maintain relationships with other functions and disciplines within the organization.
Lc.3 Encourage and help others to develop their competencies relevant to a marketing role.

Glossary

Cultural empathy – An understanding of and a true feeling for a culture.

Cultural environment – Institutions and other forces that affect society's basic values, perceptions, preferences and behaviours.

Cultural universals – Cultural characteristics and attributes that are found in a wide range of cultures: that is, features that transcend national cultures.

39

Culture – The set of basic values, perceptions, wants and behaviours learned by a member of society from family and other important institutions.

Groupthink – A term to describe one process by which a group can make bad or irrational decisions. In a groupthink situation, each member of the group attempts to conform his or her opinions to what they believe to be the consensus of the group. This results in a situation in which the group ultimately agrees on an action which each member might normally consider to be unwise.

ICT – Information and Communications Technology.

International division – A form of international marketing organization in which the division handles all of the firm's international activities. Marketing, manufacturing, research, planning and specialist staff are organized into operating units according to geography or product groups, or as an international subsidiary responsible for its own sales and profitability.

International market – Buyers in other countries, including consumers, producers, resellers and governments.

Strategic alliance – A formal relationship, short of a merger or acquisition, between two companies, formed for the purpose of gaining synergies because in some aspect the two companies complement each other.

Team selling – Using teams of people from sales, marketing, production, finance, technical support and even upper management to service large, complex accounts.

Teams

Introduction

A number of factors are contributing to an increasing emphasis on teams, including the increasing availability and affordability of Information and Communication Technology (ICT) and demands for making work more flexible by reducing its dependence on location. Many organizations have flattened their structures and delegated responsibility in order to cut costs and to utilize the skills of the workforce more effectively. Shifting authority and responsibility down the organization allows teams to take over roles and functions previously performed by management. There are also changes in relationships – among employees, between employees and employers, and between all kinds of organizations and their customers and business partners. Companies that formerly developed products solo are now forming development alliances with suppliers, customers, contractors, consultants and even competitors.

Most teams are created to increase productivity, maximize co-operation and communication, and minimize conflict. Work teams, which are part of larger systems like managerial or production systems, perform a wide array of activities within the organization. Teams often have well-defined boundaries, and norms or rules governing interaction and behaviour.

The internal leader may be a full-time team member. Management may appoint an external leader, who serves as co-ordinator, facilitator or mentor. The leadership role may also be shared by several people, or the leader may perform several functions.

Insight

Four types of Leader

There are two main Leadership Drives:

1. *Dominance* – Desire to dominate (manage) other people.
2. *Eminence* – Desire to achieve status through competition based on ability.

These two drives can be combined in four ways.

And each combination creates a different type of leader.

Type	Dominance drive	Status drive
A: Dominant Boss	High	High
B: Ambitious Professional	Low	High
C: Informal Influencer	High	Low
D: Reluctant Leader	Low	Low

Type A: Dominant bosses have the desire to dominate plus the desire to achieve status through competitive striving. Included here are political and business leaders like, Bill Gates and Steve Jobs.

Type B: Ambitious professionals have little interest in dominance over others. They are leaders because they possess some technical ability.

Examples: Faceless technocrats running investment banks and science-based firms. Or colourful creative people who lead media and arts organizations but have no real interest in managing people.

Extreme A's are often followed by B's because B's are not so pushy.

Type C: Influencers do not want to compete because they fear failure. But their high dominance drive makes them want power. So they gravitate to roles in which they have power without responsibility.

They can be cheerleaders for the boss or rebellious dissidents who sit on the sidelines working the crowd against him.

They only become leaders if there is little risk attached (e.g. in organizations which are run collectively or where the leadership role merely represents a higher power).

Type D: Reluctant leaders prefer a safe, rewarding niche free from competition. They become leaders when no one else is available or when the leader role confers little status or power.

They can also come to power via natural succession in a family firm but when they do they are usually awful.

Reluctant leadership is also common in bureaucracies in which people automatically inherit the role via rules of seniority.

Source: www.recruiting.com/recruiting/2004/12/hrfont_colorred_2.html.

Teams differ in many ways, including size, purpose, type of work performed, structure, leadership, influence and decision-making ability.

Types of teams include:

- Natural work group
- Management
- Project improvement
- Process redesign or re-engineering
- Cross-functional, for example design and production include people of various skill levels from throughout the organization
- New product and service design teams.

More and more work is performed in new ways, so as to exploit the possibilities of co-operative work across national boundaries and time zones. Many tasks are too complex for individuals to handle alone and teams are potentially more effective in solving problems and learning more quickly than individuals. When a team works well, it can improve problem-solving, become more creative and generate acceptance, support and commitment. However, teams can also be inefficient, indecisive, frustrating and, ultimately, inferior to what a collection of individuals working on their own can accomplish. Equally, some people are more comfortable working on their own than when they are in a group.

Teams can be used as *integrating mechanisms* that co-ordinate and integrate information across an organization by enabling co-ordination and integration, or as *self-contained units* (self-managed or autonomous work teams, self-directing teams) that manage aspects of an organization's work.

In knowledge-based organizations both integrating teams and self-contained teams are common and cross-functional project teams are needed to integrate the work of different functions while being as self-contained as possible.

As mentioned previously, a key part of the Marketing Management in Practice unit is working within a team to develop the marketing plan and managing teams implementing the plan by undertaking marketing activities and projects. Unit 4 of this book looks at Project Management in detail but one of the key aspects of project management is the recruitment of a team or teams of people who are able to work together effectively.

Effective product and process development requires the integration of specialized capabilities. This can be achieved, with varying advantages and disadvantages with various team structures.

Clark and Wheelwright (1997) identify four types of project teams:

1. *Functional teams* – Members are grouped by discipline, working under the direction of a functional manager. Primary responsibility for the project passes sequentially from one function to the next. An advantage of this type of organization is that managers control resources and performance in their functional areas, and team members bring specialized expertise to the project. A disadvantage is that a task must be subdivided according to functions and team members may be judged independently of the success or failure of a project.

2. *Lightweight teams* – Like a functional team but with a liaison representative. Members stay in their functional areas but each function designates a liaison person to represent it on, for example, a project co-ordinating team to co-ordinate different function's activities. There is likely to be improved communication and co-ordination compared to a functional team but Project leaders may have no real control.

3. *Heavyweight teams*, in which the project manager has direct access to and responsibility for the work of all those involved in the project, managed by leaders who may have a higher status than the functional managers. An advantage of this type of team is the integration of a project that may require fewer members compared to a more traditional team. However, it may conflict with the functional organization and be seen as an 'elite' group, alienating the rest of the organization.

4. *Autonomous team structure*, often called 'tiger teams', in which individuals from different functional area are formally assigned, dedicated and co-located to the project team. Tiger teams tend to be very focused but it can be difficult to integrate their 'solutions' into the 'parent' organization.

Tiger teams can be used in various aspects of marketing but is particularly suited to customer-focused initiatives where quick solutions may be needed. The following extract provides an example of its use in the context of Tiger teams.

Insight

Don't give up on the Hubble Space Telescope and its stunning cosmic images just yet. After NASA's reluctant decision to let one of the most productive and well-known astronomical instruments in history die early, scientists are showing that one of the best inspirations is desperation.

Stunned by the decision, 'tiger teams' of scientists and engineers have been appointed to find technological loopholes in the bad news. The search is on for new power-conserving procedures to extend battery life, ways to keep the telescope pointing at targets with as few as two gyroscopes (two of six are already kaput), and, most daring, 'teleoperated' service robots. Sent on unmanned rockets, they would be controlled from the ground like imitation astronauts to replace batteries and gyros and upgrade cameras and detectors.

But a reprieve is what astronomers want most. With one more round of service plus clever conservation, Hubble might operate until 2011 or longer, says Bruce Margon, the telescope institute's science director. That's when, if current plans hold, the even larger James Webb Space Telescope should be ready to pick up Hubble's torch. 'Do we really want to go several years with no space telescope at all?' he asks.

Effective project management requires planning and co-ordination. In vertical management, employees are organized along top–down chains of command and may have little opportunity to work with other functional areas. In horizontal management, work is organized across various functional groups that work with each other. This should lead to improved co-ordination and communication among employees and managers. When people are able to work horizontally and vertically there are more opportunities to understand the operations of other functions and how they relate to each other. The vertical aspects of organizations can limit the ability of a project manager to pull together the horizontally integrated teams that are often important for project success.

The team ideal

Robbins and Finley (2001) in their provocatively entitled book *Why Teams Don't Work: What Goes Wrong and How to Make It Right* maintain that in the 1980s the functional or specialist team worked in its organizational 'silo' in parallel rather than with other teams. These teams included, for example, accounting, finance, advertising and marketing who spoke their own functional language and did not really communicate across their functional boundaries. In contrast, today there is more variety and a cornucopia of different types of teams. For example, there are teams where everyone has the same skills but people perform different tasks, teams where people with different expertise each tackle a different part of a task, functional teams, cross-functional teams, inter-organizational teams and intra-organizational teams. Some teams work together for long periods of time while others form for a week or two then dissolve. There are self-managed teams, leader-led teams and teams where leadership is distributed within the team so that everyone leads. Clearly, what is meant by the concept of a 'team' can vary considerably and cover various organizational arrangements. However, teams are not the answer to all organizational ills and if used inappropriately they can mean that less, rather than more, is achieved.

Insight

The great sin of the age of teaming is to ask teams to do everything. A job done by a team is better than a job done by a single individual. You get that synergy going, you know, all that shared information. The truth is that teams are inherently inferior to individuals, in terms of efficiency. If a single person has sufficient information to complete a task, he or she will run rings around a team assigned the same task. There are no handoffs to other individuals. No misunderstandings or conflicting cultures. Beware. Teaming can be bad. Sometimes managers prefer teaming because it spreads accountability around, makes blaming more difficult. Or it means hand-picking team members. The saddest thing we hear is 'We were told we had to do everything as a team.' The CEO is all ga-ga about teams, so now unless you do something as a team you're a pariah in your organization. It is team tyranny and people resent it.

Source: Robbins and Finley (2001).

Types of marketing teams

Examples include,

Sales teams which can consist of one or a mix of the following:

- o Field sales people
- o Sales engineers
- o Sales technicians
- o Office sales staff
- o Sales manager
- o Export sales force.

Marketing research teams which can consist of one or a mix of the following:

- o   Market analysts
- o   Market researchers
- o   Interviewers.

Product management teams which can consist of one or a mix of the following:

- o   Research and development engineers
- o   Design engineers.

Activity 2.1

Identify key stakeholders and their expectations

- o   Stakeholders in this exercise are individuals and groups with whom you work to achieve your work objectives. This can include other teams in the organization, for example, support functions such as Finance, HR or suppliers.
- o   Who are your key stakeholders and what do you need to do together to produce your product, service and so on?
- o   What are your key stakeholders' expectations of your team and how do you know?
- o   What is your team's purpose and role in the organization?
- o   What products and/or services do you provide?
- o   What skills and capabilities does your team contribute to customer value?
- o   Who are your customers?

However, if teams are comparatively inefficient they should be more effective because they enable the collective talents of people to be brought to bear on issues, problems and situations. They can also ensure that the organization presents a consistent and coherent face internally and externally and that plans are developed to make the best use of organizational resources. There are synergies that can be derived from working together that can produce efficiency and effectiveness. Few people could deny that a marketing campaign is more effective if people in the organization are working together to ensure that it is integrated with schedules for production, operations, sales and merchandising.

All parts of an organization should have a common focus and work together purposefully to pursue the organization's overall objectives. In practice, however, relationships between different parts of an organization can be characterized by rivalry and distrust. This can affect all types and sizes of organization and give rise to what is often referred to euphemistically as office politics, or 'the informal and sometimes emotion-driven process of allocating limited resources and working out goals, decisions and actions in an environment of people with different and competing interests and personalities' (Dobson, D. and Dobson, M., 2000). Sometimes conflict arises from differences in view about what is in the organization's best interests; sometimes it is from trade-offs between what is seen to be best for the organization as a whole against what is best for a particular part of it and sometimes it arises from stereotypes and prejudices about the relative worth of different functional specialisms. In organizations staffed by professionals, the conflict can sometimes occur around who feels that they know best about what is in the interests of the customer. The customer might be a patient, a parent, a client or other service-user but in the tradition of paternalistic public services, the professional may feel that they know much better what is best rather than managers, customers or clients.

The wisdom of cross-functional teams

Don H. Lester, an operations manager for Hoechst, developed criteria for staffing cross-functional new product teams.

- What team leadership style and level of expertise is required?
- What team member skills and expertise are needed?
- What is the level of interest in the particular product concept? – Is there a Champion? – Is there a high level of ownership and commitment?
- Motivation – What will motivate individuals to want to take part in the product development project?
- Diversity of team members? – The greater the diversity, the greater the range of viewpoints represented.

Source: Lester (1998).

The role of the manager in a team

The role of the manager is important in creating, co-ordinating and maintaining the team. This requires an understanding of the specific skills and abilities of team members, and their ways of working. Managers need to understand their staff and use their influence over the way the team works, transforming them from a group of individuals to a team that is able to work together. It is also the manager's responsibility to oversee the assimilation of new recruits into a team.

Most teams are created to increase productivity, maximize co-operation and communication, and minimize conflict. Work teams that are part of larger systems, like managerial or production systems, perform a wide array of activities within the organization. The manager may be a full-time team member. Management may appoint an external leader, who serves as co-ordinator, facilitator, mentor, encourager, cheerleader or consultant, but not as a foreman or supervisor. The management role may also be shared by several people, or the manager may perform several functions. Teams differ in many ways, including size, purpose, type of work performed, structure, leadership, influence and decision-making ability. Figure 2.1 gives an indication of the range of stakeholders with whom a product manager may need to interact, although the extent to which this might be called a meaningful team is questionable. More realistically it is likely that the product manager and his or her team need to relate these to other teams in the organization and/or the product manager forms a middle management team with other managers from other functions.

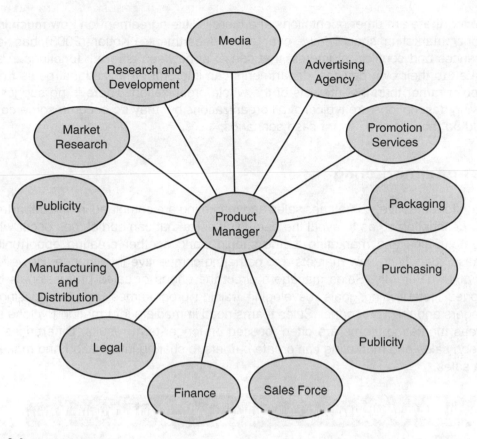

Figure 2.1

Relations between teams in an organization

Managers see teams as a way of accomplishing some or all of the following:

o Providing a structure where people with a range of technical skills, functional special-isms and different perspectives can come together, exchange ideas, learn from each other and, ultimately, provide a better service to internal and external stakeholders.
o Providing a forum in which issues or problems can be aired and dealt with.
o Encouraging acceptance and understanding of a problem and a proposed solution.
o Enable people to develop their roles.

Each part of an organization can have an impact on customer satisfaction. If it has a marketing orientation, all departments should focus on the customer or service-user and work together to meet needs, wants and expectations. An organization with a marketing orientation sees the needs of customers and consumers as central to everything and, depending on the size, may have something like the following structural characteristics:

Activity	Function
Identifying customer/consumer needs and wants	Marketing research
Developing products to meet customer/consumer needs and wants	R&D and production
Deciding on the value of the product to customers	Pricing (sales and marketing)
Making the product available to customers at the right time and place	Distribution
Informing customers/consumers of the existence of the product and persuading them to buy it	Promotion

However, there are other orientations and there is little agreement on how much influence and authority marketing should have over other departments. Kotler (2003) has identified the differences and conflicts of interest that can exist between different functions in an organization. Left to their own devices, departments can interpret organizational goals from their own viewpoint rather than the interests of the whole organization. There is no suggestion that the following descriptions are typical of all organizations but they do occur in some contexts. They should be thought of as worst-case scenarios.

Sales and marketing

As mentioned above, sometimes sales and marketing are combined in one department, section or job description so as to avoid the damaging splits that can sometimes occur when they are separate. Sales and marketing teams should work together creating opportunities for new business, identifying new markets and gathering competitive intelligence. However, they may work quite differently. Sales managers direct the efforts of sales professionals by assigning territories, establishing goals, developing training programmes, and supervising local sales managers and their personnel. Sales teams need immediate information to close sales quickly whereas marketing teams are often focused on longer-term results. Differences in approach between sales and marketing can create barriers to sharing information and make it difficult to close sales.

Sales and marketing

A key aspect of developing and maintaining effective relationships with people in other functions and disciplines within the organization is how the sales and marketing functions work together. This is a critical relationship and can take different forms depending on factors such as the size of the company, number of products and services and the geographical reach of the organization. Greater complexity creates greater demands on the co-ordination of activities.

According to IT market analysis firm Aberdeen Group Inc., as much as 80 per cent of marketing expenditures on lead generation are wasted because these efforts are ignored by sales people. Marketing teams overlook critical input from sales people regarding customer data and needs. Marketing exists to support sales. A marketing department can develop a good product strategy, but it is up to sales staff to implement it. And when the marketing and sales departments fail to share the right information, the organization suffers.

Sales people are required to spend the bulk of their time in the field meeting with customers, in the office on the phone, or at the computer. Marketing people are under pressure to solve challenges quickly and creatively while analysing the available information on the competition, the marketplace, the company's products and services, and the target audience. They rarely interact with customers, unless it is through second-party reports from surveys or focus group research. To succeed, marketing people and sales staff both need to be involved in the development of sales and marketing programmes and planning marketing activities – from product launches through promotional campaigns – if the sales force is not involved programmes are likely to fail. Sales staff need to share customer insights as well as candid information on the usability and effectiveness of marketing tools and campaigns.

Source: http://www.entrepreneur.com/Magazines/Copy_of_MA_SegArticle/0,4453,314251,00.html.

R&D

The drive for successful new products is often hindered by weak working relations between R&D and marketing. This can arise because of different professional and organizational cultures meaning that they operate with different priorities. R&D scientists and technicians may pride themselves more on scientific curiosity and detachment whereas marketing and sales personnel are likely to have a more practical set of concerns and look for products and services with features that can be promoted and sold in the marketplace. In some companies, R&D and marketing share responsibility for market-oriented innovation. R&D staff take responsibility for innovation and product launch, and marketing staff must take responsibility for new sales features and for correctly identifying customer needs and preferences.

Engineering and purchasing

Engineering is responsible for finding practical ways to design new products and production processes. Engineers, who may be focused more on technical quality and manufacturing simplicity, may be in conflict with the marketing function if they are asked for products with slightly different features, adding to manufacturing complexity. Purchasers want to obtain materials and components in the right quantities and quality at the lowest possible cost. They may have a perception of marketers as people who want products with small quantities of many components rather than large quantities with fewer components. They can also be critical of the forecasting inaccuracy of marketing personnel.

Manufacturing and operations

They may see marketers, stereotypically, as people who complain about delays in production, poor quality control and poor customer service. They may also see marketers as providing inaccurate sales forecasts who promise a higher level of service than is reasonable. Marketers are seen as not particularly interested in production problems but focused much more on the problems of customers who need goods and services quickly, who may receive defective merchandise, and who do not receive the service they need. In marketing-driven companies, the company will do all it can to satisfy its customers but this can result in high and fluctuating manufacturing costs. Organizations that have a balanced orientation ensure that manufacturing and marketing jointly determine what is best for the organization. Managing operations in service industries is concerned with service levels, and it is necessary for marketing and operations to work together. Marketing people must fully understand the capabilities and mindset of those delivering the service, and continuously try to improve attitudes and capabilities.

Finance

Financial executives evaluate the profit implications of proposed business activity. Marketing executives ask for substantial budgets for advertising, sales promotions and the sales force, without being able to prove how much this expenditure will contribute to the bottom line. They believe marketers are too often tempted to reduce prices to win orders instead of pricing to make a profit. However, marketers can see finance as conservative, risk-averse and the cause of lost opportunities because of a failure to invest in long-term development.

Insight

Marketing departments coming under greater financial scrutiny

27 September 2004 Within the financial services sector, 94 per cent of marketing heads surveyed say they are under greater pressure than ever to demonstrate a return on investment (ROI) for marketing initiatives, but the majority do not have the tools to accurately track marketing spending and measure returns, according to new research.

The findings come from a survey of 50 marketing directors and managers within the UK financial services sector. The research reveals that while marketing departments are today being held more accountable, even keeping track of spending is difficult with 88 per cent of companies forced to rely on spreadsheets and 80 per cent relying on company-wide financial systems.

Accounting

Accountants may not be very keen on the special deals sales people make with customers because these require special accounting procedures. Marketers may dislike the inflexible way that accountants allocate fixed costs to products and services. They would also like accounting to produce special reports on sales and profitability by segments, important customers, individuals and products, channels, territories, order sizes and so on. Marketers may feel that credit standards are too high and when they do find customers, they may not be able to sell to them because of a low credit rating.

Concerns about working in teams

- o Few companies know how to properly implement a team process. Many managers lack the necessary skills to provide strong leadership in a team environment.
- o Managers too frequently select people in their own image.
- o Managers do not understand the strengths of their team members and do not allocate work appropriately.
- o Members of unbalanced teams often feel that their particular talents and abilities are not being used to the full. Managers do not know how to motivate people because they do not understand individual needs.
- o Groupthink drives out critical judgement, for example illusion of invulnerability, illusion of unanimity, self-censorship.

What are effective teams?

Mike Woodcock identified a number of characteristics in his Team Development Manual as follows:

Openness and confrontation – Where the team is working well, people can express themselves openly and confront mistakes, confusions or frustrations. Such feedback can be received without recrimination and act as feedback to team members and management.

Support and trust – Trustful working relationships stem from positive orientations to others. In reality there is often too much at stake between people at work (personal rivalry, politics). Concerns such as being helpful, endeavouring to understand the perception and difficulties of others are important for team leaders responsible for giving feedback to members whose actions generate difficulty within the team.

Co-operation and conflict – Healthy competition can stimulate ideas and energy but unhealthy competition and conflicts, hidden agendas and stereotyping of people and problems need to be avoided.

Sound procedures – Effective teams need sound procedures for calling meetings, drawing up agendas, managing meetings and ensuring that follow-up action is implemented. Sound procedures include, for example, chairing skills, briefing, summarizing, questioning and exploration skills. Decision-making arrangements also need to be clear. Should the team vote on issues? Does the chair have the final say?

Appropriate leadership – The team leader has to focus on the task, the team and the needs of individuals, ensuring that the team works effectively and efficiently, and achieves its aims and objectives. The range of styles that a leader or manager can use has been captured by Tannenbaum and Schmidt.

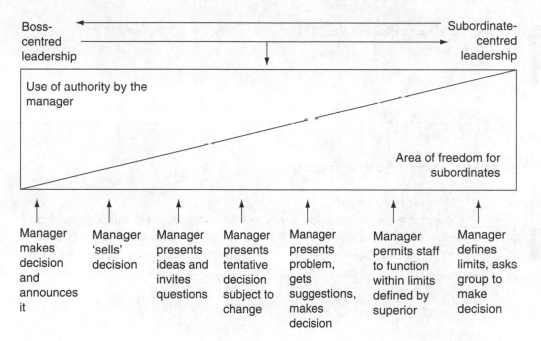

Figure 2.2

There is no one best style to adopt, rather it depends on the nature of the context, the type of work tasks undertaken and the people who make up a team and the relative importance of the decision. Styles are also contingent on factors such as timescales for making a decision. Therefore, fitness for purpose means that different approaches might be used according to how this range of factors varies.

Regular review – A team regularly reviews where it is going and focuses on issues such as: Are we achieving our objectives? Are we being effective? How well are we working together? How can we improve?

Individual development – Members' needs for growth, all-round ability, satisfaction of needs, opportunity and experience need attention.

Sound inter-group relations – Effective teams have good relationships with other departments/ teams. Each values and respects the other. The respective leaders themselves comprise an effective team. Inter-group processes require shared information and an open approach to problem-solving.

The following case study is an example of an effective team but it is one that is very different from many teams that are found in organizations.

Case study

Team formation at Honeywell Scarborough Manufacturing Operations, Canada

The implementation of an empowered workforce, particularly within a team concept, is anything but quick. The empowered Self-Directed Work Team (SDWT) concept at Honeywell is a major contributor in helping Honeywell to achieve national recognition for quality. In some types of teams, such as task or project teams, team leaders are likely to be required. However, in an SDWT mode, leaders may simply replace the supervisor and, thus, continue the hierarchical structure. SDWT members would probably wait for the leader's guidance, deferring the development of empowering skills. Team leaders are not imposed at Honeywell but individual team members can exercise 'leadership' in particular developed skills and help others with deficiencies.

Source: Department of Indian Affairs (2001).

Activity 2.2

Choose a team in your organization.

- What is its function?
- What are the key considerations to take into account in building the team?
- How would you rate its effectiveness using Woodcock's criteria, above?
- What, if any, are the key barriers to effectiveness in your chosen team?

Virtual teams

A virtual team is a group of people who are working together, even though they are not all in the same geographical location. Specifically, teams may be distributed for a variety of reasons:

- Organization-wide projects or initiatives.
- Alliances with different organizations, some of which may be in other countries.
- Mergers and acquisitions.
- Emerging markets in different geographic locations.
- The desire of many people and government organizations for telecommuting.
- The continuing need for business travel and information and communications technologies available to support this travel.
- A need to reduce costs.
- A need to reduce time-to-market.

Team members use communication technologies such as e-mail, videoconferencing and telephone more often than face-to-face meetings to communicate with each other. Common reasons for forming virtual teams are to integrate expertise from different locations, to save on travel time and travel costs, and to build relationships, shared understanding and shared identities across workplaces or organizations. Virtual teams face both the same challenges that traditional teams do and some unique ones such as those relating to communication technologies and working at a distance. The dispersion of team members can make it difficult to establish a strong team identity, and it can be more of a challenge for the team members to work towards a common goal. Examples of virtual teams include a team of people working at different geographic sites and a project team whose members telecommute.

Seven things virtual teams can do to work better:

1. Have face-to-face meetings with all the members as soon as possible after the team is formed.
2. Find ways of building trust between the team members.
3. Clearly define goals, roles and tasks.
4. Ensure all team members are trained in cultural awareness and interpersonal skills.
5. Encourage informal communication between team members.
6. Set standards for responding to communications frequency, and acceptable times to call those in different time zones.
7. Rotate the team members.

Leaders of virtual teams need to be proactive in building the team, and should anticipate and resolve misunderstandings and conflicts before they are allowed to develop. Difficult areas for dispersed teams include co-ordination and collaboration, and dealing with conflict and performance problems when team members cannot be observed directly.

Managing diversity

The trend towards a global economy is bringing people of different ethnic and cultural backgrounds together. The development of greater intercultural understanding should be an important element in all organizations because of the nature of the societies in which we live, the markets in which organizations operate, and the customers and clients that are served. Organizational culture encompasses the shared values, beliefs, behaviour and background of people, and includes race, gender, sexual orientation, age or disability. Ethnocentricity is the inclination for majority group members to view their beliefs, behaviours and values more positively than those of other minority 'out' groups and to evaluate the latter's beliefs, behaviours and values negatively from the perspective of the majority group. The members of virtual teams often include people from different countries, cultures, disciplines or organizations. Such differences mean that people have different expectations, for example about how things should be done or said, or how people should behave. This can make it difficult to build and maintain trust and personal relationships between the team members. Bringing the team together for face-to-face meetings can help here, but one of the most important things is to ensure that team members have a good degree of cultural and interpersonal awareness and are prepared to give each other the benefit of the doubt and thus avoid a blame culture.

People of different ethnic backgrounds do not always share the same attitudes, values and norms. The contemporary organizational trend is to acknowledge, accept and value the differences among diverse groups. This raises interesting questions about how best to manage people in a workforce which becomes increasingly diverse.

Insight

The term 'Latino' covers some two dozen nationalities, and includes a variety of cultures, physical types and racial backgrounds. Cuban, Mexican, Puerto Rican, Dominican and other Central and South American groups are included under the Latino umbrella. It is the fastest growing minority in the USA and presents some major challenges to marketers. However, there are also common elements such as strong family values, product loyalty and a concern for product quality. Spanish language TV is the best medium for reaching Latinos, who tend to watch more TV than their American counterparts.

Source: Wynter (1997).

One area that has been researched extensively is the contrast between individualism and collectivism. Compared to individualist cultures, collectivist cultures emphasize the needs of the group, social norms, shared beliefs and co-operation with group members. In general, Asians, Hispanics and Blacks have roots in nations with collectivist traditions, while Anglos have roots in the European tradition of individualism. Groups composed of people from collectivist cultural traditions tend to exhibit more co-operative behaviour than groups of people from individualistic cultural traditions.

Geert Hofstede conducted perhaps the most comprehensive study of how values in the workplace are influenced by culture. He analysed a large data base of employee value scores collected by IBM between 1967 and 1973 covering more than 70 countries, from which he first used the 40 largest only and afterwards extended the analysis to 50 countries and 3 regions. Subsequent studies validating the earlier results have included commercial airline pilots and students in 23 countries, civil service managers in 14 counties and 'elites' in 19 countries. He developed different axes for measuring cultural factors and found considerable differences from one nation to the next.

Power Distance Index (PDI)

This focuses on the degree of equality, or inequality, between people in the country's society. A High Power Distance ranking indicates that inequalities of power and wealth have been allowed to grow within the society. These societies are more likely to follow a caste system that does not allow significant upward mobility of its citizens. A Low Power Distance ranking indicates the society de-emphasizes the differences between citizen's power and wealth. In these societies equality and opportunity for everyone is stressed.

Individualism (IDV)

This is the degree the society reinforces individual or collective achievement and interpersonal relationships. A High Individualism ranking indicates that individuality and individual rights are paramount within the society. Individuals in these societies may tend to form a larger number of looser relationships. A Low Individualism ranking typifies societies of a more collectivist nature with close ties between individuals. These cultures reinforce extended families and collectives where everyone takes responsibility for fellow members of their group.

Masculinity (MAS)

This refers to the degree the society reinforces, or does not reinforce, the traditional masculine work role model of male achievement, control and power. A High Masculinity ranking indicates the country experiences a high degree of gender differentiation. In these cultures, males dominate a significant portion of the society and power structure, with females being controlled by male domination. A Low Masculinity ranking indicates the country has a low level of differentiation and discrimination between genders. In these cultures, females are treated equally to males in all aspects of the society.

Uncertainty Avoidance Index (UAI)

This focuses on the level of tolerance for uncertainty and ambiguity within the society – that is unstructured situations. A High Uncertainty Avoidance ranking indicates the country has a low tolerance for uncertainty and ambiguity. This creates a rule-oriented society that institutes laws, rules, regulations and controls in order to reduce the amount of uncertainty. A Low Uncertainty Avoidance ranking indicates the country has less concern about ambiguity and uncertainty and has more tolerance for a variety of opinions. This is reflected in a society that is less rule-oriented, more readily accepts change, and takes more and greater risks.

Long-Term Orientation (LTO)

This focuses on the degree the society embraces, or does not embrace, long-term devotion to traditional, forward thinking values. A High Long-Term Orientation ranking indicates the country prescribes to the values of long-term commitments and respect for tradition. This is thought to support a strong work ethic where long-term rewards are expected as a result of today's hard work. However, business may take longer to develop in this society, particularly for an 'outsider'. A Low Long-Term Orientation ranking indicates the country does not reinforce the concept of long-term, traditional orientation. In this culture, change can occur more rapidly as long-term traditions and commitments do not become impediments to change.

Hofstede's data revealed an Anglo culture of management based on high individualism, low to medium power distance between bosses and their subordinates, low to medium uncertainty avoidance and high masculinity. However there are also considerable differences within Anglo cultures. Of the 52 countries in his study, Australians were the most likely to say that leaving staff alone to get the job done was the attribute that made for a good manager. Canada ranked next, while the United States was not far behind. In relationships with suppliers, Europeans are more likely to develop a long-term relationship based upon ideas of partnership, whereas both Americans and Australians perceive contracts with suppliers as 'deals'.

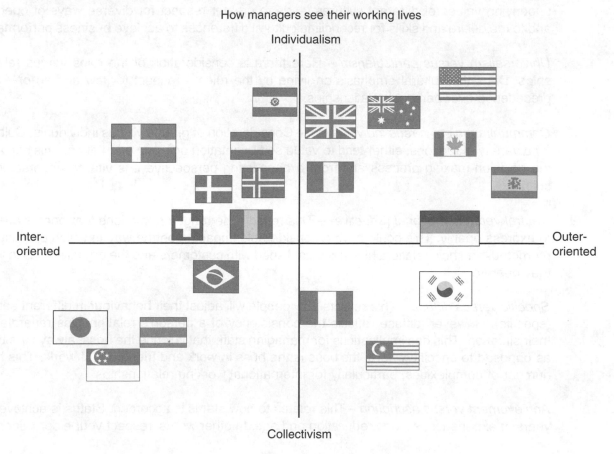

How managers see their working lives

Figure 2.3

International Marketing activities are usually organized in three ways: through export departments, international divisions or a global organization

- A global strategy looks upon the world as single market.
- A multinational strategy treats the world as a portfolio of national opportunities.
- A 'global' strategy is based on standardizing some aspects and localizing other aspects of a Company's products and services.

Source: Bartlett and Ghoshal (1989).

Trompenaars's seven-dimensional model

Trompenaars developed a model to analyse cultural differences, the 'Seven Dimensions of Culture Model', to show how managing complexity in a heterogeneous environment is a major challenge for today's international managers and corporate leaders as well as a critical component of long-term success. He explains how reconciling cultural differences will lead to competitive advantage.

He worked for the Royal Dutch Shell Group handling operations in nine different countries and undertook research over a 15-year period. His work discusses the implications for managing or being managed, working together, building relationships, team working, negotiating and communicating with people from other cultures. His basic premise is that an understanding of the underlying values of different cultures leads to greater respect for diverse ways of operating and to the desire and skills for reconciling cultural differences to achieve business performance.

Universalism versus particularism – Here there is consideration of the rules versus relationships. Does the cultural emphasis on living by the rules – respect for law and so on – take precedence over personal relationships.

Communitarianism versus individualism – Consideration of groups versus individuals. Cultures, for a variety of reasons, either tend to value self-orientation or group orientation. This can affect the decision-making process and from a negotiating perspective it is vital to understand the culture.

Neutral versus emotional (affective) – This reflects the range of emotions that people are able to express openly. This could have a considerable impact upon the way in which products are promoted, and how relationships are established with customers and the organizations in which they operate.

Specific versus diffuse – This reflects how people will adjust their behaviour in different settings (specific). However, diffuse reflects the consistency of a person's relationships regardless of their situation. This has implications for managing staff, that is 'once the boss, always the boss', as opposed to specific where 'the boss is the boss in work and friend out of work'. This has a number of complexities, particularly for international working relationships.

Achievement versus ascription – This relates to how status is accorded. Status is achieved via years of experience, service, education and age. In other words 'respect your elders' scenario.

Sequential time versus synchronic time – This is essentially the difference between a sequence of events or simultaneous events. It is a question of being able to juggle a lot of balls in respect of time, or needing to operate in a sequence to differentiate activities. This can indicate a lot about an individual's ability to work individually, within a team, on a self-motivated basis, or on a delegated activity basis.

High context and low context – High context behaviour will have a form of ritual behaviour in everyday life. Priorities, status and so on will be important. Low context will see little in the way of ritual behaviour and can generally cope with a number of events happening at any one time.

Fons Trompenaars and Charles Hampden Turner (2001) interviewed 15 000 managers in 28 countries to explore the cultural differences between what they called universalist societies and particularist societies. In universalist societies people follow the rules and assume that the standards they support are the correct ones. Further, they believe that society works better if everyone conforms to them. Particularist societies believe that particular circumstances are more important than general rules, and that people's responses depend on circumstances and on the particular people involved. In universalist countries written contracts are taken seriously. Teams of lawyers are employed to make sure that a contract is correctly drafted, and once signed it must be policed to ensure it is kept. Particularist countries think that the relationship is more important than the contract and that a written contract is not always necessary – the particular people and the particular situation matter more than the universal rules. Different cultures have different ways of coping with life, a different set of responses to the same underlying dilemmas. In Far Eastern cultures, books start 'at the back' and are read from right to left in vertical columns. To Westerners, this seems a reversal of normal practice. Managers need to display cross-cultural competence and reconcile cultural differences. Successful leaders are those who are flexible, sensitive and skilled enough to be able to ride what they call 'the waves of culture'.

Insight

Even in the best of teams individual agendas can sometimes get in the way of progress. All marketing professionals understand the importance of teamwork, and 'integrated marketing communications' (IMC) is a concept all of us are familiar with by now. It is the rather simple, but surprisingly elusive, concept that organizations should plan all of their communications efforts in tandem so that they not only contribute to the same overall business objectives, but actually reinforce each other. Synergy should make $1 + 1 + 1 = 5$.

1. Synergy occurs only when all parties are working towards the same, clearly articulated marketing objectives.
2. Measure results according to outcome, not output or glitz. Make it clear that results are all that count.
3. Assemble your IMC team before setting strategy. Involve your team during the early stages of strategic planning.
4. Manage competition between partners. Specialists tend to accentuate the advantages of their particular discipline.
5. Beware of sacred cows.

Source: Adapted from GS Insight: http://www.gibbs-soell.com/insight/GS_InsightV6-6Aug98.pdf.

Activity 2.3

o Do you have experience of working with international organizations, or does your own organization have international divisions? – If not, try to find out about the business culture in a very different country from the one in which you work.

o What are the key differences in culture between each country that have an impact on working life, for example are there different approaches to teamwork, team leadership, management style, delegation, making mistakes?

o What do you think will be the key differences that would have an impact on the manager's role? There are many aspects of culture to pay attention to, particularly in marketing activities.

Role of the HRM function

All large organizations have developed HRM departments, and their managers can rely upon the existence of clear personnel policies and back-up through every aspect of concern to personnel management. For many managers, however, there is likely to be little formal support and it is for them to recruit, select and manage. Even for managers with HRM support, there is a need to understand fully the systems and procedures so that they have sufficient understanding to be able to exert control as needed. In this, the relationship with HRM is exactly the same as with any other specialist function.

Recruitment and selection

The process involves clearly defined stages and the use of a systematic approach should ensure that you do not overlook anything important and, significantly, it will reduce the area of subjective judgement where people's biases, prejudices and weaknesses can creep in. This is important for several reasons. Firstly, on grounds of natural justice, there is the obvious point that everyone needs to be treated fairly and equitably. One of the most depressing situations that can arise in organizations is when people are denied opportunities for reasons beyond their personal control such as their age, ethnicity, disability or gender. This may deny the organization the opportunity to appoint the best candidate. Other weaknesses in the recruitment process can mean that weak or unsuitable people may be appointed on superficial criteria. There are also legal, recruitment and poor public relations consequences that can follow if a recruitment process is flawed. Who is the best candidate for a post depends on the nature of the job, the people with whom the person will need to work and interact, and the context in which the work is carried out. It is a matching process between the existing strengths and weaknesses of team members, future requirements of the role, and the qualities and capabilities of the prospective candidates.

Recruiting externally

Businesses could choose to search using the following media:

o Advertising in papers, magazines or locally
o Employment agencies
o Executive 'head-hunters'
o Job centres
o Colleges/universities
o Careers fairs.

These are all useful, but there are some disadvantages:

- ○ Companies might be overlooking and frustrating talented internal candidates.
- ○ External recruitment can be expensive.

Internal recruiting

Internal recruiting has traditionally been done by a manager appointing or promoting people. Some organizations use formal internal advertising to find the best candidate. They will advertise on noticeboards, via intranets or newsletters.

Not everyone agrees with formalized internal recruitment:

- ○ Employees may think it is an empty exercise, believing decisions are already made.
- ○ Some managers anticipate problems in succession planning if they must use open internal markets.

To avoid problems, businesses can bring someone impartial – managers from other departments, someone from HR – into the procedure. Internal recruitment can be efficient because:

- ○ The person and the firm know each other.
- ○ Savings on commercial advertising rates for recruitment can be made.
- ○ Employees are motivated because they can see the possibility of progression.

Whilst there is a cost in building on existing skills internally, this can be more reliable and less expensive than external recruitment. On the downside:

- ○ Good people outside could be overlooked.
- ○ Unsuccessful internal candidates can feel slighted.
- ○ Entirely new skills may need intensive training.

Insight

McDonald's

Recruiting, selecting and training for success

McDonald's employs on a large scale. A typical McDonald's employs about 60 people. Most are hourly paid. Managers and office staff are paid a salary. For each job there is a job description which describes these duties of the job and a person specification that describes the skills and personal qualities needed for the job.

Hourly paid workers are recruited through adverts in restaurants, job centres and career fairs. Interviews are planned using the McDonald's interview guide. Candidates are rated on a scale. Jobs are offered to those with higher ratings. The management department recruits managers. They come from two main sources. Over half are promoted hourly paid workers. Most of the rest have degrees. People can apply on line, via a recruitment hotline or by post. The online process includes a psychometric test. A good first stage interview is followed by two days on site called 'On the Job Experience'. If the OJE is a success there is a final interview after which whether or not to appoint a particular candidate [Q1]is decided. Those who are successful are inducted into the business. The Welcome Meeting gives an outline of the Company. It includes the job role and food, hygiene and safety training. Standard policies and methods of doing things are explained. The Meeting also covers administration, benefits and training. McDonald's provides for workers to further their careers through a development programme.

McDonald's puts great emphasis on On-the-Job training. Staff are given a training card on which to record their achievements. They are expected to check with their managers to ensure progress is properly recorded and that they gain experience in all work areas. New employees are teamed up with a 'buddy', a member of the training team. Job rotation is practised and there are 19 work areas to which staff can be assigned.

Observation and questioning are used to assess staff and two observations must be passed before someone is regarded as 'competent'. Restaurant managers spend a lot of time on a one-to-one basis with new recruits. Managers have training responsibilities and can spend 60 per cent of their time on the floor with the crew. Their own training involves learning everything a crew member needs to know and further classroom training.

Advertising and the use of agencies

Advertising is a major marketing activity and marketers use agencies regularly. The concepts of positioning, segmentation and targeting apply just as much to recruitment as to any other form of advertising. The agency's job is to translate your needs into short-listed candidates. The aim is to design an advert so that only those who have a realistic chance of being successful apply for the position. It is as important for unsuitable candidates to rule themselves out as it is to encourage eligible people to apply. Having a large field of candidates is of little use if many of them would stand little chance of being appointed.

Question 2.1

What are the recruitment methods used in your organization for:

○ Administrative jobs?
○ Sales jobs?
○ Professional jobs?
○ Managerial jobs?

Applications

After the closing date, a long list of possible candidates can be drawn up. From the long list you can use your personnel specification to compile a short-list. It is good practice to respond to all applicants, but some organizations feel they cannot afford it. Applicants are consumers in the marketplace so it is important to create a favourable impression with everyone who applies for a job.

Discrimination: What the law says

There are a number of Acts of Parliament which are relevant to the recruitment of staff. The main provisions are the Sex Discrimination Acts of 1975 and 1986, the Race Relations Act 1976, the Race Relations (Amendment) Act 2000 and the Disability Discrimination Act of 1995. These Acts seek to promote equality of opportunity and to ensure that no person is treated less favourably than another person on the grounds of disability, colour, race, nationality, ethnic or national origins, sex or marital status. The Disability Discrimination Act 1995 gives disabled people the right not to be treated less favourably than others. Special care must be taken in the wording and placing of recruitment advertisements to avoid seeming to prefer one type of person over another. From December 2005, third-party publishers, for example newspapers, are liable for publishing discriminatory advertisements. The government will introduce legislation to combat age discrimination in employment and vocational training by October 2006. It will cover both employment and vocational training. It will include every member of the workforce, young and old. Employers will have to adopt age positive practices. This means it will no longer be possible to recruit, train, promote or retire people on the basis of age unless it can be objectively justified.

The new legislation covers young and old alike throughout their working lives.

The Sexual Orientation Regulations apply to discrimination on grounds of orientation towards persons of the same sex (lesbians or gays), the opposite sex (heterosexuals) and the same and opposite sex (bisexuals). They cover discrimination on grounds of perceived as well as actual sexual orientation and the sexual orientation of someone with whom the person associates.

As with other forms of discrimination, the new legislation recognizes both direct and indirect discrimination on the grounds of sexual orientation. From December 2005, this definition has been extended to include civil partner employees – that is a partner in a same-sex couple that has registered their relationship under the Civil Partnership Act 2004.

Age – key business issue

'The key business issue within the framework of equality over the next few years will be the introduction of the age discrimination regulations in 2006. The CBI wishes to encourage people to work beyond the age of 65 where there is a business case for doing so. We want to see workable age legislation and will be working as part of the Age Partnership Group to inform employers of their new responsibilities under the regulations.'

Source: John Cridland, Deputy Director-General, CBI.

You should check there are no hidden age barriers in your selection and promotion processes – for example aim to place advertisements in publications read by a range of age groups. You should also make sure that redundancy procedures are based on business needs rather than age.

In certain circumstances discrimination may be allowed if it is seen to be a genuine occupational qualification for the job in question.

When interviewing people for a job there are certain questions you should not ask, either directly or indirectly, including whether a candidate is married, a partner in a same-sex civil partnership, or plans to have children. You must not attempt to elicit information about a person's sexual orientation or their religion. Read about the actions you should take to give equal treatment to civil partners in your policies, forms and other material on the ACAS website.

Care should also be taken when asking about a disability. Whilst the Disability Discrimination Act does not prohibit an employer from seeking information about a disability, that information must not be used to discriminate against a disabled person. An employer should only ask such questions if they are relevant to the person's ability to do the job, after a reasonable adjustment, if necessary.

Discrimination

The main forms of discrimination are:

Direct discrimination – that is where a woman is treated less favourably than a man or vice versa, a married person is treated less favourably than a single person or vice versa, or someone is treated less favourably on grounds that they are intending to undergo, are undergoing or have undergone a gender reassignment. Direct discrimination can occur where someone is treated less favourably on the grounds of their sexual orientation.

Indirect discrimination – that is applying a requirement or condition which, although applied equally to all groups, is such that a considerably smaller proportion of a particular racial group, sex or married persons can comply with it and which cannot be shown to be justifiable. Possible examples are unjustifiable age limits which could discriminate against women who have taken time out of employment for child rearing and rules about clothing or uniforms which disproportionately disadvantage a particular racial group.

Both types of discrimination are unlawful irrespective of whether there has been any intention to discriminate.

Disability discrimination – While legislation covering discrimination on grounds of race and sex makes discriminatory conduct unlawful, the Disability Discrimination Act 1995 goes further by requiring employers to make 'reasonable adjustments' to the workplace where that would help to overcome the practical effects of disability. Failure to carry out this legal duty amounts to discrimination unless an employer is able to justify it. People with disabilities who feel that they have been unfairly discriminated against can seek redress through the Employment Tribunals.

Sexual orientation

The Employment Equality (Sexual Orientation) Regulations 2003 outlawed discrimination in employment and vocational training on grounds of sexual orientation. The law means that it will be unlawful to deny lesbian, gay and bisexual people jobs because of prejudice. The legislation provides protection throughout the employment relationship – during the recruitment process, in the workplace, on dismissal and, in certain circumstances, after the employment has finished. They apply to terms and conditions, pay, promotion, transfers, training and dismissals.

Religion and belief

The Employment Equality (Religion or Belief) Regulations 2003 outlawed discrimination and harassment on grounds of religion or belief in large and small workplaces in England, Scotland and Wales, both in the private and public sectors. They cover all aspects of the employment relationship and outlaw treating people less favourably than others because of their religion or belief.

Equal pay

The Equal Pay Act 1970, as amended by the Equal Pay Regulations, covers all contractual conditions of service, not only pay. It gives both sexes the right to an 'equality clause', which means that if any term in their contract is less favourable than that in a contract of the opposite sex, it must be modified to make it equitable.

1. 'Like work', that is work of the same or a broadly similar nature.
2. Work rated as equivalent under a non-discriminatory evaluation scheme.
3. Work of equal value in terms of the demands made, for example under such headings as effort, skill and decision-making.

Job description

A job description is the focus of any employee's relationship with the employer. In establishing what the job is, the manager provides the foundation for all the stages of recruitment, selection, training and appraisal that follow. The job description describes the tasks and responsibilities which make up the job. As well as being a prerequisite to the recruitment process, it provides a standard against which the performance and development needs of the post-holder can be assessed. It also enables the department to focus on the characteristics of the post rather than those of the previous occupant. Job descriptions have several standard components, provided in greater detail as needed:

Job title – Accurate titles reflecting the function and level of the job – modest duties should not have grand titles. 'Engineer' should only describe a qualified engineer.

Position – Stating the job title of the person to whom the employee is responsible as well as those who report to the job holder.

Areas of responsibility – Stating the overall purpose of the job – the principal role of the job holder and the expected contribution to achieving objectives.

Main tasks – Identifying the tasks, grouping together related ones. Includes the objective or purpose of each task but not how it is done.

Description of tasks – In short numbered paragraphs, with no more than two sentences per description. Gives details of measures of work involved and proportion of time involved for any task. Descriptive headings to group together related tasks: organizing or planning.

Special requirements – Equipment, tools, special skills.

Location – of the job and travelling needed.

Special circumstances – Lifting, dangerous or unpleasant conditions, night work, overtime, weekend working.

Challenging aspects of the job – This can be useful in attracting applicants.

What is the overall purpose of the job? – Describe in one sentence, for example 'to assist the Head of Department in the efficient running of the departmental office'.

What are the main tasks of the job? – Try to use active verbs, for example 'producing', 'planning', rather than vague terms such as 'deals with', 'handles'.

What are the main responsibilities involved? – 'Responsibilities' define the scope of the job, for example for managing staff, materials, money and so on.

The key result areas of the job and the standards expected – These may include such aspects as the degree of precision required and/or the consequences of error.

With whom does the post-holder work? – These may include other staff, students and so on.

Terms and conditions of the post – Unsocial hours, necessity to work regular overtime, and any restrictions on periods during which annual leave can be taken and so on.

The job description and person specification provides a basis for drawing up a 'person specification', that is the skills and experience required to carry out the duties of the job.

The person specification

Purpose – The person specification forms the basis of the recruitment process from the advertisement through to the final interview stage. It describes the skills, aptitudes and experience needed to do the job and should be based on the job description, rather than a subjective view of the sort of person you would like to see filling the job. Generally, person specifications are laid down under standardized headings.

Qualifications and training

1. *General education* – It may be more appropriate for applicants to have certain levels of literacy or numeracy rather than academic qualifications. If qualifications are stipulated, equivalent qualifications that would be considered must be included.
2. *Specific training* – For example vocational certificates, professional qualifications, apprenticeship certificates and so on.

Knowledge – This is knowledge without which the job cannot be done, for example of computer systems. It should not include knowledge that can be imparted in an induction programme.

Experience – Either directly relevant or similar experience in a different environment might be considered. The type, range and depth of experience should be qualified (e.g. staff supervision). Specifying length of experience is usually unhelpful as some people learn more in a shorter time while others will take a longer time to learn.

Skills and abilities – This includes such aspects as the ability to communicate effectively, numeracy, analytical skills, attention to detail and so on. However, these skills must be clearly measurable as part of the selection process.

Special requirements – This should only form part of the specification where it is relevant to the job, for example a special type of driving licence if fork lift truck driving is to be part of the job, travelling, staying away from home and so on. The required characteristics are then entered against the appropriate heading, and subdivided into essential and desirable categories. The candidate who meets both the essential and desirable criteria will do the job particularly well, but obviously this person may be hard to find. Training and development may be needed in some areas. The person specification should be realistic. Too high an ideal will mean that potentially good candidates are excluded.

The Rodger seven-point plan

This was devised by Alec Rodger who developed a systematic approach for constructing person specifications. Having defined the demands of the job and evaluated the knowledge-base, skills, personal orientations, pre-dispositions and preferred values, the recruiter identifies the ideal 'qualities' needed for the job. Using the seven headings, the aim is to determine whether the candidate satisfies the essential criteria (factors that should disqualify candidates if they do not possess them). Desirable factors are ones that could be developed through training or development activities but could help in the process of distinguishing one eligible candidate from another – Does one candidate present a better profile than another?

1. *Physical make-up*

   What does the job demand in the way of general health, physical strength, stamina, eyesight, hearing, speech, appearance and so on? Legislation to prevent discrimination has stopped most of the specifications for 'attractive', 'young' and so on. The increasing number of disabled people in the workforce has encouraged many managers to re-evaluate just what physical attributes are necessary for a post.

2. *Attainments*

   What general education, technical knowledge, specialized training and relevant experience are required? To avoid becoming too overpowered by qualifications and diplomas, it is more useful to list specific knowledge areas, for example a marketing research job holder needs a proven knowledge of statistical sampling techniques. Conversely, sometimes there is an unwillingness amongst employers to recognize the value of working hard to achieve formal marketing qualifications when appointing marketing professionals. Questions need to be asked to establish the job, candidate's experience. Experience indicates knowledge and skill and how these have been used together. Much personal development comes from experience.

3. *General intelligence*

   What level of reasoning and learning ability is required? This can be a difficult area to evaluate since it is subjective in nature. For some jobs, the need is for people who prefer to have clearly structured rules and procedures to follow. For other jobs, the need may be for someone who does not mind ambiguity where little is clear-cut and each situation is different.

4. *Special aptitudes*

   Aptitudes and abilities are difficult to quantify, but they can be specified as the ability to be creative in generating solutions, to work under pressure, to think strategically, to negotiate contracts and so on. Once specified, it is possible to devise ways for assessment and evaluation.

5. *Interests*

   Are any general interests likely to be relevant to job success?

6. *Disposition*

   Does the job require people to get on with people, to be a self-starter, work on their own initiative, to accept responsibility, to work under pressure, to influence others? What attributes are needed to be able to fit into the culture of the department, section and so on. Disposition is important when individuals are going to be working as part of a team. An attempt should be made to assess how they might fit in and what contribution they might make. Characteristics such as loyalty and reliability may be more suited to the role of a product manager than to a sales person who needs to be outgoing and independent, self-motivated and confident.

7. *Candidate's circumstances*

   What domestic circumstances are relevant? – daily travel from home to work, time spent away from home on business. Is working overtime possible, if needed? However, care needs to be taken when asking such questions and the following are to be avoided – 'Are you married?', 'Do you have children?', 'Are you intending to start a family?' These are not relevant to the selection decision and could be perceived as discriminatory because they are about the person rather than the ability to do the job.

The following advertisement is for a marketing manager working for a leader in online recruitment.

Advertisement for a Marketing Manager

This is an opportunity to be part of one of the most highly regarded companies in an exciting and fast-moving industry. We are currently looking for a passionate Marketing Manager with heaps of initiative to oversee all marketing activities and communications. You'll be responsible for devising and implementing the company's annual marketing plan and helping to ensure continued growth in our client, user and subscriber numbers.

The Person

You must have:

- At least 3–4 years' experience in a similar Marketing role.
- Extensive experience of planning, buying and monitoring online marketing expenditure.
- Experience of devising and executing trade marketing campaigns to new and existing clients.
- Experience of managing a marketing budget of several hundred thousand pounds.
- Ideal, but not essential, are exposure to and understanding of the (a) accountancy and finance sectors, (b) the online recruitment industry and (c) some exposure to search engine optimization.

You must be:

- Enthusiastic, with a hands-on approach to Marketing.
- Self-motivated and adaptable with a can-do attitude.
- An excellent communicator, with creative, accurate written skills.
- Able to act as part of a wider management team, interfacing with all parts of the business especially Sales.

Munroe Fraser – 5 Point Plan

This focuses more upon a candidate's career to date as an indicator of future potential.

The 5 points:

1. *Impact on others* – Whether a person's appearance and demeanour are important.
2. *Qualifications and experience* – Skills and knowledge required.
3. *Innate abilities* – How quickly and accurately a person's mind works.
4. *Motivation* – The kind of work that appeals to a person and the amount of effort they are prepared to put into it.
5. *Emotional adjustment* – Capability of working with others.

Activity 2.4

Using one of the sets of headings identified above, draw up a person specification for the Media Relations post below:

1. *Job purpose*
   The Media Relations Executive will work in conjunction with the Trust's senior executives to develop and implement a comprehensive communications strategy. This will require building sound media contacts to ensure positive media coverage for the Trust's activities.

2. *Tasks*

   (a) Conduct a comprehensive review of media relations, and provide a diagnostic report for the Board of Directors.
   (b) Develop and implement a Trust media relations strategy.
   (c) Provide a quarterly analysis of media coverage with recommendations to improve coverage.
   (d) Arrange and publicize corporate events and host media representatives.
   (e) Anticipating and responding to events by issuing press releases, giving professional advice and guidance to other Trust managers.
   (f) Co-ordinate press conferences as necessary.
   (g) Provide in-house training on media relations and skills to trust staff according to need.
   (h) Establish robust relationships with key media representatives.

Interviews

In relation to the focus of an interview there are three principal interview models:

1. **Biographical interview** – exploring the candidate's experiences.
2. **Behavioural interview** – eliciting information about how applicants have behaved in similar situations.
3. **Situational interview** – comprising a series of job-related questions.

Many interviewers (or organizations) prefer to use one technique, but these different models can be useful in different situations and an Interview can combine all three aspects.

With regards to the process of interviewing there are, again, various models that can be used, for example Panel interviews.

Panel interviews can provide a better picture of a candidate than a one-on-one interview. There is more chance to think about a candidate's responses because the interviewer is more of an observer than a participant. This increases the validity of the assessment. In most one-on-one interviews, the interviewer is often thinking about what question to ask next; rather than listening to a candidate's answer. Many people hate these sort of interviews and find them a bit of an endurance test. To do well you will need to identify the important figures on the panel and which role each is fulfilling. The chairperson is easy to identify as they will generally make the introductions. You will also need to identify the person whom you will be working for directly – make sure you give them plenty of eye contact. When you are talking to the panel, remember that you are talking to all of them and not just the person who posed a particular question – your answer has to be the correct one for each panel member! If there is one particular panel member who everyone else seems to agree with, you should make sure you impress him or her.

Source: http://www.alec.co.uk/interview/panel.htm.

The interview room

It is essential that candidates be made to feel relaxed so that a proper assessment of their suitability for the job can be made. In the case of interview panels, care should be taken to ensure that the candidate is not seated too far away from the interviewees so as to feel isolated, nor so close as to be able to read the interviewers' notes.

Planning the interview

For an interview to be successful, it should be conducted in an orderly, empathetic but efficient manner. It is recommended that interviewers should undertake the following preparation:

o   Compare the candidate's application form with the person specification and pick out the points which need investigating further, for example experience, qualifications, gaps in a career history and inconsistencies.
o   Once the interview panel has done this, they should then prepare a plan of how the interview is to be conducted to ensure that nothing is omitted.
o   Questions need to be planned. These should be designed to probe the selection criteria of the person specification; namely a candidate's knowledge, ability and experience. Other questions should be aimed at a more general assessment of the candidate.
o   Where a candidate is attending an interview and they have informed you of any disability that they have, which may affect them during the interview process, it is a requirement of the Disability Discrimination Act to carry out 'reasonable' adjustments in order to ensure they can perform to their maximum potential; for example, if access is a problem for a candidate, the interviews should be held in a room accessible to all.
o   Identify key questions pertinent to the job that is asked of all candidates. This ensures that they have been asked equivalent and relevant questions.
o   Allocate the subjects to be explored. Each interviewer can cover different areas, for example work experience and training.
o   The candidate should have an opportunity to ask questions and interviewers should be prepared for the more obvious ones, such as hours of work and annual leave.

Objectives for an interview

Interviewers should be clear on the objectives of the interview:

o   To find out whether a candidate is suitable for the job advertised.
o   To find out whether the job and the department/organization are suitable for a candidate's needs (an aspect which is often overlooked).
o   To fairly select the most suitable candidate.

Conducting the interview

The interviewer should control the focus of the interview:

- o Introduce the members of the panel. Start the interview slowly, to allow the candidate to relax.
- o Explain the structure of the interview and what it is trying to achieve.
- o Give an overview of the context of and brief background for advertising the job.
- o Put the candidate at their ease and begin your questioning by identifying areas that are familiar, for example their present job before working through to the candidate's thoughts on the job for which they have applied.

Questioning

Encourage the candidate to speak freely, by asking open-ended questions such as 'tell us what you think about ...?' or 'how do you deal with ...?' Closed questions do not encourage the candidate to express their opinions in their own way.

Open-ended questions start with: 'how', 'what', 'why', 'when' or 'where'.

Behavioural questions are a good way of exploring what candidates have actually done in areas relevant to the job, for example:

'Give us an example from your last job when you had to persuade others to adopt a particular course of action.'

Hypothetical questions, for example, 'what would you do if?', should be used with care.

- o Allow the candidate time to think of their answers.
- o Summarize if you need to clarify ambiguous answers and to keep the interview on course.
- o Listen closely to what is being said and how it is expressed; as, by observing keenly, an interviewer can pick up clues that will enable them to explore an issue in more depth.
- o Be aware of your own biases for or against certain types of dress, appearance and so on as this could impair your judgement on the candidate's ability to do the job.
- o Make sure the candidate is aware of any special requirements of the job and that these are acceptable.
- o Allow time for the candidate to ask questions and invite them to do so.
- o Take brief notes which will allow you to return to a point later and to deliberate at the end.
- o To make comparative judgements of candidates, you must be able to remember the key points that each candidate made.

Finishing the interview

Once the interviewers have obtained all they need from the interview, they should check that the candidate has no further questions and then signify the end of the interview. They should then:

- o Tell the candidate when they can expect to know the outcome.
- o Check the candidate's expenses are covered, if appropriate.
- o Thank the candidate for attending the interview and see them out.

Key points

- Remove as much stress from the interview as possible.
- Ask open-ended questions.
- Ascertain all relevant facts, and probe ambiguous or vague answers.
- Listen to what the candidate has to say.
- Provide information relevant to the job.
- Provide opportunities for the candidate to ask questions.
- Tell the candidate when to expect to know the outcome of the interview.

The interview assessment

When a succession of candidates are seen over a period, it is essential to record accurate views on each immediately after each part of the process. Never allow interviewers to rely on memory.

The interview assessment allows each of your defined categories to be rated and a justification noted. This greatly facilitates the discussions that must take place at the end of the session as the short-list is constructed or the successful applicant is identified. Do not allow any sharing of views about candidates until after individual assessments have been recorded in writing.

Debriefing

Arrange a debriefing to:

- Short-list or reject candidates
- Make improvements to the recruitment and selection procedures
- If possible, provide advice to the unsuccessful candidates – this is good for public relations and is used routinely in the public sector.

Other aspects of interviews

The following examples of different selection techniques are not mutually exclusive and can be used in different combinations with each other.

Second interviews or follow-up interviews

Employers invite those applicants they are seriously considering as an employee following a screening or initial interview. These interviews are generally conducted by middle or senior management, together or separately. Applicants can expect more in-depth questions, and the employer will be expecting a greater level of preparation on the part of the candidate.

One-on-one interviews

Candidates are interviewed by one person. These interviews tend to be more informal; however, it depends on the employer's style. The interviewer will often have a series of prepared questions, but may have some flexibility in their choices.

Group interviews

Employers may bring several candidates together in a group situation to solve a problem. These may be aimed at testing your ability to work in a team environment or other interpersonal or problem-solving skills. It is difficult to prepare for this type of interview except to remember what is being tested and demonstrate team member or leadership skills.

Presentations

Asking candidates to make an oral presentation about a relevant topic can measure both their presentational and analytical skills.

Report writing

Candidates can be asked to write something on or before the interview day. This could test writing skills, subject knowledge or both.

Simulation exercises

An interpersonal exercise with a particular agenda and objectives, to observe how the candidates perform in a typical work situation such as a manager faced with an industrial relations issue.

Group discussions

Typically, all candidates are put together to deal with a particular problem, and are observed and evaluated doing so, such as a planning meeting on next year's appeal.

Psychometrics

These tend to measure current or potential skills levels, or personality profiling, which shows work styles and preferences and can be used to assess how well candidates will fit into the organization. Psychometric testing describes a range of exercises used by employers to find out about an individual's aptitude or personality. They usually form part of an overall selection process.

Ability tests may consist of one or more of numerical, verbal reasoning, spatial awareness and diagrammatical reasoning. Those used depend on the type of role for which someone is being assessed. Verbal and numerical tests are used in selecting graduates for a wide range of jobs including most business and management functions. Diagrammatic tests are used mainly for computing/IT jobs. The earlier in the selection procedure candidates are asked to sit a test, the more important the results are likely to be to the outcome. Employers who use tests only at second interview stage are likely to look upon the results as one of the number of criteria to be used in the selection process.

The following case study describes a more informal kind of process at the Apple Company.

Case study

Recruitment process at Apple

In marketing, you have the unique opportunity to work on revolutionary products from concept to launch with the best creative minds in the industry. Working with the most creative people in the business on breakthrough products is as satisfying as it is challenging. Our marketing department is comprised of the best and brightest, and we're always looking for stand-out talent to add to our team.

The Marketing division spans a variety of different disciplines including:

Developer relations, Events, Graphic Design, Marketing Communications, Product Marketing, Public Relations, Research and Analysis, Worldwide Markets.

Take a look at our website at www.apple.com. Explore the site and get to know our products. If you're a Software Engineer, make sure to visit our Developer site. Interested in Sales? Learn how our customers are using our products in creative ways in the Education, Pro and Business sections. Make sure you take the time to explore the website, it will tell you a lot of what you need to know about Apple and our customers.

Try our products in person at one of our retail stores or resellers. Listen to music on an iPod. Ask questions of one of the Mac Specialists. When you're at home, download our iTunes software to your Mac or PC and check out the iTunes Music Store. It's important that you familiarize yourself with our products to see what makes Apple unique. Once you're in the interview, relax and be yourself. The interview process is designed for us to make sure that we're a good fit for each other, which means that you should ask questions of us in addition to answering the questions that we ask you. Come prepared to discuss a variety of topics, not just your past experiences and accomplishments. And don't forget, we don't have a dress code, so wear clothes that make you comfortable.

Source: http://www.apple.com/jobs/marketing/interview.html.

Numerical critical reasoning

Numerical critical reasoning tests look at how well you can reason with numbers and understand information presented in a numerical form. In this sort of test you are presented with information followed by a number of questions. Your task is to select the right response from a range of possible responses.

Typical behaviour

Employers often want to assess aspects of personality, and in particular the way in which you work in a team situation. One way of doing this is to complete a 'self-report' questionnaire. This asks questions about the sort of role you tend to take when working in a team or group.

1. If it is not at all like you
2. If it is a bit like you
3. In between
4. Quite a lot like you
5. Very like you.

Sample statements

1.	I like to talk about new ways of doing things	1 2 3 4 5
2.	I am good at spotting mistakes	1 2 3 4 5
3.	I prefer to work with people I know well	1 2 3 4 5
4.	I make sure people know what to do	1 2 3 4 5
5.	I often use tried-and-tested methods	1 2 3 4 5
6.	I can be very forceful when I need to be	1 2 3 4 5

Assessment centre approach

One of the advantages of assessment centres is that it allows key job behaviours to be directly observed and measured. An assessment centre is a programme that organizes a range of tests for a group of candidates. The rationale for the approach is that multiple assessment techniques are more valid and reliable compared to single-method approaches such as interviews and personality questionnaires. The following dimensions are often assessed in assessment centres:

o Planning and organizing
o Leadership
o Analytical
o Problem-solving
o Sensitivity
o Decision-making
o Creativity
o Sociability
o Management control and delegating.

Assessors have to demonstrate the capability to observe and record the behaviour of candidates. Video is frequently used to aid assessors in gathering behavioural information. Assessors also need to be able to integrate information from various exercises, to discuss the ratings with fellow assessors and to be able to compare candidate performance.

Drawbacks of selection interviews

There is some doubt that an interview is the most appropriate mechanism for assessing candidates' suitability with accuracy, witness:

o First impressions are often lasting impressions; decisions tend to be made early on in the interview.
o Interviewers may prefer candidates who are like themselves, which may lead to discrimination.
o There is a danger of the interviewer only hearing information which supports preconceptions or first impressions.
o Interviewers can get jaded and confused if too many interviews are held in one day – early interviews get forgotten and later ones are less effective.

Online recruitment

Employer website

An employer website may be used as the mechanism for communicating details of job opportunities as well as collecting the data that an organization requires from candidates. Such a website usually provides some or all of the following features for candidates:

- Search for jobs
- Core details of the candidate
- Apply for jobs online
- Set up job 'alerts' (enables the candidate to receive e-mail notification when specified types of jobs become available)
- View status of online applications
- Job basket (allowing a single application to be submitted for multiple job vacancies).

Job boards

A job board is rather like the recruitment advertising section of a newspaper or magazine. It will carry many jobs from a combination of employers and agencies. As with traditional print media, decisions regarding which job boards to use are based on a number of factors: cost, sector, geography and so on. Some job boards offer services such as CV databases that employers and agencies can search. For candidates, job boards offer many of the same features as employer websites mentioned above.

Activity 2.5

How have those who have interviewed you performed in their role?

What would you have done differently?

What was good/bad about the best/worst interview you've ever had?

Summary

Teams differ in many ways, including size, purpose, type of work performed, structure, leadership, influence and decision-making ability. It is important to recognize that teamworking is not the best solution in every situation, and teams are not always more effective and efficient than individuals working to solve a problem. However, in many business situations, the ability to work in teams is valuable and teams can accomplish more than individuals who plough their own furrow. Criteria for an effective team were identified. An effective team has cohesion and a common purpose. Recruitment and selection guided by a personnel specification and proper preparation for interviews is of key importance. There are a wide range of selection procedures that can be used depending on the nature of the job and its importance to the organization. Recruitment and selection can be expensive but so can appointing the wrong person to a post.

Do's and don'ts for successful selection interviewing

Do's

- Prepare thoroughly.
- Check the organization's policies.
- Watch for inconsistencies between verbal and non-verbal behaviour.

Don'ts

- Make decisions based on a gut reaction.
- Break your schedule.
- Allow interruptions.
- Talk too much.

Working with diversity is an important skill for managers and team members, and they need to have good cultural and interpersonal awareness. The differences amongst individuals and groups should be acknowledged, accepted and valued. Working with people in different countries raises particular issues of cultural awareness.

Further study

Read Boddy, D. (2002) *Management: An Introduction*, Chapter 4, 'The international context of management' and Chapter 15, 'Teams'.

Hints and tips

It is always good to demonstrate your broader knowledge of marketing. So try to include examples from the marketing press, textbooks, journals and the Internet to support your answers. This is one way to demonstrate your knowledge and understanding to the senior examiner. Marketing is a highly practical activity and using examples to illustrate theory in practice is important. However, do make sure that your examples are relevant to the question in hand. Many questions do not explicitly ask for examples, but, where it is appropriate, do use them.

Bibliography

Achrol, R. and Kotler, P. (1999) 'Marketing in the network economy', *Journal of Marketing*, **62**, 146–163.

Adler, L. (2002) *Hire with Your Head*, New York: John Wiley & Sons.

Ashton, C. (1998) Strategic considerations in facilitative evaluation approaches [Internet], The Action Evaluation Project. (Available from www.aepro.org/inprint/conference/ashton.html [23 April 2000]).

Bartlett, C.A. and Ghoshal, S. (1989) *Managing Across Borders*, Cambridge, Mass: Harvard Business School.

Department of Indian and Northern Affairs, Canada (2003). <http://www.ainc-inac.gc.ca>. These ideas are adapted from the Department of Indian and Northern Affairs' website.

Department of Indian Affairs (2001), www.nqi.ca/english/ex8_spring _2001_empowerment.htm.

Dobson, D. and Dobson, M. (2000) *Enlightened Office Politics*, AMACOM.

Earley, P.C. (1993) 'East meets west meets mid east: Further explorations of collectivist and individualist work groups', *Academy of Management*, **36**(2), 319–348.

Hamel, G., Doz, W.L and Prahalad, C.K. (1991) 'Collaborate with your competitors and win', *Harvard Business Review*, **67**(1), 133–139.

Hofstede, G. (2001) *Culture's Consequences, Comparing Values, Behaviors, Institutions, and Organizations Across Nations Thousand Oaks*, CA: Sage Publications.

Hofstede, G., *Cultures and Organizations: Software of the Mind* (London: McGraw-Hill,1991; New York: McGraw-Hill,1997). Entirely re-written third Millennium edition, by Hofstede, G. and Gert, J. forthcoming (New York: McGraw-Hill, 2004).

Katzenbach, J.R. and Smith, D.K. (1993) *The Wisdom of Teams*, Harvard Business School.

Kotler, P. (2003) *Marketing Management*, 11th edition, Prentice Hall.

Lester, Don H. (1998) 'Critical success factors for new product development', *Research Technology Management*, January–February, pp. 36–43.

Maclaurin, I. (1999) 'Strategic direction', *Human Resource Management International Digest*, July/August.

Pettigrew, A. and Whipp, R. (1991) *Managing Change for Competitive Success*, Oxford: Basil Blackwell.

Robbins, H.A. and Finley, M. (2001) *The New Why Teams Don't Work: What Goes Wrong and How to Put it Right*, San Francisco: Berrett Kohler.

Trompenaars, F., Hampden and Turner, C. (2001) 21 *Leaders for the 21st Century: How Innovative Leaders Manage in the Digital Age,* London: Wiley & Sons. This is the latest book from the authors. Their best known book is Riding the Waves of Culture (1997), Nicholas Brealey Publishing.

Wertheim, E.G. (2000) Surviving the group project: A note on working in teams. [Internet] <http://www.cba.neu.edu/_ewertheim/teams/ovrvw2.htm> [20 April 2000].

Wilcox, D. (1994) 'The guide to effective participation', *Partnership*, Brighton, UK. (Available at www.partnerships.org.uk/guide/index.htm.)

Wynter, Leon E. (1997) 'Business and race: Hispanic buying habits become more diverse', *Wall Street Journal*, 8 January, B1.

Past examination papers for the Marketing Management in Practice module can be found in Appendix 5.

unit 3
developing the team

o Explain how you would use the techniques available for selecting, building, developing and motivating marketing teams to improve performance. This objective was partially covered in the previous unit (1.4).

o Allocate and lead the work of marketing teams, agreeing objectives and work plans with teams and individuals (1.5).

o Respond to poor performance within a marketing team by minimizing conflict, supporting team members, overcoming problems and maintaining discipline (1.6).

o Evaluate individual and team performance against objectives or targets, and provide constructive feedback on their performance (1.8).

Statements of Marketing Practice

Lc.1 Manage a *marketing* team.

Lc.2 Maintain relationships with other functions and disciplines within the organization.

Lc.3 Encourage and help others to develop their competencies relevant to a *marketing* role.

Study Guide

Teams – Differ in many ways, including size, purpose and type of work performed, structure, leadership, influence and decision-making ability.

Types of teams include:

1. Natural work group
2. Management
3. Project improvement
4. Process redesign or re-engineering

5. Cross-functional, that is, design and production include people of various skill levels from throughout the organization
6. New product and service design teams.

Stages of team development

In the 1960s, Psychologist B.W. Tuckman developed this model and suggested that there are four team development stages that teams have to go through in order to be productive (Tuckman, 1965).

Some teams may go through the four stages fairly rapidly and move from forming through to performing in a relatively short space of time. A lot depends on the composition of the team, the capabilities of the individuals, the tasks at hand, and the team management and leadership.

Forming

Polite but not yet trusting. Formalities are maintained and members are treated as strangers. This can be a stressful phase when new teams come together. Everyone is a bit wary of each other, particularly if they do not know anyone and particularly if the manager is new. At this stage, each individual tends to want to establish his or her personal identity within the group.

Storming

Testing others. Members start to communicate their feelings but probably do not yet view themselves as part of the team. Most groups go through a conflict stage when initial consensus on purposes, leadership, norms of behaviour and work is challenged and re-established. No matter how clear the team was in relation to the goals, roles and rules during the forming stage, it is often the case that individual interpretations of these are somewhat different in reality. At this stage, personal agendas are revealed and a certain amount of interpersonal hostility is generated. If successfully handled, this period of storming leads to a new and more realistic setting of objectives, procedures and norms. This stage can be important for testing the norms of trust in the group.

Norming

Valuing other types. People feel part of the team and realize that they can achieve work if they accept other viewpoints. Norming is characterized by acceptance. The group needs to establish norms and practices. When and how it should work, how it should take decisions, what type of behaviour, what level of work, and what degree of openness, trust and confidence is appropriate. Whereas in the storming stage, people were apt to rebel very quickly; this is not the case now and if someone has a grievance, complaint or suggestion then the proper processes are used. Goals are understood and roles are clarified. The rules and regulations are being adhered to and people are working together positively. Relationships become stronger as people are more aware of each other.

Performing

Flexibility from trust. The team works in an open and trusting atmosphere where flexibility is the key, and hierarchy is of little importance. Not every team makes it to this stage. Many get stuck at norming and although everything appears normal, there is a lack of momentum and motivation towards achieving all the important team goals. At the performing stage, team members are focused on team goals and are aware of the strengths and weaknesses of the team. Only when the three previous stages have been successfully completed, will the group be at full maturity and be able to be fully and sensibly productive. Some kind of performance will be achieved at all stages of the development but it is likely to be impeded by the other processes of growth and by individual agendas.

Roles in a team

Based on research with over 200 teams conducting management business games at the Administrative Staff College, Henley, in the UK, Belbin (1996) identified nine team types. People usually have a mix of roles and will have dominant and sub-dominant roles.

Co-ordinator

The co-ordinator is a person-oriented leader. This person is trusting, accepting, dominant, and is committed to team goals and objectives. The co-ordinator is someone tolerant enough to always listen to others, but strong enough to reject their advice. This is a person who calls meetings, keeps people on track and pays attention to group processes. For example, the co-ordinator makes sure that everyone is involved and notices when someone is upset. Some of the things that successful co-ordinators try to do are:

- o Focus team on task
- o Engage participation from all members
- o Protect individuals from personal attack
- o Suggest alternative procedures when the team is stalled
- o Summarize and clarify the team's decisions.

Shaper

The shaper is a task-focused leader who has a high motivation to achieve and for whom winning is the name of the game. The shaper is committed to achieving ends and will 'shape' others into achieving the aims of the team. He or she will challenge, argue or disagree and will display aggression in the pursuit of goal achievement. According to Belbin, two or three shapers in a group can lead to conflict and in-fighting.

Plant

The plant is a specialist idea maker characterized by high IQ and introversion, while also being dominant and original. The plant tends to take radical approaches to team functioning and problems. Plants are more concerned with major issues than with details.

Weaknesses are a tendency to disregard practical details and argumentativeness.

Resource investigator

The resource investigator is the executive who is never in his room, and if he is, he is on the telephone. The resource investigator is someone who explores opportunities and develops contacts. Resource investigators are good negotiators who probe others for information, and support and pick up other's ideas and develop them. They are characterized by sociability and enthusiasm, and are good at liaison work and exploring resources outside the group.

Weaknesses are a tendency to lose interest after initial fascination with an idea, and they are not usually the source of original ideas.

Company worker/implementer

Implementers are aware of external obligations, and are disciplined, conscientious and have a good self-image. They tend to be tough-minded and practical, trusting and tolerant, respecting established traditions. They are characterized by low anxiety and tend to work for the team in a practical, realistic way. Implementers figure prominently in positions of responsibility in larger organizations. They tend to do the jobs that others do not want to do, and do them well: for example, disciplining employees. Implementers are conservative, inflexible and slow to respond to new possibilities.

Monitor evaluator

According to the model, this is a judicious, prudent, intelligent person with a low need to achieve. Monitor evaluators contribute particularly at times of crucial decision-making because they are capable of evaluating competing proposals. The monitor evaluator is not deflected by emotional arguments, is serious-minded, tends to be slow in coming to a decision because of a need to think things over and takes pride in never being wrong.

Weaknesses are that they may appear dry and boring or even overcritical. They are not good at inspiring others. Those in high-level appointments are often monitor evaluators.

Team worker

Team workers make helpful interventions to avert potential friction and enable difficult characters within the team to use their skills to positive ends. They tend to keep team spirit up and allow other members to contribute effectively. Their diplomatic skills together with their sense of humour are assets to a team. They tend to have skills in listening, coping with awkward people and to be sociable, sensitive and people-oriented.

They can be indecisive in moments of crisis and reluctant to do things that might hurt others.

Completer/finishers

The completer/finisher dots the i's and crosses the t's. He or she gives attention to detail, aims to complete and to do so thoroughly. They make steady effort and are consistent in their work. They are not so interested in the glamour of spectacular success.

Weaknesses, according to Belbin, are that they tend to be overanxious, and have difficulty letting go and delegating work.

Specialist

The specialist provides knowledge and technical skills within the team. They may be introverted and anxious but tend to be self-starting, dedicated and committed.

Significance of Belbin team roles

Where there is an uneven spread of roles in a group there may be problems in addressing the task allocated. Team members need to be aware of their main team role, know their second-best role and see if these can complement the other group members' roles. In this way, an effective team can be constructed. A person's team role may alter over time and he or she may play different roles in different teams.

There is a tendency in top teams for too many 'shapers' and 'plants' with few if any 'completer/finishers'. This means that everyone likes to talk, wants their own ideas to be accepted by all and relies on others to take the follow-through actions. Another role that is often lacking in top teams is that of 'monitor/evaluator' – this person may be perceived as trying to prevent things from happening by introducing balance and reality into the discussions.

Specific teams

Knowing the predominant Belbin roles of your team may provide an explanation as to why a particular team does not work well. Where there is a role that is not fulfilled at all in the team, then either the leader will need to ask someone to take on the role, or it needs to be covered by the team members.

Leadership and management of teams

Not all leaders are managers and not all managers are leaders. However, managers can be leaders and vice versa. Leadership is derived from an Anglo-Saxon word meaning the road or path ahead. Managing comes from a Latin word 'manus', meaning hand, and is more associated with handling a system or machine of some kind.

As indicated above, some managers will do some of the same things that leaders do and vice versa. It is more a question of the balance of activities that comprise a job, and the expectation is that leaders would spend more time focusing on the strategic direction of the organization. However, there are many different theories about leadership and in the 1980s a new paradigm emerged called transformational leadership as opposed to transactional leadership. The relative instability and unpredictability of the environment has given rise to this new conception of leadership, and there is a premium on leadership to ensure that an organization can adapt to and be successful in a world of constant change. The transformational leader motivates and inspires staff and ensures that staff understand the vision for the future of the organization.

Five characteristics of leadership
   o *Challenging the process* – encouraging others to develop new ideas and judicious risk-taking.
   o Inspiring a shared vision about the future.
   o *Enabling others to act* – encouraging collaboration, co-operation, building teams and empowering others.
   o *Modelling the way* – planning and reviewing progress and taking corrective action in a way that gains the respect of others. Clear about values and act in a manner consistent with them.
   o Recognizing and celebrating others' achievements.

Source: Kouzes and Posner (2002).

Team leadership

John Adair's (1988) Action-Centred Leadership model is based on three parts:

1. Defining the task
2. Managing the team or group
3. Managing individuals.

People need to be briefed properly about the objectives that need to be achieved, what needs to be done, why, how and when. The extent to which all of this needs to be spelled out by the leader or manager will depend on the people involved, the work context and the nature of any particular tasks. In a situation where there is an expectation that tasks will be delegated, there is no need to go into great detail about how something should be done because this will be the responsibility of the person carrying out the task. The purpose of the business is to deliver something of value to people. The leader is responsible for ensuring that the marketing task determines what that value is, and then organizes work in the most effective and efficient way to deliver it (see Figure 3.1).

Figure 3.1 Team Leadership: John Adair, What a Leader has to do? (1988)

Core functions of leadership

Adair sets out the core functions of leadership that are central to the Action-Centred Leadership model (see Figure 3.2):

o *Planning* – Seeking information, defining tasks, setting aims, initiating – briefing, task allocation, setting standards.
o *Controlling* – Maintaining standards, ensuring progress, ongoing decision-making.
o *Supporting* – Individuals' contributions, encouraging, team spirit, reconciling, morale.
o *Informing* – Clarifying tasks and plans, updating, receiving feedback and interpreting.
o *Evaluating* – Feasibility of ideas, performance, enabling self-assessment.

The Action-Centred Leadership model, therefore, does not stand alone, it must be part of an integrated approach to managing and leading. There should be a strong emphasis on applying these principles through training.

Adair's Leadership Checklist

	Key Functions	Task	Team	Individual
C o m m u n i c a t i o n	Define objectives	❑ Clarify task ❑ Obtain information ❑ Identify resources and constraints	❑ Assemble team ❑ Give reasons why ❑ Define accountability	❑ Involve each person ❑ Gain acceptance
	Plan & Decide	❑ Consider options ❑ Establish priorities ❑ Plan time	❑ Consult ❑ Encourage ideas ❑ Agree standards	❑ Listen ❑ Assess abilities ❑ Delegate ❑ Agree targets
	Organize	❑ Establish control ❑ Brief plan ❑ Obtain feedback	❑ Structure ❑ Answer questions ❑ Prepare and train	❑ Check understanding ❑ Counsel ❑ Enthuse
	Control & Support	❑ Maintain standards ❑ Report progress ❑ Adjust plan if necessary ❑ Set personal example	❑ Co-ordinate ❑ Maintain external co-operation ❑ Relieve tension	❑ Guide and encourage ❑ Recognize effort ❑ Discipline
	Review	❑ Evaluate results against objectives ❑ Consider action	❑ Recognize team's success ❑ Learn from setbacks	❑ Appraise performance ❑ Identify further training needs ❑ Aid personal growth

Figure 3.2 Adair's leadership checklist

Generic role definition for Team Leaders (Armstrong, 1996)

Purpose of role – To lead teams in order to attain team goals and further the achievement of the organization's objectives.

Key result areas:

- o Agree targets and standards with team members which support the achievement of the organization's objectives.
- o Plan with team members work schedules and resource requirements which will ensure that team targets will be reached, indeed exceeded.
- o Agree performance measures and quality assurance processes with team members.
- o Co-ordinate the work of the team to ensure that team goals are achieved.
- o Ensure that the team members collectively monitor the team's performance in terms of achieving output, speed of response, and quality targets and standards.
- o Agree with team members any corrective action required to ensure that team goals are achieved.
- o Conduct team reviews of performance to agree improvement plans.
- o Conduct individual reviews of performance to agree areas for improvement and personal development plans.
- o Recommend appropriate team performance rewards and individual rewards related to the acquisition and effective use of skills and capabilities.

Capabilities:

- o Builds effective team relationships, ensuring that team members are committed to the common purpose.
- o Encourages self-direction amongst team members but provides guidance and clear direction as required.
- o Shares information with team members.
- o Trusts team members to get on with things – not continually checking.
- o Treats team members fairly and consistently.
- o Supports and guides team members to make the best use of their capabilities.
- o Encourages self-development by example.
- o Actively offers constructive feedback to team members, and positively seeks and is open to constructive feedback from them.

Contributes to the development of team members, encouraging the acquisition of additional skills and providing opportunities for them to be used effectively.

Managing team behaviour

Behaviour to avoid is self-serving behaviour that has nothing to do with the team performing. For example:

- o *Attention getting* – nobody seems interested in what I have to say.
- o *Aggression* – don't care what you say, you're wrong.
- o *Withdrawal* – we're getting nowhere, why don't we each work on the problem by ourselves.

Managing team behaviour requires skill and a clear understanding of what is required. Again good communication skills can significantly improve team behaviour. Communication skills that help encourage team members to focus on the task include:

- o *Initiating* – where shall we start?
- o *Clarifying* – isn't Jo suggesting that …?
- o *Direction* – don't you think we should be moving the discussion along?
- o *Information seeking* – don't you have some sales figures on …?
- o *Information giving* – the latest marketing research report shows …

A team leader is accountable for the effective functioning of the team. The leader monitors team performance and takes action to improve team effectiveness. Teams tend to perform best when responsibilities are shared and leadership tasks are distributed among members.

Evaluation of team performance

Developing a process plan for the way a team will work together can provide a useful reference point to evaluate how well a team is doing. A team's process plan should describe how the team will approach its work, including how the team will resolve conflict. Controlling politics is critical to team decision-making because internal politics produce poor team performance and restrict information flow within the team. Techniques for controlling internal politics include:

- o Conduct open and frank discussions
- o Fully share information
- o Make meetings open to all members.

When a team approach to work is in place, the focus of performance management is on the accomplishments of the team as well as the individual's contributions to those accomplishments. Team effectiveness is improved when both team and individual performance are recognized as significant and factored into the performance management process. Team performance standards refer to skills which make employees effective team members as well as the standards expected of individuals. Performance management of a self-directed work team may be undertaken by the team itself but this can vary from organization to organization, or department to department. The organization should provide guidelines and a framework for that performance management, but within this, the team may be responsible and accountable for its own performance. A self-directed work team may be able to describe its own jobs, set its own standards, give feedback to its own members about work performance and team skills, appraise itself and identify and support the training and development needs of its members. However, this is likely to be a rare occurrence because of the greater demands of accountability that have developed in the past couple of decades.

The ability to provide effective observation and feedback is important because it is through observation that areas for improvement can be identified and the team made aware of them. Whether the team is self-directed and managing its own performance, or team members that report to one or more line managers, teams will benefit from observation and feedback. If the team as a whole has a formal reporting relationship with a line manager, he or she will be concerned with observing and giving feedback about the work-related behaviour and outputs of the team as a whole, as well as that of individual team members. If team members report to different line managers, or if the line manager is not present when the team does its work, he or she will need to establish procedures and relationships for learning about the work the team is doing and how it is working together. This could involve receiving input from the team leader, team members and customers of the team.

Performance standards and statistical data relating to the achievement of objectives and targets help in providing 'objective' feedback. However, statistics never speak for themselves and should only be used as the platform for a discussion as to why targets have or have not been reached. There may be a host of extraneous and unforeseen factors that have influenced the attainment of targets. For example, no one could have predicted what would happen to the airline industry in 2001 when the Twin Towers were attacked in New York. Another source of feedback for teams is customers. This feedback may come in a variety of forms: surveys, feedback cards, suggestion boxes, in-person interviews, telephone interviews, and focus groups.

When the basis for appraisal is the performance of individual team members, the incentive to work effectively with other team members may be missing. Because of this some organizations appraise team performance and not individual performance but this can undermine a sense of individual responsibility. Some organizations appraise team performance and individual performance. The main issues regarding the performance management of teams relate to the variety of reporting relationships and degree of independent responsibility that teams may exercise, as well as the need to reinforce team values and efforts without undermining individual responsibility. Typically, a line manager will be involved in some or all of the following activities:

- Allocating work to teams and individuals
- Agreeing objectives and work plans with teams and individuals
- Assessing the performance of teams and individuals
- Providing feedback to teams and individuals on their performance
- Dealing with poor performance in a team
- Supporting team members who have problems affecting their performance
- Implementing disciplinary and grievance procedures
- Dismissing team members whose performance is unsatisfactory.

Constructive feedback

Feedback is a way of learning more about ourselves and the effect our behaviour has on others. Constructive feedback increases self-awareness, offers options and encourages development.

Start with the positive

Most people need encouragement to be told when they are doing something well. If the positive is identified at the beginning, negative points are more likely to be acted upon.

Be specific

Generalized comments are not very helpful. Try to be specific about particular examples of behaviour that are not acceptable. Try to identify what a person did well or behaviour that can be praised.

Refer to behaviour that can be changed

Give feedback about something that the person can change.

Offer alternatives

If you give negative feedback, suggest what the person could have done differently. Turn the negative into a positive suggestion.

Be descriptive rather than evaluative

Tell the person what you saw or heard and the effect it had on you rather than merely saying that something was good, bad and so on. Explain fully.

Own the feedback

All that anyone is entitled to give is their own experience, of that person, at a particular time. Comments such as 'you always . . .' or 'you are . . .' as if they are agreed statements about what a person is like are not productive. It is important that we take responsibility for the feedback that we offer.

Leave the receiver with a choice

Feedback which demands change may meet with resistance. Skilled feedback offers people information about themselves in a way which leaves them with the choice about whether to act on it or not. It can help to examine the consequences of any decision to change or not to change.

This will keep the individuals motivated to give their best.

Insight

The 12-minute interview

A regular meeting with an employee to talk one-on-one about issues, problems and progress in work and the workplace.

Why should it be used? – To make sure that employees have direct contact with the team leader. Talking to staff regularly encourages each employee to contribute to the team effort. If time is invested, it will help to avoid losing touch with people when it is a busy time.

How can this tool help? – One of the concerns of front-line staff is a lack of direct contact with their supervisor or manager. This tool helps to build meeting time into the daily routine.

How does it work? – Create a rotating schedule so that, for example, every day at a particular time the team leader meets with a different member of staff.

Doing – Ensure that 12 minutes at the set hour. Do not try to control the session; what is important will come up.

Follow-up – Once the 12-minute interview becomes part of workplace culture, it will enable better and more planned use of time. Staff will keep note of questions, problems and issues that can be addressed during their regular interview and only ask for special meetings for more urgent or complex matters.

Allocating responsibilities

In order to allocate work to teams and individuals, the manager needs to decide with the team how to distribute tasks and responsibilities. This means ensuring that the allocation makes best use of team members' abilities, and provides opportunities for them to learn and develop in their roles. The manager needs to make it clear what is expected of team members. Where resources are limited, a manager may have to prioritize objectives or reallocate resources while minimizing the disruption this may cause.

Objectives and work plans

In order to agree objectives and work plans with teams and individuals, they need to be SMART, that is, specific, measurable, realistic, time-bound and consistent with the organization's overall objectives and policies. Ways of working need to be explained, and there is a need to update objectives and work plans in the light of progress and changes. In order to assess the performance of teams and individuals, the manager needs to make it clear why performance is monitored and assessed. Individuals and teams need to be encouraged to evaluate their own performance wherever possible.

Motivation

Work motivation refers to the forces within a person that affect his or her direction, intensity, and sustainability of voluntary behaviour in the workplace. As a new generation of employees enters the workplace and as globalization creates a more diverse workforce, companies may need to rethink their motivational practices. Content motivation theories explain why people have different needs at different times. These theories also warn against relying too heavily on financial rewards as a source of employee motivation. Process theories of motivation describe the processes through which needs are translated into behaviour. According to Maslow's needs hierarchy theory, the lowest needs are initially most important, but higher needs become more important as the lower ones are satisfied. Goals are more effective when they are specific, relevant, challenging, accepted by the employee, and accompanied by meaningful feedback. Goal setting can be less effective when tied to financial rewards. It also creates the risk of focusing employees on measurable dimensions of their job to the detriment of more complex and long-term performance dimensions.

McClelland

One of the best-known theories is McClelland's motivational theory (McClelland *et al.*, 1953) which is based on three types of motivational need that are found to varying degrees in all workers and managers. McClelland's theory argues that people have secondary needs or drives that are learned rather than instinctive, including need for achievement, need for power, and need for affiliation.

Achievement motivation – The 'achievement motivated' person seeks attainment of realistic but challenging goals, and advancement in the job. There is a strong need for feedback about achievement and progress, and a need for a sense of accomplishment.

Authority/power motivation – The 'authority motivated' person needs to be influential and effective to make an impact. There is a strong need to lead and for their ideas to prevail. There is also motivation and need towards increasing personal status and prestige.

Affiliation motivation – The 'affiliation motivated' person has a need for friendly relationships and is motivated towards interaction with other people. The affiliation driver produces motivation, and need to be liked and held in popular regard. These people are team players.

Most people possess and exhibit a combination of these characteristics. Some people exhibit a strong bias to a particular motivational need, and this affects their behaviour and working/ managing style. McClelland felt that people with a strong 'achievement motivation' made the best leaders although there was a tendency to demand too much of their staff in the belief that they too are highly achievement-focused and results-driven.

McClelland suggested that for achievement-motivated people:

- ○ Achievement is more important than material or financial reward.
- ○ Achieving the aim or task gives greater personal satisfaction than receiving praise or recognition.
- ○ Financial reward is regarded as a measurement of success, not an end in itself.
- ○ Security is not the prime motivator, nor is status.
- ○ Feedback is essential, because it enables measurement of success, not for reasons of praise or recognition (the implication here is that feedback must be reliable, quantifiable and factual).
- ○ Achievement-motivated people constantly seek improvements and ways of doing things better.
- ○ Achievement-motivated people will logically favour jobs and responsibilities that naturally satisfy their needs, that is, offer flexibility and opportunity to set and achieve goals, for example, sales and business management, and entrepreneurial roles.

McGregor XY Theory

In 1960, Douglas McGregor advanced the idea that managers had a major part in motivating staff. He divided managers into two categories – Theory X managers who believe that their staff are lazy and will do as little as they can get away with; and Theory Y managers who believe that their people really want to do their best in their work. Theory X managers believe that staff will do things if they are given explicit instructions and plenty of stick if they do not do what they are supposed to do. Theory Y managers believe their people work their best when empowered to make appropriate decisions.

Achievement-motivated people tend towards X-Theory style, due to their high task focus.

1. *Theory X assumptions*:

   (a) People inherently dislike work
   (b) People must be coerced or controlled to do work to achieve objectives
   (c) People prefer to be directed.

2. *Theory Y assumptions*:

   (a) People view work as being a natural activity
   (b) People will exercise self-direction and control towards achieving objectives to which they are committed
   (c) People learn to accept and seek responsibility.

Since McGregor, Theory Z has been advanced by William Ouchi. This is Theory Y on steroids, and states that employees crave responsibility and opportunities for growth all the time. It is strongly influenced by Japanese management styles.

Hertzberg motivators and hygiene factors (Hertzberg *et al.*, 1959)

Herzberg's motivator–hygiene theory states that people are only motivated by characteristics of the work itself, whereas 'hygiene' factors only reduce dissatisfaction. However, evidence suggests that hygienes can motivate to some extent.

Hertzberg (1959) constructed a two-dimensional paradigm of factors affecting people's attitudes about work. He concluded that such factors as company policy, supervision, interpersonal relations, working conditions and salary are hygiene factors rather than motivators. According to the theory, the absence of hygiene factors can create job dissatisfaction, but their presence does not motivate or create satisfaction. In contrast, motivators are elements that enriched a person's job; he found five factors in particular that were strong determiners of job satisfaction: achievement, recognition, the work itself, responsibility and advancement. These motivators (satisfiers) were associated with long-term positive effects in job performance while the hygiene factors (dissatisfiers) consistently produced only short-term changes in job attitudes and performance, which quickly fell back to its previous level.

Satisfiers describe a person's relationship with what he or she does, many related to the tasks being performed. Dissatisfiers, on the other hand, have to do with a person's relationship to the context or environment in which he or she performs the job. The satisfiers relate to what a person does while the dissatisfiers relate to the situation in which the person does what he or she does. A manager may not be able to easily influence all the hygiene factors of a person's job but he or she can have a big influence on many of the motivators.

1. *Motivator factors that increase job satisfaction*:

   (a) Achievement
   (b) Recognition
   (c) Work itself
   (d) Responsibility
   (e) Advancement
   (f) Growth.

2. *Hygiene factors – absence of 'good' factors can create job dissatisfaction*:

(a) Company policy
(b) Working conditions
(c) Salary
(d) Peer relationships
(e) Security.

Source: Frederick Hertzberg, *Work and the Nature of Man* (1966).

Expectancy theory

Expectancy theory states that work effort is determined by the perception that effort will result in a particular level of performance (E –> P expectancy), the perception that a specific behaviour or performance level will lead to specific outcomes (P –> O expectancy), and the valences that the person feels for those outcomes.

The E –> P expectancy increases by improving the employee's ability and confidence to perform the job. The P –> O expectancy increases by measuring performance accurately, distributing higher rewards to better performers, and showing employees that rewards are performance-based.

Equity theory

Equity theory explains how people develop perceptions of fairness in the distribution and exchange of resources. The theory also explains what people are motivated to do when they feel inequitably treated. People react differently to inequitable situations based on their equity sensitivity. These differences are influenced by personality and cultural values.

Adams' Equity Theory is based on the principle that individuals want a fair balance between the inputs, or what they give to their job, and the outputs, or what they get from it. Employees develop a view of what is fair by comparing their own situation with other people who they regard as 'referents'. Typical inputs might be effort, loyalty, hard work, commitment and skill. Typical outputs are obvious ones such as pay and expenses and also more intangible ones such as recognition, praise, responsibility, sense of achievement and so on.

If people feel that their inputs outweigh the outputs then they may become demotivated. In this situation, some people switch off and do the minimum that they can, or even become disruptive. Others aim to seek to improve the outputs by making pay claims or looking for other work. The key aspect of the theory is that extrinsic rewards such as level of pay are neither motivating nor demotivating in themselves. Rather it is how fair we perceive them to be when we compare ourselves with significant others, that is people who we feel should be paid less than or about the same as ourselves, or people whom we expect to be paid more than us.

If we feel that inputs are fairly and adequately rewarded by outputs (the fairness benchmark being subjectively perceived from market norms and other comparable references) then we are happy in our work and motivated to continue inputting at the same level.

Creating a culture of teamwork

To make teamwork happen, these actions need to occur:

- Leaders need to communicate the clear expectation that teamwork and collaboration are expected. No one completely owns a work area or process all by himself. People who own work processes and positions are open and receptive to ideas and input from others.
- Leaders and managers model teamwork in their interaction with each other and the rest of the organization. They maintain teamwork even when things are going wrong, and the temptation is to slip back into former behaviour.
- Teamwork is rewarded and recognized. The lone ranger, even if he or she is an excellent producer, is valued less than the person who achieves results with others. Compensation, bonuses and rewards depend on collaborative practices as much as individual contribution and achievement.
- The performance management system needs to emphasize and value teamwork. Often 360-degree feedback is integrated within the system; this feedback from colleagues, direct reports and managers can have a powerful impact on work behaviours.
- Teams need to be formed to solve real work issues and to improve real work processes. Provide training in systematic methods so that the team expends its energy on the project, not on how to work together to approach it.
- Hold department meetings to review projects and progress, to obtain broad input, and to co-ordinate shared work processes. If group members are not getting along, examine the work processes they mutually own. The problem may not be the personalities of the people. Rather it may be the fact that they often have not agreed on how they will deliver a product or a service or the steps required to get something done.
- Celebrate group successes publicly.
- A team leader should be focused on achieving the task, building and maintaining the team and developing the individual.

Are there situations in which teamwork can be detrimental?

YES! If the group is not primarily interdependent, then teamwork can be detrimental to the effectiveness of the group. For instance, teambuilding programmes for sales people will usually be counterproductive. Sales people are typically independent and self-motivating. Therefore, teambuilding activities will be seen by the group as a waste of time. More effective training for a group which is not interdependent would be communication training, leadership training or other forms of personal development.

If the group is interdependent, but doesn't realize that the actions of the individual affect the group, then teambuilding activities will also meet with resistance. This may occur in an organization where departments are autonomous. Department heads may begin to see themselves in competition with other department heads for resources including budgets, capital and personnel. Before implementing teambuilding activities with this type of group, spend some time helping the group realize how interdependent they really are.

Building and maintaining the team

A team-based organization relies on self-directed work teams rather than functional departments as the core work units. Traditional departments may be teams where employees are encouraged to directly interact and coordinate work activities with each other. However, unlike traditional departments, team-based organizations tend to rely on cross-functional, autonomous teams with less need for supervisors as a communication or coordination role.

Virtual teams operate across space, time and organizational boundaries with members who communicate mainly through information technologies.

Three team design elements are task characteristics, team size and team composition. Teams work best when tasks are clear, easy to implement and require a high degree of interdependence. Teams need to be large enough to perform the work, yet small enough for efficient coordination and meaningful involvement. Effective teams are composed of people with the competencies and motivation to perform tasks in a team environment.

Individuals are often required to move between working with many different groups of people during their working lives. Most teams are created to increase productivity, maximize cooperation and communication, and minimize conflict. Work teams, which are part of larger systems like managerial or production systems, perform a wide array of activities within the organization. Teams usually have well-defined physical and task boundaries, matching technical systems, and norms or rules governing interaction and behaviour. The internal leader may be a full-time team member. Management may appoint an external leader, who serves as coordinator, facilitator, mentor, encourager, cheerleader or consultant. The leadership role may also be shared by several people, or the leader may perform several functions. There are two critical elements to effective team building: a connection between all members of the team, and a shared understanding between the leadership and each team member.

Cross-functional teams consist of people from many parts of an organization. Organizations tend to have flatter structures and functional departments may not be well defined. The rise of self-directed teams reflects these trends. Cross-functional teams require a wide range of information to reach their decisions. They need to draw on information from all parts of an organization's information base. This includes information from all functional departments. Cross-functional teams require information from all levels of management. Technical, financial, marketing, and all other types of information must come in a form that all members of a cross-functional team can understand.

Team building is any formal activity intended to improve the development and functioning of a work team. Four team-building strategies are role definition, goal setting, problem-solving, and interpersonal processes. Some team building events succeed, but companies often fail to consider the contingencies of team building. Cohesiveness is the degree of attraction people feel toward the team and their motivation to remain members. Teams need some level of cohesiveness to survive, but high cohesive units have higher task performance only when their norms do not conflict with organizational objectives.

The six deadly sins of team building (Bacal, 2002).

If the need for team development is recognized, there are some pitfalls to avoid.

1. *Lack of a model* – It is not uncommon for people leading a team-building process to focus on a single aspect of team functioning. Often the emphasis will be on communication practices, to the exclusion of other elements that are critical to team success and effectiveness. A one-dimensional team-building process may increase frustration, and destroy the credibility of the process.
2. *Lack of diagnosis* – Each team is different. Each team has distinct strengths and weaknesses, and team building must build on these specific strengths and address weaknesses. Without knowing these strengths and weaknesses, the team-building leader runs the risk of using a process that will be irrelevant.
3. *Short-term intervention* – It is not uncommon for a manager to arrange for a team-building day, without developing a longer-term strategy for team development. At best, a single day on its own will result in a brief motivational surge that quickly fades. At worst, the day will bring to light issues that cannot be solved during that day, and are left to fester.
4. *No evaluation of progress* – It is common for team-building efforts to take for granted that things are improving without putting in place a mechanism for regular evaluation of team functioning. The team-building leader must be able to identify barriers so that the team can work to eliminate them.
5. *Leadership detachment* – Management sometimes enters into team building in a somewhat detached way. The detached manager treats it as something that will help others change, so that the team will function more effectively. However, team effectiveness cannot be improved unless the manager is willing to look at his or her contributions to the team. Management usually has to change too.
6. *Doing it all internally* – Team building generally will not succeed unless conflicts and problems can be brought into the open and dealt with properly. The problem is that poorly functioning teams are characterized by a climate of blame, defensiveness and a lack of ability to deal with conflict. Poor teams lack the ability to improve themselves.

Conclusion – Whether you are leading team-building activities or hiring someone, it is important that you stay away from the six deadly sins.

Insight

The stand-up

A tool to help create a group identity and a sense of shared purpose.

A regular, standing-up, 15-minute team session.

To make sure that everyone is aware of all the important things in your workplace that affect you and your work.

How can it help?

It helps to address the 'Why am I never told?' syndrome. The stand-up is an easy way to make sure that everyone is up to date. There is no time for long descriptions of the progress of each person's work.

How does it work?

It requires a shared understanding among the members of your group about what this 'anti-meeting' should accomplish and how it works.

Planning

There is no chairperson and no agenda but only raise those items that concern the whole group. Meet regularly in a central location where everyone has room to stand.

Doing

Keep it simple, optimistic, focused and fun. It is better to say nothing than to talk about something of no concern to the group. Talkers learn to listen and listeners have an opportunity to talk.

Conflict in organizations

Conflict is inevitable but it can be minimized, diverted and/or resolved. Workplace conflict can lower morale and productivity, increase turnover and employee burnout, and add greatly to sick pay costs. Some conflicts are good and some not so good. Conflict occurs naturally when people interact, and teams, organizations and even individuals can grow as a result of the new ideas and the new ways of thinking that can emerge through conflict. However, conflict can also be destructive for individuals and for organizations. Organizational change can require members of an organization to work together in new ways and under new rules. Competition can exacerbate personality conflicts and the complexities of communication can make it more difficult for culturally, economically and socially diverse workers to resolve the issues and problems they encounter on the job.

Source: Lankard Brown (1998).

Different people have different ways of dealing with situations but, in general, human beings share certain characteristics that are very similar – even across gender, racial and socio-economic lines.

- ○ People tend to like it when people agree with them
- ○ People tend to not like it when people disagree with them
- ○ People tend to like other people who agree with them
- ○ People tend to dislike other people who disagree with them
- ○ People who are good at resolving conflicts look for some point of agreement and use good people skills to get others to see a different point of view.

Conflict occurs when individuals or groups do not obtain what they need or want and are seeking to look after their own self-interests. Sometimes the individual is not aware of the need and unconsciously starts to act out. Other times, the individual is very aware of what he or she wants and actively works at achieving the goal.

Conflict is destructive when it:

- ○ Takes attention away from other important activities
- ○ Undermines morale or self-concept
- ○ Polarizes people and groups, reducing co-operation
- ○ Increases or sharpens difference.

Conflict is constructive when it:

- Results in clarification of important problems and issues
- Results in solutions to problems
- Involves people in resolving issues important to them
- Causes authentic communication
- Helps release emotion, anxiety and stress
- Builds co-operation among people through learning more about each other
- Joining in resolving the conflict
- Helps individuals develop understanding and skills.

Some strategies for dealing with conflict

1. *Non-verbal alert* – Non-verbal behaviour can be an early warning sign of conflict. Ask people to verbalize their feelings wherever possible.
2. *Team development phase* – See (p. 80) the Tuckman forming, storming, norming, performing model. Sometimes conflict is predictable because that is what happens at one particular phase of group development.
3. *Resort to authority* – This means bringing in someone using a legitimate power base (and perhaps other power bases) to lay down the law. This may be necessary if team members are playing destructive roles.
4. *Planning* – Planning techniques, such as task scheduling, timelines and project diaries and meetings may provide an authoritative and neutral way of sequencing tasks to be performed by different individuals or sub-groups, thus reducing potential for conflict.
5. *Use communication skills more effectively* – Sometimes it is best to utilize what you know about good communication skills. Try to control destructive role-playing. Acknowledge individuals by praising their input.
6. *Conflict management techniques*
7. Collaborating: win/win

    (a) Compromising: win some/lose some
    (b) Accommodating: lose/win
    (c) Competing: win/lose
    (d) Avoiding: no winners/no losers.

Collaborating
I win, you win

Fundamental premise – Teamwork and co-operation help everyone achieve their goals while also maintaining relationships.

Strategic philosophy – Working through differences will lead to creative solutions that will satisfy both the parties' concerns.

When to use:

- When there is a high level of trust.
- When you don't want to have full responsibility.
- When you want others to also have 'ownership' of solutions.
- When the people involved are willing to change their thinking as more information is found and new options are suggested.
- When you need to work through animosity and hard feelings.

Drawbacks:

- o Takes lots of time and energy.
- o Some may take advantage of other people's trust and openness.

Compromising
You bend, I bend

Fundamental premise – Winning something while losing a little is OK.

Strategic philosophy – Both ends are placed against the middle in an attempt to serve the 'common good' while ensuring each person can maintain something of their original position.

When to use:

- o When people of equal status are equally committed to goals.
- o When time can be saved by reaching intermediate settlements on individual parts of complex issues.
- o When goals are moderately important.

Drawbacks:

- o Important values and long-term objectives can be derailed in the process.
- o May not work if initial demands are too great
- o Can create cynicism, especially if there is no commitment to honour the compromise solutions.

Accommodating
I lose, you win

Fundamental premise – Working towards a common purpose is more important than any of the peripheral issues.

Strategic philosophy – Appease others by downplaying conflict, thus protecting the relationship.

When to use:

- o When the issue is not as important to you as it is to the other person.
- o When you know you can't win.
- o When it's not the right time.
- o When harmony is extremely important.
- o When what the parties have in common is a good deal more important than their differences.

Drawbacks:

- o One's own ideas don't get attention.
- o Credibility and influence can be lost.

Competing

I win, you lose

Fundamental premise – Associates 'winning' a conflict with competition.

Strategic philosophy – When goals are extremely important, one must sometimes use power to win.

When to use:

- ○ When you know you are right.
- ○ When you need a quick decision.
- ○ When a strong personality is trying to steamroller you.
- ○ When you need to stand up for your rights.

Drawbacks:

- ○ Can escalate conflict.
- ○ Losers may retaliate.

Avoiding

No winners, no losers

Fundamental premise – This isn't the right time or place to address this issue.

Strategic philosophy – Avoids conflict by withdrawing, sidestepping or postponing.

When to use:

- ○ When the conflict is small and relationships are at stake.
- ○ When more important issues are pressing and you don't have time to deal with this one.
- ○ When you see no chance of getting your concerns met.
- ○ When you are too emotionally involved and others around you can solve the conflict more successfully.
- ○ When more information is needed.

Drawbacks:

- ○ Important decisions may be made by default.
- ○ Postponing sometimes makes matters worse.

Source: Culbert (2002).

Managing conflict between teams

Teams don't have to like each other to work together, but they do need to respect and value each other's existence. Find common goals and work out a compromise. Ultimately, the groups share a common goal: Both want the company to succeed. If both teams contribute to the same product, having a successful product launch is a shared goal. Even though product developers may not write ad copy, they must still support marketing's goals if they want employment this time next year. Product developers do have strengths they can offer. They may be good at building systems or analysing problems. Have each team identified the strengths they have that they can offer across the company?

After celebrating their own strengths, have the teams brainstormed the strengths of some of the other teams and designed a request they might make of another team? Keep each team focused on the strengths of other teams. Have the teams kept their own written record of this part of the strengths conversation, especially the strengths they discover in other teams? If they put it in writing themselves and share it, it will have much more psychological power than a one-time discussion.

Bring the groups together. Frame the meeting as a joint exploration of how you can, as a group, move past conflict and reach the shared goals that the groups have already owned individually.

Source: Adapted from *Managing Conflict Between Teams*, 16 June 2003, by Steve Robbins, http://www.entrepreneur.com/article/0,4621,309225,00.html.

Copyright © 2006 Entrepreneur.com. all rights reserved. Reprinted with permission from Entrepreneur.com

Groupthink

Groupthink is a concept that was identified by Irving Janis, referring to faulty decision-making in a group. Groups experiencing groupthink do not consider all alternatives, and they desire unanimity at the expense of quality decisions. Janis listed seven symptoms that show that consensus seeking has led the group astray. The first two stem from overconfidence in the group's prowess. The next pair reflect the tunnel vision members use to view the problem. The final three are signs of strong conformity pressure within the group.

- Incomplete survey of alternatives
- Incomplete survey of objectives
- Failure to examine risks of preferred choice
- Failure to reappraise initially rejected alternatives
- Poor information search
- Selective bias in processing information at hand
- Failure to work out contingency plans.

Case study

An illustration of groupthink

Report of the presidential commission on the space shuttle Challenger disaster

1. *Illusion of invulnerability* – Despite the launch pad fire that killed three astronauts in 1967 and the close call of Apollo 13, the American space programme had never experienced an in-flight fatality. When engineers raised the possibility of catastrophic O-ring blow-by, NASA manager George Hardy nonchalantly pointed out that this risk was 'true of every other flight we have had'. Janis summarizes this attitude as 'everything is going to work out all right because we are a special group'.

2. *Belief in inherent morality of the group* – Under the sway of groupthink, members automatically assume the rightness of their cause. At the hearing, engineer Brian Russell noted that NASA managers had shifted the moral rules under which they operated: 'I had the distinct feeling that we were in the position of having to prove that it was unsafe instead of the other way around'.

3. *Collective rationalization* – Despite the written policy that the O-ring seal was a critical failure point without back-up, NASA manager George Hardy testified that 'we were counting on the secondary O-ring to be the sealing O-ring under the worst case conditions'. Apparently, this was a shared misconception. NASA manager Lawrence Mulloy confirmed that 'no one in the meeting questioned the fact that the secondary seal was capable and in position to seal during the early part of the ignition transient'.

4. *Out-group stereotypes* – Although there is no direct evidence that NASA officials looked down on Thiokol engineers, Mulloy was caustic about their recommendation to postpone the launch until the temperature rose to 53 degrees. He reportedly asked whether they expected NASA to wait until April to launch the shuttle.

5. *Self-censorship* – We now know that Thiokol engineer George McDonald wanted to postpone the flight. But instead of clearly stating 'I recommend we don't launch below 53 degrees', he offered an equivocal opinion. He suggested that 'lower temperatures are in the direction of badness for both O-rings . . .' What did he think they should do? From his tempered words, it's hard to tell.

6. *Illusion of unanimity* – NASA managers perpetuated the fiction that everyone was fully in accord with the launch recommendation. They admitted to the presidential commission that they didn't report Thiokol's on-again/off-again hesitancy with their superiors. As often happens in such cases, the flight readiness review team interpreted silence as agreement.

7. *Direct pressure on dissenters* – Thiokol engineers felt pressure from two directions to reverse their 'no-go' recommendation. NASA managers had already postponed the launch three times and were fearful that the American public would regard the agency as inept. Similarly, the company's management was fearful of losing future NASA contracts. When they went off-line for their group meeting, Thiokol's senior vice president urged Roger Lund, vice president of engineering, to 'take off his engineering hat and put on his management hat'.

8. *Self-appointed mindguards* – 'Mindguards' protect a leader from assault by troublesome ideas. NASA managers insulated Jesse Moore from the debate over the integrity of the rocket booster seals. Even though Roger Boisjoly was Thiokol's expert on O-rings, he later bemoaned that he 'was not even asked to participate in giving input to the final decision charts'. Conflict within groups or teams can often lead to bad decision-making and problem-solving, rash decisions, inadequate consideration of alternative solutions and poor perception of what is happening in a given situation.

Source: Griffin (1999).

Another related phenomenon is the Abilene Paradox which describes a situation when a group of people act in a way that none of them wants but no-one intervenes to stop what is occurring. Sometimes people feel uncomfortable acting in a manner contrary to the trend of the group. Sometimes the theory is used to help explain poor business decisions and groups are urged to ask themselves – 'Are we going to Abilene?' to make sure that the decision is what the group members want or whether it is a result of groupthink.

The Abilene Paradox

In 1988 *The Abilene Paradox and other Meditations on Management* was published by Jerry B. Harvey. The essence of the Paradox is that the limits of a particular situation force a group of people to act in a way that is directly the opposite of their actual preferences. It occurs when groups continue with activities that no group member wants but no-one is willing to raise any objections.

A family is playing dominoes when the father-in-law suggests that they take a trip to Abilene (53 miles away) for dinner. The wife says, 'it's a great idea'. The husband has reservations because it is a long drive but thinking he must be out-of-step he says, 'Sounds good to me. I just hope your mother wants to go.' The mother-in-law then says, 'Of course I want to go.'

The drive is hot, dusty and long and the cafeteria food is bad. They arrive back home four hours later, exhausted. One of them dishonestly says, 'It was a great trip, wasn't it.' The mother-in-law says that, actually, she would rather have stayed home, but went along since the other three were so enthusiastic. The husband says, 'I wasn't delighted to be doing what we were doing. I only went to satisfy the rest of you.' The wife says, 'I just went along to keep you happy.' The father-in-law then says that he only suggested it because he thought the others might be bored.

The group sits back, wondering how they managed to take a trip which none of them wanted. They each would have preferred to sit comfortably, but did not admit to it.

Developing the team

Activity 3.1

Here is an activity for evaluating your team. Circle the number that is appropriate for your team. What are your priorities for development? – You could also ask a trusted colleague to complete a form like this about you so that you can compare your responses with his or her perceptions. If there were large gaps in perception you might want to pursue this further to understand why your perceptions are different.

Evaluate your team development

Rating team development
How do you feel about your team's
    progress? (Circle rating)
1. Team's purpose
    I'm uncertain   1 2 3 4 5   I'm clear
2. Team membership
    I'm out   1 2 3 4 5   I'm in
3. Communications
    Very guarded   1 2 3 4 5   Very open
4. Team goals
    Set from above   1 2 3 4 5   Emerged through team interaction
5. Use of team member's skills
    Poor use   1 2 3 4 5   Good use

6. Support
   Little help for individuals 1 2 3 4 5 High level of support for individuals
7. Conflict
   Difficult issues are avoided 1 2 3 4 5 Problems are discussed openly and directly
8. Influence on decisions
   By few members 1 2 3 4 5 By all members
9. Risk-taking
   Not encouraged 1 2 3 4 5 Encouraged and supported
10. Working on relationships with
    others
    Little effort 1 2 3 4 5 High level of effort
11. Distribution of leadership
    Limited 1 2 3 4 5 Shared
12. Useful feedback
    Very little 1 2 3 4 5 Considerable

Team effectiveness includes the group's ability to survive, achieve its system-based objectives and fulfill the needs of its members. The model of team effectiveness considers the team and organizational environment, team design and team processes. The team or organizational environment influence team effectiveness directly, as well as through team design and team processes. Elements in the organizational and team environment that can influence team effectiveness include reward systems, communication systems and physical space. Team decisions are impeded by time constraints, conformity to peer pressure, groupthink and group polarization. Conformity keeps team members aligned with team goals, but it also tends to suppress dissenting opinions. Group polarization refers to the tendency of teams to make more extreme decisions than individuals working alone. Team decision-making problems can be minimized by ensuring that the team leader does not dominate, maintaining an optimal team size, ensuring that team norms support critical thinking, and introducing team structures that support more creative decision-making.

Learning in teams
Team learning is essential for organizational learning. Learning between teams, and the structures for this shared learning, is how organizational learning builds. Different people learn in different ways and therefore a training programme that suits one type of person might not suit another. Training should contain a variety of activities so that everyone finds something that is suitable for them. One of the best-known approaches to learning styles is the work of David Kolb through his 'Learning Styles Inventory'. Peter Honey and Alan Mumford published *The Learning Styles Questionnaire* (1982) which extended Kolb's work.

Insight

Learning and development

Developing our people is one of our most important goals. Essentially, if we do not have the right people, with the right skills and capabilities, at the right time and in the right places, our business will suffer. After all, Serco only has two kinds of product: its processes and its people.

We are committed to developing our people – and we encourage them to learn and grow throughout their careers. In a business as diverse as ours, it is vital that we can share more widely the best practice developed in one market or region. That is why we are using the latest technology to give everyone access to the same information and resources.

We are always being joined by new people as we phase-in new contracts – so we have devised ways of helping them assimilate our values and adopt the Serco culture. Because we have a diverse portfolio of contracts, our training and development processes are designed to produce staff who are versatile, flexible and inventive.

As Serco becomes increasingly global, distance learning is likely to become more important. We are currently investing in solutions that will enable us to deploy and track learning in geographically diverse locations – enabling us to reach all our people, everywhere. Combined with powerful diagnostic tools, including performance appraisal and development centres, this will ensure we deliver learning solutions that meet today's business needs – and help us anticipate future needs.

SERCO: Our World, December 2005.

Induction training

All new employees need some form of introduction to the organization and the job. A well-planned system of induction provides regular training and/or development sessions. For example, large department stores have a continuing programme of induction with a new course starting every week and special provision for part-time workers. This leaves individual managers in the comfortable position of receiving staff who have at least received training that is specific to their job. Some training, such as health and safety awareness, should be given to all employees.

In larger organizations line managers may take responsibility for monitoring and encouraging each individual at their place of work and for off-the-job training. However, there may be a specialist training and development section that is usually part of the Human Resources Department.

The benefits of training and development

o *Improved motivation* – Individuals see their skills base extending and their promotion prospects being enhanced.
o *Lower turnover* – Opportunities for self-improvement, leads to people staying longer in one employment.
o *Higher levels of performance* – Trained and motivated staff are more likely to give of their best, which, in the end, justifies the training budget.

Insight

The Polestar Group is the UK's leading commercial printer and the fourth largest in the world. The Group aims to be the most innovative and profitable printers in Europe. This means that its staff need to be trained to use the latest high-tech digital equipment. Polestar's employees experience training at work that includes:

o Induction training
o Training in new ways of working, technology and software
o Multi skilling – employees are trained to do several different interrelated jobs
o Learning management, organizational and leadership skills
o Developing skills through a wide range of personal enhancement programmes.

Skilled print workers are in short supply, and the average age of the workforce is high. Polestar has developed a training programme called 'Printdynamics' which is designed to both attract and retain good workers. It is an interactive CD-Rom and online training package that offers comprehensive coverage of the print industry. It guides the trainee through the different print processes. Ensuring that employees are multi-skilled leads to increased job satisfaction and flexibility. Ongoing training often results in improved productivity by eliminating waste and avoiding delays.

On-the-Job training (OJT)

Although people's learning styles differ, learning theory suggests that most people learn and retain more through doing and practising activities. OJT is the most common form of training in organizations. To be effective it needs to:

o Be properly planned and specified in advance
o Take place at trainees' normal work positions
o Be accepted that there will be 'downtime' when little is being produced by the people carrying out the training.

It is often carried out with a line manager or other experienced staff but often they will not have received any training in this role so the quality can be variable. OJT is not always the best approach to developing broader transferable skills but it is good for job-specific skills. Training that takes place at or near the job can be more easily tailored to meet specific needs and arranged at convenient times. The involvement of colleagues, supervisors or managers in OJT can also help to build a strong team spirit. OJT is often associated with the development of new employees, but it can also be used to update and widen the skills of existing employees.

Off-the-Job training and development

A key issue is making sure that the event matches up to the values the organization is trying to promote and the expectations of the staff who are taking part in the training. One aspect of this is the venue and, for example, if the intention is to focus on customer care it is important that the participants are treated well as customers. Everything about the training needs to model the behaviour it is trying to promote.

Online training and education

Online training can be used as a supplement to face-to-face encounters. In some instances, instructors can supplement their material by placing related material on the Web. Some uses include:

o Aspects of induction training which are routine and technical such as health and safety procedures.
o Business training on procedures used to protect information within the company.
o Teaching the use of common business applications, such as Microsoft Office.

Managers need to understand their own Learning Style preferences and those of the people they manage. Responses to e-learning may be according to Learning Style preference. E-learning is more likely to deliver knowledge-type learning, rather than skills development. It may not be the most suitable answer to a particular individual's learning needs.

Introduction

To succeed, businesses need to monitor the changing business environment and respond accordingly. They also must ensure that the workforce is developed so that it can respond to changing requirements and provide good customer service. Quality customer service is a complex process that leads to competitive advantage. Travis Perkins was formed in 1988. The two businesses that merged had histories stretching back 200 years. It is one of the UK's biggest distributors of building materials. It uses customer service as a basis for growth. It trades under a number of brand names that have helped to establish its reputation with customers.

Growth

Many organizations benefit by economies of scale when they grow sufficiently large. These may be Internal – made within the organization such as discounts through bulk buying or using techniques and equipment unavailable to smaller firms – or external – arising outside the organization such as access to a skilled labour force, specialist trade associations and being close to specialist suppliers. Travis Perkin's business strategy has been successfully based on growth and it aims to continue to grow.

Business culture

Every business has a particular way of reaching its objectives and its own way of working embodied in its culture. Travis Perkin's culture is based on the assertion that quality of service is paramount. Good service and reliability are particularly important in the building trade when contractors may be fined for late completion.

Training

Travis Perkins continuously improves its workforce. After being inducted, employees go through customer service training. Their performance is continually reviewed and they receive training from managers. There is also skills training to develop effectiveness, ICT, customer care and accounting. In 2003 Travis Perkins launched Excel, a programme for all employees, aimed at continuously improving services to customers. It links training processes to the need to provide high quality customer care. The business has also set up a Development Zone where employees can book sessions to complete training courses.

Management training

This includes programmes developed in-house for trainees and middle managers. Outside providers run courses for senior managers. Programmes vary according to need. For example, high performance managers can develop a tool kit for performance to help them to analyse, manage, delegate and work in teams.

Conclusion

Travis Perkins recognizes that it is its employees and their understanding of quality customer service that makes the organization distinct. Good training is vital.

Evaluation of training

Most management and employee training is only assessed by the individuals involved in the process and much of the feedback is taken from questionnaires. Although many organizations have developed strategies for developing managers, the evaluation of their training and development is often ineffective. Over a decade ago, research undertaken in the UK entitled 'Training in Britain: A Study of Funding, Activity and Attitudes' revealed that 85 per cent of UK employers made no attempt to assess the benefits gained from undertaking training. The reasons for this are:

○ Difficulty in quantifying the effects.
○ Difficulty in disentangling the effect of a number of variables which might affect performance.
○ Cost of evaluation that could outweigh the value of the benefit achieved.
○ Sensitivity of the trainers who are keen to ensure that their training is shown to have had a positive effect.

The ultimate goal of training and development is to effect change in an individual's knowledge, understanding, skills and behaviours. However, for practical reasons of time and resources, often it only focuses on knowledge and to a lesser extent on understanding.

A model of effective evaluation: Joyce and Showers model

The first of five components of this model is the presentation of theory or the description of a new skill or behaviour deemed useful or desirable.

The second component of the Joyce and Showers model is demonstration or modelling of the new strategy or skill. This could be achieved by observing someone.

The third component is initial practice in a protected or simulated setting – most often in a workshop session. The individual or the group participates, trying out the new skill.

The fourth component is providing structured and open-ended feedback about performance.

The fifth component is coaching. As the new idea or skill is being applied and tried in a real setting, follow-up help with implementation is given to the participant.

When participants were given only the first component, a description of the new skill, 10 per cent of the persons could transfer or use the skill in the workplace. When the second component, demonstration of the skill, was included, 2–3 per cent more persons could perform the skill in the classroom. When practice, the third component, was added, 2–3 per cent more transfer occurred; similarly, when the fourth component, feedback, was included, another 2–3 per cent transfer occurred. Thus, four components resulted in 16–19 persons out of 100 able to perform the new skill in the classroom. However, when coaching, the fifth component, was part of the staff development process, up to 95 per cent of the participants transferred the skill into their actual practice. The coaching component was a critical one in effecting a change in the skills of an exceedingly large number of persons.

Coaching

Coaching is a learning opportunity and individual learning preferences need to be considered as part of this. To be an effective coach, the team leader needs to build trusting relationships. Focused listening is one of the most important skills for establishing such a relationship.

There are three levels of understanding and skill required for effective coaching:

o Recognizing managerial situations as opportunities
o Creating an effective learning process
o Establishing an acceptable helping relationship.

Organizational benefits of coaching

o To improve individual performance – to expand an individual's range of skills, knowledge and insight in order to help them do the job better
o To provide a supportive working environment
o To value people
o To improve communication
o To promote effective teams
o To ensure appropriate allocation of tasks and projects
o To develop managerial skills, for example, to improve the skills of team leaders
o To expand the range of skills, knowledge and insight of someone in order to enhance their prospects for a different job
o To develop people for more senior jobs
o To increase organizational effectiveness and efficiency
o To enable best use of resources.

Benefits of coaching to the individual

o Support for individual learning needs – tackling the tasks and the issues that concern people in their day-to-day job
o On-the-job development for both coach and individual – it can be a learning experience for both participants in the opportunity to reflect on skills, knowledge and behaviour
o Increased motivation
o Improved capability at work
o Potential to support career development.

 ## Activity 3.2

Tick any items where you feel you have a need for coaching. Put them in order of priority for you. Next to your priorities, write the names of people in your organization who might help you with these activities. Work out a strategy for approaching the people concerned.

Coaching checklist

1. Providing guidance and support —— ——
2. Helping to get the 'big picture' in the organization —— ——
3. Helping with networking/making contacts —— ——
4. Interpreting organizational politics —— ——
5. Translating organizational jargon —— ——
6. Being a sounding-board for action plans —— ——
7. Appraising/reviewing performance —— ——
8. Providing day-to-day advice on problems —— ——
9. Listening and questioning —— ——
10. Being a resource person – able to point to opportunities/learning resources
11. Evaluating progress.

Mentoring

Mentoring can be provided in various ways but its aim is to develop people and organizational effectiveness.

Management development

Torrington and Hall (1998) show that management training and management development can be differentiated in four important ways:

1. Management development is a broader concept. It is more concerned with developing the whole person rather than emphasizing the learning of narrowly defined skills.
2. Management development emphasizes the contribution of both formal and informal work experiences.
3. The concept of management development places a greater responsibility on managers to develop themselves than is placed on most employees to train themselves.
4. Although in training generally there is always a need to be concerned with the future, this is especially emphasized in management development. Managers are developed as much for jobs they will be doing, as for jobs that they are doing. Both the managers and the organization benefit from this approach.

K Shoes first implemented teams in 1990, and 45 per cent of the employees are in teams of 5–8 people. Their responsibilities include: managing team resources based on marketplace demand for styles of shoes, understanding the business and marketplace issues and their impact on demand, and the handling of materials and equipment budgeting. Other responsibilities are controlling team profit and loss, identifying team training needs, and conducting cross-training and problem-solving during non-production time. Also described in the case study are the training and compensation of teams, member selection, performance evaluation and the impact of teams on the organization.

The primary benefits of undertaking a management development programme for the individual is the modification of their management style, technical or professional skills, while the primary benefits for the organization of such a programme focus on its ability to act as a catalyst in transforming the organization by providing the skills and knowledge to manage innovation and change (Doyle, 2000). These benefits are complementary in developing both the individual and the organization. A significant trend in management development in the 1990s has been the move away from case-based programmes to problem-solving, focusing on real-life issues.

1. The individual participating must see the issue involved as important
2. It must involve some analysis
3. It must involve some aspect of creativity
4. There must be practical application of the suggested improvement.

Goals of management development

Given that there is some uncertainty about what successful managers actually do, it is difficult to establish clear goals for management development. In general, however:

- o Management development will focus on the abilities to do, rather than on pure knowledge.
- o Management development will focus on the needs of individuals and tailor 'developmental opportunities for each'.
- o Individuals will be expected as a matter of course to take the initiative in their own self-development.

Team reward

Team reward aims to reinforce behaviour which leads to effective teamwork. It encourages group endeavour rather than just individual performance. Most team reward systems emphasize team pay rather than non-financial rewards. However, teams may respond to all types of reward from pay, bonuses and public recognition. An advantage is that team pay can encourage co-operative work and behaviour, and develop self-managed and directed teams.

Team pay works best if teams stand alone with agreed targets and are composed of people whose work is interdependent. For it to work well, everybody must understand and accept the targets and the reward must be linked clearly to effort and achievement.

Teams may be able to plan and implement their own improvement programmes if they receive feedback and meet regularly to discuss performance. Team reward is a way for organizations to demonstrate that they value teams and individuals who perform well, and that high levels of performance are important. The quality of teamwork depends on:

- o Culture
- o Structure and operating processes
- o Values
- o Performance management
- o Management style
- o Employee development programmes.

Discipline

A disciplinary interview can be thought of as having three stages:

- o *Establishing the gap* – Future performance is the main concern, so any discussion about present behaviour should be focused on changes that are needed for the future and how to achieve them. It is important to be specific about concerns and to provide evidence or examples of how there is a gap between present behaviour and what is required.
- o *Exploring the reasons for a gap* – It is important to allow the person subject to a disciplinary interview to explain the circumstances and to put forward their point of view about the gap. This may uncover problems or issues that the manager is unaware of but will need to be dealt with in some way, for example suggesting that they seek advice and guidance or specialist help.
- o *Eliminating the gap* – There will need to be agreement to a plan of action that may involve training. Arrangements for keeping the situation under review will need to be agreed, and the person should be aware of how and when their performance is going to be monitored. The aim is to help facilitate an improvement in performance.

Summary

Members of a team can contribute to it in two distinct roles: their professional or technical role (production, sales, etc.) and their team role. The effectiveness of the team will depend on the extent to which its members correctly recognize and adjust themselves to the relative strengths within the team. Each team needs a balance of team roles and the optimum balance will depend on the tasks that the team needs to perform and its objectives. Personal attributes fit some roles well but limit the ability to succeed in other roles.

Further study

Read Boddy, D. (2002) *Management: An Introduction*, Chapter 13, 'Motivation' and Chapter 15, 'Teams'.

Hints and tips

If you are asked to interpret some information, it usually means that you need to explain the meaning of it, making it clear that you understand the data provided. This is a likely scenario if undertaking Marketing in Practice. This exam will contain data that needs interpreting.

You will need to have an appreciation of the theories and processes applicable to selection, recruitment, appointment and induction of new personnel into an organization. Specific development should reflect the nature of any particular position that is the focus of the recruitment and the context of the organization.

Lengthy description is not necessary. Focused use of theory in the particular case study context is important.

Bibliography

Adair, J. (1988) *Effective Leadership*, London: Pan.

Armstrong, M. (1996) *A Handbook of Personnel Management Practice*, London: Kogan Page.

Bacal, R. (2002) *'The six deadly sins of team building'*, <http://www.work911.com/articles/teambuildings.htm>

Belbin, R.,, Meredith (1996a) *Management Teams: Why they Succeed or Fail*, London: Butterworth-Heinemann.

Belbin, R.,, Meredith (1996b) *Team Roles at Work*, London: Butterworth-Heinemann.

Bennis, G., Warren (1994) *On Becoming a Leader*, 2nd edition, New York: Perseus.

Challenger Disaster, *A First Look at Communication Theory*, 3rd edition, McGraw-Hill.

Culbert, H. (2002) 'Conflict management strategies and styles: Improving group dynamics', <http://home.snu.edu/>

Doyle (2000) *Value-based Marketing: Marketing Strategies for Corporate Growth and Shareholder Value.*

Griffin, Em. (1999) 'Report of the presidential commission on the space shuttle', www.firstlook.com

Herzberg, F. et al., (1959) *The Motivation to Work*, New York: John Wiley.

Kouzes, J.M., Posner B.Z. (2002) *The Leadership Challenge*, 3rd edition, New York: Jossey Bass.

Lankard Brown, Bettina (1998) 'Conflict management', <http://ericave.org/docs/conflict.htm>

McClelland, D. et al. (1953) *The Achievement Motive*, New York: Appleton Century Crofts.

McGregor, D. (1960) *The Human Side of Enterprise*, New York: McGraw-Hill.

Ott, Daniel, J. (1999) <http://www.egsa.org/powerline/past/MA99relmktg.htm>

Tuckman, B.W. (1965) 'Developmental sequences in small groups', *Psychological Bulletin*, **63**, pp. 384–399. Tuckman later revised his model to include a fifth stage but this is not as well known as his 4 stage model. See Tuckman, B.W. and Jensen, M.A.C. 'Stages of small group development revisited', *Groups and Organization Studies*, **2**, pp. 419–427.

Past examination papers for the Marketing Management in Practice module can be found in Appendix 5.

unit 4
managing change

Learning objectives

Explain the sources and nature of change affecting organizations, and the techniques available for managing change (1.7).

Related Statement of Marketing Practice

Lc.4   Embrace change and modify behaviours and attitudes.

Introduction

Organizations face change all the time, driven by internal and/or external influences. Most changes in organizations are minor and incremental. A few changes are major and involve completely new ways of operating. Managing change means taking active control of change because many problems are those of adaptation, that is they require of the organization only that it adjusts to an ever-changing set of circumstances. Factors from outside the business include: technological developments; changing market conditions, such as exchange rate movements, supplier price increases and demand from customers for new services; and legislation, such as the working time regulations and the minimum wage. Factors from inside the business include: personnel changes, such as key employees leaving and new senior appointments. New management processes such as customer service initiatives are also a source of change, and there are constant pressures to improve efficiency in both the public and private sectors. Change management is the process of developing a planned approach to change in an organization.

Change management can be either 'reactive', in which case management is responding to changes in the macro-environment, or 'proactive', in which case management is initiating the change in order to achieve a desired goal.

A key part of managing change is being able to select and apply appropriate tools and techniques that enable an organization to understand its strengths and weaknesses in relation to its competitors as well as understanding how the world is changing and its implications for a business. This kind of analysis helps an organization to develop a rationale and understand the factors that are driving change.

Much depends on how different models are used because each model helps to illuminate an organization's position in its own way. However valuing the acquisition of useful information is different from relying entirely on information gained from one model to base a strategy. Thus, despite the criticisms of different models, they each have something to offer when applied judiciously.

Factors driving change

The macro-environment

This includes all factors that can influence an organization, but that are out of their direct control. A company does not generally influence any laws (although it is accepted that they could lobby or be part of a trade organization). It is continuously changing, and the company needs to be flexible to adapt. There may be aggressive competition and rivalry in a market.

The PEST analysis is a useful tool for understanding market growth or decline. A PEST analysis is a business measurement tool. PEST is an acronym for Political, Economic, Social and Technological factors, which are used to assess the market for a business or organizational unit.

A PEST analysis (also sometimes called STEP, STEEP or PESTLE analysis) looks at the external business environment. Technological factors include ecological and environmental aspects – the second E in STEEP and PESTLE, while the L in PESTLE stands for legal. A PEST analysis examines the impact of each of these factors and the interplay between them on the organization. The results can then be used to take advantage of opportunities and to make contingency plans for threats when preparing business and strategic plans.

The PEST analysis headings are a framework for reviewing a situation, and can be used to review a strategy or position, direction of a company, a marketing proposition, or an idea.

PEST is useful than SWOT because it helps to identify SWOT factors. There is an overlap between PEST and SWOT, in that similar factors would appear in each. PEST assesses a market, including competitors, from the standpoint of a particular proposition or a business. SWOT is an assessment of a business or a proposition, whether your own or a competitor's. PEST becomes more useful and relevant the larger and more complex the business or proposition, but even for very small local businesses a PEST analysis can still throw up significant issues that might otherwise be missed. The four dimensions of PEST vary in significance depending on the type of business, for example social factors are more obviously relevant to consumer businesses or a B2B business close to the consumer-end of the supply chain.

A market is defined by what is addressing it, be it a product, company, brand, business unit and so on, so be clear about how the market being analysed is defined. The PEST subject should be a clear definition of the market being addressed, which might be from any of the following standpoints:

o A company looking at its market
o A product looking at its market
o A brand in relation to its market
o A local business unit
o A strategic option, such as entering a new market or launching a new product
o A potential acquisition
o A potential partnership
o An investment opportunity.

PEST is not only relevant to environment analyses – it can also be used to help assess the feasibility of a proposal for business change. Thus a business analyst, when considering a solution in a department or division of a company, might perform a PEST analysis. The analyst would examine the organizational strategy, board make-up and organizational structure for political influences.

Political

Political factors include government regulations and legal issues and define both formal and informal rules under which the firm must operate. Some examples include:

- Ecological/environmental issues
- Current legislation in the home market
- Future legislation
- European/international legislation
- Regulatory bodies and processes
- Government policies
- Government term and change
- Trading policies
- Funding, grants and initiatives
- Home market lobbying/pressure groups
- International pressure groups.

Economic

Economic factors affect the purchasing power of potential customers and the firm's cost of capital. The following are examples:

- Home economy situation
- Home economy trends
- Overseas economies and trends
- General taxation issues
- Taxation specific to products/services
- Seasonality/weather issues
- Market and trade cycles
- Specific industry factors
- Market routes and distribution trends
- Customer/end-user drivers
- Interest and exchange rates.

Social

Social factors include the demographic and cultural aspects of the external macro-environment. These factors affect customer needs and the size of potential markets. Some social factors include:

- Lifestyle trends
- Demographics
- Consumer attitudes and opinions
- Media views
- Law changes affecting social factors
- Brand, company, technology image
- Consumer buying patterns
- Fashion and role models
- Major events and influences
- Buying access and trends
- Ethnic/religious factors

Technological

Technological factors can lower barriers to entry, reduce minimum efficient production levels and influence outsourcing decisions. Some technological factors include:

- Competing technology development
- Research funding
- Associated/dependent technologies
- Replacement technology/solutions
- Maturity of technology
- Manufacturing maturity and capacity
- Information and communications
- Consumer's buying mechanisms/technology
- Technology legislation
- Innovation potential
- Technology access, licensing, patents
- Intellectual property issues.

External opportunities and threats

The PEST factors combined with external micro-environmental factors can be classified as opportunities and threats in a SWOT analysis.

PEST is useful than SWOT – not generally vice-versa. PEST helps to identify SWOT factors. There is an overlap between PEST and SWOT such that similar factors would appear in each However, PEST and SWOT are two different perspectives. PEST assesses a market, including competitors, from the standpoint of a particular proposition or a business. SWOT is an assessment of a business or a proposition, whether your own or a competitor's. PEST becomes more useful and relevant the larger and more complex the business or proposition, but even for very small local businesses a PEST analysis can still throw up one or two very significant issues that might otherwise be missed. The four quadrants in PEST vary in significance depending on the type of business, for example social factors are more obviously relevant to consumer businesses or a B2B business close to the consumer-end of the supply chain, whereas political factors are more obviously relevant to a global munitions supplier or aerosol propellant manufacturer. All businesses benefit from a SWOT analysis, and all businesses benefit from completing a SWOT analysis of their main competitors, which can then provide some feedback into the economic aspects of the PEST analysis.

Activity 4.1

Using an organization or industry of your choice collect examples of environmental changes in each of the quadrants of the grid (Political, Economic, Social, Technological) that may affect the way in which the organization operates.

Insight

Technology

- At the end of 2003, one in two UK homes had Internet access, compared with one in ten in 1999. Regular adult Internet use has also grown significantly, rising to 56 per cent in 2003, representing consistent year-on-year growth of over 5 percentage points. Sixty one per cent of the population reports that they have used the Internet at some time.
- Increased ease of physical access has fostered this progress. Over £400 million has been invested in the national network of 6000 UK online centres, located in local libraries. Ninety six per cent of Britain's population are aware of a place where they can access the Internet.
- Eighty per cent of the population has access to a mass-market broadband solution; from less than 50 000 in 2000 there are now over 2.6 million broadband subscribers in the UK.
- e-Commerce has become more popular. In 2000, 28 per cent of Internet users had purchased goods or services online; by 2003 this figure had reached 52 per cent.
- UK's lowest income households are, at 12 per cent of the population, over seven times less likely to be online than those in the top income group, of whom 86 per cent have home Internet access. While over 78 per cent of 16–24-year-olds are regular Internet users, only 16 per cent of those over 65 are online.
- Fewer than one in twelve Internet users have ever carried out an online transaction with the government. This, despite the following facts: over two-thirds of government services are now online; every local council has a website; and more than 3000 gov.uk websites have surfaced.
- The government pledges that every home in Britain will have access to online services by 2008. The plan includes both narrowband and broadband services as well as digital, terrestrial, cable, satellite TV.

Porter's five forces of competitive position

Michael Porter's Five Forces of Competitive Position is a perspective for assessing and analysing the competitive strength and position of a corporation or business organization.

The five forces that, Porter suggests, drive competition are:

1. Existing competitive rivalry between suppliers
2. Threat of new market entrants
3. Bargaining power of buyers
4. Power of suppliers
5. Threat of substitute products (including technology change).

The model can be used to good analytical effect alongside other models such as the SWOT and PEST analysis tools.

The value chain

Another model that can be used is Porter's Value Chain. It is a model which helps break down the business cycle into strategic activities that add value to a product or service. Through this analysis, the company can identify where costs are too high, or are reasonable, and also understand where and how differentiation from competitors can be achieved. In the context of managing business information, the company can also decide where information systems can help reduce costs and deliver competitive advantage. The Value Chain refers mainly to the handling of physical goods, often in a manufacturing or retail context.

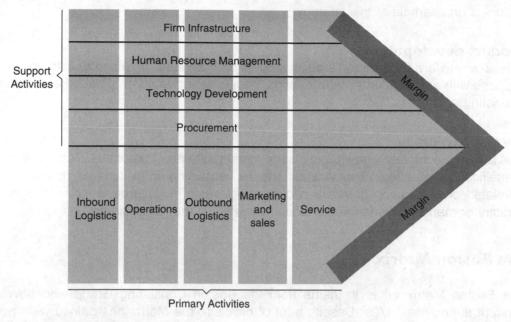

Figure 4.1 The value chain
Source: M E Porter (1980)

Ansoff's matrix – planning for growth

This marketing tool is used by marketers who have objectives for growth. Ansoff's matrix offers strategic choices to achieve the objectives. There are four main categories for selection.

Product ╲ Market	Present	New
Present	Market Penetration	Product Development
New	Market Development	Diversification

Figure 4.2 Ansoff's matrix

Market penetration

This is based on marketing existing products to existing customers. This could mean increasing revenue by, for example, promoting the product or repositioning the brand. The product is not altered and new customers are not sought.

Market development

An existing product range is offered in a new market. This means that the product remains the same, but it is marketed to a new audience. Exporting the product, or marketing it in a new region, is an example of this strategy.

Product development

This is where a new product is developed to be marketed to existing customers. This often happens with auto markets where existing models are updated or replaced and then marketed to existing customers.

Diversification

This is where completely new products are marketed to new customers. There are two types of diversification. Related diversification means remaining in a familiar market or industry. Unrelated diversification is where a company invests in an area where it has no previous industry or market experience, for example invests in the rail business.

The Boston Matrix

The Boston Matrix takes its name from the Boston Consulting Group who developed the concept during the 1970s. Despite a lot of criticism, the Matrix has gained wide acceptance as a useful concept. The theory underlying the Boston Matrix is the Product Life Cycle concept, which states that business opportunities move through 'life-cycle' phases of introduction, growth, maturity and decline. They are cash poor at the beginning of their lives and require significant investment until they achieve widespread market acceptance. Meanwhile, mature business opportunities should generate a surplus of cash.

A business opportunity will start out as a 'Question Mark', that is the host company has a low market share and spends a great deal of cash establishing itself as a lead player. The opportunity will then move anticlockwise around the matrix through 'Star', and ultimately to 'Cash Cow' status by which time the host company should be dominant and see a significant return for its efforts! The host company may ultimately loose market share as new competitors enter the market with lower cost (or better) alternatives, in which case the Product/Market opportunity relegates to a 'Dog' status.

Directional Policy Matrix

The Directional Policy Matrix (or GE–McKinsey Matrix) illustrates which segments a company should actively pursue, and which segments should be divested. Development of the Directional Policy Matrix came about through recognition of the potential limitations of using only a single variable within the Boston Matrix. The matrix shows the relative position of each segment using 'Relative Competitive Strength' as the horizontal axis and 'Relative Segment Attractiveness' as the vertical axis. The host company should invest in Product/Market opportunities that appear to the top left of the matrix. A company should invest in segments that are both attractive and in which it has established some measure of competitive advantage. Product/Market opportunities appearing in the bottom right of the matrix are both unattractive and the company competitively weak. Opportunities appearing in between these extremes are more problematic and decisions need to be made about whether to increase the marketing effort in the hope of achieving market leadership or maintaining them to generate cash, or to divest from the market altogether.

Shell Directional Policy Matrix

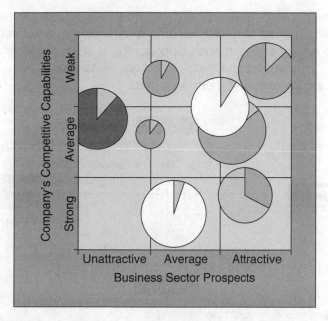

Figure 4.3 Shell Directional Policy Matrix

Gap analysis

Gap analysis is a tool for helping marketing managers to decide upon marketing strategies and tactics. The first step is to decide how a gap will be measured over time. For example, market share, profit, sales. Two questions are asked – *where are we now?* and *where do we want to be?* The difference between the two is the Gap.

Gap Analysis

Figure 4.4 Gap analysis
Source: www.marketingteacher.com

The next step is to close the gap.

Perceptual maps

Whilst it has been criticized for oversimplifying what can sometimes be complex problems, the two-dimensional Perceptual Map has become a particularly useful vehicle for management to draw attention to an emerging market opportunity, a new strategic direction or a changing market condition. Perceptual mapping is a way of taking results from brand association research surveys and presenting them on a map.

Figure 4.5 Two-dimensional Perpetual Map
Source: http://www.brainmassreports.com/perceptualmap.php

Balanced Scorecard

The Balanced Scorecard is an approach that can be used by strategic marketing managers to control, and keep track of, key performance indicators. There are four zones in a balanced scorecard namely financial, customers, processes and learning and growth. Each measure is part of a longer chain of cause and effect, and all of the measures eventually lead to outcomes (read on and this will become clearer). So the scorecard is 'balanced' in that outcomes are in balance with each other.

Figure 4.6 Balanced scorecard
Source: www.MARKETINGTEACHER.COM

Learning and growth

Learning and growth deals with measures of corporate success in relation to how it learns as it develops over time. So if the company makes mistakes in any way, then it must learn from them and there must be mechanisms in place to make sure that it happens. Growth also includes the way in which it develops employees with the necessary skills that will ultimately sustain its business.

Internal business processes

Internal business processes include all operations within the organization. Examples of internal business processes include Information Technology, manufacturing, marketing operations such as customer service, procurement and quality processes.

Customer

Examples of customer measures include customer retention and recruitment and their satisfaction.

Financial

Financial measures are important for any business, but information on customers, markets and technology also needs to be used. Resources, individuals and teams within a business need to be aligned with the scorecard objectives, measures, targets and initiatives for each of the four areas of measurement.

Globalization

Globalization is helping to remove restrictions on where people can go, what they can buy, where they can invest, and what they can read, hear or see. Economic integration is driven by two forces: advances in technology and decisions to liberalize trade. Globalization means that there is always the threat of substitute products and new entrants. The wider environment is also ever-changing, and the marketer needs to take account of changes in culture, politics, economics and technology.

However, there are unanswered questions concerning those people who lose out economically, socially and culturally. Globalization has had a mixed press and has been violently denounced at demonstrations during World Trade Organization meetings. The growth in availability of Fair Trade products signals greater interest in the ethics of trade. Critics argue that globalization has led to rising global inequality and exploitation of the poor by transnational companies.

Supporters of globalization argue that the number of people in extreme poverty – living on less than a dollar a day – fell from about 30 per cent of the world population in 1980 to 20 per cent in 1997, according to the World Bank. They also argue that the relatively rapid growth of China and India has led to an improved income distribution, not a deterioration.

A series of corporate scandals that began with the collapse of Enron has caused a crisis of legitimacy and the business of wealth creation has been tarnished. At Enron, this took the form of generating phony profits, whilst at WorldCom, accountants turned operating expenses into capital assets.

The micro-environment

This environment influences the organization directly. It includes suppliers, consumers and customers, and other local stakeholders. Micro-environment describes the relationship between organizations and the driving forces that control this relationship. It may be more of a local relationship, and the organization may be able to exert its influence. Some external influences like globalization affect all organizations, directly or indirectly, whilst other influences may be more specific to particular sectors. For example, at present the Government has a 'modernization agenda' that claims to be aimed at improving public services, as the following case study demonstrates.

Case study

The public sector is faced with the challenge to improve the service it delivers to its customers. A gap has opened up between what commercial services can deliver and what we can expect from public services. For example, two-thirds of the people in this country now own mobile telephones and the cost of calls has fallen by nearly one-quarter over the past 2 years. We can buy cheap fresh food from around the world at any time of the day or night at a local supermarket or, if we prefer, over the phone or the PC. Meanwhile, it is still difficult to find a public library open before or after work or at any time on Sundays, and GP surgery hours are similarly limited. For increasing numbers of us today, the widening gulf between what we can buy as customers and what we get as public service users has created a credibility gap. Moreover, the public sector must serve all sections of society, not just those with money in their pockets. Change is not a simple, linear process, and improving the experience of users requires not only changes to systems and procedures in what are often huge, complex and interdependent organizations, but also changes in the attitudes and behaviour of individual members of staff. Change is painful and destructive as well as positive and creative. It challenges vested interests: personal, professional and institutional. Change is unavoidable; potentially both exciting and rewarding, but at the same time a messy and difficult enterprise, frequently confounding the intentions of managers, politicians and policy-makers. There is no magic formula for change management, but there is a body of useful experience about what works and that can help build long-term capacity for the future.

Source: Managing for Excellence in the NHS (2002) Department of Health.

Managing change can be aided by undertaking a stakeholder analysis.

Stakeholder analysis

Stakeholder analysis is the technique used to identify the key people who have to be won over. By communicating with stakeholders early and frequently, you can ensure that they fully understand what you are doing and understand the benefits of your project – this means they can support you actively when necessary.

Identifying your stakeholders

The first step in your stakeholder analysis is to brainstorm who your stakeholders are. As part of this, think of all the people who are affected by your work, who have influence or power over it, or have an interest in its successful or unsuccessful conclusion.

- Your line manager
- Shareholders
- Senior executives
- Your co-workers
- Suppliers
- Your team
- Interest groups

- o Customers
- o The public
- o Prospective customers
- o Future recruits.

Prioritize your stakeholders

You may now have a long list of people and organizations that are affected by your work. Some of these may have the power to either block or advance. Some may be interested in what you are doing, others may not care. For example, your line manager is likely to have high power and influence over your projects and high interest.

Key questions that can help you understand your stakeholders

- o What interest do they have in the outcome of your work? Is it positive or negative?
- o What information do they want from you?
- o How do they want to receive information from you? What is the best way of communicating your message to them?
- o What is their current opinion of your work? Is it based on good information?
- o If they are not likely to be positive, what will win them around to support your project?
- o If you don't think you will be able to win them around, how will you manage their opposition?

Write your responses to these questions.

Estimate attitude and confidence in a particular change

Estimate the stakeholder's attitude, from supportive to opposed

- o Strongly in favour
- o Weakly in favour
- o Indifferent or undecided
- o Weakly opposed
- o Strongly opposed.

How confident you are about your estimate

- o Fully confident
- o Reasonably confident (some missing information, perhaps)
- o An informed guess
- o Wild guess.

Your best estimate of the influence of the stakeholder

- o H – High; this person or group has power of veto, formally or informally.
- o M – Medium; you could probably achieve your goals against this person's or group's opposition, but not easily.
- o L – Low; this person can do little to influence the outcomes of your intended actions.

Plan strategies

Plan your strategies for approaching and involving each person or group. It usually takes the form of obtaining more information, or of involving the stakeholder in the planning for the change. Highly influential people need to be involved in some way, or their influence needs to be neutralized. The people or groups who require the most attention are those who are influential and opposed to change.

The internal environment of the organization

As mentioned above, factors that are internal to the organization are known as the 'internal environment', these can include, for example, personnel changes or new management processes or demands to improve efficiency. They are sometimes ascertained by applying what is called the 'Five Ms' which are Men, Money, Machinery, Materials and Markets. The internal environment is as important for managing change as the external. Change is likely to be needed when, for example, responding to newly identified markets, or taking up the cost-saving opportunities offered by new technologies. Successful organizations are those that are effective at managing cultural change. However, many organizations do not recognize the need for cultural change.

Insight

Today's world of work in the UK

○ Today's world of work is much less satisfying to employees than the one they were experiencing 10 years ago. What is also striking is the apparent but significant deterioration that has taken place among workers in having any sense of a personal commitment to the company that employs them. Today's managerial rhetoric emphasizes the importance of enhancing human capital, the concept of partnership at work, the need to improve the learning and skills of employees as well as provide a wider range of benefits and incentives to attract and retain staff.

○ The survey provides little evidence, however, that many of these progressive ideas usually associated with enlightened human resource management techniques are being translated into practical measures that are ensuring the growth of more high-commitment workplaces.

○ The largest falls in job satisfaction over the number of hours worked was the most pronounced at both ends of the occupational grading – among senior managers and professionals and the unskilled and semi-skilled. The disgruntled manager has joined the disgruntled manual worker, at least in complaints about the long hours culture.

○ Most people still leave their homes for paid employment. In fact, a larger proportion of workers were employed in one specific workplace in 2000 (78 per cent) compared with 10 years ago when 76 per cent were. Only 3 per cent of employees said they worked partly at home in 2000 and a further 1.1 per cent solely or mainly at home. The overwhelming majority of workers in Britain do not feel insecure in their jobs.

○ We have much greater job stability, longer employment tenure and far less evidence of new forms of flexible employment contracts than many may realize. The extent of labour flexibility is also questionable in the way that work is being organized. The overwhelming majority of managers, administrators and professionals see their job as having a career structure with a clearly recognized promotion ladder. By contrast only a tiny minority of manual workers take any similar view of the career potential in their jobs and they are becoming a dwindling part of the labour force with the advance of information technology.

○ The most striking sign of significant workplace innovation can be seen in the dramatic growth in the proportion of workers across all occupational categories who now make use of modern technology in the jobs they do. The use of computers and other forms of information technology at work advanced significantly during the 1990s.

o But many employers have not yet recognized that the emergence of a more demanding work-force in future will mean they will have to adopt a more sensitive attitude towards how their employees should be treated. The survey suggests that while a trend exists to greater freedom for the worker on the job, the degree of control and surveillance by management has also increased.

o We do not have the flexible labour market which we think other European countries ought to admire and emulate. On the contrary it is hard not to draw the conclusion that we need to reappraise our whole approach to employment.

o *Policies* – If employees are going to co-operate in a positive and active manner with the management of workplace change they are going to need a greater sense of well-being, status and control over the work they perform.

Source: Robert Taylor (2002) Britain's World of Work – Myths and Realities.

Implications for marketing

Some of the implications have been discussed in other units, for example being sensitive to cultural differences when working in a multinational environment and the impact of information and communications technology on approaches to marketing. Marketing management is the process of planning and executing the conception, pricing, promotion and distribution of goods, services and ideas to create exchanges with target groups that satisfy customer and organizational objectives. The emphasis is shifting from transaction-oriented marketing to relationship marketing, and organizations need to retain customer loyalty through continually satisfying their needs in a superior way.

Marketing teams must implement processes that co-ordinate all marketing and sales activities and achieve the level of data access, collection and sharing that is critical to consistent messaging, lead tracking, sales conversion and ongoing marketing intelligence. With the availability of websites, e-mail and mobile devices, and the introduction of high-powered packages for targeting customers, marketing should be easier than ever. However, the increase in marketing contact causes prospects to feel overloaded, reducing response rates and the value of marketing effort. Lack of co-ordination further erodes marketing effectiveness.

Marketers need to know when to:

o Cultivate large markets or niche markets
o Launch new brands or extend existing brand names
o Push or pull products through distribution
o Protect the domestic market or penetrate aggressively into foreign markets
o Add more benefits to the offer or reduce the price
o Expand or contract budgets for sales force, advertising and other marketing tools.

A product is anything that can be offered to a market for attention, acquisition, use or consumption that might satisfy a want or need.

The change problem

At the heart of change management lies the change problem. It might be large or small in scope and scale, and it might focus on individuals or groups, on one or more divisions or departments, the entire organization, or on one or more aspects of the organization's environment. Problems may be formulated in terms of 'how', 'what' and 'why' questions. Which formulation is used depends on where in the organization the person posing the question or formulating the problem is situated, and where the organization is situated in its own life cycle.

For a change programme to be successful and sustainable (C), there must be:

- o A compelling reason for change (R)
- o A clear vision of the future (V)
- o And a coherent plan for getting there (P)

$$R + V + P = \text{Sustainable Change}$$

When all these elements are not in place different scenarios can be envisaged

$$R + V = \text{Leap of Faith}$$

No coherent plan means that the outcomes are precarious

$$R + P = \text{Tower of Babel}$$

According to the narrative in Genesis Chapter 11 of the Bible, the Tower of Babel was a tower built by a united humanity in order to reach the heavens. To prevent the project from succeeding, God confused their languages so that each spoke a different language. They could no longer communicate with one another and the work could not proceed. After that time, people moved away to different parts of Earth.

$$V + P = \text{Doomed Crusade}$$

Without having a compelling reason to change it difficult to gain 'buy in' from the various stakeholders.

Why change agendas often fail?

- o Complacency
- o Failing to create teams with enough power to lead the change
- o Underestimating the power of vision
- o Failing to communicate the vision
- o Allowing obstacles, real or imagined, to block the vision
- o Failing to create short-term gains
- o Declaring victory too soon
- o Neglecting to embed the changes in the culture
- o Failure to consult.

Source: Adapted from John P. Kotter (1996), *Leading Change*.

Change programmes benefit from a 'champion' to galvanize the plan and the action. Select a team with a mix of competences not necessarily all at senior levels. Develop an outline of what the organization will look like at the end of the change programme. Others need to be persuaded of the need for change. Relate this need to organizational objectives linked to a vision of where the organization will be if change is successful. Persuading people of the need for change can be difficult and it may be useful to bring a facilitator from the outside to act as a catalyst. Changes are best owned by the people implementing them, so it is more effective to encourage people to identify the change factors themselves. In any organization, there will be forces driving and forces restraining change. Try to reinforce the drivers and lessen the restraining forces through education. Communicate continuously with stakeholders – employees, customers, suppliers and owners.

Activity 4.2

Is an assessment of what the customer wants at the heart of your change strategy?

Do you have relevant measures to indicate your efficiency and effectiveness?

Do you have a realistic assessment of staff morale?

Making change

The U.S. Mint needed an enterprise resource planning (ERP) system that would let our business units get at all the customer information hidden in our systems. And we had just 12 months to get it up and running. Three years into the process, we kept running into the wall of our systems. Even though the customer data was there, only a few people had access to it. The biggest challenge was to convince them to sacrifice some of their most talented people to the project. If I could do it all over again, I'd spend more money educating the organization on what life was going to be like after the implementation. We invested a lot in training, but we probably should have spent twice as much time and money. To other executives, I would say, the most critical thing is to start with a business requirement. What does your business lack that such a solution will provide? If the business requirement doesn't justify the pain, don't do it.

Source: Adapted from Philip Diehl, Making Change: HEADFIRST. www.darwinmag.com\read\060100\head_content.html.

Because change causes fear, a sense of loss of the familiar, for example, it takes time for employees to understand and commit themselves to it in a meaningful way. Some writers (Bacal, 2000) argue that people tend to go through stages in their attempts to cope with change.

Stage 1: Denial

One way that people cope with change is to deny that it is happening, or that it will continue or last. People tend to avoid dealing with the fear and uncertainty of prospective change because they are hoping they would not have to adapt. This stage is difficult because it is hard to involve people in planning for the future. Moving out of the denial stage occurs when they see tangible evidence that things are different.

Stage 2: Anger and resistance

When it is no longer feasible to deny that something is happening or has already happened, people may move into a state of anger, accompanied by forms of resistance. Leadership is needed to help people work through this and on to the next stage. If leadership is poor, anger and resentment may last indefinitely.

Stage 3: Exploration and acceptance

This is the stage where people are beginning to develop a better understanding of the change and are more willing to explore further, and to accept it. They are more willing to participate in the process.

Stage 4: Commitment

This is the stage where people are willing to work towards making it succeed. They have adapted sufficiently to make it work. While some changes, for example downsizing, may never be accepted, eventually people do commit themselves to making the organization effective within the constraints arising from the change. The change process can take some time to stabilize.

The following insight highlights some of the problems that people leading change may face.

Insight

New or different ideas often run into trouble before they reach fruition. However, change leaders need to help teams overcome blocks to change.

Forecasts fall short – A plan is needed but it is difficult to predict timing and cost. Change leaders need to accept departures from plans.

Expect the unexpected – A new path is unlikely to run straight and every change brings unanticipated consequences. Change leaders need to respond, to make adjustments and to make their case.

Momentum slows – You do not have solutions to problems, and the team is discouraged and enmeshed in conflict. Critics emerge. Even if a coalition has been built and key stakeholders are involved, you will be challenged. When the impact of change becomes clear, those threatened by it will formulate objections. This is when change leaders need to respond, remove obstacles and push forward. Actual progress will produce more believers than doubters.

Source: Adapted from Kanter, Rosabeth Moss (1999) 'The enduring skills of change leaders', *Leader to Leader*, **13** (Summer 1999), 15–22.

Change management: The skill requirements

Managing the kinds of changes encountered by and instituted within organizations requires an unusually broad and finely honed set of skills, chief among which are listed below.

Political skills

Organizations are first and foremost social systems. Without people there can be no organization. Organizations are intensely political. Change agents need to understand it.

Analytical skills

A rational, well-argued analysis can be ignored and even suppressed but not successfully contested and, in most cases, should be successful. If not, the political issues have not been properly addressed.

Case study

Decide exactly what you want – Unclear goals create unclear outcomes. Succumbing to the temptation to start work without thought and planning wastes energy and produces disillusionment. Clear goals direct energy, give a sense of purpose and provide a context for resolving any problems.

Decide that you really want the change – Don't see the change as an option, decide that it must happen. Believe that there is no alternative, no matter how busy the organization, no matter what might crop up 2 months from now. If there is an alternative, don't bother starting it. Many change projects start life as 'a pretty good idea' that is 'probably worth the effort in the long run'. All too often, people begin with the intention of seeing if anything crops up later along the line. Such saintly efforts are easy prey for people keen to play the role of change assassins. Don't let your project take a mugging.

Own it – Someone must make this change happen and take responsibility for everything it produces – whether the consequences are anticipated and manageable, or not. Someone has to be clearly identified with the project, not only when it is fashionable and full of hope and the best players, but also when it begins to annoy people and your best people leave to work on something that 'cropped up later'.

Be realistic – The change may be as painful and costly for you as for the people around you. The pain and cost may come before, during or after the project – but it will come. Realism means understanding the volume of work involved in keeping individuals and organizations aligned with the change vision, especially when their instincts are screaming at them to get back to the old way of doing things.

Understand what blocks change – Become fascinated by the current practices or behaviours in your organization that resist change. Get to know them intimately. Give power to the strong and take power from the weak. In this context, strong means the positive things you want to achieve. Praise them, reward them, reinforce them, celebrate them, repeat them and publicize them when they happen. By contrast, punish old behaviours when they happen – and make it clear why you have corrected them.

Be positive – Attitude and self-belief are drivers of change. Don't play the 'but' or 'maybe' game; doubt slaughters change. Try not to be sidetracked by fear.

Be optimistic – 'If you want to achieve excellence, you can get there today. As of this second, quit doing less than excellent work.' So, allegedly, said Thomas Watson, the founder of IBM.

Deciding to make a change takes an instant, but sustaining it is the challenge. Most change programmes are long and complex. Some are so long that there's a good chance that you won't be around to see it end, while some change destinations alter as the project is in motion. So focus on the journey as well as the destination.

Be aware – raise awareness by asking key questions.

What is happening to take us towards the goal?

What happened last week that failed to move us forward, or took us down old paths that we agreed we wanted to change?

What can each of us do next week that will move us towards our goal?

Let it happen – It seems a contradictory thing to say, as I do, both that a clear sense of what you want gives you a motivating direction and purpose, and that you should let go of what will happen. Allowing your purpose to unfold as it will is an exhortation to 'stay flexible'.

Source: Adapted from Firth (2003), www.treefrog.ws.

Planning for a change programme

Before embarking on a change programme it is important to work on creating favourable conditions for implementing the change. Some of these things may be easier said than done but it is still important, wherever possible, to maximize support and minimize opposition.

- Ensure that there is a receptive climate towards the proposed change.
- Identify a champion or a team of champions that will help to promote change and oversee its implementation.
- Audit team capabilities and competences and identify any gaps that may need to be filled through training and development.
- Market the change to the target audience.
- Develop the plan, including a budget.
- Try to anticipate arguments against change, and identify positive responses to them.

The following case study exemplifies this process in a library context.

Before we can effectively market our libraries to our customers, we have to market within to library staff. Each member of staff markets the library with every single interaction they have with customers. Friendly staff can often make up for shortcomings elsewhere in the service. Staff are also the most potentially damaging part of the marketing equation. Customers do not always notice good service, but they invariably notice and remember poor service, which is often a consequence of limited interpersonal skills. If employees do not care about their company, they will in the end contribute to its demise. Even if you don't have the time, staff or budget for a formal, full-blown marketing plan, you can make progress on internal marketing.

Step 1: Staff buy-in

Get staff involved, energized, and feeling ownership for your library. Your staff members have a personal stake in your library, and therefore in this process every customer interaction is a marketing moment.

Step 2: Mission statement

Do you have a mission statement? Does it explicitly support the mission of your organization? The needs of your customers? Link the work of individual staff members to your mission. Post your mission statement prominently in your library; use it on documents such as fax cover sheets, e-mail, business cards, etc.

Step 3: Image/Brand

A brand is the emotional connection you have with your customers.

Your library's image is created by the collective actions of the library staff.

What expectations do you want to create for your customers?

How will you deliver on those expectations?

Step 4: Identity

Create an identity for your library – Place your identity stamp on intranet banner ads, library brochures and publications, presentations, e-mail signatures, and partner intranet sites.

Step 5: Key customer messages

Identify the key messages you want to communicate to your customers, for example I know the library has an intranet site; I can easily navigate the library's site; I know the library staff can provide consulting and analysis for my projects.

Step 6: Vision

Do you have a vision of where your library is going? What it will look like in 2 years? In the real world, you need to have a clear picture of your vision – and then communicate that vision to your staff.

What will success look like? – library staff will understand that they are selling or hurting your library during every interaction with customers? – feel increased personal ownership for your library? – know how your mission supports your organization's goals?

In conclusion, every customer interaction is a marketing moment. All staff must know, support and be able to articulate your library's mission, vision and key customer messages.

Source: Adapted from Internal Marketing: Inside Job. Laura Zick, Library and Information Services, Lilly University, Eli Lilly and Company. http://www.sla.org/division/dpht/Spring2003/presentations2003/Laura_Zick.ppt.

Preparing for change

- Current attitude of staff?
- How big a change is needed?
- Who are the 'influencers'?
- How big is resistance likely to be?

Internal marketing is an important 'implementation' tool. It aids communication and helps to overcome resistance to change. It informs and involves staff in new initiatives and strategies. Internal marketing has a structure similar to external marketing. The main differences are that the customers are the employees.

The marketer's skills are traditionally associated with the interface between organization and customer/consumer. But management also have a need to communicate with those within the organization – and the stakeholders associated with it. It is unlikely that an organization will be truly successful unless these buy in to management plans. There needs to be a common focus, and goals need to be understood and accepted. The prime marketing skill is communication – marketers are the specialists in identifying target audiences, assessing needs and in managing communications plans. Applying these skills internally means that a consumer-centred approach, with the employees identified as the consumers, needs to be adopted.

Change management tools

Lewin's freeze phases

In the early 20th century, psychologist Kurt Lewin identified three stages of change.

Unfreeze

A basic tendency of people is to seek a context in which they have relative safety and feel a sense of control. In establishing themselves, they attach their sense of identity to their environment. Talking about the future is rarely enough to move them from this 'frozen' state and significant effort may be required to 'unfreeze' them and get them moving.

Example of an unfreezing method
Stimulate the need for change by creating instability that leads people to seek somewhere other than where they are at present. For example:

- Make the current safe place less safe.
- Show that which is held to be true is not true, at least not in all important areas.
- Open the doors of the house to show the real terrors just outside.
- Get in angry customers to berate people for poor products and service.
- Show them the realities of financial instability.
- Show them competitors' products
- Reorganize to break up cosy groups.
- Give jobs that are outside of their current skills.

When people are comfortable (in their 'comfort zone'), there is no driving need for them to change. If they are shocked too much then they may freeze or rebel. If, however, they are simply made less comfortable by some destabilization technique, then when change is announced they are more likely to be ready for it and are less likely to resist.

Whole-system Planning

Gather together the participants in the Whole-system Planning so that everyone can work together as equals. The number of people are sufficient to represent all groups, but small enough to discuss matters as a whole.

Past
The first part is focused on the past. Delegates tell stories of success and struggles. The past is honoured and recalled. Attention to the past also can be used to take a view of the culture of the organization, understanding its roots and why it holds its present form.

Present
The next part is focused on the present. The external forces on the organization are explored. Customers and markets are considered, with information about how market share is going up or down, how products and services are faring, what customers are saying about the company (quotes and examples are good here). Focus then moves further in, to how the organization is responding to these forces, how it is coping and how it is structured. Strengths and weaknesses are explored, in all departments as well as in the leadership.

Future
Finally, the third part focuses on the future. This may start with a visioning exercise to determine a desired future state. This vision is shared and developed and given local meaning. Plans are then built to reach this desirable future. These may start with overall strategic thoughts, developed collaboratively, then broken down into more localized plans that are discussed in smaller groups.

Blocks are identified and discussed and risks are explored. Finally, a management structure for implementing the changes is identified.

The Whole-system Planning approach is useful for collaborative change settings where there is a need to engage a large audience in planning for the future and taking forward action plans. Not all plans may be developed in detail but involving everyone makes it easier to address problems that are identified.

Transition

Part of Lewin's model is the notion that change is a journey rather than a simple step. This journey may not be that simple and the person may need to go through several stages of misunderstanding before they get to the other side.

Transitioning requires time and leadership is often important and some form of coaching, or other support, is needed.

Example of a transitioning technique
First steps
Make the first steps of change particularly easy and keep everyone focused on the next steps. Starting something can be the hardest thing and people often see change as a single monolithic effort. Making the next step small and straightforward can remove objections to implementation. Having clear steps in the change and dividing work into distinct elements means that change may not be seen as a single, monolithic entity but more as a set of activities, each of which gains specific value.

Refreeze

At the other end of the journey, the final goal is to 'refreeze', putting down roots again and establishing the new place of stability. In practice, refreezing may be a slow process as transitions seldom stop cleanly, but go more in fits and starts with a long tail of bits and pieces.

Example of a refreezing technique

Burning a bridge behind you stops any thought of retreat and is a deliberate way of preventing any reversion to old ways of working. It can concentrate minds and managers who may not be fully committed to the change and are now strongly motivated to continue. Plan for change projects to reach milestones and deliver real results in a regular and predictable stream of communications. Avoid the trap of requiring that people change whilst keeping the reward system that is driving their behaviour unchanged. Requesting teamwork and rewarding individuals are examples of this.

Get people to maintain interest in a change by giving them new challenges that stimulate them and keep them looking to the future. A marketing organization that wants to stop people from drifting away back to old ways could plan a series of moves to inspire and engage its people in beating its competitors. One of the key things that people respond to is a challenge.

Five Whys

This tool can help teams understand the underlying causes of problems or issues. The technique begins with a clear statement of a problem or issue and then allows teams to interrogate this statement with the question 'Why?' The tool breaks down large issues into their component parts, allowing teams to respond with focused actions and initiatives.

When changes are instituted, it is not uncommon for people to seek ways to go back to the old way of working, particularly after the eagle eye of change agents has moved onto change projects anew.

Problem-solving, team-building (PSTB)

The tool can be applied when a team faces a problem or issue that requires a solution. It is a structured approach to problem-solving. The tool begins with a clear problem statement by an identified problem owner. The problem is usually expressed as a question, 'How do I?' Other members of the team act as a resource for the problem owner and there is also a facilitator who ensures that the tool process is followed through a series of time-limited stages:

- Idea generation
- Idea selection
- Benefits and concerns analysis
- Identifying and working critical concerns
- Initial action plan.

Fishbone analysis

This can be used to deepen a team's understanding of a problem or issue. It takes its name from the form it takes with a problem statement on one side of the paper and a 'spine' extending from this and lines branching off it on which the team records sub-issues. Working in this way teams can understand the elements which contribute to a perceived problem.

Force field analysis

The force field analysis is used to map the sometimes opposing forces within an environment where change is taking place. It can be particularly useful when issues have already been identified and teams want to analyse and understand the prevailing forces, which should be dealt with and start to inform an action plan.

It begins with a statement of a problem or issue. The team also needs to make a statement of the goal or outcome that it is seeking. The team lists those forces which drive towards the desired outcome and the restraining forces that impede achieving that outcome. Each of these forces is then given a score of 1 to 4 (where 1 is a weak force and 4 a strong one). Totalling the driving and restraining forces can give the team an indication of which set of forces would prevail in the current environment. A team can begin to look at what actions can be taken to reduce restraining ones.

Internal marketing

Internal marketing is an ongoing process whereby an organization aligns, motivates and empowers employees at all functions and levels to deliver a consistent and positive customer experience that helps achieve business objectives.

You should be able to demonstrate that you are able to use marketing communications techniques for an internal marketing plan to support the management of change within an organization. The basis of internal marketing is focusing on the relationship that exists between the organization and its employees. One of the success factors for the implementation of the marketing plan is to treat internal staff as if they are customers who all need the same consideration and attention as external customers. The aim of internal marketing is to develop a unified sense of purpose among employees. It plays an important role in ensuring that the organization is marketing- and customer-focused. Internal marketing is based on a communications programme, and there are a number of steps that an organization can take in order to achieve internal synergy and employee co-operation:

- Creating an internal awareness of the corporate aims, objectives and overall mission
- Determining the expectations of the internal customer
- Communication to internal customers
- Changes in tasks and activities
- Internal monitoring and control.

It is as important to segment the market internally, as it is segmented externally. A key aim of the marketing plan should be the successful motivation and retention of the internal customer so that the organization can meet the needs of the external market.

Internal marketing aids communication and can help to overcome resistance to change. It can be used to help inform and involve staff in new initiatives and strategies.

The Internet can help to foster the sharing of information but an extranet, that is a computer network that provides communication across selected organizations, enables sharing in a more controlled and secure manner. Often, companies use extranets as part of a search for better ways to communicate with their channel members and reduce costs. Because the extranet is interactive and easily accessible, it has the potential to transform the way channel members communicate with each other. For example, it can make information-sharing and communication frequency more timely than the same information obtained from more traditional methods of communication.

Internal relationship marketing techniques

Internal marketing projects can be considered in four phases.

Understanding the nature of the internal market
An assessment phase that aims to find out the attitudes and beliefs of employees and managers towards each other, the company, customers and marketing mix components.

Communicating with staff
A review of communications activities and their effectiveness, including a 'mapping' of communications channels.

Developing the plan
Devising strategies for meeting the objectives of the internal marketing campaign.

Evaluation
Evaluating the success of the plan according to the set objectives.

Internal marketing can contribute to helping organizations achieve good relationships with their external customers. The key success factors of internal marketing success are:

- Create an internal awareness of the corporate aims, objectives and overall mission.
- Determine the expectations of the internal customer.
- Communicate to internal customers.
- Provide appropriate human and financial resources to underpin the implementation of the marketing strategy.
- Provide training in order that employees have the appropriate skills and competences to undertake the task at hand.
- Implement a change in tasks and activities appropriate to the objectives of the organization.
- Provide a structure whereby cross-functional integrated teams across business units can work together, in order to aid communication of business activity relating to the achievement of corporate goals.
- Provide the systems and processes that enable successful delivery of services and products, enabling employees to successfully implement them and achieve organizational success.
- Maximize the opportunity for customer interaction through effective management of service levels, for example response times, reply processes.
- Internal monitoring and control.

For internal marketing to be successfully implemented, a planned approach is essential to allow evaluation and measurement of the successful execution of a plan. The plan could be designed with the following headings:

- Internal vision
- Aims and objectives
- Internal marketing strategy
- Segmentation, targeting and positioning
- Marketing programme (to include all elements of the marketing mix)
- Implementation.

Planning for internal marketing

Internal marketing requires a similar kind of approach to that used in external marketing. An internal marketing audit is needed to discover who are the target audiences and to identify what are their needs. Channels of communication, both formal and informal, need to be identified. The same kind of questions that are used in any marketing audit can be used. Payback will be in terms of commitment rather than cash. Objectives should be SMART but couched in terms of changed behaviour rather than increases in market share and so on.

Strategy

Establishing a strategy for change will require a long-term view to be taken. What is the long-term need, and what are the short-term issues? Within the long-term strategic goal(s) will be the short-term need to introduce new products, to change operating procedures and so on. New product introduction may not be seen as an internal issue but internal staff need to know about, and be familiar with, new products before the outside world is notified. (One can be sure the telephone calls will start within hours of a launch. Internal staff must not respond 'Is that one of our products? I didn't know.')

Targets

Just as in marketing communications, there is need to identify target audiences. These will range from internal groupings such as individuals, sections, departments and so on to include those 'exterior' stakeholders such as the organization's shareholders, bankers, lawyers, agencies, consultancies and so on. An internal marketing communications plan can be far more complex than one used to promote a product. The target audiences are more diverse.

Promotion

Two-way communication means that the target audience members should be able to have some input into proposed change. Internal communication media includes meetings, newsletters and noticeboards, but there is a need to achieve impact. Change has to be marketed effectively, and training and development offers a good opportunity to do this.

Price

Faced with 'selling' an idea or proposal to senior managers, the same process should be adopted but the needs of the management team and the stakeholders need to be considered, and benefits such as raised profitability quantified and communicated. The price to an internal audience is measured in terms of inconvenience, extra work, coping with unfamiliarity and so on. The question 'Why bother?' must be answered, and answered well.

Product

The product consists of market strategies and the marketing plan. Therefore, the 'product' needs to be 'sold' in terms of values, attitudes and behaviour to employees so that they can buy into it.

Place

For the internal marketer, place can be interpreted as when and where a change will be introduced. For example, it may be better to introduce a new computer system in the off-season rather than at peak times.

Promotion – As has been said above, promote the benefits to those in each target audience.

Process – All aspects of the change need to be thought through carefully, piloted, evaluated, modified and re-piloted. It should ease the burden of adapting to change and, if possible, should simplify an employee's task. The introductory process, similarly, should be timetabled and then managed so that what is announced actually happens as planned and in the way it was intended.

Participants – All involved, from top management to junior staff, must follow the same procedures. If a senior manager does not comply it is unlikely that others will bother.

Managing the implementation of internal marketing (Jobber, 1995)

- ○ Set objectives for internal marketing, for example to persuade 100 staff to join a new Performance-Related Pay (PRP) scheme.
- ○ Tactics would include an internal application of the marketing mix, and could include staff forums, presentations, an intranet, away days, videos, personal visits by company directors or newsletters.
- ○ Evaluation would consider the take-up of PRP against your objectives, attendees at away days, visits to an intranet page and so on.

Internal marketing involves selling marketing plans to key internal staff or employees. Piercey and Morgan's model (Piercey and Morgan, 1997) of internal marketing indicates the implications for the marketing mix.

Price – this relates to the benefit to the employee of taking this marketing planning information on board. It relates to the personal psychological cost of adopting different key values, and changing the way jobs are done. Often it requires asking managers to step outside their comfort zones with new methods of operation.

Place/Distribution – this concerns the physical and socio-technical venues at which organizations will have to deliver the product and its communications, that is where should employees be targeted, for example Internet, staff canteens and so on.

Promotion/Communication – this is the most tangible aspect of internal marketing – communication media and the messages used to inform and persuade employees. There will be work on the attitudes of the key personnel in the internal marketplace and a two-way methodology must be employed.

Service quality is influenced by employees because of the inseparability of services production and consumption in relation to the provider, that is staff. Good communication, motivation and training are central to service quality, and this is influenced by internal marketing.

Internal marketing is like 'change management'. Firstly, internal customers need to be identified. As with external customers, they will have their own buyer behaviour, or way of 'buying into' the changes which you are charged to implement. As Jobber (1995) explains, three different segments, namely 'supporters', 'neutral', and finally 'opposers', can be targeted.

Each segment requires a slightly different internal marketing mix to achieve the internal marketing objectives.

For example, if the change was that a company was to relocate closer to its market, 'supporters' could be targeted with information about lower property prices; 'neutral' internal customers could be targeted with incentives such as better rewards. With 'opposers', a choice would need to be made between inaction or forcing acceptance of change. It depends on a calculation of what the impact would be between these two courses of action.

Critical incidents can also be used to improve service quality. For a critical incident report to be useful, at least three pieces of information must be collected:

1. A description of the situation that led to the incident
2. The actions of the focal person in the incident and
3. The results or outcomes of the incident.

How to plan for a change programme

The approach needs to be properly considered before starting the implementation. The climate needs to be accepting of change.

- Appoint a change agent, or a champion for change, that will help to ease changes through.
- Audit the skills and capabilities of the team. Train and develop as necessary.
- The change must be correctly marketed to your target audience.
- Decide upon the plan.
- Work out a realistic budget and stick to it.
- Try to anticipate the arguments against change.
- Ensure that there is a receptive climate towards the proposed change.
- Identify a champion or a team of champions that will help to promote change and oversee its implementation.
- Audit team capabilities and competences and identify any gaps that may need to be filled through training and development.
- Market the change to the target audience.
- Develop the plan, including a budget.
- Try to anticipate arguments against change, and identify positive responses to them.

Activity 4.3

Think about a change which has recently been introduced in your organization. Would you say it was marketed effectively internally?

What was the change?

What was effective about this approach?

How could this approach have been improved?

What kind of issues did you identify?

Case study

Employees are the company. Particularly in the services sectors, they represent the culture, the brand and the customer experience with the company. Employees are the best form of marketing during change. If people don't feel good about the change, customers will know it quickly.

Segment the benefits of the change. What factors are beneficial to employees, shareholders, customers and other stakeholders? Use these benefits to create key messages about the changes to be marketed to the appropriate audience.

Be truthful and genuine. It only takes one example of misdirection or dishonesty to create employee distrust of management's messages. Spin is spin, and people generally know when they are being spun. Be willing to show that a particular change isn't necessarily 'good' for everyone.

Change requires strongly embracing the future and a quick release of the past. Keep the organization's 'eyes' looking forward. Keep it thinking about what the customer wants. Those who have worked at the company for a long time tend to pull the company back into issues of tradition. Customers care little about the past. What will you do for them today or tomorrow?

Focus communications around the people who will remain after any staffing cuts or changes.

Deal with 'survivor syndrome', that is the phenomenon of those who keep their jobs feeling guilty that they have kept their jobs while many lose theirs.

Focus the organization externally. Work to eliminate the inwardness that comes with change.

Recognize that change is a personal issue. It involves a loss of control and employees, once content with their careers, now have to ask 'Will I have a job when this is finished?'

Make changes quickly, decisively and as fairly as possible. Spreading bad news over a longer period is more painful than making that one decisive action.

Focus on customers. Show a true concern for customer issues, but the change is not a customer vote. Communicating to your people, who will in turn reassure your customers, is the best defence.

Source: Adapted from Change Marketing: The Universal Truths for Marketing the Benefits of a Merger/ Acquisition (Bedford Consulting Group, June 2002).

Summary

Change is a natural part of the environment, but is seldom popular and is often resisted. Change, as a process, can and should be managed. It is as much subject to management planning and control as any other process. All change should be taken seriously, and planned and implemented with care. Major changes include a switch from a product/sales to a marketing/customer approach, and from a domestic to an international orientation. Internal marketing is of crucial importance in securing change and is best handled from a corporate level, possibly with marketers seconded for the purpose. Change always requires a price to be paid in human terms.

Hints and tips

Marketing, with its outward focus, is in the vanguard of change in an organization. Candidates need to have an understanding of change management theory or contexts. Winning marketing is about driving change, to face new market opportunities and threats. Marketers are agents of change.

You should be both familiar with models in their traditional form but also be able to apply them to different scenarios. Although textbooks describe what could be called the 'classical' application of models, the value of the models often lies in their flexibility. The evolving business environment and the range of business strategies used mean that these models should be used with thought and flexibility.

Bibliography

Bacal, R. (2000) 'Understanding the cycle of change and how people react to it', www.work911.com/articles.htm

Bedford Consulting Group (June, 2002) www.bedfordgroupconsulting.com

Firth, D. (2003) '10 rules of change', *People Management,* 6 March.

Grove, A.S. (1999) 'Managing segment zero', *Leader to Leader,* **11**, Winter.

Jobber (1995) *Principles and Practicing of Marketing*, McGraw-Hill.

Kanter, Rosabeth Moss (1999) 'Enduring skills of change leaders', *Leader to Leader,* **13**, Summer, pp. 15–22.

Kanter, R.M. (1999) <http://drucker.org/leaderbook/L2L/summer99/kanter.html>

Piercey, N. and Morgan, N. (1997) 'Internal marketing', *International Journal of Bank Marketing.*

Whittington, P.R. and Mayer, M. (2002) *Organising for Success*, London: CIPD.

Past examination papers for the Marketing Management in Practice module can be found in Appendix 5.

unit 5
project management

Learning objectives

o Describe the main stages of a project and the roles of people involved at each stage (2.1).

o Describe the main characteristics of successful and less successful projects and identify the main reasons for success or failure (2.2).

o Explain the importance of, and techniques for, establishing the project's scope, definition and goals (2.3).

o Use the main techniques available for planning, scheduling, resourcing and controlling activities on a project (2.4).

o Explain the importance of preparing budgets and techniques for controlling progress throughout a project to ensure it is completed on time and within budget (2.5).

o Explain the main techniques for evaluating the effectiveness of a project on its completion (2.6).

Statements of Marketing Practice

Jc.1   Plan *marketing* projects and prepare budgets.

Jc.2   Manage and report on delivery against plan and objectives.

Kc.1   Define measurements appropriate to the plan or business case and ensure they are undertaken.

Kc.2   Evaluate activities and identify improvements using measurement data.

142

Glossary

Business case – This is used to define the information that justifies the setting up, continuation or termination of the project. It answers the question 'Why should this project be undertaken?' It can be updated at key points throughout the project.

Critical path – The series of tasks that must be completed on time for a project to finish on schedule. Each task on the critical path is a critical task; any delay to it would delay the project's schedule. Often displayed as:

Critical path analysis – A method for scheduling when tasks will happen. Comprising of a forward pass and a backward pass, it determines how quickly and how slowly the tasks can be accomplished.

Customer – Customer is used to represent the person or group who has commissioned the work and will be benefiting from the end results.

Gantt chart – A graphical representation of the project's current schedule. It will often contain bars for normal tasks, summary tasks, milestone tasks and slack values. Gantt charts are also referred to as bar charts as they depict task bars against a timescale.

PERT analysis – It is a simple form of quantitative risk analysis and can be applied to a schedule to help estimate the duration of a task. After the entry of optimistic, pessimistic and expected durations for each of the tasks, Microsoft Project will calculate a weighted average of the three durations, and determine a single duration estimate for each task. Gantt charts can display the results of critical path analysis taking all tasks at their optimistic, pessimistic and expected values. A button on the analysis toolbar provides access to PERT commands.

Product, deliverable or outcome – Terms used to describe everything that the project has to create or change, however physical or otherwise these may be. Results of projects can vary from physical items such as buildings to intangible things such as culture change.

Programme – This is a collection of projects that together achieve a beneficial change for an organization.

Project objectives – Three basic objectives that a project must meet to ensure its successful conclusion:

1. Time objective
2. Cost objective
3. Quality objective

Project objectives are often a contractual agreement between the project manager, the project's sponsor and the project's stakeholders.

Project definition – What a project will deliver and how it will be judged.

Project resources – Work, time and cost are resources of the project that are consumed in its execution. For example, doing some work will take some time and incur some cost, as its accomplishment adds to meeting the project's overall objectives.

Supplier – This refers to the group that is providing specialist resources and skills to the project, or goods and services, to create the project outcome required by the customer and user(s).

User – A user is the person or group who will use or operate the final product. In some situations, the customer and the user may be the same group of people.

Introduction

Some of the underpinning knowledge for this is covered in other modules and units, and a key part is contained in the final unit – Developing marketing plans. When studying the Marketing Management in Practice module, CIM recommends that two-thirds of the sessions should be allocated to a significant practical project involving the formulation and implementation of an operational marketing plan. This should cover the management of information, communications and human resources. The emphasis should be the application of this theory within a marketing team. A typical project will consist of:

- ○ Planning the project to be undertaken to meet the brief given.
- ○ Undertaking the task. This will involve collecting and analysing information and developing a marketing plan.
- ○ Planning, scheduling and resourcing marketing activities within the plan, identifying and overcoming problems during implementation.
- ○ Measuring and evaluating the outcomes.
- ○ Reflecting on the performance of the team and the individuals in it.

The basic approach to project management should be the same regardless of the type of project or sector in which the project is carried out. Services marketing professionals, in particular, are facing greater complexity in managing programmes and projects. Typical marketing programmes within large IT services organizations involve teamwork with different functional areas such as research and development, training, manufacturing, communication, as well as with business partners. Global marketing organizations require managing collaboration across numerous cultures and time zones.

What is a project?

The application of knowledge, skills, tools and techniques to a broad range of activities. Project management knowledge and practices are best described in terms of their component processes, for example initiating, planning, executing, controlling and closing.

Key roles in the project process

Sponsor
The person who WANTS the change AND has the POWER to legitimize it.

Advocate
Someone who thinks the change is a good idea. Generally helpful but not to be confused with a sponsor.

Expert
Someone who is qualified to comment on technical issues. Everyone thinks they're one of these, but it's important to listen to a real expert.

Target
The group of people who HAVE TO change. The difference between them and stakeholders is that stakeholders have a greater degree of choice.

Stakeholders
Beneficiaries of the change or people who may affect or be affected by it.

Change agent
Someone charged by the sponsor to bring the change about, but who has no power on his or her own.

Overview

Project management
- It should be collaborative
- The methodology should be capable of being applied to any project
- It should be results-oriented
- It should be easy to use.

Stages of a project
In recent years, project teams and a project management approach have become common in many organizations. The Initiation – The limits, constraints and priorities need to be defined.

Planning
- Team members need to be selected
- Scope of the project should be defined
- Potential 'risks' identified and planned for
- Resources required determined
- Execution
- Deliverables created
- Progress monitored and communicated
- Issues resolved and changes managed.

Closeout
- Customer satisfaction measured
- Lessons learned, analysed.

Criteria for success
- Customer satisfaction – expectations need to be managed
- Organization satisfaction – for example profit, development of capability
- Team learning – can lessons be learned and taken forward to other projects.

Reasons for failure
- Lack of appropriate expertise and approach from the project leader
- Lack of support from project sponsor – need to communicate resources needed and reasons
- Lack of ability/necessary expertise of team members – need to select carefully
- Lack of 'buy-in' from end-users – need to involve them in the project.

Scope, definition and goals
- Project name
- Business case
- Objectives
- Deliverables
- Identify customers' requirements and needs
- Resources needed
- Planning, scheduling and resourcing.

Project plan
- *Who* – recruit the right skill base
- *How* – identify the interim deliverables
- *When* – schedule of delivery
- *How much* – the costs.

Budgets
- Staff costs
- Overheads
- Equipment needed
- Outside services
- Supplies
- Travel.

Controls
- Project team meetings
- Regular reviews
- Team member accountability
- Milestones
- Stakeholder meetings.

Post project evaluation
- Customer and stakeholder evaluation
- Reviewing final status report with project team
- Recording lessons learned
- Reviewing final report with sponsor
- Celebrating success.

Seven steps to success
1. Use an effective method
2. Invest in planning
3. Involve the customer
4. Make it manageable
5. Involve the team
6. Communicate effectively
7. Learn from mistakes.

Project management may not always come easy to marketers, who may want to focus more on the 'creative' side of the work. Without a project management method, those who commission a project, those who manage it and those who work on it will have different ideas about how things should be organized and when the different aspects of the project will be completed. Those involved will not be clear about how much responsibility, authority and accountability they have and, as a result, there will often be confusion surrounding the project.

A project should possess identifiable goals, and a definite starting and finishing point. Project goals should be defined clearly. The major constraints on the completion of projects are time, resource availability and the need to achieve the required standard of performance for the project.

While marketing projects are getting more complex, marketing managers need to demonstrate a clear and strong return on marketing investment (ROI). One response to these pressures is the establishment of a 'project management office' – a team of people that uses management methodologies and tools. Although such a structured approach might not be necessary or appropriate for every organization, many marketing professionals need to understand project planning and implementation.

Feasibility studies

Before a project is given the go-ahead, a feasibility study might be conducted before the launch of a project. Support for a project could be important, so the aim of a feasibility study is to carry out a preliminary investigation to help determine whether a project should proceed further and how it should proceed.

The questions asked and the focus of a study will depend upon, for example, such things as the nature of the project that is being contemplated, the risk factors involved and its cost. The cost of carrying out a feasibility study needs to be weighed against the cost of a project not delivering what is expected of it. There is no point in carrying out an actual feasibility study if the cost of it would exceed the actual cost of the project. In this situation, the feasibility of a project would need to be determined in other ways on the basis of information that is already available.

However, a feasibility study will need to consider the following:

Cost – Is it within the budget set by the organization or within the capabilities of the organization to finance it?

Timing – Are there any time constraints and will it be possible to complete the project within these constraints?

Performance – Will the project deliver the benefits that are claimed for it?

Effect on the organization – Is it feasible in the context of the organization and the effect which it will have upon it? – Does it fit the culture of the organization? – Will it draw resources away from other important activities?

Resourcing – Are the necessary skills, technology and physical infrastructure available? Or, if not, can they be easily recruited?

Stages of a project

Project definition

Once the project has received formal approval to proceed, the objectives of the project and how the work will be undertaken can be determined. The project manager will carry out this work, in consultation with the client, and any sub-project manager if there are sub-projects. Large projects may be divided into sub-projects, with each sub-project requiring its own sub-project definition. The aim is to identify if all prerequisites are in place. Before a definition can begin, there should be a project brief or terms of reference signed off by all parties involved in the project and giving the authority to proceed.

This is the stage where objectives, assumptions and constraints need to be identified so that everyone can be clear about the basis on which the project will proceed. As the project gets underway, there are likely to be changes to it because it is very difficult to know everything at the outset. Some of the assumptions made may need to change in the light of experience or, for example, the availability of resources or key personnel, and the original scheduling may need to be revised. All this is easier if the objectives, assumptions and constraints have been identified in the first place.

A project covers interrelated activities or tasks with definite start and finish times, identifiable objectives and an integrated system of complex but interdependent relationships. An activity or task is a unit of work whose scheduling is overseen by a project manager.

Projects have three elements:

1. Budget
2. Schedule
3. Deliverables.

The aim of project management is to ensure the effective scheduling of tasks and use of resources to deliver the objectives of a project on time, within cost constraints and with outcomes that meet the needs of the end-users.

Determine project scope

Determining the scope of the project helps to clarify objectives and set the boundaries of the project. It is often useful to state limitations, that is what the project will not cover.

Project brief

A project brief should take the objectives and translate them into targets and goals. Any key constraints should also be identified and stated at this stage. This brief should be agreed by the client and communicated to the project manager. Success criteria should be established for the project, preferably criteria that are tangible and measurable. The success criteria should be provided in response to the conditions adhering to the project.

Contents of a project brief

A project brief will identify:

- *Objectives* – Why you are doing it, as listed in the client requirements definition, the business benefits that the project will provide when it is completed – often broken down to three basic project objectives: Time, Cost and Quality.
- *Scope* – Project boundaries.
- *Deliverables* – What it will provide.
- *Accountability* – Success criteria.

How you will be performing it – major milestones, change control procedures.

- *Constraints* – Question of how would you know if your project had been successful.
- *Assumptions* – Listed unknowns about the project.
- Resources.

Key personnel – Who is responsible for what? Who are the stakeholders?

Objectives – Three basic objectives that a project must meet to ensure its successful conclusion:

1. Time
2. Cost
3. Quality.

The objectives form the basis of the project's strategic information. They also relate to one another; for example, a reduction in time may incur additional cost or may reduce overall quality. Project objectives are often a contractual agreement between the project manager, the project's client and the project's stakeholders.

The client is one of the project's stakeholders who will receive the benefits that the project will provide. He usually provides or authorizes the terms of reference and communicates strategic information to and from the project manager. Stakeholders are individuals or organizations with a vested interest in a project. The most obvious stakeholder is the sponsor.

Assumptions

Project assumptions can be checked with stakeholders who can critique them and, if necessary, a revised set of assumptions agreed when there are changes. A schedule can be revised when new information becomes available.

Areas where assumptions may need to be made include:

- The materials, resources, people and equipment that will be available.
- How long particular tasks will take to complete – Are the assumptions based on realistic information or are they the result of inspired guesses?
- How important is cost to the project – What are the arrangements if a budget needs to be increased?
- Will all the project tasks be completed in the timescale available and to an acceptable quality level?

- ○ Are the project aims deliverable in line with what the key stakeholders are expecting?
- ○ What are the management arrangements for overseeing the project – Will there be a steering group to whom the project director or manager will report?
- ○ What kinds of reports will be needed, by when?

Constraints

There can be constraints on the completion of projects, arising from the different objectives of:

- ○ Timescale
- ○ Resource availability
- ○ Quality factors
- ○ Human factors
- ○ *Performance specifications* – These may be set out in terms of the ability to deal with certain demands. For example, this could be number of patients or transactions processed, or the number of enquiries dealt with.
- ○ *Specific quality standards* – This could relate to technical standards and tolerance, or may be the achievement of a favourable report from an outside inspection agency.
- ○ *Meeting deadlines* – For example, a new system may need to be implemented, ready for the start of the financial year, or a new development may have to meet time requirements as laid down in contract specifications.

Calculate resource requirements

Calculate requirements for each time period. Identify needs for each resource type (e.g. systems analyst, user staff) and identify needs for special skills or scarce resources.

Calculate costs

Calculate costs for the sub-project. This should include 'hardening up' items such as cabling, training and so on for which an order of costs had been produced previously.

Determine overall costs of the project

The cost/benefit justification should have already been stated in the feasibility study. This stage provides the opportunity to review the case in the light of more detailed information. An important criterion may be to complete the project within a cost limit or budget which has been determined. Additionally, there may be requirements in terms of the ongoing cost of the completed project. For example, a new system may be required to make savings for the organization on a continuing basis.

Deliverables

A deliverable is a tangible verifiable outcome of work done to produce a product or service. To be verifiable, the deliverable must meet pre-determined standards for its completion, such as design specifications for a product or a checklist of steps that is completed as part of a service. Deliverables have external stakeholders who receive the finished product or service such as customers and internal stakeholders like a project manager and team members who work directly on the deliverable. A project may have only one or many deliverables.

Define key project tasks

To help in breaking a project down into smaller and more manageable pieces of work, the project's objectives and scope are broken down into more detail in terms of duration, work and links. The most common approach is to plan from the overall objective and then to break this down into sub-objectives (or phases). Sub-objectives may relate to products, functions, disciplines and cost areas. The sub-objectives need to be broken down further into lower levels of detail until quantifiable tasks are at the bottom of the structure. The smaller the task, the more accurately it can be estimated. Tasks should be allocated to a named person, group or organization for implementation.

Once a project's tasks have been defined, the next stage is to determine how the tasks relate to one another. This creates sequences of tasks within the project and identifies when each of the tasks can occur.

In determining the sequence of tasks – the tasks that must be accomplished before a particular task can take place – its predecessor(s) needs to be identified. This technique is known as precedence analysis and is the common way of determining how tasks relate.

These relationships are referred to as dependencies or precedences, and when planning a project it is important to establish the order of precedence of dependent activities, and to establish those activities which can be performed in parallel with other activities.

Not all tasks within a project start at the same time. There will always be some form of sequence. The simplest relationship is where the commencement of one task depends upon the completion of just one task that precedes it. This is a dependent relationship.

Building a project plan

The complexity of the project plan will depend on the size of the project, as larger projects demand greater planning and structure than smaller ones. Software such as Microsoft® Project can be used to build project plans and will help with listing the project tasks, organize them into phases, schedule tasks, set dependencies, deadlines and constraints, and specify and assign the resources to tasks.

If the timeline indicates that the project will run over its deadline, a check should be made to ensure that resources are not under- or over-allocated. Resolving this is called Resource Levelling and it may assist in sorting out the timeline. If it does not work, more resources may be needed. However, adding another person to a task does not necessarily mean that the task will necessarily be completed more quickly if the person needs to be trained and familiarized with the specific project. It may also slow down an existing member of the team if they need to brief and coach the newcomer. The timeline might be shortened through working overtime, though excessive overtime reduces productivity. If this does not work and the deadline really is unmovable, the project requirements may need to be reworked to meet the date. When the project plan is agreed, it becomes a baseline that can be used to compare with the progress of the project.

RACI chart

RACI stands for:

R = Responsible (the role responsible for performing the task)

A = Accountable (the role with overall responsibility for the task)

C = Consulted (the roles that provide input to help perform the task)

I = Informed (the roles with vested interest who should be kept informed).

Responsibility Charting is a technique for identifying functional areas where there are ambiguities, It enables managers from the same or different organizational levels or programmes to participate in a discussion about actions that must be accomplished in order to deliver a successful end product or service.

A RACI chart can help to ensure that the right people are involved in the right activities.

Action items	R	A	C	I
1._____	(Name)	(Other name)	May be	May be
2._____			More than	next in
3._____			one person	line
4._____				
5._____				
Etc.				

Determine work structure

Large projects are more likely to be successful if they can be divided into smaller units of work (sub-projects). Identify tasks which can be arranged into logical groups to form sub-projects. Grouping could be on the basis of, for example:

- Tasks Relating to one functional area
- Tasks to be performed by staff in one geographic location
- Tasks Relating to a particular deliverable
- Tasks to be performed by team members belonging to the same division or department.

Ensure project structure and responsibilities are established.

Determine management systems

These will vary according to the size and nature of the project but should always include:

- A progress control system for recording planned and actual times. This could be an automated system or a manual one.
- Agreed procedures for formal review and agreement of each project deliverable.
- Scheduled management checkpoints.

If the project is divided into sub-projects, it is important that consistent management systems are used across them all.

Assign sub-project managers where appropriate. Clarify composition and responsibilities of the project steering group, and responsibilities of the project sponsor and the project manager.

Produce a project organization structure to show reporting lines.

Assemble and organize the project team

Projects are sometimes carried out by a team of people assembled for that specific purpose. The activities of this team may be co-ordinated by a project manager. Project teams may consist of people from different parts of the organization, and in some cases, people from different organizations. The selection of the team will be dependent upon the skill requirements of the project, and upon the matching of those to individual members of the team. Within a project, roles and responsibilities define the relationships between the project team and the work that has to be done. Project work is often multifaceted, requiring a combination of skills and activities for planning, execution and completion. Every key project activity should be clearly defined in terms of roles and responsibilities. Some team members will have dual responsibilities of involvement in the project, in addition to a commitment to other projects or management of a functional area on a day-to-day basis. It is at this stage that a project manager should be appointed and responsibilities made explicit for all members of the team.

Project scheduling

Scheduling the project
The aim is to ensure that resources are available when they are needed. This needs to be checked before building a project plan.

Creating a cost schedule
This phase is primarily concerned with attaching a timescale and sequence to the activities to be conducted within the project. Materials and people needed at each stage of the project are determined, and the time each is to take will be set. When resources are assigned to tasks, they create measurable work. This work in turn can incur cost. One common occurrence when working with resource assignments is that demand will invariably exceed supply. Some key people will be overworked and others will have time to spare. This inefficiency can be overcome by firstly looking at how people are utilized, and then by looking at the tasks within the project and determining how much free time (slack) they possess. Once these factors are understood, actions can be taken and decisions can be reached regarding who does what (most efficiently) and when.

Resource conflicts
If resource demand exceeds supply, this is known as a resource conflict and needs to be resolved. An assignment is the relationship between a task and a resource. This relationship creates work – somebody doing something to achieve the objective of the task. Work, time and cost are resources of the project that are consumed in its execution. Doing some work will take some time and incur some cost.

Milestones
Milestones – measurable objectives that signal the completion of a major deliverable and indicate that you have reached a significant point in the project. Milestones can be established quickly if the project is on schedule, and can be useful when reporting on progress to management and clients.

Milestones are used to signify that something significant has been completed or something significant is ready to occur; for example, the start or beginning of a phase or the achievement

153

of a key deliverable. The milestones and the information that need to be received and provided for different parts of the project need to be agreed with the project stakeholders. The information can be strategic and tactical.

Strategic

Strategic information would normally be provided for and by key stakeholders and would include:

o   Timing reports for the start and finish of major project phases
o   Start and finish dates for discrete tasks within a project phase
o   Cost schedules summarized by phase
o   Start and finish dates for tasks assigned to a particular skill or resource
o   Milestone date schedules a task's sub-deliverables, or a to-do list.

Tactical

Tactical information would normally be shared between the project manager and members of their workgroup. This should include:

o   Start and finish dates for discrete tasks within a project phase
o   Cost schedules summarized by phase
o   Start and finish dates for tasks assigned to a particular skill or resource.

Gantt charts

Gantt charts are particularly helpful when scheduling and controlling a project which has a number of repetitive activities within it. The graphic display afforded by the Gantt chart not only helps the operations management of the project but also helps to co-ordinate the various activities in an efficient way.

The Gantt chart takes its name from Henry Gantt, the American engineer who created it. It is a technique that can be used for sequencing project activities. The chart is the most common report in all project management systems. It is a form of bar chart with horizontal bars drawn against a timescale for each project activity. The length of each bar represents the time taken to complete an activity.

To construct a Gantt chart, the various activities are listed on a vertical axis, and the horizontal axis is used to represent time. Activity precedences are taken into account by starting a horizontal bar to represent the next activity at an appropriate point after its preceding activities, that is those activities which must take place before the next activity can start, have taken place. Normally, this would be at the earliest time that it could start after its preceding activities had finished.

The timescale should cover the duration of the project – from the start to the project finish date. In between these dates, it should be divided into equal increments. Gantt charts are sometimes known as milestone plans and they provide a useful way of monitoring the progress of a project (Figure 5.1). The advantages of using them are:

o   All activities are planned for
o   The sequence of activities is accounted for
o   The activity time estimates are recorded
o   The overall project time is recorded.

Task Name	1 2 3 4 5 6 7 8 9 10 11 12 13 14 15 16 17 18 19 20 21 22 23 24 25 26 27 28 29 30

Figure 5.1 A Gantt timescale of 30 days

Once the chart's timescale has been created, tasks can be added. These tasks should be the complete list of sub-tasks as described within the network diagram, or from the lowest level of the outline (Work Breakdown Structure). The chart's timescale can be in days, weeks, months and so on. It must be linear and in equal increments, for Figure 5.2 increment per day or one increment per week.

Task Name	1 2 3 4 5 6 7 8 9 10 11 12 13 14 15 16 17 18 19 20 21 22 23 24 25 26 27 28 29 30
Design structure	■ ■ ■ ■ ■
Write body text	■ ■ ■ ■ ■ ■ ■ ■ ■ ■ ■ ■ ■ ■ ■
Set page layouts	
Create exercises	■ ■ ■ ■ ■ ■ ■ ■ ■
Test exercises	
Create contents & index	

Figure 5.2 Example of a schedule for developing an online course

Displaying link lines between tasks

When a Gantt chart has a lot of links between tasks (especially cross-project links), the chart can become very busy with detail. When producing a Gantt chart for a client or a sponsor, decide if it is appropriate to tell them how tasks relate. They probably only need to know when tasks are scheduled to occur.

Once the project's schedule has been calculated (with critical path analysis) and a Gantt chart created, the next step in the planning process is to create some resource assignments. These assignments add the people dimension – someone doing something. What is important is a general understanding of the relationship between the task (something that needs to be achieved) and the resource (the individual that performs the work to achieve the task's objective). Gantt charts also provide a summary of the project as a whole, and can be used as a rough and ready means of assessing progress at the project control phase. At any date, the project manager can draw a dateline through the Gantt chart and see which activities are on time, which are behind schedule and generally record project status against plans.

MONTH	APR	MAY	JUNE	JULY	AUG	SEPT
Marketing						
Broadsheet advertisements			▓			
Face-to-face meetings with clients			▓			
Direct mailing inserts into Marketing Success			▓			
Arrange corporate ID		▓				
Arrange printing of business cards		▓				

		▓				
Recruitment						
Recruitment period				▓	▓	▓
London recruitment fair			▓			
Programme starts						
Administration						
Administration support recruited			▓			
Partnership agreement signed		▓				
Arrange professional indemnity insurance		▓				
Purchase domain name	▓					
Register with Data Protection Act	▓					
Finance						
Arrange online credit card payment system	▓					
Arrange bank loan	▓					
Website						
Design website	▓	▓				
Design activities for website		▓	▓			
Write web guide			▓	▓		

Figure 5.3 Six month activity schedule

Activity 5.1

Choose a project that you will be involved with at work and, construct a Gantt chart which will provide an overview of the planned project.

When do you anticipate that you will start?

How soon could the project be completed?

Which activities need to be completed on time in order to ensure that the project is completed as soon as possible?

Show the shortest time it will take to complete the project.

Network analysis

The first step in network analysis is to divide the project into discrete 'activities' and 'events'. An event marks a point in time equating to the start or finish of an activity. An activity is a task or combination of small tasks that occurs between two events. Any activity that can be disaggregated and described by activities and events may be analysed within a network. The two most common and widely used project management techniques that can be classified under the title of Network Analysis are Programme Evaluation and Review Technique (PERT) and Critical Path Method (CPM).

PERT/CPM

There are six stages common to both PERT and CPM:

1. Define the project and specify all activities or tasks.
2. Develop the relationships amongst activities. Decide upon precedences.
3. Draw network to connect all activities.
4. Assign time and/or costs to each activity.
5. Calculate the longest time path through the network: this is the 'critical path'.
6. Use network to plan, monitor and control the project. A network diagram is used to express how all the tasks in a project relate to each other. It helps to show how all the project tasks interrelate. A network diagram is also good for showing cross-project links.

Both models can help to answer the following questions for projects with thousands of activities and events, both at the beginning of the project and once it is under way:

1. When will the project be completed?
2. What are the critical activities (i.e. the tasks which, if delayed, will affect time for overall completion)?
3. Which activities are non-critical and can run late without delaying project completion time?
4. What is the probability of the project being completed by a specific date?
5. At any particular time, is the project on schedule?
6. At any particular time, is the money spent equal to, less than or more than the budgeted amount?
7. Are there enough resources left to complete the project on time?

Probability analysis

Once the expected completion time and variance have been determined, the probability that a project will be completed by a specific date can be assessed. The assumption is usually made that the distribution of completion dates follows that of a normal distribution curve. If the project is to be completed in a shorter time, what is the least cost means to accomplish this and what are the cost consequences?

Critical path analysis

This is a method for scheduling when tasks will happen. A critical task is one that must be completed on schedule for the project to finish on time. If a critical task is delayed, the project finish date might also be delayed. A series of critical tasks make up a project's critical path.

As the tasks within a project have links between them, they cannot all happen at the same time. Critical path analysis (CPA) can be used to determine what can happen when. It calculates how quickly and how slowly the tasks can be performed, taking into account the sequence of tasks and the interrelationships between them. Gantt charts are created as a result of CPA.

Critical path analysis is a procedure that calculates a project's schedule. Taking each task in turn, it first calculates how quickly the task can be accomplished – its early start and early finish dates. Once all these dates have been calculated, the project finish date can also be determined. With this finish date known, CPA can then calculate how slowly each task can be accomplished (late start and late finish dates). Once all this information is known for each task, CPA will also calculate the slack that the task possesses.

The objective of CPA is to determine times for:

ES = Earliest Start Time. This is the earliest time an activity can be started, allowing for the fact that all preceding activities have been completed.

LS = Latest Start Time. This is the latest time an activity can be started without delaying the start of subsequent activities which would put the entire project behind schedule.

EF = Earliest Finish Time. The earliest time an activity can be finished.

LF = Latest Finish Time. The latest time that an activity can finish for the project to remain on schedule.

ZS = Activity Slack Time. The amount of slippage in activity start or duration time which can be tolerated without delaying the project as a whole.

Once these values are known, the overall project can be analysed. The critical path is the group of activities in the project that have a slack time of zero. This path of activities is critical because a delay in any activity along it would delay the project as a whole. Finding the critical path is a major activity in controlling a project. Managers can derive flexibility by identifying the non-critical activities and replanning, rescheduling and reallocating resources such as manpower and finances within identified boundaries.

PERT

The major difference between CPM and PERT is that the latter employs three time estimates for each activity. Probabilities are attached to each of these times which, in turn, is used for computing expected values and potential variations for activity times. CPM assumes that activity times are known and fixed, so only one time estimate is given and used for each activity. The three time estimates specified for each activity in PERT are:

1. The optimistic time
2. The most probable time
3. The pessimistic time.

The optimistic, most likely and pessimistic time estimates are used to calculate an expected activity completion time. In addition, the three time estimates can be used to calculate the variance for each activity. The formulae used are as follows.

When using PERT, the expected times are calculated first from the three values of activity time estimates, and it is these values that are then used exactly as in CPM. The variance values are calculated for the various activity times and the variance of the total project completion time is the sum of the variances of the activities lying on that critical path.

Reviewing progress

It is the job of the project manager to make sure that the project stays on track and the deliverables meet the specifications detailed in the project definition document, as well as managing client expectations by keeping all relevant parties informed about the project's status. The project has a greater chance of success if the client is actively involved. The broad aims of reviewing are to:

Compare – Find variances between the baseline schedule and actual progress – cost variances and work variances.

Evaluate – Are the project's objectives still able to be met? Do the variances indicate the development of a trend?

Decide – Perform a 'what-if' analysis to overcome the variances and get the project back on track. This is a method of experimentation to determine the optimum schedule of tasks or utilization of resources. A 'what-if' analysis may need to be carried out more than once.

Inform – Inform all project team members of revisions to the project's schedule, individual schedules and deliverables met. If certain tasks or resources are constantly going over budget or always taking longer than planned, could a trend be developing?

Managing communication

Effective communication with the relevant parties is the key to a successful project. The project manager should develop a communications plan in order to gather progress information from the team, supply timely reports and gather feedback from the management and the client.

Collecting information from team members

Regular contact is needed with individual team members to evaluate the status of their work and to deal with any questions they have or issues that need to be resolved. There is no need to waste time by insisting on written reports when information can be gathered easily in other ways from face-to-face meetings, e-mail or telephone calls.

Information should be gathered at regular intervals and any issues that are raised by the project team should be dealt with promptly.

159

Project meetings

Project meetings give the team, including management and the client representative, an opportunity to evaluate the project's status as a whole and to highlight issues that the team as a whole need to deal with. These meetings provide an opportunity to raise issues that concern the big picture even if they are only noted to be dealt with at a later time.

Reports to management and the client

Depending on the size of the project, status reports should be submitted to the management and the client to keep those who do not attend the project status meetings up to date. These may not be necessary for small projects, but for medium and large projects bi-monthly or monthly reports would be appropriate.

Managing client expectations

Managing client expectations is one of the tasks of the project manager and the project definition document is a tool that is useful in this process. By identifying clear project deliverables and constraints, the client should know what to expect from the outset of the project.

Once the project is under way, you then need to carefully manage scope change. Any changes to scope, whether suggested by the client or a member of the team, should be carefully discussed with the client. Pros and cons of the change should be weighed up, and if it is decided to go ahead, a formal scope change document should be presented to and signed by the client.

Managing the project plan

The progress of the project can be tracked by noting the status of each task at regular intervals. Software such as Microsoft Project offers three methods for tracking progress:

1. *Percentage of work complete* – This is the least accurate but fastest way to track. Asking team members to report their progress according to this method can result in misleading reports due to the human tendency to at times be 'almost done' for prolonged periods.
2. *Actual work completed* – This is more accurate, but also more time consuming.
3. *Hours of work completed per time period* – This is the most accurate but most time consuming, as people need to specify the exact hours they have worked in particular time periods.

Adding tasks

Sometimes the project will demand the addition of tasks that had not been previously identified, or the scope of the project may have changed. The project plan will need to be adjusted to create a new baseline.

Take note of when milestones are met and review the plan to ensure that it will meet the delivery date. If not, remedial action will be needed. Problems with the budget need to be resolved quickly, so it needs to be reviewed on a regular basis and reports submitted to the relevant parties.

Managing the scope of the project

The project manager is in charge of managing the scope of the project, so that only what was agreed is delivered unless changes have been formally agreed. The project manager needs to ensure that everybody involved remembers the project objective.

Mission creep occurs when the client or team members lose sight of the agreed project objectives. This can be avoided by creating a clear and unambiguous project and scope definition at the outset, and by constantly referring to this definition during the course of the project. The project's scope may also change upon request. Changing the scope of a project often means that a client has asked for extra work.

Budgeting

A budget is an expression of an organization's planned activities and serves a number of purposes. It is a forecast of the resources likely to be available to the organization and a plan for utilizing these resources to achieve the organization's objectives. It is also a framework for authorizing the expenditure of resources and for maintaining control over that expenditure.

Budgeting is the most common control mechanism of any planning process. Control is based on comparing actual against planned expenditure and investigating any variances calculated. It is important that sales and production targets are met and budgeting provides a standard against which the performance of the organization as a whole and the performance of individuals may be judged.

Budgeting systems also need to be flexible in enabling resources to be deployed quickly in response to changing demands from the environment and also motivate staff to use resources effectively and efficiently.

The control process

Monitoring and control effectively contains four key activities:

1. Development or adjustment of marketing objectives
2. Setting of performance standards
3. Evaluation of performance
4. Corrective action.

The first stage in the process after setting the objectives, by which performance will be measured, is setting performance standards. Performance standards are principally the level of performance against which actual performance can be compared. In the main, performance standards are presented in the form of budgets. The sole purpose of this will be to ensure that the amount of money given over to expenditure is not exceeded and that the proposed targets for income and profit are actually achieved. There are a number of methods of measuring performance overall, such as performance management. This consists of reviewing performance, giving feedback and, if necessary, re-examining and re-setting objectives and targets. To make monitoring easier, budgets are often broken down into a number of smaller manageable areas, often termed cost centres. For each of these, planned income and expenditure are monitored and compared with the actual results. In some organizations, each function may be a cost centre. For example, headings on a monthly or annual budget report could be as shown in the following table:

INCOME BUDGET – Marketing and sales division

Income	Actual year	Month	Budgeted amount	Variance under	Variance over
Sales					
Interest earned					
Sales commission					
Licence fees					
Royalty payments					
Property rentals					
Total Income					

EXPENDITURE BUDGET – Marketing and sales division					
Income	**Actual year**	**Month**	**Budgeted amount**	**Variance under**	**Variance over**
Sales					
Rent					
Advertising					
PR					
Sales promotions					
Travel					
Sales commission					
Total Expenditure					

Variance analysis

One of the main things that control is likely to expose is constant variances from the planned budget. Variance analysis is used along with budgetary control. It compares a planned budget with an actual budget and seeks to explain any variations from what has been planned. A variance in itself is not good or bad, it is the interpretation and explanation of why there is a variance that will determine whether it is good or bad. As mentioned previously, figures do not speak for themselves, they need to be interpreted. The key to using variance analysis as a control tool is to be aware that variance in budgets is inevitable.

Benchmarking

In the words of Drummond and Ensor, *Strategic Marketing Planning and Control*, benchmarking is defined as

> *A systematic and ongoing process of measuring and comparing an organization's business processes and achievements against acknowledged process leaders and/or key competitors, to facilitate improved performance.*

Benchmarking is concerned with demonstrating a commitment to continuous improvement and show that the organization is a learning organization, willing to learn from past mistakes and also past successes and develop an approach to best business practice. It falls into three categories:

1. *Competitive analysis* – reviewing on an ongoing basis competitor activities in order to learn from their success.
2. *Best practice* – here the organization should involve itself in reviewing the best way of undertaking activities across the whole of the organization.
3. *Performance standards* – ensuring that targets are either met or surpassed.

Managing quality

The project manager should ensure that the project's quality standard is understood by everyone concerned and that deliverables meet that standard. Checklists and regular reviews focusing on the subject can assist in this process.

Post project reviews

Some issues to consider:

- Were the main objectives met?
- Was enough time allocated to each task?
- Were there any warning signs that were ignored?
- Did everyone understand the project definition and their roles?
- Was the project on time and to budget and why?
- Was the relationship with the client satisfactory, or did unforeseen problems arise?
- Was the quality control process sufficient?

Successful project management

The effectiveness of project management is critical in assuring the success of any substantial undertaking. Areas of responsibility for the project manager include planning, control and implementation.

Knowledge, skills, goals and personalities are all factors that need to be considered within project management. The project manager and his/her team should possess the necessary interpersonal and technical skills to control the project activities.

The stages of implementation must be identified at the project planning phase. In addition to planning, the control of the project is also a necessary condition of success. This means adequate monitoring and feedback mechanisms to facilitate comparisons of progress against projections. Monitoring and feedback also enables minor problems to be anticipated and addressed before they become major ones. Consulting with end-users is important for ensuring the success of a project.

Activity 5.2

Can you think of any examples where your organization needs to respond to change and a project management approach may be valid?

The reasons for project failure

Common reasons are as follows:

- Project goals are not clearly defined.
- The assumptions that are made at the outset of the project are incorrect but remain unchallenged.
- The project team is not sure of the project objectives or the deliverables.
- The planned schedule overruns.
- The budget is exceeded.
- Lack of co-ordination of resources and activities.
- Lack of communication with interested parties, leading to products being delivered that are not what the customer wanted.
- Poor estimation of duration and costs, leading to projects taking more time and costing more money than expected.
- Inadequate planning of resources, activities and scheduling.
- Lack of control over progress, so that projects do not reveal their exact status until too late.
- Lack of quality control, resulting in the delivery of products that are unacceptable or unusable.

Problems with project goals

o   The project sponsor or client has an inadequate idea of what the project is about at the start.
o   Failure of communication between the client and the project manager. This may be due to a lack of technical knowledge on the part of the client or an overuse of jargon by the project manager.
o   Specifications may be subject to constant change. This may be due to problems with individual clients, decision-making processes at the client's end, or environmental changes. For example the government may change the basic 'rules of the game' before the completion of the project.
o   The project goals may be unrealistic and unachievable, and it may be that this is only realized once the project is under way.
o   Projects may be complex and objectives may contradict each other.

There are perhaps two stages which can help in ensuring that goals are properly defined and achievable:

Ensuring that the client specification is clear and understandable. To do this the following objectives of the project must be established:

o   What is it that the organization is setting out to achieve or is being asked to achieve?
o   Will the suggested project fulfil these objectives?
o   Have all the alternatives been considered, and is the chosen option the best one available?
o   Have the full effects of the project, both inside and outside the organization, been considered?

Constraints on the completion of projects

Time

The definition of a project stated that it was an activity which had a defined beginning and ending point. Most projects will be close-ended in terms of there being a requirement for completion by a certain point of time. This point may be the result of an external factor such as new legislation, or may be derived from organizational requirements. It may also be partly determined by other constraints. There is likely to be some relationship between the time taken for a project and its cost. A trade-off between the two constraining factors may then be necessary.

Resource availability

There is likely to be a budget for the project and this will clearly be a major constraint. Cost constraints may be set in a number of ways, for example as an overall cash limit or as a detailed budget broken down over a number of expenditure headings. Labour resources in particular may be a limiting factor on the completion of the project. Whilst the overall resource available may be, in theory, sufficient to complete the project, there may be difficulties arising out of the way in which the project has been scheduled. That is, there may be a number of activities scheduled to take place at the same time and this may not be possible, given the amount of resources available.

Quality factors

Whether the project delivers the goods to the right quality. There are techniques which can be used to overcome the problems referred to above. These include:

o   Budgeting and the corresponding control of the project budget through budgetary control
o   Procedures
o   Project planning and control techniques such as Gantt charts and network analysis.

The various constraints on project completion are likely to be interlinked with each other. For example, problems with time constraints or resource constraints may be overcome by spending more through working overtime, employing more people or purchasing better machines. Budget problems may have a knock-on effect on the achievement of deadlines.

Provided the project is not too complex in its activity relationships or simply too big to be mapped on reasonably sized graph paper, Gantt charts can be very useful tools for the project manager and are graphically superior to the network analysis methods of CPM and PERT.

They allow the critical activities to be found, that is those activities which must be performed on time if the project duration is not to increase, and any 'slack' or 'float' in the sequence of activities can easily be shown.

By timetabling the activities by horizontal bars whose lengths represent the activity times, the earliest completion date for the entire project can be mapped out by the Gantt chart, and then used as indicated above by the operations manager to check on progress as the project proceeds.

Management of projects

Gantt charts, PERT, CPM and other scheduling techniques have proven to be valuable tools in the management of large and complex projects. A wide variety of software packages are available for project managers, for use on micro or larger computers, to assist in the handling of complex network problems. PERT and CPM, however, cannot ever purport to be able to solve all project scheduling and management problems in service or manufacturing industries. Good management practices, clear responsibilities for tasks, and accurate and timely reporting systems are the most essential qualities for successful project completion. As useful as these techniques are, they are only tools to assist the manager in making better, more calculated decisions in the process of conducting large-scale projects.

The role of the project manager falls into three areas:

1. Management of stakeholders
2. Management of the project life cycle
3. Management of performance.

Management of stakeholders

Stakeholders' interests must be monitored to ensure that their:

- Interest and support is maintained
- Views and ideas are being adequately reflected in the project development
- Personal success criteria are being pursued and achieved.

Management of the project life cycle

Feedback systems need to be set up to monitor key areas.

Management of performance

This is the least tangible but possibly the most important of the three categories. How it is tackled will depend upon what kind of project is being carried out. It is likely that they will work apart most of the time, meeting up only occasionally and meeting only with the project manager from time to time. Issues that need to be considered are:

- How to get the best out of the team when they are together
- Ensuring people work when the team is apart
- Disseminating information and keeping everyone informed is important

        ο Ensuring continuing commitment by the team
        ο Communicating change to team members quickly and effectively
        ο It is important to look at the team and also for the project leader to look at his or her own performance.

Project management and network techniques such as CPM and PERT are valuable tools for showing relationships between project activities, and identifying critical activities but the management of people is a major factor in whether a project will be a success or not. The ability to motivate staff, to create the structures and conditions in which they can be motivated and work effectively, and dealing with any people problems that arise are also essential features of project management. The human factors are as important as having the right tools and techniques. Working in teams and motivation have been looked at in other units so they would not be repeated here, but they are very important.

Five rules for delivering criticism

Project managers need to create and maintain good working relationships but they also need to monitor others' performance and act if there is a problem.

1. *Think it through before you say something* – A problem worth solving demands concentrated attention and focus to gain desired outcomes. This may mean not saying anything at all until you have mentally rehearsed your delivery and envisioned the receiver's response.
2. *Criticize in private* – Public criticism offends the receivers and observers. When a problem arises during a team meeting, acknowledge it and say that this is something that needs to be addressed 'later' 'without taking up everyone's time'.
3. *Respond to problems in a timely fashion* – Realize your own propensity to put off discussing problem behaviours. Remember the difficulty in reconstructing problems because everyone remembers them differently. Compare that to the benefits of a timely focus on correcting one problem at a time.
4. *Criticize without comparison* – Broad, unfavourable comparisons mean that individuals will end up finding fault with you rather than dealing with the ambiguous criticism levied at them.
5. *Criticize with specificity, not labels* – Examples of specific behaviours are: inaccuracy, lateness, absenteeism, interrupting, missed timelines, incompleteness, incorrectness, assumptions, data and so on. Criticism or feedback that cites specific examples such as these requires no interpretation of meaning. A missed commitment is a missed commitment. These concrete descriptions focus on quantifiable problems and achievable improvements.

Source: Paris (2000).

 Activity 5.3

For a project that is already under way in your organization, identify the key areas requiring monitoring, and suggest the kind of information and procedures that would be involved.

Differences between a functional manager and a project manager

A functional manager is likely to be a specialist in the area being managed, such that when technical knowledge is required or a difficult issue arises in an area, he should be able to make some realistic recommendations about how to tackle it. In contrast, a project manager is more likely to be a generalist who can bring various specialist resources together in order to complete a project (Meredith and Mantel, 1995).

Responsibilities of a project manager

- o To plan the project, soliciting the active involvement of all functional areas involved, in order to obtain and maintain a realistic plan that satisfies their commitment for performance.
- o To control the organization of human resources needed by the project.
- o To control the basic technical definition of the project, ensuring that 'technical' versus 'cost' trade-offs determine the specific areas where optimization is necessary.
- o To lead the people and organizations assigned to the project at any given point of time. Strong positive leadership must be exercised in order to keep the many disparate elements moving in the same direction in a co-operative manner.
- o To monitor performance, costs and efficiency of all elements of the project and the project as a whole, exercising judgement and leadership in determining the causes of problems and facilitating solutions.
- o To complete the project on schedule and within costs, these being the overall standard by which performance of the project manager is evaluated.

The skills of a project manager

The PM is expected to integrate all aspects of the project, to ensure that the proper knowledge and resources are available when and where needed, and above all to ensure that the expected results are produced in a timely, cost-effective manner.

A project manager is more likely to be a generalist who is required to bring together a number of functional areas, each comprising specialists in their own fields. The PM's task is to bring them together to form a coherent whole. The project manager needs to be able to synthesize a wide range of information, whereas a functional manager must be more skilled in analysing a narrower area. The functional manager needs a depth of experience whilst the project manager needs breadth. The authors argue that an analytical approach breaks a system down into smaller and smaller parts, but a systems approach tries to understand the links between different elements. However, there is no doubt that an effective project manager needs the skills of analysis and synthesis.

Skill dimensions that a project manager needs to use at different points in the project management cycle (Elbeik and Thomas, 1998):

Administrator

- o Accomplishment of project tasks and goals
- o Strong management of repetitive tasks and procedures
- o Adhering to routines and systematic controls
- o Focus on stability and consistency
- o Able to meet deadlines and cope with workloads
- o Organizing skills
- o A concern for detail and accuracy.

Analyst
- Strong problem-solving orientation
- High level of critical thinking ability
- Ability to synthesize other people's thought and actions
- A strategic outlook – able to see the 'bigger picture'
- Able to balance short-, medium- and long-term requirements.

Negotiator
- Influencing and persuasion skills
- Diplomatic
- Willingness to challenge and tackle others
- Able to 'read' situations and identify motives and needs
- Determination to achieve objectives.

Verbal communicator
- Able to present arguments persuasively
- Able to communicate effectively with people from different backgrounds and levels of seniority
- Effective range of responses to most situations and able to think on his or her feet
- Able to secure people's attention
- Political sensitivity.

Written communicator
- Able to keep written communications brief and to the point
- Able to express complexity in a form that makes it accessible to the audience for whom it is intended
- Can write persuasively
- Can write with accuracy and precision
- Political sensitivity.

Listener
Those who are answering questions need to be convinced that someone:

- Is listening to them
- Is interested in what they say
- Understands what they are saying
- Active listening is the skill of demonstrating to the person who is speaking that you are listening
- Empathy and the ability to develop rapport.

Motivator
- Commands respect
- Persuasive and influential
- Able to enthuse people
- Highly developed interpersonal skills
- Able to achieve results through others
- Different people may respond to various techniques of persuasion in different ways, and it is important to know how to approach people so that they will be motivated to take appropriate action.

Decision-maker
- Capable of making decisions in the face of incomplete information
- Able to absorb a lot of information and identify what is significant about it
- Able to keep project aims and objectives in mind and avoid becoming bogged down in detail.

Three questions face the PM at the outset of a project:

1. What needs to be done?
2. When must it be done?
3. How are the resources needed by the project to be obtained?

Using IT
Computer software for project management
A wide variety of software packages is available to help with the scheduling and controlling of projects. Examples of the kind of software which an organization uses are:

o ABC Flowchart
o Harvard Project Manager III
o On-Target
o Microsoft Project
o Suretrak
o Project Scheduler V5
o Super Project V2
o Time Line
o InstaPlan.

Managing large team projects
When managing a project it may be necessary to bring together partner firms, suppliers, subcontractors and team members who do not sit in the same building, or even in the same state or country. This presents challenges of monitoring, managing and integrating:

o Information flow (up, down and across the team)
o Scheduling, change control and logistics
o Work planning and staffing requirements.

All project team members need to be able to contribute their part of the project at the right time and place. This synergy of time, information and action depends on communication, collaboration and reporting. All of this is influenced by software capabilities.

Using a workgroup messaging system
The success of a project often depends on quick and effective communication between team members. Members of a team can be linked through a workgroup messaging system; for example, Microsoft Project allows for almost instant exchange of project information. A workgroup messaging system is a network that is used to send and receive information about task status and assignments. Each team member should have access to this network, and be able to receive and send workgroup messages.

PRINCE
PRINCE (Projects in Controlled Environments) is a project management method covering the organization, management and control of projects. Since its introduction, PRINCE has become widely used in both the public and private sectors. Although PRINCE was originally developed for the needs of IT projects, the method has also been used on many non-IT projects. PRINCE2 is designed as a generic approach for the management of all types of projects. Each process is defined with its key inputs and outputs together with the specific objectives to be achieved.

Project evaluation

The main reasons for project evaluation and feedback are:

○ To ensure that the project remains on track
○ To confirm whether the project meets user needs
○ To determine whether the project delivers value for money
○ To transfer the knowledge and any lessons from one project to other projects.

One reason for carrying out evaluation as an ongoing process during the project, rather than as a single post project evaluation at the end of the project, is to ensure that important information and lessons are not forgotten.

Post Project Review

A Post Project Review is performed by a project team at the end of the project's life cycle to gather information on what worked well and what did not, so that future projects can benefit from that learning. Participants in the Post Project Review process are members of the project team, key stakeholders and users of the project deliverables or results. Lessons learned from the Post Project Review should be archived so that it is easy for project team members, process improvement teams and managers to find useful information. This is a formal review of a programme or project. It helps to answer the question of whether what was planned for has been achieved and if not, what should be done? It is undertaken when there has been time to demonstrate the business benefits.

Outputs and outcomes

There is a difference between outputs and outcomes. It is often possible to identify outputs during and not long after a project has been completed. With outcomes it takes longer to assess the impact of a project because objectives are often long term as well as short term. Implementation of outcomes-based monitoring can be difficult because while an organization may be able to control inputs (which resources are allocated in what amounts at what times to what activities) and to some degree outputs (in terms of products that are controlled by the organization), it cannot control the outcomes (impact) of a project. Traditionally, success is measured by input-output analyses. Thus, for example, an anti-smoking campaign may be measured to see how many column inches of press coverage and other media coverage is generated (an output) but does it stop people smoking and lead to healthier people (an outcome)?

Post Implementation Review (PIR)

The scope of the PIR will be dictated largely by the business case that will have identified the areas of business change and where benefits were to have been realized. A PIR will usually include an assessment of:

○ The achievement (to date) of objectives
○ Costs and benefits to date against forecast, and other benefits realized and expected
○ Alignment with the overall business strategy
○ Ways of maximizing benefits and minimizing cost and risk
○ Business and user satisfaction.

Common problems

There are a number of common problems that may be encountered in carrying out PIRs. These include:

o When more than one organization is involved there may not be a common standard for measuring and recording the benefits and costs.
o A lack of documentation about aims and objectives.
o A lack of baseline measures. Measures of success can only be made accurately by comparing the level of performance before the project implementation against that at the time of the PIR.
o Management of expectations. The review process may lead to raised expectations of changes that may cost more to implement than the value of the benefits they would deliver.
o An organization may be too busy to undertake a systematic PIR and lessons may not be learnt or passed on when another project is implemented.

Some key success factors

o Focus on achieving continuous improvement through direction setting, evaluating achievements and identifying improvement actions.
o Performance management and measurement is an integral part of the business life cycle, helping the organization to evolve and change.
o Openness to constructive criticism and advice.
o Management commitment and readiness to learn lessons by adopting recommendations.

The Post Implementation Review/Post Project Review

The purpose of the Post Project Review is to find out whether the expected benefits of the project have been realized and if lessons learned from the project will lead to recommendations for improvements.

Fitness for purpose checklist:

Are all benefits mentioned in the Project Brief and is the Business Case covered?

Does it describe each achievement in a tangible, measurable form?

Are there recommendations in any case where a benefit is not being fully met, a problem has been identified, or a potential extra benefit could be obtained?

Has this been conducted as soon as the benefits and problems were measured?

Was this scheduled in the project/programme plan?

Project review checklist

When the project was complete, did the project outcomes meet user requirements without additional work?

How close to scheduled completion was the project actually completed?

What factors enabled the team to stay on schedule?

What factors caused delays?

Overall, what did you learn about scheduling on this project that will help you on the next project?

Budget

How close to the budget was the final project cost?

What did you learn about budgeting that will help you on the next project?

Team issues

What did you learn about staffing that will help you on the next project?

What worked or didn't work about team communications?

What was effective or ineffective about how information was distributed? Did you have the right skill mix?

Managing relationships

What lessons did you learn about managing the working relationship with your client?

What lessons did you learn about managing working relationships with other departments or divisions?

What techniques or systems did you develop for this project that could be used on other projects?

List any recommendations you have for future development.

If you could do the project again, what would you do differently?

Summary

In recent years, project teams and a project management approach have become common in many organizations. The basic approach to project management should be the same regardless of the type of project or sector in which the project is carried out. Project management is associated with a precise set of techniques, definitions and practices that can be used. These are all useful and demonstrate how a systematic approach can be used. However, skills in managing people are equally important. Many people are involved in managing projects as only part of their job and have to carry it out alongside other activities. A project should possess identifiable goals, and a definite starting and finishing point. Project goals should be defined clearly. Managing stakeholders' expectations is a major part of a project manager's role. The major constraints on the completion of projects are time, resource availability and the need to achieve the required standard of performance for the project.

Further study

Read, Elbeik and Thomas (1998) *Project Skills*, Chapters 2–4.

Hints and tips

It is useful to have an overview of the principles and techniques of project management. There are no surprises in the techniques that are used and they can be applied to a wide variety of situations where a systematic approach is needed.

Good answers integrate some project management theory and context specific development.

There is not the time for very detailed development of Gantt charts or budgets in the examination. An appreciation of their role is necessary.

Too much detailed development eats into time that could be spent better on other issues of project management.

Bibliography

Elbeik, S. and Thomas, M. (1998) *Project Skills*, Oxford: Butterworth-Heinemann.

Meredith, J. and Mantel, S. (1995) *Project Management – A Managerial Approach*, New York: Wiley.

Paris, Claudine, E. (2000) <http://www.4pm.com/>.

Past examination papers for the Marketing Management in Practice module can be found in Appendix 5.

unit 6
knowledge management and market research

○ Explain the concept of information and knowledge management highlighting the role of marketing and employees within the organization (3.1).

○ Design a research project aimed at providing information as part of a marketing audit or for marketing and business decisions (3.2).

○ Manage a marketing research project by gathering relevant information on time and within the agreed budget (3.3).

○ Make arrangements to record, store and, if appropriate, update information in the market information system (MkIS) – a database created for a purpose or another system (3.4).

○ Analyse and interpret information and present, as a written report or an oral presentation, appropriate conclusions or recommendations that inform the marketing and business decisions for which the research was undertaken (3.5).

○ Give examples of the application of information and knowledge management (3.6).

○ Design a research project aimed at providing information as part of a marketing audit or for marketing and business decisions.

○ Review and evaluate the effectiveness of the activities and the role of the individual and team in this process (3.6).

Key skills

Communication

○ Develop a research brief

○ Develop a research proposal or plan

- o Present research results to decision-makers

- o Present and justify a marketing or communications plan

- o Produce effective marketing communications

- o Assess the impact of a campaign.

Study Guide

In order for organizations to make informed decisions about the future, information is needed about a wide range of issues. This unit looks at information and knowledge management, and market research. Marketing research provides a useful link between the supplier and the customer by keeping up to date with customer needs and wants. The unit also looks at the range of issues that needs to be taken into account when conducting a market research project, and in using the results of such projects.

Glossary

Agency – An agency can be any individual, organization, department or division (which includes those belonging to the same organization as the client) responsible for or acting on all or part of a market research project.

Data mining – The practice of automatically searching large stores of data for patterns. To do this, data mining uses computational techniques from statistics and pattern recognition.

Distribution – This is one of the four aspects of marketing. A distribution business is the middleman between the manufacturer and retailer. After a product is manufactured by a supplier/factory, it is typically stored in a distribution company's warehouse. The product is then sold to retailers or customers.

Knowledge management – Refers to the technology, techniques, or social practices for organizing and collecting 'knowledge' so that it is applied at an appropriate time or place. It includes the technology of databases and software applications collecting information.

Marketing research – It is a form of applied sociology which concentrates on understanding the behaviours and preferences, of consumers in a market-based economy.

Market research – Broader in scope and examines all aspects of a business environment. It asks questions about competitors, market structure, government regulations, economic trends, technological advances, and numerous other factors that make up the business environment.

Knowledge management

Knowledge management develops an organization's capacity to acquire, share and utilize knowledge in ways that improves its survival and success. Intellectual capital is knowledge that resides in an organization and can be an organization's main source of competitive advantage. Knowledge use occurs when employees realize that the knowledge is available and that they have discretion to be able to apply it. In recent years, the concept of knowledge management has become widespread in the business and management literature. Given marketing's focus on the effective gathering, analysis and use of information to yield insights into the behaviour of consumers in different markets, it is an important area.

Although there is agreement that it is a 'good thing', implementing a system for managing knowledge is by no means a straightforward proposition.

Knowledge management is concerned principally with how people are managed to collaborate and share their knowledge. Managing knowledge is concerned with developing a culture where people within the organization are willing to share knowledge so that the organization can be successful. This may involve changing the culture of the organization and putting processes in place to enable knowledge creation and transfer.

Knowledge management is the process through which organizations generate value from their intellectual and knowledge-based assets. This involves sharing them among employees, departments and sometimes with other companies. Knowledge-based assets can be explicit or tacit. Explicit assets usually refer to items that can be documented and archived such as patents, trademarks, business plans, marketing research and customer lists. Tacit knowledge refers to the know-how contained in people's heads. The challenge consists of being able to recognize, generate, share and manage it. ICT tools such as databases, access tools, e-learning applications, e-mail, groupware, instant messaging and related technologies, synchronous interaction tools, and search and data mining tools can all help to facilitate the dissemination of tacit knowledge but identifying it in the first place is a major challenge for most organizations.

Differences between data, information and knowledge

Data is unorganized words, numbers and images. It has no meaning and context. Information is data that has been organized or categorized and has meaning or value added to data. Knowledge refers to the use of information. Therefore, organizations can gather/capture information about their customers and competitors but they can only become knowledge driven only if they have the systems in place to use the information. Whether the organization becomes a knowledge-driven organization depends on leadership, culture and trust. Organizations such as management consultancies and R&D centres rely almost completely on their employees' skills and know-how for their success. Knowledge-intensive firms need employees who are able to spread knowledge across organizational boundaries.

However, the following case study provides an indication of some of the barriers to sharing knowledge across organizations.

Why ideas don't travel well?

There are a number of reasons why good ideas that emerge in one part of an organization don't get picked up elsewhere. These include:

- *'What's in it for me?'* – To get people to transfer or take on a good idea there must be something in it for them, which could be recognition, thanks, career progression or learning.
- *The 'not invented here' syndrome* – Why should I learn from people I don't know much about? How do I know that what worked there will work here?
- *Lack of leadership* – Many leaders do not spend any time promoting idea-sharing or rewarding those who contribute to it.
- *Lack of time* – This is often a way of saying 'not enough of a priority'.
- *Failure to apply learning design expertise* – Good ideas or business practices are turned into long documents that capture facts but are not designed to help people learn.
- *Lack of context sensitivity* – Many organizations believe that what works well in one part of the organization (often the biggest part, such as the home country) can be applied without any modification in very different business environments.
- *Underinvestment in facilitating knowledge transfer* – Leaders may say that 'sharing best practice' is a business priority but fail to give anyone the accountability or resources to make it happen.

All companies contain knowledge that they need to exploit and new technology makes it easier to share it. For example, conference calls mean that several people in different places can talk together and videoconferencing means they can see each other while they talk. Electronic databases make it possible to store vast amounts of knowledge, to which others can be given access. E-mail means people can communicate quickly, cheaply and over long distances. Company intranets mean staff can be given access to more information more quickly, and extranets enable organizations in the marketing channels to communicate more effectively.

Data mining can help businesses to handle and interpret large volumes of data so as to develop marketing, customer relationship and communication strategies. Advanced software can be used to analyse data in a fraction of the time needed for human analysis. One of the challenges for companies that are serious about knowledge management is how to address the people and cultural issues. In an environment where an individual's knowledge is valued and rewarded, establishing a culture that promotes sharing can be difficult. It can seem as if people are being asked to give up something that enhances their value as individuals. Companies that manage knowledge most effectively tend to have three main characteristics:

1. Knowledge management programmes that are an intrinsic part of their overall business strategy.
2. Human resources and information technology policies that support the sharing of information.
3. A corporate culture that encourages staff to share what they know.

Case study

Nokia dominates the world mobile phone industry with a market share of around 35 per cent. One of the keys to its success is its focus on knowledge management, on making sure that all parts of the organization communicate continuously with each other and with their suppliers. A large part of Nokia's success is ensuring that different groups constantly share their knowledge. A user-interface team is an eclectic group, made up of engineers, graphic designers, psychologists, sociologists and even a theatre director, who look at how people use mobile phones. While the design team thinks about what the phone should look like and the manufacturing group considers how it could be made, the user-interface team worries about how the customer will interact with it. While technology, such as e-mail, is important, it is not the foundation of the company's knowledge management. What is crucial is the constant attempt to break down barriers – between designers and engineers, or between factories and suppliers – and this is a task that never ends. What is important is seeking out the knowledge contained within the company and making it available to others in the organization so that they could use it. Many companies run up against a problem: their staff do not want to share what they know. They want to keep it for themselves. This is the most substantial obstacle to knowledge management.

'Dos' and 'don'ts' for effective knowledge management

1. The idea is to improve something or create new value so start with the business itself, the role of knowledge in it and work from there. Focus knowledge building on tools that justify the investment:

   (a) *In-house Yellow Pages* – This system connects inquirers to experts and experience you can use, reduces errors and guesswork, and prevents the reinvention of countless wheels.

   (b) *Lessons learned* – Insist that no project is complete until time has been spent providing insights into what went right and wrong and guidelines for others undertaking similar projects. Allow access via the company intranet.

   (c) *Competitor intelligence* – Organize a database of customers, competitors and suppliers so that they are searchable and widely accessible and in a consistent format.

   (d) Use technology to its fullest, but don't use it in place of human contact. In particular, don't rely on databases, encyclopaedias and libraries if there aren't 'librarians' who can help with navigation through the sea of information.

2. Share with people how the company makes money. Many people are not aware of how this is achieved.
3. Deal fully with the obstacles to sharing knowledge inside the organization.
4. Speed up knowledge flows. Encourage interactions via e-mail, in-house training programmes, cross-functional projects, and sharing best practices across departments and business units.
5. Don't manage knowledge for the sake of managing knowledge.
6. Leverage the knowledge you have. The most important function of knowledge management systems should be connection of people to people, of questions to answers.
7. Technology is an enabler but don't think about knowledge management or knowledge management technology until it is clear what needs to be enabled.

Information

In his book *Marketing Research*, Alan Wilson (2003) identifies three main areas where information is needed by marketers if decisions are to be effective – information about customers, other organizations and the marketing environment.

Customers

Who are customers? – what are their characteristics? – what are the main influences on what, where, when and how they buy or use a product or service.

Other organizations

Comparison of performance relative to other organizations is used in the private and the public sector to improve competitiveness or, generally, to improve the quality of services. Benchmarking is an example of this. It involves learning, sharing information and adopting best practices to bring about step changes in performance.

Marketing environment

The environment consists of many influences that are beyond the power of organizations to shape and control but have an impact on the organization. This includes factors such as social changes in the size and composition of households, age structure, legal framework, government policies and guidelines, economy and technology. The power of alliances such as the European Union, NAFTA, and ASEAN means that individual countries are less able to influence the trading environment in any significant way.

Market Information System (MkIS)

Information underpins successful marketing and can be of strategic importance as well as contributing to tactical and operational decision-making. Kotler defines an MkIS as:

> ... *consisting of people, equipment and procedures to gather, sort, analyse, evaluate and distribute needed, timely and accurate information to marketing decision makers.*

A typical MkIS comprises:

The Marketing Research System – The system used for gathering information about specific issues that are of interest to a marketer such as testing products and evaluating the success of communications strategies.

Marketing Intelligence System – For example, published data, including government statistics, research reports, the national and trade press. A Market Intelligence System (MkIS) gathers and processes critical business information, transforming it into intelligence to support marketing decisions.

Decision support system – The tools needed to make sense of data, statistical packages, the intranet and other tools that help marketers make decisions.

Internal records – Sales records, account records, and other information that is available in the company.

Source: Housden 2003.

An MkIS can contain many different sources and types of information and, for example, it has a role in support of information gathering, evaluation, processing, dissemination, analysis and control. A good MkIS should encourage people throughout the organization to focus externally and provide quick, efficient and cost-effective information that is easily accessible. It can serve a number of purposes – it can help sales and service personnel in the field who want pricing information; marketers and planners who want to know about market and product trends so as to be able to develop marketing plans and adjust the marketing mix; and directors and senior managers who are interested in market developments that affect investment and other strategic decisions. Knowing what kind of information to obtain and how to make effective use of it are key skills of strategic marketing.

Marketing research is an important element of the MkIS and is concerned with the provision of information about markets and customers and how they may or do react to different marketing strategies. Marketing intelligence is concerned with information available from the marketing environment and may be less focused on immediate decision-making. Marketing productivity analysis uses internal information to quantify marketing inputs and outputs, for example measuring the response to a promotional campaign. Marketing modelling may involve, for example, the synthesis of profile and transaction information to develop profiles of individual customers. The MkIS is concerned with many areas of data collection.

Activity 6.1

How would you respond to these questions if they were asked about your organization?

Some questions for establishing the scope of an MkIS

What types of decisions need to be made regularly?

What types of information are needed to make these decisions?

Is this information available in a timely fashion?

What types of information are needed but aren't available at the moment?

What information is needed on a daily basis? weekly? monthly? yearly?

What reports are needed on a regular basis?

What types of data analysis programmes need to be made available?

What are the four most helpful improvements that could be made in the present marketing information system?

The critical function is how the organization uses information not the information system used to develop the information or the technology supporting it. Short-term advantage can accrue from IT but the results are not sustainable. Since the early 1980s, competitive advantage's focus has moved towards systems and away from technology. Systems that enable a business to create value for its customers include customer relationship management, supply chain management and knowledge management.

MkIS and CRM trends

The development of technology is bringing closer the time when a company's information systems will lead to the generation of integrated profiles of individual customers. However, there are considerable difficulties in realizing the potential of technology. Whilst it is an important tool for marketers, human factors will always have a big influence on how effectively technology is utilized. The following trends are mostly enabled by increased technological capacity but still need an appropriate organizational structure and culture in order for any benefits to be realized.

1. *Highly successful companies will invest more in customers, not less* – Successful companies will focus on using customer information and applying technology and strategies to keep high-value customers, convert moderate-to-low-value customers to higher value, and minimize investments in customers that detract value.
2. *Companies will compete for customer share, not market share* – Companies will need to focus on how they are going to increase or maximize the individual share of each customer's spending by managing and increasing the value delivered to each customer.
3. *CRM will evolve to CVM* – Customer value management (CVM) will become the standard approach to maximizing the return on customer investments. The measurement of customer value will evolve from revenue-based metrics to individual customer profitability.
4. *Companies will heighten their focus on data analysis and organization to avoid information roadblocks* – Companies will place a much greater emphasis on the analysis and organization of data so they can better differentiate their customers, establish clear customer value (profitability based) segments, and create richer and more measurable marketing campaigns.
5. *Companies will realize customer satisfaction doesn't translate to loyalty* – Companies will no longer be able to assume that a satisfied customer will remain a loyal customer. That's because people often make purchasing decisions based on shifting and migratory preferences with satisfaction being just one factor among many.
6. *Companies will focus on thoughtware, not software* – There's a reason why 55–75 per cent of current CRM projects don't meet their objectives. It's because companies often confuse CRM strategy with technology implementation, when in fact, CRM is a broader business strategy that technologies can enable.
7. *Companies will stitch their customer channels together* – The trend will be to create seamless interplay among all customer channels (customer service, field service, Web, marketing, sales, etc.) in order to create a consistent experience for customers regardless of how they choose to interact with an organization. As these channels are integrated, the marketer will have one comprehensive view of the customer.
8. *Companies will embrace PRM as a means to maximize value to end-customers* – Organizations finally integrate their customer channels and focus on partner relationship management (PRM), a strategy to better serve end-customers by leveraging a company's business partner network.

9. *Companies will create CRM platforms* – We will start to see the integration and convergence of the Internet platforms with CRM platforms.
10. *Companies will shift to a long-term focus* – Organizations will think about long-term application viability, and focus on IT strategy to enable integrated CRM solutions.

Source: Adapted from Braun Consulting (www.braunconsult.com).

Relationship marketing (RM) and customer relationship management (CRM)

This is an area of marketing that has been influenced considerably by the availability of IT solutions, particularly large interactive databases to enable companies to gather and maintain large amounts of data about individual customers and to enable more individualized marketing. Customer databases and database marketing are the key to effective CRM.

Database uses include:

o Identifying the best prospects
o Matching offers to customers
o Strengthening customer loyalty
o Re-activating customer purchasing.

Relationship marketing sees the concept of ongoing customer loyalty at the core of its customer relationship marketing strategy. The key aims are to ensure existing customers to continue purchase from them on a lifelong basis, that is achieving lifetime value to both the customer and the organization, rather than just one-off transactions. Sometimes, organizations concentrate solely on their customers, but there are other important relationships that should be considered. Typically, these groups are known as the stakeholder audience and include the following:

o *Internal markets* – If employees are treated as customers it should be possible to improve levels of customer service and quality throughout the organization.
o *Influence markets* – These are any bodies or groups that influence or have the potential to influence the organization's operations. This includes government and regulatory bodies.
o *Employee markets* – The recruitment, retention and succession of skilled staff are important to the continuing success of the organization and companies need HR strategies to address this.
o *Supplier markets* – In recent years, there has been a lot more emphasis on partnerships and alliances, and the synergy that is created from different forms of co-operative relationship.
o *Referral markets* – This is where organizations refer potential customers to third parties, for example, banks may refer mortgage customers to insurance companies and vice versa.

In order to implement successfully the ethos and culture of relationship marketing, the organization needs to look at internal markets – that is the employees and management of the organization. This aspect is considered in more detail in Unit 3.

Knowledge management – At the heart of a CRM implementation is the acquisition of information about a customer, its analysis, sharing and tracking. Employees need to know what actions they need to take as a result of this knowledge.

Database consolidation – The consolidation of customer information in a single database and the re-engineering of business processes around the customer. All interactions with a customer need to be recorded in one place to drive production, marketing, sales and customer support activities.

Integration of channels and systems – Customers should be able to interact with a company through the former's channel of choice. The aim is to integrate all communication channels with the customer database. It also means the integration of CRM with other parts of a company's business systems and applications.

Technology and infrastructure – Tools exist to automate and streamline online customer service but there is a need to ensure that the technology infrastructure is able to cope with increased volumes.

Change management – Customer relationship management involves a change in philosophy and attitudes. A process for managing this change is needed to help a company move from a product centric focus to a more customer centric one.

 Activity 6.2

Visit CRM Update at http://techupdate.cnet.com/enterprise/0-6133427-724-20156564.html and answer the following questions:

1. The site contains information about CRM. How could a CRM manager benefit from the site?
2. Read one of the related articles on CRM found on the site and describe how a company can benefit from the information you found.

Customer relationship management is a subset of RM and focused on the management of customer relations only. Relationship marketing is a broader type of marketing, encompassing relationships with customers, suppliers and intermediaries as well as strategies for the overall picture. Internal marketing can also be regarded as a sub-type of RM, focusing on the relationships within the company. A database is a tool in RM and might be able to provide information about trends that will help an organization to individualize its offer. Customization involves creating products and service offers specific for a particular individual or target group rather than analysing buying patterns to produce a 'best-fit' option. Thus, a prerequisite of customization is a detailed understanding of clients' needs and wants and this poses a considerable challenge for a marketing information system.

Benchmarking

Another complementary approach to an audit would be to use a benchmarking approach that compares one organization with another that is regarded as being very successful. Obviously, in some organizations, this can be difficult because of commercial sensitivities and the need to retain competitive advantage. However, a table could be constructed that could compare the organization along the dimensions that are felt to be important for marketing. The precise details will vary for each organization but, for example, it might look something like Table 6.1.

Table 6.1 Comparing the organization with high and low performing organizations

Poor	Good	Excellent
Product driven	Market driven	Market driving
Mass-market oriented	Segment-oriented	Niche-oriented and customer-oriented
Product offer	Augmented product offer	Legendary

The EFQM Excellence Model

Another way of contributing to an audit is to use a recognized quality model. Usually, these kind of models are very comprehensive and too detailed for a marketing audit because they cover the whole of an organization's activities. One of the most widely used models in the private and public sectors is the EFQM Excellence Model. It was introduced at the beginning of 1992 as the framework for assessing applications for the European Quality Award. It is a non-prescriptive framework that recognizes many approaches to achieving sustainable excellence. Increasingly, organizations use the outputs from self-assessment as part of their business planning process and as a basis for reviewing the organization.

Within this non-prescriptive approach, there are some Fundamental Concepts which underpin the model. It is a non-prescriptive framework based on nine criteria. Five of these are 'Enablers' and four are 'Results'. The 'Enabler' criteria cover what an organization does. The 'Results' criteria cover what an organization achieves. 'Results' are caused by 'Enablers', and feedback from 'Results' helps to improve 'Enablers'. The model is based on the premise that:

'Excellent results with respect to Performance, Customers, People and Society are achieved through the enablers of Leadership driving Policy and Strategy, which is delivered through People Partnerships, Resources, and Processes' (Figure 6.1).

Figure 6.1
Source: http://www.efqm.org.

Results orientation – Achieving results that delight all the organization's stakeholders.

Customer focus – Creating sustainable customer value.

Leadership and constancy of purpose – Visionary and inspirational leadership, coupled with constancy of purpose.

Management by processes and facts – Managing the organization through a set of interdependent and interrelated systems, processes and facts.

People development and involvement – Maximizing the contribution of employees through their development and involvement.

Continuous learning, innovation and improvement – Challenging the status quo and effecting change by using learning to create innovation and improvement opportunities.

Partnership development – Developing and maintaining value-adding partnerships.

Corporate social responsibility – Exceeding the minimum regulatory framework in which the organization operates and strives to understand and respond to the expectations of their stakeholders in society.

An example – Partnerships and Resources Element of the EFQM Model
How is information and knowledge managed in the organization?

Areas to address
This could include:

- ○ How information and knowledge is collected, structured and managed in support of policy and strategy?
- ○ How unique intellectual property is cultivated, developed and protected in order to maximize value?
- ○ How appropriate access to relevant information and knowledge for both internal and external users is provided?
- ○ How the organization seeks to acquire and use information and knowledge effectively?
- ○ How the organization assures and improves the validity, integrity and security of its information?
- ○ How the organization generates innovative and creative thinking within the organization through the use of relevant information and knowledge resources?

RADAR

The method of assessment is based on the RADAR model, which looks at the evidence of what the organization achieves. This is based on documenting what it sets out to do, what evidence there is that its aims and objectives are actually translated into practice; whether it assesses the appropriateness of its approach and how successful its reviews have been. In this way, the self-assessment goes beyond what an organization claims it is doing to look for evidence that it is actually being implemented in practice.

Results – What an organization achieves.

Approach – What is it we are trying to do in order to address the issue?

Deployment – How widely is the approach used across the organization?

Assessment – Do we ever think about how appropriate the approach is?

Review – Can we/do we measure success of the approach?

An example of the kind of format in which information could be collected is given in Table 6.2.

Table 6.2 Recording the outcomes of the process

Review your descriptions of the approaches as a whole, then record your views on where things have been successful, where improvements could be made and actions to be taken based on this analysis
Strengths (+) Areas for improvement (−)

Activity 6.3

Use the Areas to address (above) to find out how your organization acquires and uses information. What are the strengths and weaknesses of its approach and how could it be improved?

Market research is a cost-effective way of finding out what people believe, want, need or do. It is information that cannot usually be obtained from any other source. Until recently, limited budgets kept most types of market research out of reach of small organizations, but through the Internet there are more research options. The most important role of market research is to minimize risk by researching a product or service before it reaches the market. Thus, market research is a fundamental part of the marketing planning process.

This is dealt with in more detail in the CIM Advanced Certificate book, Marketing Research and Information 2005–2006, Butterworth-Heinemann. A market research project should include some form of a marketing audit, that is an appraisal of an organization's marketing activities. This involves a systematic assessment of marketing plans, objectives, strategies, programmes, activities, organizational structure and personnel. There are a number of models that can be used for a marketing audit, for example a SWOT or a PESTLE analysis can each yield useful data that can inform an audit. The marketing audit and the models that contribute to it are discussed in Unit 8.

In conducting an audit the following are examples of the kinds of questions that could be asked.

Objectives
- Are the marketing objectives of your department consistent with the overall company objectives? Should these objectives be altered to fit changing environmental variables?
- Are objectives consistent with one another?
- How do objectives relate to marketing strengths and market opportunities?

Strategy
- What is the relationship between objectives and strategies?
- Are resources sufficient to implement the strategies?
- What are the company's weaknesses?
- How do you compare your strategies with those of competitors?

Product decisions

o How are new products developed within your business unit?
o How are existing products evaluated?
o How are products phased out of the line?

Pricing decisions

o How are pricing decisions made?
o How do pricing decisions reflect the influences of competitors and the concerns of channel members?

Distribution decisions

o How are channel members selected, evaluated and dropped, if necessary?
o How are channel members motivated?
o How are decisions to modify channel structures reached?

Promotion decisions

o How are promotion mix decisions made?
o How are sales people selected, monitored and evaluated?
o How are pay-offs associated with promotional efforts estimated?

Market information

o How is marketing research information transmitted to, and used within, the business unit?
o Is a global information system in place?

Activities and tasks

o How are tasks scheduled, described and planned? How are the responsibilities of individuals determined?
o What spans of supervision, reporting relationships and communication patterns exist? How are they evaluated?

Personnel

o What level of competence has been attained by personnel in each position?
o Are remedies to problems, if necessary, being planned? What are they?
o What is the state of morale? motivation? What are the present plans in these areas?
o Describe career development paths. Have potential replacements for personnel in key positions been identified?

The term 'marketing research' covers market research, marketing research, product research and research to support pricing, distribution and promotional activity. Market research is used to supply information about the market for particular products and services. Therefore, market research has a narrower focus compared to marketing research.

Characteristics of good market research

Scientific method – The principles are careful observation, formulation of hypotheses, prediction and testing.

Research creativity – Research should develop innovative ways to solve a problem.

Multiple methods – The research should use more than one method to increase confidence in the results.

Interdependence of models and data – A recognition that data is interpreted from underlying models that guide the type of information sought.

Value and cost of information – A concern for estimating the value of the research against its cost. Costs are easy to determine but the value of the research is harder to ascertain.

Ethical marketing – Marketing research should be conducted according to a recognized code of practice that respects informants.

The most important distinguishing characteristics of marketing research are that:

- o Its primary objective is to apply research methods to the collection of information that will help in describing and understanding markets, planning strategies and monitoring outcomes.
- o In most cases, it achieves this by studying relatively small, and usually representative, samples of the relevant populations.
- o It is primarily, but not exclusively, concerned with analysing and reporting on aggregated groupings of those interviewed; it does not report information which can be linked to identifiable individuals.
- o It guarantees the confidentiality of the information provided by respondents. Such information can be disclosed only with the respondent's consent, and then only for research purposes and to research organizations involved in the project.

Market research is concerned with a one-way channel of communication, from respondents to the client via the confidential filter of the researcher. It does not provide a facility for any form of commercial or similar communication in the opposite direction, from client to individual respondent, nor does it seek to influence the respondent's views or behaviour as a result of the research. It only tells us about today and customers are not necessarily a good guide to the future. Many people see the future as more of the same: faster and smaller computers, better cars and more TV channels. They can't easily envision how things might be different. For example, in the mid-1990s when British Airways asked business fliers what they wanted very few respondents mentioned data sockets on satellite phones or power supplies in arm rests so they could use PCs without needing spare batteries. It proved to be much more expensive to reengineer existing planes than it would have been to design these features into the building of planes in the first place.

The characteristics of direct marketing are different from those of market research

- o The primary objective of direct marketing is to conduct promotional and selling activities directed at specific individuals and organizations. Marketing analysis provides aggregated and cross-analysed information of various kinds – but this is normally a secondary rather than the primary objective of collecting the data, and does not affect the other characteristics of direct marketing referred to here.
- o It normally involves the collection and use of personal data from very large numbers of the general population or from as many as possible of a specific group (e.g. customers). The emphasis is on maximizing the total number of the target audience covered rather than on the representativeness of the final data.
- o The data collected is purposely stored and made use of on an individually identified, disaggregated basis since it would not otherwise be fully exploitable in direct marketing.
- o Since the personal data collected is permanently linked to the individuals who have supplied the data, there can normally be no guarantee of anonymity. In many cases, the

personal data will be made available to a variety of users, most often for non-research purposes such as promotion and direct selling.

o Unlike marketing research, direct marketing is usually a two-way process whereby the individual who provides the data receives promotional and/or sales approaches based on the use of that data. Direct marketing is a form of 'commercial communication'.

Stages in the market research process

Stage 1 – Defining the marketing problem to be addressed and research objectives

This includes specifying the objectives of the specific research project or projects, to formulate the problem precisely. The art is to strike a balance between too broad and too narrow a definition of a problem. Too broad a definition can lead to a lot of information that is superfluous, whilst too narrow a definition means that some necessary information about issues that impact on the subject is not collected. It depends on how much is known about the problem. If relatively little is known, exploratory research may be used, for example qualitative research as well as secondary research. Some research is causal – its purpose is to test a cause and effect relationship. A marketing problem needs to be formulated as a marketing research problem. So, for example, a marketing problem might be that sales are too low but the marketing research problem could be to assess customer perception of the price of the product in terms of its perceived value relative to the competition.

Sometimes, a researcher will be designing a research programme according to a research brief. However, the brief may not exist in a definitive form, and the researcher may need to work with the client to refine it and make sure that it can be operationalized.

Research briefs

When drafting a research brief for an agency to respond, as much detail as possible should be given. This helps to refine and clarify thinking about the project, including the target audience, the kinds of questions and issues that ought to be addressed, and why. Specify the deliverables expected. Below is a checklist of questions which could be used by the researcher to draw out the background to design a research programme.

Checklist to guide a researcher when taking a brief.

History

o How long has the company been established?
o How long has it concentrated on its present product/service range?
o Has the company always been sited in its present location?
o What factors have influenced its location?

Company background

o What is the principal business of the company? What are its subsidiary activities?
o What is its total turnover?
o Describe any holding companies/subsidiary companies.
o How many employees are there at the establishment?

Product details
- What are the important products (or services) in the range (by size, capacity, shape, material, etc.)?
- What proportion of the total turnover does each of the above groups account for?
- To what extent are the products standard/custom built?
- What proportion of an assembled product is made in-house or bought out?
- How important are spares in terms of revenue versus profit?
- Are any of the products built under licence?

Pricing
- What are the prices for each of the important products or services?
- How do prices compare with those of the competitors?
- Is there a published price list?
- What is the discount policy?
- What power does the sales representative have to alter prices?
- How price-sensitive is the product?

Sales force
- Number of representatives.
- Are they a general or a specialized sales force – in what way are they specialized?
- How many calls a day do they make?
- Does the sales force bring back orders or, are they sent in independently?

Markets
- What are the major user markets for the products?
- What proportion of total sales is there to each of these markets?
- Are any markets known for the product, where the company currently does not/cannot sell?
- Which markets are believed to offer the greatest scope for expansion of sales?

Decision-makers
- Who are the key decision-makers who specify and buy this type of product? What roles do they play?
- What do decision-makers look for from suppliers? PROBE price, quality, delivery, sales service?

Competition
- Who are the most important competitors? Where are they based?
- What is their rank order/market share?
- What are the perceived strengths and weaknesses of each company (including the client's)?
- To what extent do competitors rely upon this market for their turnover and profit?

Quality
- Where does the product fit against the competition in its quality?
- What are the special features of its quality?
- Where is it weak on quality?
- How long will the product last?
- When it finally fails, why will it do so?

Deliveries
- What is the current delivery period?
- What is the competition's delivery?
- What is the ideal delivery?

Distribution
- How is the product distributed?
- What proportion goes direct/indirect? What is the policy which leads to this split (e.g. size of account – OEM versus replacement, etc.)?
- What are distributors' margins?
- What other products do distributors sell?
- Do distributors actively sell, or just take orders?
- Who are the major distributors

  - used by the company?
  - not used by the company?

- What is the average size of a direct account and a distributor account?

Promotion
- How big is the promotional budget?
- How does this break down between: (a) media (b) exhibitions (c) PR (d) print (e) direct mail (f) websites?
- Which media are used? Which are most successful?
- What proportion of sales leads come from promotion? How many? What is their quality?
- Which exhibitions are attended? What is their perceived value?
- What opportunities exist for e-commerce?

Other data
Full details of names (initials as well) of persons present at briefing; date of briefing; address of company; address to which proposals should be sent; how many copies of the proposal are required to be sent.

Preparing a research proposal
Having received the brief, the researcher, whether in-house or from an agency, must submit a written proposal to the sponsor which states an appreciation of the problem, the objectives, the research method and the timing. If an agency is preparing the proposal, a statement of cost must be given. An in-house job may omit this but many managers still like to see an estimate as a benchmark to compare with other surveys and as a perspective that they can use to relate to the size of any decision which may be taken. If the proposal is accepted, it becomes the contract between the researcher and the sponsor.

The following case study is an extract from one of the many produced by the US Department of Commerce. Note what it says about the importance of language even though English is spoken in both countries. When conducting market research that has an international focus, all the cultural factors that were mentioned in previous units need to be taken into account.

Entering the UK market

The British still tend to buy package tours put together and advertised in catalogues and brochures by tour operators. Travel agents use these catalogues and brochures to help clients choose where to go and to decide virtually every detail of their vacation.

Tour operators and travel agents therefore are pivotal in the U.K. travel industry. Consumer marketing should be the last, never the first, step.

It can be a costly error to assume that, because English is a shared language, materials developed for the U.S. market are automatically suitable for use in the U.K.

Many words have subtly or radically different meanings in U.K. and American English, which can lead to confusion or misunderstanding. For example, 'cheap' in American parlance is often used to mean 'inexpensive'. To a Briton, however, 'cheap' means 'shoddy'. 'Homely' to an American means 'ugly'; to a Briton it has the very positive meaning of 'homelike'. 'Mean' to an American means 'unkind', while to a Briton it means 'tight with money'.

Source: STAT-USA on the Internet, US Department of Commerce, http://strategis.ic.gc.ca/.

Stage 2 – Develop the research plan and determine research design

This involves developing an efficient plan for gathering the necessary information. A marketing manager needs to know the cost of the research before agreeing it can go ahead. One of the issues to be considered is what is the need for primary and/or secondary research. If primary research is needed, then what type? Research design specifies the type of research required. Secondary research usually precedes primary research to see whether the problem that needs to be investigated can be addressed without having to spend resources on acquiring primary data.

Exploratory research

The goal of exploratory market research is discovery. The underlying questions are 'What is new?' and 'What are we missing?'. The goal of confirmatory techniques is resolution: 'Is this the right choice?', 'What results can we expect?'. Exploratory market research is used to broaden a vision, whilst confirmatory research is used to narrow options and concentrate efforts (McQuarrie, 1996).

Exploratory and confirmatory market research techniques are used at different stages in a research project's decision cycle (Table 6.3). The decision cycle calls for sequential market research activities and questions as the research design and strategy are developed and implemented. Each activity requires different market research techniques as the researcher's informational needs change from initial exploratory information to final confirmatory information.

The four decision cycle activities in Table 6.3 are further described in relation to each activity's objectives and suggested market research techniques.

Research design

Table 6.3 Four decision cycle activities

Activity/Questions	Objectives	Techniques
Scan the environment How are we doing? What is going on? Supporting: Focus groups, surveys	Identify, describe, monitor	Main: Secondary research, user visits
Generate options What are the possibilities? Supporting: Secondary research	Generate, define, explore	Main: User visits, focus groups
Select an option What is the explanation? Which option is best? Supporting: Secondary research	Evaluate, test, select, prioritize	Main: Experiments, surveys, choice models, usability tests
Evaluate success What will we achieve? How are we doing? Supporting: User visits	Measure, track, assess	Main: Surveys, secondary research

Source: Adapted from McQuarrie (1996, p. 24).

A survey of the literature will usually precede all research designs.

This is to:

- Learn from previous research in the area.
- Prevent expensive primary research being undertaken when research results are available.

Surveys of people with particular experience, or knowledge of the subject under investigation should be undertaken. For example, interviews of commercial directors to find out about trends in football merchandising. Examine the best and the worst examples to see if any conclusions may be made. For instance, a detailed investigation of top and bottom sales people to try to understand the factors that contribute to success or failure.

- Repeated investigations over time; for example, monthly opinion surveys of consumers.
- Single investigation; for example, a single survey of 100 business leaders to find out their attitudes to the training of their employees. Field experiments are carried out in the normal context, such as in a store, while a laboratory experiment is undertaken in an artificial environment.
- A field experiment is where, for example, the store changes the price of products in store and assesses changes in the quantity and value purchased. In this context, the experiment is in a normal environment and the consumer is unaware that it is taking place.

Sampling

Organizations will target specified customer groups for their marketing activity. These customer groups, or segments, will be the basis on which any marketing research is undertaken. They will be the focus of any sampling activity. The potential population in this context could be any target group ranging from large populations, such as the potential purchasers of television sets, to relatively small markets, such as widescreen plasma TV sets. Sampling allows conclusions to be drawn about the wider market, without the need to talk to everyone in the marketplace. Sampling estimates the numbers, attributes and beliefs of a population. The key to a good sample is to define the population of customers that are of interest and to select enough random members of that population. If the attitudes of buyers to a new type of hand-held computer were needed before planning a marketing campaign, the target population will be those who are affluent. This target population could be found, for example, by buying a mailing list from a computer magazine and specifying postcodes in a 30-mile radius of the store with the highest incomes.

However, what you really need to know is who has the highest disposable income with an interest in electronic gadgets. This may not coincide with the most affluent. A young person in a well-paid job, living at home with his parents may have more disposable income than an older person with twice the annual income. Therefore, you might want to cross-refer salary data with other data relating to marital status and age. However, marital status is not much of a guide to anything because many people are unmarried but living with partners. These latter points serve to illustrate the complexity of some of the factors when drawing up a relevant valid and reliable sample. The main decisions to be made when selecting a sample are:

1. The process by which the sample is to be selected is known as the sample design. The quality of all statistical analyses and procedures is governed by the quality of the sample data. If the sample data is not representative of the population, analysing the data and drawing conclusions from it will be unproductive and invalid. A representative sample will require the introduction of randomness in the sampling procedure.
2. From which list to draw a sample? This involves selecting a sample frame (i.e. a list of all members of the population) – unless people are just being interviewed randomly in the street.
3. How large a sample to select?

Sample design

The main approaches to sample design:

○ Non-probability sample design.
○ Probability sample design.

A key issue is the cost of sampling versus the benefits. The main difference between probability and non-probability sampling is that with the former the result of a sample can be projected to the whole population whereas this cannot be done with non-probability samples.

Probability samples

Probability sampling requires the researcher to know the size of the population, and for each individual in the population to have a known and equal chance of being selected (using a sampling frame). The most commonly used sampling frames are telephone numbers and postcodes. There are four major ways to contact those being surveyed:

1. Telephone
2. Personal (e.g. door to door)
3. Mail
4. Internet.

Telephone, mail and e-mail provide the most control over the characteristics of those who are surveyed. The Internet and e-mail are the cheapest, and the respondents may not be representative of your target population.

Random sample – Everyone has the same chance. The advantage of the random sample is that it is the best representation of the population that can be obtained. The disadvantage is the difficulty of obtaining an entire population list. It works better with a small population because it is easier to get hold of that list.

What does it mean to be random?

Stratified random sample – The population is divided into groups/levels of interest, for example socio-economic status. This is a more representative type of sample.

Cluster sampling – This is based on subsets of the population, for example geographic regions.

Non-probability samples

These are samples in which you do not know what is the chance of being selected. The precise size of a population or even who is in the population is not known. Examples of non-probability samples include:

Convenience sample – Samples are selected for interviews based on the ease of finding a sample from the researchers' point of view, that is from their convenience. They are not random and they use readily available subjects, for example students.

Quota sample – Respondents are recruited because they possess particular characteristics – perhaps they may be selected on the basis of age or gender if these are believed to be important influencing factors in purchase decisions. Different individuals with different characteristics are sampled to meet the quota – for example gender: 50 male, 50 female. This type of sample design attempts to reflect key attributes of the general population in the selection of the sample to be researched. It is a common sampling technique used by commercial marketing research companies.

Judgement sampling – In this approach, the researcher believes that the results of the research will be improved if some judgement is exercised in selecting a sample, may be by asking 'experts'.

Stage 3 – Data collection methods

Market research works because, by talking to a relatively small number of people, it is possible to find out about a far larger number, but it only works if the people who are interviewed (the sample) are a representative subgroup of the total group of interest (the universe), and if the right questions are asked. The universe might be the population as a whole or, parents, car drivers, the elderly, shoppers, voters, IT managers and so on.

There are four basic data collection methods employed for surveys: (1) personal interviews; (2) telephone interviews; (3) mail surveys and (4) Web-based surveys. The choice of the data collection method will depend on the objectives of the survey, and the relative importance of factors such as level of accuracy required, the amount of data to be collected, the sample bias acceptable, the budget required, speed and any administrative issues.

Market research information can be obtained from a variety of sources. Basically there are two types of research: 'Primary' and 'Secondary'. The latter involves using information that is already readily available, for example by utilizing your local library you will have access to reference materials, magazines, directories of associations, etc. Primary research is where a bespoke piece of market research is conducted.

Secondary research

Compared with primary research, secondary research is generally:

- o Quicker
- o Cheaper
- o Less relevant to the topic under investigation
- o Out of date if it refers to fast-changing contexts or issues.

As someone else has conducted the secondary research, users of this material must look carefully at how the data was derived and how valid and reliable are the conclusions.

Evaluating secondary information

1. *What was the purpose of the study?* – Was it undertaken by an impartial source or by a pressure group that is attempting to put across a particular point?
2. *Who collected the information?* – In the UK, it is possible to obtain statistics on the number of vegetarians from the Vegetarian Society or from the meat industry. These two sources of information do not provide the same estimate for the number of vegetarians!
3. *What information was collected?* – Figures from two sources may differ because of the use of different sources of information, or because different timescales are used. However, sometimes it can be because each wants to prove a point.
4. *When was the information collected?* – If there has been a recent food scare, for example mad cow disease, consumption levels of beef will be low and consumption of substitutes will be high.
5. *Is the information consistent with other information?* – Most secondary information tends to be quantitative rather than qualitative.

Activity 6.4

Identify secondary research sources for your organization's products, services and markets. List specific reports that would be useful for marketing.

Primary research

There are four main types of primary research:

1. Surveys
2. Observation
3. Experimentation
4. Simulation.

Personal interviews

Benefits

- o Interviewer can select a good quality sample.
- o Interviewer can interpret strange answers and ask for clarification.
- o The interviewer can classify interviewees to save time.
- o Longer questionnaires can be asked with this method.
- o Can use visual images.

Problems

- o Costly.
- o Possible interviewer bias.
- o Possibility of fake interviews.

Focus groups

This is one of the most frequently used techniques in marketing research. Successful research requires a skilled moderator (i.e. the person who directs the topics of discussion and creates a balanced environment to encourage the contribution of all members of the group). Members of the focus group should be selected from the target population for the firm's products and services.

Benefits

- o A wide range of ideas can be obtained.
- o In-depth understanding of consumer attitudes and purchase motivations may be obtained.
- o Ideal when managers are looking for ideas or need to clarify some details.
- o A certain synergy can be obtained from a group discussion that allows a deeper probing of issues.
- o Can use visual images.
- o Relatively easy to record (video and audio tape) for future analysis.

Problems

- ○ Costly.
- ○ Success is highly dependent on the skill of the interviewer and on the selection of the sample to attend the focus group.
- ○ Possible problem of domination of the group by a strong and forceful individual, which will result in group conflict or only the views of the forceful individual being obtained.

Focus groups can be used to cover a variety of topics, but they are best used to understand 'why' a particular group feels or acts in a particular way. If an interviewee says something of particular interest during a focus group, the interviewer can probe deeper into the topic, uncovering the information. Topics often covered in focus groups include reactions to product ideas and product prototypes, messaging tests, ad testing and customer-needs identification. The groups are taped (video and audio) for later analysis and can be observed during the focus group – either at a specially designed facility, or via a videoconference or Web-based hook-up when the session proceedings can be viewed remotely. Sometimes hard-to-reach people will not come to a focus group but they may be reached by depth interviews which are one-on-one discussions with a researcher. While qualitative data is very accessible, it can fall short on reliability.

Telephone surveys
Benefits

- ○ Quick and easy to do.
- ○ Reach geographically dispersed sample.
- ○ Ease of sampling, for example random digit dialling.
- ○ Complex routing through questionnaire is automated.
- ○ Low cost.
- ○ Possibility of recording to confirm that interview took place.

Problems

- ○ Method can only handle very short, simple questionnaires.
- ○ Sample obtained can be biased, depending on the type of people who are willing to complete a telephone interview.
- ○ Lack of access to households without telephones.

 Activity 6.5

What do you think of the advantages and disadvantages of using a telephone survey for this kind of work? Do you think the sceptics are being unrealistic in expecting in-depth interviews in the workplace, or do they have a point?

Postal surveys
Benefits

- Low cost.
- Ease of contacting geographically dispersed sample.
- More complex questions can be asked.

Problems

- Usually quite a low response rate.
- The interviewee can misinterpret the questions.
- It can take a long time to get back replies.
- Minimal chance of interpreting the extent to which the respondent is answering truthfully.

Internet surveys
Benefits

- Very fast: instant analysis may be undertaken.
- Very low cost.
- Highly targeted.
- Ease of contacting the sample.

Problems

- Method can only handle very short, simple questionnaires.
- Very limited potential for 'open' questions.
- People with access to the Internet are not representative of the total population for all markets. They tend to be higher income and higher socio-economic groups. This is less of a problem for business–Internet surveys.

Quantitative data

- Tends to be on large numbers of people.
- Findings are expressed numerically.
- Concerned with 'how many', 'how often' and 'what' rather than 'why'.
- Quantitative research problem: How many consumers buy the company's shampoo?

Qualitative approaches

- Fewer people.
- Deals with data difficult to quantify – concerned with 'why' rather than 'how many', or 'how often'.
- Concerned with attitudes and motivations.

Some of the more important criteria, when selecting research method, include:

- Cost
- Speed
- Access to target population (including ability to sample the target population)
- Type of questions that can be asked
- Quantity of data
- Response rate.

Qualitative research tends to be exploratory and directional in nature. It is designed to bring out issues associated with the subject matter as well as the best general direction to proceed. Qualitative methods can be useful in all stages of development and are very tangible to marketers and developers.

Observation

This is literally where the individual's behaviour is monitored and recorded. One of the most popular applications of this technique recently is in researching in-store shopping. Consumer movement through the store is observed and recorded. Researchers have been able to classify individuals in supermarkets according to their speed of movement through the store, their willingness to scan the shelves for products and to divert from a preplanned shopping list, where one exists.

In-depth interviews involve one-to-one contact with respondents and are usually conducted face to face, although telephone interviews are sometimes used. The in-depth interview is different from the tightly structured interview used in quantitative surveys or opinion polls – it is not only longer (45–60 minutes), but also more discursive and open-ended. The interviewer also has a greater level of flexibility since they are not constrained by the order or wording of questions; she or he is able to cover the issues specified in the topic guide in a more context-sensitive way, as they 'naturally' emerge, and to probe responses to gain a full understanding of their meaning and/or implications.

Experimentation

This is where the researcher attempts to establish causality between two factors by varying one factor and holding all other factors constant.

Laboratory experiments

Laboratory experiments take place in an artificial environment created by the researcher, which allows one factor to be varied. For example, an advert can be placed within a magazine that has been created specially for research purposes. Consumers can be given the magazine to look through, and are then asked to comment on the advertising. If unfavourable comments are made, then the advert is changed and consumers are asked to repeat the procedure. In this way, researchers are able to assess changes in advertising on consumer response.

Field experiments

Field experiments take place in a more natural environment. Researchers often change a factor in order to observe the influence on purchase quantity/sales revenue. Examples of experimentation in a retail environment include changing:

- o Shelf location
- o Price
- o Pack design
- o Sales promotion activity.

As each of these factors is varied, the researcher observes the effect on sales volume and on revenue.

Simulation

Simulation is where researchers build a model (usually a computer model) of an environment and use this as the basis for experimentation. Simulation is employed when a problem is judged to be too complex for ease of mathematical formulation. In building a simulation, the researcher sets the framework (parameters) of the model and within that framework, the researcher or business manager may experiment.

Insight

The power of images

Pictures selected by tongue-tied shoppers can help companies learn what consumers really want. When words fail, the images consumers choose can serve as a window into their thoughts. These images can be used to tap non-verbal reactions and to probe below the surface for deeper feelings. The insights gleaned can be incorporated into marketing campaigns that resonate with consumers on an emotional level.

Source: American Demographics, November 2001, p. 32.

Cross-section versus longitudinal research

Researchers need to be clear about the type of data they require. Cross-sectional data is where a 'snapshot' picture of the current situation is obtained. A survey undertaken this month reports on the situation as it is for this month. For various reasons, the results may not be relevant at any other time. Longitudinal data is obtained over a period of time, often over many years.

Tracking studies

A tracking study may involve conducting a survey every month, or even every week, to establish and track consumer reaction. In such studies, advertising managers want to assess the peak level of response, such as awareness, and the rate at which this decays between advertising activities. As longitudinal research is very expensive for individual companies to buy, groups of companies join together to purchase the same data using 'syndicated research'.

Syndicated research

Only companies within the syndicate have access to the data. A relatively low-cost method of collecting 'cross-sectional data usually' is the omnibus survey. A company will run a regular survey (say, every month) with a specified target population. Often a theme is specified, such as financial services or children. Any company is then able to pay to add their own questions.

Stage 4 – Data collection

The most common approach to collecting information is the questionnaire. There are two main types of questions used in questionnaires: open questions and closed questions.

Open questions are used when the researcher wants to explore some ideas. They may be used when trying to design a new product or explore consumer opinion about the company brand, for example what features would you like in a robot vacuum cleaner?

Closed questions are most frequently used to count the number of people who exhibit a particular trait.

Closed question, for example:

Do you buy products made by the firm?

- o Never?
- o Once per year?
- o Once per month?
- o More frequently than once per month.

There are many types of closed and open questions. Some closed questions are able to achieve more than simply a count of people or attributes. They may be used to investigate attitudes held by consumers, in particular the intensity of attitude.

Closed questions

Closed questions may include two (dichotomous) or more (multichotomous) options from which the respondent selects an answer.

Semantic differential scale

Semantic differential scale respondents are presented with a set of bipolar adjectives and asked to indicate the point on the scale which best describes the intensity of their feelings.

Open questions

Open questions gather ideas and attitudes but they are time-consuming to analyse and require knowledgeable analysts.

Open questions invite facts and opinions, whereas closed questions seek either the answer 'yes' or 'no'.

The danger of using too many closed questions is that they:

- ○ Prevent people from expressing views
- ○ Restrict the flow of information.

Simple Open questions

These leave the respondent free to answer as they wish.

Leading questions

These are phrased in such a way that makes it clear that you only expect one answer: 'I'm sure we all agree that ...?' 'Isn't it true that ...?' 'Don't you think that ...?'. They are to be avoided because they can cause resentment at trying to put words into their mouths or trying to persuade them, against their own judgement, to agree with you. Ultimately, the data gathered is flawed because it may not represent what the respondent really thinks or believes.

Multiple questions

People can only answer one question at a time, so do not fall into the trap of issuing a stream of questions, such as:

'What's the situation with ... and how will we ... and when by?'.

Listening

Questioning skills will not bring results unless equally effective listening skills are being practised. There are three levels of listening:

1. Hearing the words – You must be able to actually hear and understand the words that are being spoken.
2. Understanding the meaning – You must understand the overall meaning.
3. Perceiving the inference – You must be able to perceive the inferences that lie behind the words.

Influence of Researcher

When listening, and when you are being listened to, you should be aware of the stream of signals which are given off by somebody who is speaking. These verbal and non-verbal signals can transmit a significantly different message to other members of the meeting than the literal meaning of the spoken words.

Facial expression – If the speaker's expression does not match the words, it is the expression which carries more weight.

Body language – Shrugged shoulders or dismissive hand gestures have the same impact as facial expression.

Tone of voice – Listeners can perceive strong signals through tone of voice and emphasis on certain words. The tone of voice, consciously or subconsciously, can significantly influence the way in which the question is perceived. For example, the question: 'Do you think this is achievable?' is apparently a neutral, closed question which seeks without expectation the answer 'yes' or 'no'. However, in a different tone, it could also imply that there is the slightest chance that the results can be achieved. Conversely, the same question spoken in an enthusiastic voice would convey the impression that you were looking for a 'yes!' If you want the honest opinion of other members, you should take care to keep any expectation – either positive or negative – out of your voice.

Stage 5 – Analysing the data

Quantitative research is numerically oriented and often involves statistical analysis of a large number of respondents compared to qualitative research which provides more in-depth analysis of fewer responses. Analysing quantitative data is more straightforward compared to qualitative data although for all research the acid test is neatly summed up.

> *Internal validity, the degree to which findings correctly map the phenomenon in question; external validity, the degree to which findings can be generalized to other settings similar to the one in which the study occurred; reliability, the extent to which findings can be replicated, or reproduced, by another inquirer; and objectivity, the extent to which findings are free from bias.*

Source: Denzin, N. and Lincoln, Y. (Eds.) (2000).

Adding value

Descriptive data is the most basic level of analysis. Further analysis allows more depth and means that specific themes can be explored within the data. Techniques include:

Factor analysis

This means taking particular themes, for example service, price, value for money and identifying whether there are any significant patterns that will help to structure the analysis.

Cluster analysis

Cluster analysis helps identify 'segments' or 'clusters' from a sample with particular attitudes, behaviours or demographic profiles. Statements relating to the topic of interest, are presented to respondents and responses are analysed by looking at correlations between the latter to assess which categories each respondent falls into in terms of behaviour and/or attitudes towards a product, service and so on. Each respondent is allocated a cluster number and the data is run against a demographic profile data (e.g. gender, age, socio-economic status) to identify the characteristics of people with differing attitudes/behaviours. This technique is useful for identifying target audiences for marketing purposes.

Strategic priority analysis

This technique allows businesses to identify priorities for action. Respondents are presented with a list of different aspects of service and/or product information which they rate in terms of satisfaction/dissatisfaction. The analysis identifies which of these issues cause an increase or decrease in overall satisfaction levels (the issues can be ranked in order of impact or importance to customers).

Stage 6 – Present the findings

The market research report should present findings that are relevant to the major marketing decisions facing management.

Online research

Online research covers all digital interactive media, including digital TV, WAP and new entertainment technologies. Online research can be appropriate if the target market is visitors to a specific website or Internet-users in general – but it is still not a medium for general public surveys. This may change eventually as penetration grows among women and older groups. Internet research has an advantage for surveys among staff, employees and customers or subscribers to online services in any situation where the universe is known, and the e-mail addresses are available and up to date. Business e-mail addresses tend to be less volatile compared to consumers. The barriers to conducting online research are very low. The most important issue for research is declining respondent co-operation rates. Approaches like showing interactive stimuli material such as clips from ads all work well on the Internet. But while it is feasible to show TV clips, they can slow download times. With interactive digital TV, there is a lot more potential.

Insight

Online research will dominate in the future

Today

- Most research uses 'cold' unsolicited approaches, for example 'Excuse me, can you help us?', 'Sorry to bother you. Would you mind?'
- Little use of opt-in.
- Permission not currently required for first approaches unless re-contacting respondents.

Year 2015 (tomorrow)

- Most research will be permission-based.
- Opt-in only for research.
- Online-managed Panels will be the primary research tool.
- Research channels will still vary by research requirements.

PEST analysis/reasoning for the changes

Politics: government legislation/policy (anti-cold calling, anti-spam, etc.)

Economics: commercial pressures. cost, speed, repetition – And Quality: No fraud, reliable/good quality data: data density, open-ended questions.

Society: desire for control/personalization, wary of commercial approaches, individual privacy, reward/feedback for contributions, Internet access/use for majority.

Technology: computerization, Internet, online-managed panels.

Effects

- o Significantly less face-to-face approaches.
- o Fewer personal interviewers required.
- o Telephone will prosper in combination with panels and TAWI surveys.
- o More respondent control – Do what they want, when they want.

Some vital statistics

Today

55–65 per cent of quantitative data is collected online in USA; 15–25 per cent of quantitative data in Western Europe/UK is collected online. It was only 3–5 per cent 4 years ago.

Companies like Budweiser and Canon do virtually all their quant research online.

Source: Darren Noyce, SKOPOS, November 2005

http://www.marketresearchworld.net/
index.php?option=com_content&task=view&id=384&Itemid=42

Computer-assisted interviewing (CAI)

Computer-assisted interviewing involves the use of a computer to collect, store, manipulate and transmit data relating to interviews conducted between the interviewer and the respondent(s).

Computer-assisted personal interviewing (CAPI)

Computer-assisted personal interviewing (personal interview by an interviewer using a portable computer at the home or business of the respondent) is one component of CAI. Other components include computer-assisted telephone interviewing (CATI) and Computer-assisted self-interviewing (CASI). The three chief theoretical benefits of CAPI are: better quality, improved timeliness and lower cost after the initial investment. Computer-assisted personal interviewing has the potential to provide improvements in the areas of data quality, survey timeliness and cost-effectiveness, but cost savings directly attributable to CAPI are less well documented than the other benefits. On large-scale continuous surveys and on other operations where the hardware can be efficiently utilized and the costs spread over time, net savings might be expected but otherwise the costs might well be greater for CAPI. Computer-assisted personal interviewing also provides the opportunity to apply experimental design principles to survey testing, and the flexibility to enable collection of important policy-related data for difficult topics.

Online focus groups

An online focus group is essentially a formal chat session. A trained moderator leads a group of participants through a predetermined discussion over the Internet. Participants are often recruited through a research firm's own panel and are paid a fee for participating. A focus group could be set up inexpensively by using a chat room and recruiting your own participants. If a panel is used, the following checklist is useful to note.

Online panel users

A good online panel can offer real advantages over other approaches. But how do you know it's a good panel?

Here's a checklist of questions to ask a panel supplier.

Recruitment sources – How are the panel members found? What biases does this recruitment approach build in?

Screening – Are prospective panel members screened (off-line) to confirm age, residence and so on? Many panel members belong to several different panels, to the point where some have become almost professional respondents.

Representative membership – How well does the profile of panel members match an independently derived profile of net users as a whole? Is there a bias towards the heavier or more experienced users?

Maintenance of representativeness – What steps has the panel supplier taken to ensure that the membership profile remains up to date? Dropouts and the changing profile of net users can lead to biases in the panel membership, if it is not regularly monitored.

Sampling methods – How are samples drawn from the panel membership? Is it a random sample from the whole database? Are quotas or over-sampling used to allow for differential response rates?

Differential response rates – What monitoring has the agency done on differential response rates? Some people respond every time; some rarely, so that the achieved sample for any survey may be biased, even if the panel as a whole is representative.

Survey frequency – How often are panel members asked to complete surveys? Professional respondents are not representative.

Lifestyle profiling – Are panel members profiled according to lifestyle criteria? If not, the panel could be less cost-effective if you are only interested in, for example people who have booked travel online, or people who regularly work from home. http://www.mori.com/pubinfo/nep-onlineresearch.shtml

How are panels used – the panel should be recruited, maintained and used for Bonafide market research purposes only

Source: http://www.mori.com/pubinfo/nep-onlineresearch.shtml Online Research – ESOMAR Research World Interview.

Feedback forms

A simple way to conduct ongoing qualitative research is through a feedback form. You can gain valuable insight by asking website visitors for suggestions, and/or asking them their opinions. You can do this through a form directly on your site and/or via e-mail to those on your opt-in list.

Primary quantitative market research

Quantitative research is used when you are looking for hard numbers and precision. To produce a top-quality primary quantitative research study, you must generally work through a research agency. For a small-budget business, this type of research is expensive. The Internet has made more inexpensive means of data collection and analysis possible. With the help of software or Web-based tools, you can perform research through customer surveys and collect visitor-use patterns through Web logs.

Customer surveys

The Internet has made conducting surveys quicker and less expensive. Options range from do-it-yourself programmes to research services with screened panels. You can use surveys in a variety of ways – segmenting your customers, improving/developing your product or site and gauging brand awareness, for example.

Use patterns

Another approach to quantitative research on the Web is to look for visitor-use patterns such as routes taken through your site, pages viewed or ordering behaviour. By studying Web logs, you can know which pages are most popular, how visitors navigate through your site, common entry pages and where visitors often leave the site. You can also determine the number of different visitors to your site as well as the percentage of visitors converted to customers. By using a traffic-analysis service or software (often available through your hosting service), you can streamline the process. An alternative to conducting primary research is to find secondary research, or research that originated elsewhere. You can obtain secondary research either by purchasing the information or finding it through free resources.

Quantitative research

Quantitative research produces results that are more statistically accurate than qualitative research results. Often, companies first conduct qualitative research when developing a concept or looking for ideas, and later complete quantitative research to fine-tune and optimize. It is usually conducted via surveys or behavioural tracking. It is based on the principle that the characteristics of a randomly selected group of people will closely reflect the characteristics of the entire group from which the sample was taken. So, when marketers and site developers need to know, with relative certainty, the answers to specific questions, quantitative methods are used.

Insight

Quantitative research focuses on the left brain – objective, comfortable with logic, numbers and detailed, convergent reasoning rather than divergent reasoning. Qualitative research deals with the right brain – the hemisphere accountable for processing data such as words, emotions, feelings, colour and music. Traditional survey questionnaires are weak at eliciting follow-up data from respondents, as they usually require responses precategorized by the researcher. Often managers greeted the receipt of such surveys with the response 'So what?'. They answer questions related to such issues as market share, predicted revenue, statistical trends and past behaviour of customers well, but statistics are not good for answering questions about human behaviour, perceptions, future behaviour and involvement with a product. As a result of the need for companies to obtain richer data about their customers, prospective customers and the market as a whole, qualitative research became more in demand. While data collection techniques are now better developed, data analysis methodologies have not kept up. The new 'So what?' reaction from management is in response to the often confused summaries of the pages upon pages of focus group or interview transcripts. Running quantitative research alongside qualitative research offers a synergy, whereby objective data can provide a structure to the analysis of subjective qualitative data. Generally, quantitative and qualitative research are presented as two separate entities. Yet, the smart market researcher knows how to combine both kinds of data.

Source: Adapted from: http://www.asiamarketresearch.com/columns/market5.htm.

The market research industry

The market research industry consists of hundreds of firms and consultancies. Each of these will have their own areas of specialization. It comprises:

Market research agencies

Full service market research agencies are organizations that will be able to conduct all elements of your research project from start to finish. They are able to help design the project to ensure it meets the initial research objectives, carry out the fieldwork to collect the data, analyse the information, interpret the data and produce conclusions and recommendations.

The leading agencies, and many of the smaller ones, have directors and executives who are members of the Market Research Society. The Society has a Professional Code of Conduct which lays down rules and good practice with respect to their responsibilities to clients (confidentiality), respondents (anonymity), the public as a whole and to each other.

Market research consultancies

Consultancies are usually smaller than market research agencies and do not have their own fieldwork department, telephone unit and data processing department. Usually these aspects of a project would be dealt with by specialist fieldwork and data processing companies.

Freelancers or consultants

Market research freelancers or consultants operate on a lone basis. Some tend to support research agencies as an extra resource and/or have their own direct clients. As with a consultancy a freelancer would have to contract out some parts of the project – the fieldwork and data processing.

The main advantage of selecting a freelancer is their low overheads which usually offer very competitive rates.

Fieldwork and tabulation companies

Fieldwork companies deal with data collection only. After the data has been collected it needs to be verified, checked, processed and tabulated so that it can be analysed by the researcher.

Some companies offer both elements whilst others specialize in either aspect.

Data preparation and analysis

These are companies that specialize in verifying, checking, processing and tabulating data so that it can be analysed by the researcher but also such companies will analyse the data and present reports based on the data.

Viewing facilities

This enables interviews or group discussions to be viewed. A facilitator sits in one room with the respondent(s), whilst the client sits somewhere else out of sight. By using one-way mirrors the client see and hear the conversation. Viewing facilities also offer audio, video and DVD recordings of the interviews and group discussions.

Market research recruitment agencies

The following case study demonstrates how market research is becoming more complex and needs to become more sophisticated to match the complexity of consumers' lives.

A case study in complexity

An overwhelming majority of marketers surveyed – 92 per cent – believe that marketing has become more complicated as a result of the complexity of consumers' lives. Media fragmentation is identified as the root of their frustration, with 67 per cent of marketers citing it as the driving force behind increased complexity. The modern marketer is faced with a dramatically increased number of channels and platforms to deal with. Two-fifths of marketers believe that the increase in the number of media outlets has made consumers' media consumption less predictable and fostered a decline in consumer loyalty. Marketers are increasingly concerned that targeted outlets, which aim to capture specific consumers, have increased confusion rather than offering clarity. Marketers have to balance the need to develop an overall communications strategy with the need to target niche groups. The relationship between marketers and consumers embodies the complexity problem. The fragmentation of consumers' lives has led marketers to develop more sophisticated methods of marketing to reach them. This in turn has increased choice, making consumers' lives even more complex. Marketers are realizing that standard market research is no longer sufficient for understanding consumer needs. More than two-thirds of those surveyed agreed that there is a need for more innovative research, although only 20 per cent felt that they were already carrying out such research. Respondents to the survey believe that some companies are already getting it right: Tesco received the most praise, followed by Orange, Virgin, First Direct and EasyJet. Another interesting example is Ronseal, which is seen by marketers as a brand that achieves clarity and precision through the simplicity of its marketing.

Source: Adapted from *Marketing Week*, 18 September 2003, Caroline Parry, Emma Doniger and the Future Foundation.

On the theme of increased choice making consumers' lives ever more complex, the book Sophisticated Consumers, Intricate Lifestyles, Simple Solutions (Willmott and Nelson, 2003) reports how fourteen types of dental floss were found in one UK pharmacy, a similar range of brandies in a Spanish supermarket and there were eight kinds of orange juice available under the Tropicana brand alone.

Agency selection

It is possible to buy research and a reputable agency should give advice on the most cost-effective way of researching a target audience. It will discuss the advantages and disadvantages of different research options, and help to design and write questions. It will endeavour to achieve a representative sample and report the main findings in whatever form is preferred. The agency should also be willing to discuss the implications of any findings for the business.

Qualitative and quantitative market research: where the twain meet . . .

Why can't advertising agencies and market researchers just get on?

Advertising agencies attract creative people, often innovators and independent thinkers who also often lack pragmatic and rational thinking. On the other hand, market research agencies attract a different sort of person – methodical and objective, often more introvert, detail-minded and conservative in outlook. Advertising agencies think they can do the research better than the market research agencies, and market research agencies think they can do the advertising better than the advertising agencies. Research departments within advertising agencies often lack power and crumble under the pressure of their more extrovert advertising colleagues at meetings. The reverse is true with research-based organizations that venture into advertising. It may be difficult for the extrovert, creative people who make up advertising agencies to listen to market researchers whose research suggests that a wonderfully original and unique ad may cause a negative reaction, and similarly it is difficult for researchers to get excited by new and paradigm-challenging ideas.

Source: http://www.asiamarketresearch.com/columns/market1.htm.

Rod Davies, Orient Pacific Century, 12 February 2000.

Rod Davies, Orient Pacific Century, October 2000.

The British Market Research Association (BMRA) website lists its member agencies with their specialisms. Smaller agencies are good for niche areas but larger agencies will tend to have specialists who focus on particular sectors, such as the voluntary sector, financial services, telecommunications, education and so on.

Assessing the impact of marketing activity

Advertising
Pre-testing
Pre-testing is the showing of unfinished advertisements to representative groups of the target audience.

Post-testing
Post-testing is concerned with the evaluation of a campaign once it has been released. Examples include the return of coupons, response card and requests for further literature or actual orders. Recall tests attempt to assess how memorable particular advertisements are whilst recognition tests are based on the ability of respondents to reprocess information about an advertisement.

Evaluation of sales promotions

Evaluation methods include:

o *Consumer audits* – This will indicate if there has been a change in consumer behaviour as a result of the sales promotion campaign.
o *Sales information* – Increase in sales is one performance indicator.
o *Retail audits* – Specialist organizations can track changes in stock levels, distribution and market share immediately after the promotional campaign. This will provide an insight into the basis of an increase or decrease in sales.
o *Sales force feedback* – This is based on sales force feedback about the uptake of sales promotion opportunities in their area.
o *Voucher/coupon redemption* – Usually based on coding to relate response rate to sales promotion activities – this can be used to endorse the right selection of media, the right kind of sales promotion activity and potentially the most frequently used distribution outlet.

Evaluation of public relations

Haywood (1991) suggested that there are seven commonly used measures of results:

1. *Budget* – An assessment of whether the planned PR activity has been achieved within the budget defined and also within the timescales set.
2. *Awareness* – The measure of awareness can be quite complex and is most likely to be established through a range of marketing research activities to establish the level of brand awareness in the marketplace.
3. *Attitude* – Combined with research on brand awareness can be research on brand attitudes, whether they are positive or negative, and whether they have resulted in any change in consumer behaviour.
4. *Media coverage and tone* – First, it will be essential to establish the level of media coverage achieved as a result of planned-PR activities. Typical measures might include the number of different media which covered the case, the number of columns taken, key headings and perceived importance of the PR information. Second, the nature and tone in which the PR activities have been covered.
5. *Positioning* – Measuring the perception of the position of the organization versus that of the competition.

6. *Response generation* – Many of the enquiries or leads generated may be subject to some degree of code referencing, or sources of the enquiry will be recorded.
7. *Share price* – For large public companies, this is an indicator of public confidence in the organization.

Evaluation of direct and interactive marketing communications

Evaluation is related to the predetermined objectives of a campaign.

Typical measures for successful implementation of the direct marketing campaign will include:

- o Response rate
- o Conversion rate
- o Order value
- o Repeat orders.

This information will be gathered through a range of voucher and campaign response codes that will be able to distinguish the source of the direct mail or promotion. This may establish the most popular direct marketing technique.

Technology is developing quickly and click-through rates are a common measure for online activity. However, this evaluates only behaviour not attitudes.

Evaluation of personal sales

Sales performance needs to be measured against objectives on a regular basis. Other factors relating to sales performance that can be measured include:

- o Productivity – calls per day, calls per account, total number of orders versus calls.
- o Account development – total of new accounts, total of existing accounts and growth of sales from existing accounts.
- o Expenses – expenses versus number of calls made, cost per call.

Sales measurement techniques are becoming more sophisticated and more effective and the speed at which information becomes available is of the essence.

When assessing the impact of the marketing activity it is likely that a combination of measures will need to be used to support future expenditure. These could include:

- Sales growth
- Relationship measurement mechanism within centres (e.g. questionnaires)
- Qualitative and quantitative research
- Customer feedback mechanisms
- Footfall conversion measurement
- Indexed trading data (sales trends)
- Service charge savings
- Press cuttings with impact scoring mechanism (e.g. size of article)
- Car counting
- Dwell time measurement
- Frequency of customer visits
- Retailer demand for units
- Community relationships
- Retailer feedback mechanisms including surveys and retailer consultations
- Use of website, where appropriate.

Source: http://www.rics.org.uk/NR/rdonlyres/025B7E06-7F19-46F4-8D27-547F2095078/0/ shopping_goodpractice.pdf

Summary

There are many different approaches to market research but the most important aspect is to choose an approach that is fit for the purpose and will deliver the kind of data that will be useful. Sophisticated market research is costly so it is important to conduct a cost/benefit analysis of any proposal. No approach is perfect and the main choice is between knowing a lot about a little, or a little about a lot.

Further study

Boddy, D. (2002) *Management: An Introduction*, Chapter 7 'Managing Marketing'.

Hints and tips

You need to be able to show that you know the issue that needs to be decided when designing a research project aimed at providing information as part of a marketing audit or for marketing and business decisions. On a practical level, you will need to be able to analyse and interpret information and present, as a written report or oral presentation, appropriate conclusions or recommendations that inform the marketing and business decisions for which the research was undertaken.

Bibliography

Denzin, N. and Lincoln, Y. (Eds) (2000) *Handbook of Qualitative Research in Education* (2nd ed.), Thousand Oaks, CA: Sage Publications.

Housden, M. (2003) *Marketing Research and Information*, Oxford: Butterworth-Heinemann.

Public Sector Benchmarking Service (2004) <http://www.benchmarking.gov.uk>

Willmott and Nelson (2003) *Complicated Lives: Sophisticated Consumers, Intricate Lifestyles, Simple Solutions*, Wiley & Sons.

Wilson, D. (2003) *Marketing Research, Harlow*, Essex: FT Prentice Hall.

Past examination papers for the Marketing Management in Practice module can be found in Appendix 5.

unit 7
developing and implementing marketing plans

Learning objectives

o Develop an operational marketing plan, selecting an appropriate marketing mix for an organization operating in any context such as FMCG, business-to-business (supply chain), large or capital project-based, services, voluntary and not-for-profit, or sales support (e.g. SMEs) (4.1).

o Use the main techniques available for planning, scheduling and resourcing activities within the plan (4.2).

o Identify appropriate measures for evaluating and controlling the marketing plan (4.3).

o Review and evaluate the effectiveness of planning activities (4.4).

Related Statements of Marketing Practice

Jc2   Manage and report on delivery against plan and objectives.

Kc.1   Define measurements appropriate to the plan or business case and ensure they are undertaken.

Kc.2   Evaluate activities and identify improvements using measurement data.

Glossary

Corporate Planning – Continuous process of making present risk-taking decisions systematically and with the greatest knowledge of their futurity; organizing systematically the efforts needed to carry out these decisions, and measuring the results of these decisions against the expectations through organized, systematic feedback.

Environmental scanning – Environmental scanning is fundamental to the planning process and should form an integral part of all localized planning and strategic decision-making. The process involves the research and assessment of known or proposed changes in the areas of politics, the environment, social and demographic change, technology, economic issues or legal issues, in the short, medium and long term. A PEST analysis is part of this process.

Marketing audit – The systematic collection, analysis and evaluation of information relating to the internal and external environments that answers the question 'Where are we now?' for the organization.

PEST – A framework for analysing the political, economic, social and technological trends, issues and so on in the external environment that are likely to have an impact on the business. Sometimes this is written as 'PESTLE' where Legal and Environmental categories are added.

Strategic planning – Long-term plans based on the organizations' overall business objectives. Strategic plans are typically for multiple years and reach out 5 or 10 years (or more) using Scenarios or other planning methods that identify Assumptions, Risks, and Environmental factors.

SWOT – A matrix that categorizes information about internal strengths and weaknesses and external opportunities and threats. The aim is to minimize the threats and address the weaknesses whilst capitalizing on strengths and aligning them with the opportunities that exist.

Introduction

The Marketing Management in Practice module is intended to give participants some practice in developing and implementing marketing plans at an operational level in organizations. A key part of this is working within a team to develop the plan and managing teams implementing the plan by undertaking marketing activities and projects. Its aim is to encourage you to integrate and apply knowledge from all the modules, particularly as part of a team. The focus should be on implementing a marketing plan as a team activity and careful attention needs to be given to the issues surrounding the actual implementation of a plan.

Marketing planning and corporate planning

Corporate planning or strategic company planning comprises the following sequential steps:

- ○ *Mission statement* is a statement of the company's overall business philosophy or purpose. It is normally a set of guidelines, rather than something that is stated in hard and fast quantitative terms.
- ○ *Situational analysis* means evaluating external and internal factors that will affect the planning process and asks the question 'Where are we now?'

- ○ *Organizational objectives* describe where an organization wants to be and how it wants to fulfil its mission. They are often expressed in achievable quantitative terms.
- ○ *Strategies to achieve these objectives.* These are the concrete ideas that set about achieving the company's objectives and they relate to how the mission will be accomplished.

In large organizations, corporate planning is often a separate function reporting directly to top management. How corporate planning is organized in different organizations and sectors is influenced by factors such as the size and structure of the organization. Corporate planning provides an overview and brings planning functions together from across the organization. A key aspect of corporate planning is to ensure that there is consistency and coherence across the organization and all plans will contribute to achieving overall organizational objectives. Corporate objectives are derived from the corporate plan, and inform the direction and focus of the marketing plan. Marketing objectives cover issues such as increasing the awareness of a product or service among a target audience within a particular time frame. Marketing objectives are likely to be linked to market share or sales targets.

Strategic planning

In his book *The Rise and Fall of Strategic Planning*, Henry Mintzberg describes how strategic planners make the mistake that the future will resemble the past and tend to gather 'hard' data on their industry, markets and competitors, whilst ignoring 'soft' data such as talking with customers, suppliers and employees. Many organizations now make use of the term 'Strategic Intent' defined by Gary Hamel and C.K. Prahalad in their book *Competing for the Future* as 'an ambitious and compelling dream that provides the emotional and intellectual energy for the journey to the future, conveying a sense of direction and destiny'. Strategic Intent is more flexible than a strategic plan and recognizes that the best-laid plans may need to change in response to market conditions. The pace of change means that it is not always possible to anticipate change and, for example, cataclysmic events such as September 11 and its aftermath, which was not and could not have been anticipated, can completely transform the business context. The upshot of this is that planning is important but it needs to incorporate flexibility. The days when vast resources were put into creating gigantic strategic plans that were out of date by the time they had been produced are probably over for the present.

Marketing planning

Strategic marketing planning is the application of a number of logical steps in the planning process. There are different ways in which this can be done. One specific model would not suit every marketing planning situation. The planning process:

Example of a structure for a marketing plan linked to corporate planning

Mission Statement

Macro-Environment Situational Analysis

Political, Economic, Socio-cultural Audits of all major company and Technological (PEST) functions – Marketing, Finance, HRM, Production, Distribution

Strengths, Weaknesses, Opportunities, Threats, Analysis (SWOT)

Marketing Objectives

Forecast Market Potential

Generate Marketing Strategies

Assumptions and Contingency Plans

Prepare Detailed Marketing Mix Programmes

Budget Resources including Staffing

Agree Timescales

Implement the Plan

Measure and Control

Marketing plan components

The following are examples of what can be included in a marketing plan but it does not necessarily follow that every plan will have all of these components. Marketing plans tend to vary by industry, size of company, stage of growth and organizational goals. The process of preparing it is as important as the particular form it takes. The process should make you think about goals and the marketing strategy that will be used to achieve them. A marketing plan may contain all or just some of the following components.

Executive summary

Introduce the organization:

- ○ Explain the major points of your plan
- ○ Describe briefly the nature of the business and the products or services offered
- ○ Include a mission or values statement and objectives
- ○ List the structure of your organization and the senior management team
- ○ Summarize the marketing objectives and strategies that are in the plan.

Marketing audit

A good marketing audit is:

- ○ *Systematic* – It follows a logical, predetermined framework, an orderly sequence of diagnostic steps.
- ○ *Comprehensive* – It considers all factors affecting marketing performance, not just obvious trouble spots. Marketers can be fooled into addressing symptoms rather than underlying problems. A comprehensive audit can identify the real problems.

o *Independent* – To ensure objectivity, outside consultants are used sometimes to prepare the marketing audit. Using outsiders may not be necessary, but having an objective auditor is important.

o *Periodic* – Many organizations schedule regular marketing audits because the environment for marketing is dynamic.

A typical marketing audit consists of a number of sections, examples of which are given below.

Marketing environment audit

This is based on an analysis of the internal and external environment. It should include information about target markets, including information about other individuals or organizations that offer similar products and services. Identify key issues in the competitive environment, for example challenges, such as new legislation or the impact of technological changes.

The marketing audit is important to the planning process because it provides the analysis that supports the corporate and the marketing decision-making process. An audit should provide information on the external (macro) and internal (micro) environment. Understanding trends and trying to anticipate changes that will have an impact on markets, customers, suppliers and competitors are important aspects of strategic development. Decisions about product and service development and investment decisions should be informed by the outcome of the marketing audit. The challenge is to use data intelligently and be prepared to respond to changes that influence consumer preferences and behaviour as well as to be proactive and try to influence that behaviour.

Environmental scanning

This is the systematic collection and evaluation of information from the wider marketing environment that might affect the organization and its strategic marketing activities. It is undertaken by marketing planners.

Key issues are:

o Making sure that data is up to date, particularly for markets that are volatile and where consumer behaviour can change quickly.

o The ability to identify what is significant amongst a myriad of detail. It is important not to drown in a sea of information.

o Collecting data on a regular basis may be too expensive for an organization to undertake itself, but the data that is available to purchase from market research analysts may not be specific enough about particular markets and products.

o Marketing managers need to be able to understand the environment in which they are operating.

Marketing analysis tools

Analysis tools commonly used for this purpose are PESTLE, Porter's five force analysis, gap analysis, BCG matrix, GE matrix and so on.

A PESTLE (Political/Policy, Economic, Social/Societal, Technological, Legal and Environmental) analysis is a logical framework for identifying and assessing the various influences on the present and future development of the organization. It is usually a precursor to developing a SWOT analysis of the internal strengths and weaknesses of the organization compared with the opportunities and constraints in the external environment.

Political factors – Such as changes in government and the ramifications of their strategies such as tax levels, education and training issues, employment legislation and so on. Any changes in policy – impact on strategic direction – timing? Change of government, policy changes, legislative foreign exchange, taxation policy, interest rates, funding sources and exports.

Economic factors – Such as the impact of the trade cycle, levels of disposable income and inflation. Typical questions are:

- o What are the effects of competitors (their products, services, technologies) on your operation?
- o What major developments in income, prices, savings, taxation and credit will affect the organization?

Social/cultural issues – Such as the ageing consumer, increases in one-parent families, changing values, attitudes and beliefs to smoking.

Typical questions to ask are:

- o What population trends are expected to affect existing and planned strategy?
- o What social and psychological patterns (attitudes, lifestyle, etc.) are expected to affect buyer behaviour patterns? How are environmental trends monitored?
- o How are present and pending legal developments affecting your operation?

Technological factors – Such as the increased rate of computer capability, production methods, information management, privacy of data, reliability, updates on technology, protection of intellectual property, ease of transferring funds with technology.

Legal issues – Such as changes in advertising legislation for tobacco, regulations and codes of practice for promotions and so on.

Environmental issues – Kyoto protocol, biodiversity, climate change, desertification, nuclear test ban, ozone layer protection, safety and health, cultural heritage of the land, environmentally responsible corporate citizens, attitudes towards pollution, energy use, fair trade, slave labour and so on.

The following case study is an extract from a PESTLE analysis carried out by a national training organization that was faced with the loss of government grant and the need to become a commercial organization dependent on winning contracts.

The future development of a training organization: PEST analysis

Political issues

Learning and skills are regarded as central to economic growth and prosperity, and are underpinned by government resources.

Employers are central to the Government's agenda but UK employer networks and institutions are weak, limiting opportunities for information sharing, best practice and collaboration.

The environment of audit inspection, information and regulation will become more intense and sophisticated. Developing standards, benchmarks and quality assurance procedures will continue to be important.

Economic issues

Globalization

There will be global markets in skilled workers as well as in investment and trade. Taking advantage of globalization will require people who are able to access the resources of other people and organizations around the world.

Flexible labour markets

Non-standard employment, that is part-time work, flexi-hours, self-employment and home working will become more common.

The information economy

The information economy will be a small business; entrepreneurial economy and small firms will become more important. Knowledge is seen as a resource by businesses, governments and individuals.

Social issues

Skills

UK labour productivity currently lags behind that of other major industrialized countries. The need for 'softer skills' such as communication and team working is likely to increase because of flatter structures, more team-based operations, greater diversification of job roles and other changes to the workplace.

Demography

Young and skilled people are becoming a scarce resource, particularly in countries with tight labour markets. There is an ageing workforce.

Qualifications

A significant number of individuals and employers are not engaging with the qualifications system at all.

Developing the supply side of training

In a demand-led system, private providers, voluntary sector providers and companies' in-house training facilities will be able to compete with public sector providers.

Technological

Technological developments will mean that the provision of education and learning will become more diffuse, informal and user-driven. The Internet's use as a source of information and education will grow significantly.

SWOT analysis

This should be a summary of the marketing audit and indicate the key issues which need then to be considered further.

SWOT stands for Strengths Weaknesses Opportunities Threats.

Strengths

Every organization has some strength. In some cases this is obvious, for example dominant market shares. In other cases, it is a matter of perspective, for instance a company is very small and hence has the ability to move fast. It is important to note that companies that are in a bad position also have strengths. Whether these strengths are adequate is an issue for analysis.

Weaknesses

Every organization also has some weakness. In some cases, this is obvious; say, for example, a stricter regulatory environment. In other cases, it is a matter of perspective, for example a company has 99 per cent market share and is open to attack from every new player. It is important to note that companies that are extremely competent in what they do also have weaknesses. How badly these weaknesses will affect the company is a matter of analysis.

Opportunities

All organizations have some opportunities that they can gain from. These could range from diversification to sale of operations. Identifying hidden opportunities is the mark of an astute analyst.

Threats

No organization is immune to threats. These could be internal, such as falling productivity. Or they could be external, such as lower priced international competition.

A SWOT analysis is undertaken to help plan the marketing mix, which includes:

- Strengths of the product/service/organization
- Weaknesses of the organization
- Opportunities available to the organization (external factors)
- Threats which may come from the competition.

One way to improve upon the basic SWOT is to include more detailed competitor and business environment information in the analysis. SWOT analysis can also be augmented through surveys, for example customer awareness, interest, trial and usage levels.

SWOT analysis Starbucks

Strengths

Starbucks Corporation is a very profitable organization, earning in excess of $600 million in 2004. The company generated revenues of more than $5000 million in the same year.

It is a global coffee brand built upon a reputation for fine products and services. It has almost 9000 cafes in almost 40 countries.

Starbucks was one of the *Fortune Top 100 Companies to Work For* in 2005. The company is a respected employer that values its workforce.

The organization has strong ethical values and an ethical mission statement as follows: 'Starbucks is committed to a role of environmental leadership in all facets of our business.'

Weaknesses

Starbucks has a reputation for new product development and creativity. However, they remain vulnerable to the possibility that their innovation may falter over time.

The organization has a strong presence in the United States of America with more than three-quarters of their cafes located in the home market. It is often argued that they need to look for a portfolio of countries, in order to spread business risk.

The organization is dependent on a main competitive advantage, the retail trade of coffee. This could make them slow to diversify into other sectors should the need arise.

Opportunities

Starbucks are very good at taking advantage of opportunities.

In 2004, the company created a CD-burning service in their Santa Monica (California, USA) cafe with Hewlett Packard, where customers create their own music CD.

New products and services that can be retailed in their cafes, such as Fair Trade products.

The company has the opportunity to expand its global operations. New markets for coffee such as India and the Pacific Rim nations are beginning to emerge.

Co-branding with other manufacturers of food and drink, and brand franchising to manufacturers of other goods and services both have potential.

Threats

Who knows if the market for coffee will grow and stay in favour with customers, or whether another type of beverage or leisure activity will replace coffee in the future?

Starbucks are exposed to rises in the cost of coffee and dairy products.

Since its conception in Pine Place Park, Seattle, in 1971, Starbucks' success has led to the market entry of many competitors and copycat brands that pose potential threats.

Starbucks' mission statement is 'Establish Starbucks as the premier purveyor of the finest coffee in the world while maintaining our uncompromising principles while we grow.'

Gap analysis

A gap analysis is something which needs to be monitored and considered in terms of filling the gap, should one occur. A gap is where corporate sales and financial objectives are greater than the current long-range forecasts in marketing planning. A gap could be filled in various ways, for example by improving productivity, reducing costs, increasing prices, stimulating increased usage, increasing market share, finding new user groups, developing new market segments and by product development.

The marketing audit should ensure that the method chosen to fill the gap is consistent with the company's capabilities and builds on its strengths. For example, it would normally prove far less profitable for a dry goods grocery manufacturer to introduce frozen foods than to add another dry goods product. Likewise, if a product could be sold to existing channels using the existing sales force, this is far less risky than introducing a new product that requires new channels and new selling skills.

Marketing objectives

Corporate objectives are derived from the corporate plan, and inform the direction and focus of the marketing plan. Marketing objectives cover issues such as increasing the awareness of your product or service among your target audience within a particular time frame. The marketing objectives are likely to be linked to market share or sales targets. Long-, medium- and short-term objectives should be identified, some of which should be SMART. Examples of objectives are:

1. *Profitability objectives* – To achieve a 25 per cent return on capital employed by August 2007.
2. *Market share objectives* – To gain 30 per cent of the market for umbrellas by September 2006.
3. *Promotional objectives* – To increase awareness of the dangers of hepatitis to travellers from 15 to 30 per cent by April 2005.
4. *Objectives for survival* – To survive the current double-dip recession.
5. *Objectives for growth* – To increase the size of our operation from $200 000 in 2002 to $400 000 in 2003.
6. *Objectives for branding* – To make Y brand of bottled beer the preferred brand of 21–28-year-old females in North America by February 2006.

Goals and aims tend to be more vague and focus on the longer term compared with objectives. They will not be SMART.

Marketing mix decisions

The strategy will inform the decisions in relation to pricing, product, place, promotion and the extended Ps – people, process and physical evidence. Here, the marketing communications plan will be developed. This enables the organization to meet the needs of its target markets and achieve its marketing objectives. Consideration should be given to each of the areas of the 'four Ps' plus customer considerations in terms of segmentation, targeting and positioning. All parts of the marketing mix should work together to achieve an organization's objectives. This part of the plan is concerned with who will do what and how it will be done. In this way responsibility, accountability and action over a specific time period can be planned, scheduled, implemented and reviewed. Budget decisions will need to be taken throughout the strategic and operational areas of the plan. Marketing mix decisions describe how you intend achieving your marketing objectives. It is, essentially, the heart of your marketing plan and covers the 4 Ps of marketing.

Product – Describe your product or service in detail. Include product features and benefits.

Price – Describe your pricing strategy and payment policies. There are a range of approaches to pricing strategies considering cost, volume and profit.

There are four key factors that affect pricing decisions, also known as the 4 Cs:

1. *Cost* – Related to the actual costs involved
2. *Consumer/customer* – Related to the price the consumer will pay
3. *Competition* – Related to competitors' prices for substitute or complementary products
4. *Company* – Related to the company's financial objectives.

Promotion – Describe the promotional tools or tactics (a promotion plan) you will use to accomplish your marketing objectives (see Unit 8).

To sell an offering it must be effectively promoted and advertised. There are two basic promotion strategies, PUSH and PULL.

o The PUSH strategy maximizes the use of all available channels of distribution to 'push' the offering into the marketplace. This usually requires generous discounts to achieve the objective of giving the channels incentive to promote the offering, thus minimizing your need for advertising.
o The PULL strategy requires direct interface with the end-user of the offering. Use of channels of distribution is minimized during the first stages of promotion and a major commitment to advertising is required. The objective is to 'pull' the prospects into the various channel outlets creating a demand the channels cannot ignore.

There are many strategies for advertising an offering. Some of these include:

o Product comparison advertising – In a market where your offering is one of several providing similar capabilities, if your offering stacks up well when comparing features then a product comparison ad can be beneficial.
o Product benefits advertising – When you want to promote your offering without comparison to competitors, the product benefits ad is the correct approach. This is especially beneficial when you have introduced a new approach to solving a user need and comparison to the old approaches is inappropriate.

225

○ Product family advertising – If your offering is part of a group or family of offerings that can be of benefit to the customer as a set, then the product family ad can be of benefit.

○ Corporate advertising – When you have a variety of offerings and your audience is fairly broad, it is often beneficial to promote your enterprise identity rather than a specific offering.

Of course, making a decision about pricing, promotion and distribution is heavily influenced by some key factors in the industry and marketplace. These factors should be analysed initially to create the strategy and then regularly monitored for changes. If any of them change substantially the strategy should be re-evaluated.

Place – Describe how and where you will place your product so that customers have access to it and how you will make the sale – your sales and distribution methods.

These could include:

○ On-premise Sales involve the sale of your offering using a field sales organization that visits the prospect's facilities to make the sale.

○ Direct Sales involve the sale of your offering using a direct, in-house sales organization that does all the selling through the Internet, telephone or mail order contact.

○ Wholesale Sales involve the sale of your offering using intermediaries or 'middle-men' to distribute your product or service to the retailers.

○ Self-service Retail Sales involve the sale of your offering using self-service retail methods of distribution.

○ Full-service Retail Sales involve the sale of your offering through a full-service retail distribution channel.

Action plan – Describes what will be done, when it will begin or be completed and who will accomplish the tasks.

Budget – Lists the cost of the marketing activities you are describing in the marketing plan.

Measurements – Describes the specific numerical targets that will be used to measure the results of implementing your plan. Control involves setting standards and comparing progress against them. Corrective action needs to be taken if it looks like the standards would not be met. Includes time limits for achieving goals.

Monitoring and control – The plan will need to identify the methods of monitoring and evaluating the plan. Decides which controls are important, how they should be implemented and who should be involved.

Control factors – There are four main areas where control mechanisms should be considered within the marketing plan. These are listed below:

○ *Management control* – This includes areas such as performance appraisal for staff and the workforce, benchmarking procedures and so on against other organizations.

○ *Financial control* – This includes financial controls which most companies are adept at calculating. It could include trend analysis, comparison, liquidity ratios, debt ratios, activity ratios and so on.

○ *Efficiency control* – Here, this area considers the optimum value from marketing assets.

○ *Strategic control* – The easiest method of control is to measure marketing activities against market performance or objectives set.

Some organizations group their analysis into the following areas.

Financial analysis

This would include ratio analysis, variance analysis, cash flow monitoring and capital expenditure monitoring. Financial analysis of competitors is relatively easy to perform because the financial accounts should be readily available. The main problems arise when the competitor is a division of a major corporation, and is not a limited company in its own right, and so is not obliged to publish its accounts, or when the company is present in markets where accurate financial reporting is not in evidence.

Market analysis

This would cover analysis of total market demand and market share. Market share information may not be as easily obtainable, although most organizations have access to some means of measuring this, such as through marketing database companies, market research periodicals, trade associations and journals.

Sales analysis

Analysis of sales targets and selling cost budgets. As with market share, this information may not be easily obtainable. Checking out the effectiveness of a marketing campaign from a product sales standpoint is critical. Begin the review process early and repeat it often. The plan can be tweaked along the way to eliminate or shift schedules if some element of the mix is not working.

Physical resource analysis

This would involve analysis of plant and equipment utilization together with other measures of productivity and product quality. Operational effectiveness, for example process technology, people, information systems and so on, impacts on operational efficiency. This affects costs and business performance, including the speed and efficiency of service, customer perception, quality and reliability of product or service and warranty claims.

Systems analysis

The effectiveness of strategic implementation and analysis of marketing resource applications.

Companies may benchmark best practice at different levels of the organization in a variety of ways:

- o In an organization in another industry
- o Internally, for example comparing operations in business units in different locations
- o With competitors, though they may be unwilling to share the secrets of their success.

The way an organization prioritizes these factors has a bearing on its performance.

This leads to the following questions:

- Which factors are absent from your organization? Do these need further investigation?
- Which factors do competitors pay more attention to, compared to your organization, and why?
- Which factors are given low priority by your organization? Do these indicate areas for improvement?

Assumptions and contingency plans

Assumptions relate to external factors over which the company has little control and should be as few as possible. For each assumption, a contingency plan should be formulated. They should consist of a sentence or two that gives a general indication of what would happen if assumptions prove to be incorrect.

Budget resources and staffing

Budgeting covers general marketing expenditure and salaries and expenses for staffing. If the plan is based on increasing sales and market share this will normally have resource implications for the marketing department, perhaps in terms of more representation or increased advertising costs. Financial considerations might well cause the organization to tone down its original marketing objectives.

Timescales

Most plans are for a period of 1 year but a plan must also contain timescales which detail marketing activities normally on a month by month, or a quarter by quarter, basis. However, longer-term issues can also be addressed in the marketing plan. This will mean different things in different business sectors. In the case of technology long term may not be longer than 3 years, whereas in car production long term may mean 10 years or more. When long-term planning is addressed as part of a marketing plan it is usually a directional marketing plan which does not contain a lot of detail. Some companies have rolling plans that are modified in the light of experience. As one planning period finishes (1 month, 1 quarter, 1 year) the rolling plan will be modified in the light of what has happened and a further planning period will be added on to the end of the plan.

Implement the plan

The plan is now put into action. Those who are involved in implementation need to know what part they must play in its implementation to ensure its success.

Measure and control

The marketing information system provides information from market intelligence, marketing research and the organization's own internal accounting system. It can also be a control mechanism because customer reactions are also fed into this MkIS from market intelligence through the field sales force or from marketing research studies. Information on sales analyses is also fed into the system so assessments can be made as to whether forecasted sales are being achieved or not. The plan should be reviewed on a regular and controlled basis and then updated as circumstances change. Such controls can address the tactics in terms of sales analyses that will commence with a comparison of budgeted sales revenue against actual sales revenue. Variations might be due to volume or price variances.

Tools for monitoring and control

Control involves setting standards, measurement, evaluation and monitoring. Resources are scarce and costly so it is important to control marketing plans. A marketing manager will compare actual progress against the standards. Corrective action (if any) is then taken and an investigation undertaken to establish precisely why the difference or variance occurred.

There are many tools to help with control and monitoring:

- Market share analysis
- Sales analysis
- Budgets
- Marketing information systems (MkIS) and Customer relationship management (CRM) systems. See Unit 6
- Feedback from customer satisfaction surveys
- Cash-flow statements
- Performance of any promotional activities.

Tracking procedures

This section of the plan should include plans and procedures for tracking each type of media you are using and which seems to be the most effective.

Display advertising – With traditional consumer publications, tracking can be done through the use of different phone numbers, special offers (specific to that advertisement or publication) or reference to a specific department to call for information.

Many trade publications also include Reader Service Cards that allow the reader to circle a number that corresponds to your ad on a mail-in postcard in order to get more information about your product or service.

Direct marketing – With postal mailings, tracking is relatively simple. Include on the mailing label a code (called a key code or a source code) that corresponds with the mailing list. For telemarketing campaigns, tracking is also relatively simple since someone is communicating with the customer throughout the entire process in most cases.

Internet marketing – Usually this is easily tracked because it is based on click throughs or page impressions.

Promotions – Most closed promotions are basically 'self-tracking' because they require the customer to do something such as fill out an entry form (trackable), turn in a coupon, return a rebate slip (trackable), or log on to a website to claim a prize (also trackable).

Supporting documentation

Include any supporting documents referenced in other plan sections here, such as CVs or key management resumés, spreadsheets, market research results and so on.

Activity 7.1

Read and compare the case studies below and critically appraise them as marketing plans. They differ from each other in some respects. Your task is to decide whether these differences are because the organizations are different in size and so on and serve different markets with different products and services, or is it because of differences in the usefulness and comprehensiveness of the plan?

Would either of the plans benefit from some of the strengths of the other plan, or is the same level of detail not necessary for both plans?

Use the components of a marketing plan from above and decide:

- Are there components that have not been used in one plan which would improve the other plan if they were included?
- What gaps are there in the plans?
- How could either or both plans be improved?

Case study 1 – Diamond badges

Marketing plan

The following marketing plan is written by the solo owner of a small business. Names of some businesses and cities have been fictionalized at the owner's request.

Mission statement

Technically, the mission statement is in the opening of the entire business plan, of which the marketing plan is a part. It is included here for the reader's information.

Diamond intends to supply Oxford with the most visually interesting badges available today. They will delight their users and provide a springboard for creative activity. Diamond believes artistic expression enhances life. It appreciates the skill of human hands and the sensitivity of human hearts. It regards badges as small works of art in which we are able to see ourselves.

Diamond's marketing plan

Diamond is a specialty retail store offering a collection of antique, contemporary and hand-crafted badges from around the world. These badges are distinguished from those available in the marketplace by the quality of materials, workmanship and design.

Diamond addresses the need to have fun! Badges are wonderfully expressive objects that add unexpected vitality to clothing. Apparel manufacturers are witnessing a competitive advantage to using fun and distinctive badges.

With growth, Diamond will also establish a working studio.

Diamond opened for business on 5 August 1999, with an inventory valued at £2050. In the first 8 months of operation, another £2290 of inventory was added. Sales totalled £2376 for the same period with the average monthly total being £172. Sales have increased steadily over this 8-month period.

Organizations and businesses served include:

o Oxford Badgemakers Guild
o Badge for Profit of Oxford
o Intercom Designers
o The Workroom.

Funding for the company has come from the personal income of the sole proprietor and from the income generated by sales. Additional funding is sought for the expansion of inventory and for advertising.

Product or service description

Diamond offers hand-crafted and manufactured badges in a range of materials and finishes. A high percentage of these badges are made of natural materials such as horn, bone, wood, glass and clay. These badges are hand-crafted by artisans throughout the world and are of original design. Manufactured metal and synthetic badges are also offered, together with a collection of vintage and antique badges.

Badges are often purchased for their beauty, and collections of antique badges represent a significant investment and historical rise in value.

Location

Diamond is located in Oxford on the second floor of the Tower Building. With growth, it would like to relocate to the building's south end. The benefits of this location are first floor access, room for expansion, higher visibility from large arched windows, more convenient parking, closer proximity to area retailers and reasonable cost.

Market analysis

The industry

According to the British Badgemakers Craft Association, the home badge-making industry contributes £2.5 million in retail sales to the economy. In the 5 years from 1995 to 2002, first-time buyers of badge-making machines increased from 40 to 55 per cent. In the last 5 years (1991–1996), membership in the British Badgemakers Guild has doubled in size with a 55 per cent increase in the number of local chapters. Today's badge-making is technologically advanced and computer memories have also enhanced the creative potential of the badge-making machine.

Badge-making is one of several creative industries served by Diamond. As this country reassesses its priorities, home-oriented leisure activities enjoy increased levels of interest.

The target market

The Badgemaker's profile, as reported by the British Home Badge-making and Craft Association, looks like:

o 75 per cent female
o 35–64 years of age
o household income of £35 000 and more
o artistic, values originality.

231

This profile is supported by direct observation of Diamond's customers.

People who pursue the creative industries value objects made by hand, and purchase them for themselves, their friends and their families. They are deeply involved in home-based leisure activities such as reading and gardening. Badges are used increasingly in the home as an element of interest and design.

The competition

Direct competitors exist in three nearby cities. They are the badge factory, a high-end of the market shop located in York and two badge shops in Bath – Antique Badges and Renewal Badges. The strength of these competitors lies in the length of time they have been in business. Awareness of their product is well established.

Badges are displayed prominently at Diamond in a manner consistent with their quality and character. Again, Diamond will compete by focusing on badges. The company will also compete on the basis of location.

Antique Badges and Renewal Badges offer a product impressive in its range of quality, price and character. They are both centrally located and are the model upon which Diamond patterns itself.

Diamond will entice fans away from these shops by diligently procuring badges of high originality. Independent badgesmiths will be showcased whenever possible. Diamond will also maintain a large collection of vintage and antique badges. Indirect competition comes from Northeast Fabrics. Diamond offers badges that cannot be found in these stores and they are priced generally higher. Diamond will attract customers who may be willing to spend more on badges than on fabric to achieve a higher level of style and expression.

Promotional objectives and strategies

One of the greatest challenges facing Diamond in its first year of operation is lack of awareness. At this time, the customer base is 200 people. The company's goal is to double this number over the months of June through October for an overall goal of 400 customers.

Strategies for achieving this goal include:

- Establishing an auxiliary sales display at the local farmer's market on Saturdays throughout the summer. This can be done at a cost of £110.
- Distributing business cards and reprints of an article about Diamond which appeared in *Lifelike Magazine*. Distribution points will be the farmer's market, the Arts Alive Gallery and the Underground Studio.
- Publishing a quarterly newsletter to existing customers and selected businesses. The newsletter will solicit referrals, advertise additions to inventory and notify readers of current sales promotions.
- Establishing quarterly sales promotions in May, August, November and February.
- The April sales promotion will be in honour of Mother's Day. Customers will be treated to an afternoon tea; discounted gift certificates for mothers will be offered.
- November will focus on year-end festivities.
- February will highlight Valentine's Day.
- Advertising in the newsletters of the Woodbrook Weavers, the Oxford Guild. Costs range in the area of £10 per issue.
- Continuing to advertise in the Yellow Pages at a cost of £15.75 per month.

o   Another goal which Diamond needs to address is that of building inventory. Summer months will allow a greater portion of the company's resources to be directed towards augmenting inventory.
o   Diamond will advertise in the area weeklies, such as *Retreat*, as wanting to buy old badges.
o   Diamond will solicit handmade badges by advertising in the 'Opportunities' section of *The Art Calendar* as a consignor.

Pricing policy

Three categories of badges are purchased by Diamond for resale. They are hand-crafted badges, manufactured badges and antique badges. The standard industry mark-up is 100 per cent.

The average retail price of hand-crafted and antique badges is £4.25. Manufactured badges range in price from £1.45 to £2.00, depending on what material is used. Badges of natural materials are more expensive.

Case study 2 – Stormbreaker

Stormbreaker is a small but profitable company in the extremely competitive sportswear market. In order to grow and become even more profitable, it needs to expand its products to a wider market and consider segmenting specific areas of the marketplace. In 2000, Stormbreaker introduced a fully waterproof, fully breathable outer clothing system, virtually eliminating the condensation problems normally associated with waterproof clothing.

Turnover in 2000/2001 was £16 million, with a net profit of £182 500. The R&D investment is £250 000 with other costs being covered by co-operation with suppliers and customers.

The market environment

It is clear that many individuals will have specialist sports shoes for specialist sports (tennis, running, cycling, etc.). There are many other companies that are now well established in this market. Some specialize in sportswear alone, unlike Stormbreaker, who have a wide range of sports shoes and sportswear.

Distribution

Stormbreaker has recently been considering some options regarding the way their goods reach the final consumer. Most of the goods are actually sold through specialist retail outlets and catalogues to whom they supply leaflets and posters.

With the advent of e-commerce and the possibility of expanding their network, the company has recently been considering web-based activities much more seriously.

Stormbreaker continues to be highly active in pioneering the use of new materials in their product range. The use of 'smart' materials is particularly interesting them at present. The development of heating and cooling the wearer, utilizing specially bonded fabrics, is currently being explored.

SWOT analysis

Strengths
o Good brand
o Good range of outdoor items
o Specialist products
o New waterproof material
o Good TV exposure and PR in general
o Innovative organization.

Weaknesses
o Not well known
o R&D base small
o Marketing and branding budget too small
o Manufacturing UK-oriented
o Limited range.

Opportunities
o Expand manufacturing base
o Creating strategic alliances with companies that have produced new materials and used chip technology
o More expenditure on marketing and PR
o Segmentation and targeting.

Threats
o New entrants with products based on chip technology
o Aggressive branding by more established companies
o Me-too products.

PESTLE analysis

Political

There are hardly any political issues impinging on the company. The only thing it needs to consider is the possible ethical impact of manufacturing in the Far East. If they handle this sensitively and well, then they will be able to use this in their marketing strategies.

Economic

The possible plateauing of running shoe sales. Also, any impending recession will mean that consumers will rein back spending on possible luxury items.

Social

Society is ageing ... certainly in Europe. In considering marketing strategies, the company will have to take into account grey buying power and its impact on their marketing segmentation policies.

Technological

The technology for sports clothing is continuously developing and improving. In the long run, one can see how 'computerized/smart' materials-based clothing will come into being. Various information links within the case show how this technology is evolving. Technological changes are likely to have a far-reaching impact on the company's sportswear. They need to scan the environment continuously to monitor these changes.

Legal

Not too important, unless they produce substandard goods or infringe copyright.

Environmental

This usually relates to the production of the sportswear, whether it is environmentally friendly or not. This does not appear to be an issue for Stormbreaker.

However, their products allow a person to visit previously unexplored places, which affects the environment.

Porter's five forces analysis

Porter explains that there are five forces that determine industry attractiveness and long-run industry profitability. These five 'competitive forces' are:

1. The threat of entry of new competitors (new entrants)
2. The threat of substitutes
3. The bargaining power of buyers
4. The bargaining power of suppliers
5. The degree of rivalry between existing competitors.

Threat of new entrants

This could be a significant issue for Stormbreaker. New entrants could appear:

o Through the Web
o New brand development by some of the major companies: for example, Boots introduced their Botanics range to compete with Bodyshop products.

Power of suppliers

Supplier power largely depends on their strength in bargaining. It appears that this is not a significant issue for Stormbreaker, as the main items of use are leather and other generic materials.

Many new items such as self-wicking clothing are developed by the company itself, or in co-operation with suppliers.

Power of buyers

This is a significant area for Stormbreaker to consider and also impacts on the generic strategies they adopt (see later questions).

The customers have considerable power – whether they are the end-consumers or the retailers.

Threat of substitutes

The threat of substitutes is forever present. 'Smart' materials and 'computerized' clothing accessories could be the future for outdoor pursuits. The company, however, may not have enough R&D clout to undertake product development in this area.

Rivalry between firms

The market is *very* competitive.

Product	Stage of the product life cycle
'Smart' clothing	Introduction
Clothing and accessories	Growth
Walking and climbing boots	Maturity
Sports shoes and football boots	Decline

To gain a deeper understanding of the issues and factors affecting planning and control for Stormbreaker, utilize the following as the basis for your group discussions.

- o Product life-cycle analysis
- o The Ansoff Matrix
- o The General Electric Matrix
- o Innovation/Value Matrix
- o The BCG Matrix
- o Core Competencies
- o Gap analysis.

The life-cycle model helps to show how a product may grow and then eventually decline. The Adopter Categorization of innovators, early and late majority and laggards should also be considered in conjunction with this model. Decline is not inevitable and a number of companies halted their decline in sales in the mid-1980s by repositioning their brand and revitalizing their offer to the consumer. Improved marketing and product development, and more investment can help to halt decline.

		Products	
		Existing	**New**
Markets	*Existing*	Football/Running shoes Climbing/Walking boots Accessories/clothing	New waterproof attire Elasticated clothing 'Smart' clothing
	New	Clothing for cyclists	'Smart' clothing for different markets, including the health market

Figure 7.1 Ansoff Matrix for Stormbreaker

In Igor Ansoff's model, strategy is designed to transform the firm from the present position to the position described by the objectives, subject to the constraints of the capabilities and the potential of the organization. This model emphasizes two concepts. Gap analysis is designed to evaluate the difference between the current position of the firm and its objectives. The organization chooses the strategy that closes the gap. Synergy refers to the idea that firms must seek a combined performance that is greater than the sum of its parts, more commonly known as '2 + 2 = 5' formula.

This analysis helps identify whether the company actually has competences within attractive sectors.

Figure 7.2 Industry/Product Matrix for Stormbreaker (General Electric Matrix)

	New waterproof clothing	
Pioneers Value Innovate **Stormbreaker's position** Boots		
Migrators Improve value		Repositioning of products and businesses (high growth trajectory)
Settlers Me-too businesses		
	Current Portfolio	Planned Portfolio

Figure 7.3 The Innovation/Value Matrix

Stormbreaker needs to consider the Innovation/Value Matrix in terms of the possible threats from the me-too and migrator competitors. If it is to keep its lead then it must innovate. Its large R&D budget is indicative of this. The dotted arrow shows the threat from me-too companies. It is important for Stormbreaker to protect its innovations with a patent.

BCG Matrix

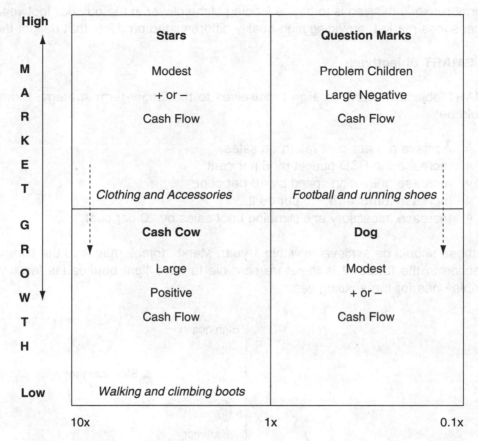

Figure 7.4 Boston Matrix

A possible BCG analysis is presented for Stormbreaker, taking into account industry growth and potential growth for Stormbreaker products. In undertaking this analysis, it would be hopeless to consider the whole market. We have to make the assumption that Stormbreaker is competing within a small sector of the specialist market and therefore the idea of a market share actually makes some sense! The potential trajectories for the products are shown in the matrix.

Market share

In addition to this, it is useful to gauge what products/markets meet the above criteria. Whatever strategy Stormbreaker undertakes, these criteria should be met to ensure continued success in the marketplace. The above analyses show the positioning of the company *vis-à-vis* its product portfolio and market attractiveness. You could continue analysing a company's situation *ad nauseum*, ending up with paralysis through analysis. You should consider issues such as available time and the most relevant models. From these analyses, Stormbreaker has several potential routes that it could follow. The route chosen will depend on the strategies that it is likely to follow.

(a) Possible mission statement

Stormbreaker's mission is to be the leading niche player in the outdoor footwear, clothing and accessories market, providing high-quality differentiated products that delight the customer.

(b) SMART objectives

SMART objectives have to align themselves to the longer-term strategy. Examples of these would be:

o Achieve a 5 per cent return on sales
o Increase the R&D budget by 5 per cent
o Increase marketing spend by 10 per cent
o Increase turnover by 10 per cent
o Increase accessory and climbing boot sales by 20 per cent.

All these should be achievable within 1 year. Market forces may lead the company to change direction in the future. It is therefore sensible to have tight boundaries for 1 year and more flexible ones for the ensuing years.

Figure 7.5

(c) Possible option for Stormbreaker to follow

o Drop the football and running shoe market
o Expand research into 'smart' clothing technology (computerized clothing)
o Consider a strategic alliance
o Concentrate on pushing forward the focused strategy (Porter)
o Improve return on sales by concentrating on the most profitable items
o Develop a communications plan that fits with the strategies adopted.

The company could decide to follow all these options or some of them, depending on its resource base. A differentiated strategy, with more manufacturing taking place in the Far East, would certainly help to increase its market share, but would it then have a negative impact on its specialist market? Once an option has been decided and the strategy set, actions need to be considered. For instance:

- Dropping the football and running shoe market will mean considerable loss in revenue.
- No one can predict the potential market for 'smart' clothing. A basic calculator now has more computing power than the Apollo spacecraft which landed on the moon in 1969. Mobile phones, smart cards, digital cameras and many more everyday items are the results of continuing developments in, and combinations of, technology.
- Alliances are usually within distribution networks for the sports and clothing industry. Whilst Stormbreaker collaborates with suppliers in the development of materials, it does not have a sufficient volume of output to have exclusive use of such materials. Stormbreaker gains a reputation for innovation from these relationships.
- Concentrating on the more profitable items can improve return on sales, but not always. Porsche improved their position by cutting back on diversity in the mid-1990s and improved their position considerably. Triumph motorcycles withdrew from the smaller bike market in the 1970s. The consequent loss of 'novice' customers led to a decline in sales of larger bikes.

Stormbreaker should not only set targets and measure performance against them, but should also benchmark these against the industry, specific competitors and best practice. Any aspect of the business can be benchmarked, providing opportunities for measurement and improvement at the tactical and local level. From this comparison, the essential attributes for delivering value to customers can be derived.

Activity 7.2

Implementation

It is important to schedule the events in your plan and assign responsibilities for implementation. Using some of the components of a marketing plan above and previous chapters in the book, draw up a simple action plan for implementing the Stormbreaker marketing plan. Try using a Gantt chart to schedule the activities.

Pay particular attention to who should be involved in the implementation. Identify the positions of people involved, for example finance manager, marketing manager and so on.

The plan should include information about:

- What needs to be done (tasks and activities)
- Who needs to do it (assembling the team)
- When does it need to be done (scheduling).

Summary

This unit has provided examples of marketing plans and demonstrated that there is no uniform pattern. However, there are key issues that a marketing plan needs to address even if the formats are sometimes different.

Hints and tips

In an exam context you may not have time to go into great detail so an outline marketing plan with some elements described in detail might be the most appropriate strategy. Remember that any tools that are used need to be applied to the context. There are no marks just for knowing about different models. Application of knowledge is the key activity.

Past examination papers for the Marketing Management in Practice module can be found in Appendix 5.

unit 8 marketing communications and customer service

Learning objectives

- ° Plan the design, development, execution and evaluation of communications campaigns by a team of marketers, including external agencies and suppliers (5.1).

- ° Use appropriate marketing communications to develop relationships or to communicate with a range of stakeholders (5.2).

- ° Manage and monitor the provision of effective customer service (5.3).

- ° Use marketing communications to provide support for members of a marketing channel (5.4).

- ° Use marketing communications techniques for an internal marketing plan to support management of change within an organization (5.5).

- ° Review and evaluate the effectiveness of communications activities and the role of the individual and the team in this process (5.6).

Glossary

Communications mix – This refers to the way in which a company allocates its marketing budget between the various communications media. It would include deciding on how much of the budget to allocate to the print, radio, visual and other forms of communications media.

Customer service – The set of behaviours that a business undertakes during its interaction with its customers. It can also refer to a specific person or desk which is set up to provide general assistance to customers.

Direct marketing – Sales and promotion technique in which the promotional materials are delivered individually to potential customers via direct mail, telemarketing, door-to-door selling or other direct means.

Introduction

Marketing communications strategy is concerned with how an organization can successfully communicate and deliver its marketing strategy. The Marketing Communications units of the CIM syllabus are intended to provide the skills and knowledge that enable marketers to manage marketing communications and brand support activities within organizations. The Marketing Management in Practice Module builds on the underpinning knowledge developed in the CIM Marketing Communications module.

The communications mix

Sometimes referred to as the promotional mix, the communications mix lists all of the communications tools available to a marketer:

1. Selling
2. Advertising
3. Sales promotion
4. Direct marketing
5. Publicity (and public relations)
6. Sponsorship
7. Exhibitions
8. Packaging
9. Point-of-sale and merchandising
10. Word of mouth
11. E-marketing
12. Corporate identity.

Different types of enterprise put different emphases on certain communications tools. An FMCG manufacturer is likely to put greater emphasis on advertising, packaging, sales promotion and point-of-sale while an industrial machine manufacturer may consider selling, exhibitions and word of mouth to be the most important.

Formats for a marketing communications plan

There are a range of formats that can be used for developing a marketing communications plan. The following is an example from a university:

Deciding where, when and how to get the right message to the right audience at the right time is the essence of a marketing communications plan. The plan is a tool to promote an event, unit or activity and is based on the following fundamentals:

o Targeted audience
o Perceived university image
o Overall marketing strategy
o Results/expected outcome
o Resources available and capabilities
o Timing of these activities
o Measuring results.

Checklist to complete a Marketing Communications Plan

Do your homework – Before you contact your account executive to begin planning, assemble the relevant background information for review. Think through your key messages and audiences, timeline, budget, challenges, resources, measurable goals, sources to contact and what you want accomplished.

Plan – Meet with your account executive and other appropriate personnel to think through communications strategies linked to the university's marketing goals, past efforts and external factors.

Assign responsibilities – Determine who will communicate all vital information, facilitate meetings among key staff, faculty and students and ensure timely approvals and reviews through plan completion.

Write – Determine who will gather information, read reports, interview key sources, review what has been done and how project relates to the university marketing goals.

Approve plan – Identify who will edit, update and approve the plan at various administrative levels.

Assign responsibilities – Determine who will carry out the plan's tactics on time, on budget and within university identity and style compliance and ensure payment of services.

Distribute – Send plan to all appropriate personnel.

Evaluate – Track, monitor and evaluate plan's effectiveness and distribute evaluation. Ensure goals are successfully met.

Source: http://www.map.wayne.edu/checklists/marketing.pdf.

Designing a communications campaign

A communications campaign is the dissemination of messages using appropriate channels, to a well-defined audience in order to educate and create an informed public. Designing and implementing a communications campaign could be carried out entirely in-house, or it could be devolved to an agency, or the campaign could involve a combination of internal and external input. Obviously the size of the campaign and that of the budget, as well as its aims and objectives, will be important factors in determining which approach to use. The key barrier to integrating the communications mix is people, and the way they work. The best way to overcome this barrier is to motivate the key players to work as a team. An effective team is one that includes client and agency, across the entire communications mix.

Full-service agency

When using an external agency the most straightforward approach is to use the services of a full-service agency that is able to assemble a team including representatives from all the agency services that the client needs. Full-service agencies can provide a comprehensive range of services such as creative, strategic planning, production, media planning and buying and market research. The advantage of using a full-service agency is the range of skills that can be drawn upon when needed, and the fact that all the elements of the promotional mix and marketing communications operation can be brought together making the whole process easier to manage and control. However, this strength is also a potential weakness because if the relationship breaks down, it will be difficult to find another agency to take on the work at short notice and still keep to the envisaged timescale.

Limited service agency

An alternative to the full-service agency is a limited service agency that specializes in particular elements of the marketing communications process. For example, an advertising agency may specialize in the design of advertisements. The advantage in using a limited service agency is that a client can use different agencies for the different skills that best suit his needs. This gives choice and flexibility but it can take a lot of time to manage the different relationships involved. Selecting an agency should be based on explicit criteria based on the aims and objectives of the communications. Key issues are whether the agency fully understands the requirements of a brief, and whether it will be able to work with the client as a team. In some cases, companies are establishing online communication services which may make it more difficult to tell whether or not the chemistry is right between the client and the agency.

Developing an agency brief

Elements that could be contained in an agency brief are:

Current situation – The history of the brand, previous campaign successes (or failures) and the reasons for mounting the new campaign.

Promotional objectives – Having set marketing objectives, the promotional objectives need to be identified. These will vary but could include, for example, encouraging product trial or direct sales or increasing distribution outlets.

Target markets – This should include socio-economic details (e.g. age, class, sex) and also psychographic information on users. This will have a bearing on the focus and content of the promotional activity.

Product/service – In providing the agency with a detailed brief, this section should include any available research that has been used to establish the perceived benefits so that these can be promoted strongly.

Budget – The budget should include funds for the cost of the media and the production of promotional material.

Competitors – Find out about these and include the results of your findings in the brief.

Timescales – Media scheduling will play an important role at this stage.

The creative team will be responsible for the direction of the artwork, ensuring that visualization and copywriting match the needs of the organization, and they will be directed by the accounts manager within the agency who will also brief the media and planning functions.

When agencies are used, the process of briefing will be followed by the 'agency pitch'. An agency will carry out research into the marketing and communications situation, and then present creative and media plans to the client.

What type of campaign is it?

There are different types of marketing communications campaign. An educational campaign targets a specific audience with information that benefits the consumer, for example health-related matters, or how to obtain benefits. A marketing campaign promotes, for example, a new service or product, or repositions an old service or product, and focuses on price, promotion and product. A public relations campaign would focus on image and name recognition. The following is an example of an integrated campaign that was the result of extensive research carried out over a year involving marketers and professionals working in the anti-drug field.

National youth anti-drug media campaign

The campaign's 5-year initiative to reduce and deglamorize youth drug use targets middle-school-age adolescents (approximately 11–13 years old), parents and other influential adults. The integrated communications campaign delivers anti-drug messages to kids and parents where they live, work and play through advertising, the Internet, movies, music and television, public education efforts and community partnerships. The campaign will spend about $180 million per year in advertising – and receive a pro bono match of equal value from the entertainment industry, media, corporations and other advertisers – to expose young people to innovative anti-drug messages that reinforce the ads. For more than a year, TV ads have run nationwide during prime time. Nearly a year of research went into designing the campaign. Hundreds of specialists were consulted, including experts in behaviour change, drug prevention, teen marketing and advertising communications, as well as representatives from professional, civic and community organizations. The campaign will be constantly monitored, evaluated and updated to ensure that it effectively reaches teens and their parents.

Who is the target audience?

Communication should be tailored to meet the needs and interests of a given audience. Is the audience potential buyers, current users, deciders or influencers, individuals groups, or the general public? Are the members of the target audience consumers, businesses, non-profit organizations or government agencies? The target audience is a critical influence on decisions about what to say to whom, when and how.

What are the aims and objectives of the campaign?

Try to devise both quantitative (measurable) and qualitative objectives. A quantitative objective would be, for example, to increase the number of users by 20 per cent per year. A qualitative objective would be to improve public understanding of the benefits of recycling by the October, measured by pre- and post-survey responses. The campaign may be trying to elicit a cognitive (attention), affective (feeling) or behavioural (doing) response.

Designing the message

This is concerned with what to say, how to say it and who should say it. The aim is to find a theme, idea, appeal or unique selling proposition. The message can try to appeal on moral, rational or emotional grounds. Rational grounds emphasize the benefits of a product or service such as quality, value or performance. Emotional appeals try to stir up negative or positive emotions to motivate purchase. Moral appeals to the audience's sense of propriety and the right way to behave. The structure of a message is important, that is, whether it is a one-sided or two-sided presentation mentioning benefits and shortcomings, and the order in which arguments are presented. The credibility of the message source depends on expertise, trust-worthiness and likeability.

Select the channels

This involves choosing between a range of personal communication channels, for example face to face or through telephone or e-mail, and non-personal communication channels which include the media.

Activity 8.1

Think of a marketing campaign that you have been involved in or which is memorable to you.

What type of campaign was it?
Who do you perceive was the target audience?
What was the key message?
What channels were used?
What made it stand out for you?

Internet marketing

Companies that have achieved the greatest success with Internet marketing have leveraged the strength of multiple marketing and sales channels. This includes the use of more traditional marketing and sales channels: brand advertising in broadcast media, demand generation and promotional communications in print media, direct mail and e-mail channels, and sales and service support from field sales, telesales and business partners.

What is the single biggest prerequisite for successful Internet marketing? – Customer-centric thinking and delivery. Marketers still talk about 'campaigns' whereas customers want to take control of the relationship. And the second biggest lesson for successful online marketing? It's a multi-channel process, not just a collection of separate web pages. Customers experience you as a journey that is a sequence of interactions across any number of channels towards their end goal.

The really successful marketers really understand that journey and how the channels, including the Internet, best work together. The real challenge here is getting your organization galvanized and incentivized to work together, as opposed to by channel or departmental silo, to help the customer towards his or her end destination, wherever that may be within your company.

Companies that have achieved the greatest successes also have defined and deployed Internet marketing strategies from a cross-functional perspective and leveraged the strength of multiple marketing and sales channels. In these companies customer-facing marketing, sales and service activities have not simply been automated or moved to the Internet. Instead, they first have been freshly re-designed to provide greater value, reliability, responsiveness and service quality to customers – and secondly to provide improved transaction economics to the company. Such a re-design, of course, suggests that the company has already gained a thorough understanding of customers' buying behaviours and their channel preferences.

The Internet has been an integrated element of the marketing mix, not an isolated or stand-alone marketing activity. Years of management research and practical experience have demonstrated that changing customers' buying behaviours and motivating them to accept and adopt innovations, like Internet marketing, can be difficult and costly. The most successful 'Internet marketing' companies have recognized that integrating new e-channel capabilities with traditional marketing and sales channels can accelerate the innovation process for customers and themselves.

Source: http://www.insightexec.com/cgi-bin/item.cgi?id=130982&u=pnd&m=phn. http://www. insightexec.com/cgi-bin/item.cgi?id=130983&u=pnd&m=phnd.

Until recently, consumers usually learned about a product and made their choice at the same time. People would often visit a department store or dealership to seek advice from a salesman, look at his recommendations and then buy. Now, for many, each of these steps is separate. Reaching these better-informed consumers with a marketing message is not easy. Some Internet search firms are offering more localized services on PCs and mobile phones. So local consumers will be able to find a local store and then check the offers from nearby outlets even as they browse the aisles, or listen to a salesman. Consumers are in a more powerful position to take control of the way they find out about products. There is more spending on 'below-the-line' advertising, or marketing services.

Proctor and Gamble

For P&G, brands are the chief medium through which it communicates with customers. Traditionally, that communication has gone in a single direction, with P&G spending billions of dollars a year to tell consumers through bold, persistent advertising.

The PG.com team successfully pushed to include two features on the site that would have been almost unthinkable in the old, world of P&G. In Try & Buy, which has become the site's most visited section, consumers can purchase new products before they show up in the supermarket or drugstore. In Help Us Create, P&G conducts virtual test markets where consumers can tell the company which kinds of new products it should make, or how it might improve existing products.

P&G has stepped up its experimentation because it has discovered an ideal laboratory for doing so: the Internet. Using test markets – auditioning a product in selected locations in order to find out what sells and what doesn't – is old-time religion at P&G. Before rolling out a new product nationally, the company typically spends several months and millions of dollars to conduct field tests in a handful of midsize, middle-American cities. But the Internet has fostered new, more efficient ways to sound out customer attitudes toward product innovation. By doing a test online P&G can do it for a tenth of the cost in a quarter of the time.

Media planning

Media planning needs to be co-ordinated with marketing strategy and with other aspects of an advertising strategy. The strategic aspects of media planning involve four steps:

1. Selecting the target audience towards which all subsequent efforts will be directed.
2. Specifying media objectives, for example, in terms of reach (What proportion of the target audience must see, read, or hear our advertising message during a specified period?), frequency (How often should the target audience be exposed to the advertisement during this period?), gross rating points or GRPs or effective rating points or ERPs (How much total advertising is necessary during a particular period to accomplish the reach and frequency objectives?).
3. Selecting general media categories and specific vehicles within each medium.
4. Buying media.

The concept of media neutral planning has been developed to counteract the perceived power of creative teams that may be regarded as considering only itself and its peers when developing new ideas. This has led to media choice, being biased towards those options deemed to show off creative talent to best effect, rather than necessarily being the best at meeting the needs of the consumer.

Is Media Neutral Planning Just Today's Buzz Word or a Genuine New World Order?

Looking back for a moment we can see that each decade through the second half of the twentieth century brought our predecessors face to face with their own key issues. Starting in the 1950s with the development of the creative team as we now know it, which then contributed in the 1960s to the move away from linear models of communication to a more humanistic approach, through the advent of account planning in the 1970s, to the break up of the full-service agency in the 1980s which, in turn, led directly to the issue of integration in the 1990s. So here we are in a new century facing our own particular issue – media neutral planning. But what is it? What, if anything, does it owe to these preceding trends? And is it just a passing fad or is it here to stay? To set my stall out from the beginning ~I should say that, in my view, media neutral planning is probably the biggest issue of all, being a culmination of all those issues that came before. To put it in its own context, I believe that media neutral planning is far greater than merely a creative or 'advertising' issue. It is fundamental to the way in which a brand does and should touch consumers' lives. It is the planning of those brand touchpoints without bias toward or against any particular mediums or channels, from conventional above-the-line media, through traditional below-the-line options to new media, ambient media, pr, sponsorship, events, design, point of sale, collateral material and so on. Currently, planning tends to be heavily media centric dependent on where the planner sits, who pays his/her wages and what his/her particular prejudices are. Media neutral planning, on the other hand, seeks to put the consumer firmly at the centre of the planning process, viewing media from his/her perspective as defined by the particular brand relationship in question.

Source: Tina Kaye, http://www.marketing-society.org.uk/downloads/MEDIA-NEUTRAL-PLANNING.pdf.

Determining the marketing communications budget

A key task within the framework of marketing communications is the appropriate determination of the levels of expenditure required to fulfil the task established. The amount of money spent on marketing communications differs widely among companies, even within the same industry. There are various methods to choose from, each with a slightly different focus, and different advantages and disadvantages.

Percentage of sales – A widely used method of budget determination is based on the calculation of a ratio between past expenditure and sales. The model creates a situation in which the budget only increases against an expectation of higher sales and fails to acknowledge that marketing can create sales for a brand.

Percentage of product gross margin – A percentage of either the past or expected gross margin – net sales less the cost of goods – is used.

Percentage of anticipated turnover – This approach is based on the allocation of a fixed percentage of future turnover to the marketing communications budget.

Unit or case/sales ratio method – This method is based on estimating sales volumes, and a fixed sum per unit is allocated towards marketing communications expenditure. Multiplying the expected sales volume by the fixed allocation gives producers the size of the budget. The expenditure patterns reflect past achievement and tend to benefit growth brands and disadvantage those that are declining.

Competitive expenditure – Another frequently used approach is to base a brand's expenditure levels on an assessment of competitors' expenditures. However, the difficulty is how to make an accurate assessment of the level of competitors' spend. While it is possible to obtain a reasonable fix on advertising spend from published information, the same is not true of sales promotional spend and other categories of marketing communications.

Share of voice – This approach is based on the relationship between the volume share of the product category and the expenditure within the category as a whole. It is primarily related to advertising expenditure.

Media inflation – This makes the assumption that the previous year's budget should be increased in line with the growth in media costs.

Objective and task method – This method is based on the specific objectives that the marketing plan needs to achieve. The objective and task method requires that specific objectives for the campaign are defined; for example, increasing brand awareness, encouraging sampling and trial, promoting repeat purchase and so on. A numerical target is given and the costs of achieving this target are calculated. The budget is based on present goals rather than past or future results.

What can be afforded – This is based on a management assessment of, for example, the return on investment, and the marketing communications budget is the amount that remains after calculating that level and other claims on the budget.

251

When engaging in media planning

There are multiple issues to consider. Some of the most important ones are:

The nature of advertising is changing: customers want to be more informed about the choices they are making, especially when the product of their interest is a costly one.

Doing some additional research on the Internet before making the final decision on a purchase is therefore more of a rule than exception these days. That's why a web presence with a reliable appearance and solid information about your product is a must these days.

Ratings from various sources always harbour a certain amount of error. For starters, the ratings are based on a sample of the population, which always entails the possibility of deviations from real outcomes. Besides, up till now, the strategies that were used to establish the ratings could be questioned for all media.

And on top of that, ratings are always a retrospective picture in a world where everything changes at the speed of the wind. One of the most risky acts in the media decision-making process is therefore: linear planning.

The act of planning which media to use for an advertising campaign should therefore be done with consideration of the numbers available, but also with a certain amount of vision and intuition.

Comparing the performance of the designated brand with that of its competitors is a good way to go, but should not be the ultimate determining factor in developing your media strategy. After all, your competitors may have a different marketing strategy – and perhaps also an entirely different budget – lying at the foundation of their campaign than you have for yours.

Length of impact of the particular media vehicles should also be looked at. Will your product still be around or in season by the time a particular media vehicle of your choice reaches its last important group of viewers? Keep the average duration of the media vehicles you want to select in mind when planning, and compare them with the availability and seasonableness of your product.

Keep multiple factors in mind when comparing and contrasting index numbers: even if your brand seems to do greatly in a certain market, you cannot solely rely on the indices: market size and purchasing power of the group under consideration should also play an important role in determining your final choice.

Considering the markets where you want your campaign to be executed is also a multi-faceted issue: what are your competitors doing, and why? If your brand is not doing well in a market but your competitors' are, you may want to find out what the reasons are before increasing your advertising budget in that market. And if neither your brand nor your competitors' are doing well in a market, you may think even harder before initiating a campaign there.

When you compare data from various sources, make sure you also consider the geographic divisions these sources handle: there are many divisions in use by various data sources. You don't want to compare apples and oranges.

Make sure you remain on top of the developments: digital is the key word of the near future. You want to be on that train. And not just with regards to new media, but also when it comes to old media going digital, such as online newspapers.

Keep all factors in mind when making final decisions. Everything is important and intertwined these days: the right time, the right audience, the duration of the impact, the availability of the product, your intuition, and the way your audience makes its decisions. Just be where they go.

Source: Marketing Monthly, November 2004, http://www.onevision.co.uk/xq/ASP/id.1078/qx/default.htm?CT=LeftNav.

Senior marketing communications manager – Job description

Responsibilities

Actively help to develop and implement a marketing communications plan that effectively reaches target users, and facilitates the job of product marketing and business development teams by generating quality customer and partner leads.

Design, co-ordinate production and implement ongoing advertising, direct mail and other promotional programmes.

Maintain overall responsibility for management of and changes to company website.

Actively contribute to the development of and regular updates to corporate and product messaging, as well as to public relations materials.

Track newsworthy events and co-ordinate with public relations agency to publicize.

Gather information for press releases and co-ordinate approval and distribution processes.

Help co-ordinate the creative process, development and production of the company's collateral materials.

Help manage development, writing and production of company newsletter.

Co-ordinate with sales teams to collect leads, integrate with sales force and manage the appropriate follow-up.

Manage development of the process to measure marketing communications results, including quality of leads generated and so on.

Hold primary responsibility for managing the company's various advertising, design and public relations agency relationships, including negotiating contracts, managing administrative and billing issues and so on.

Marketing communications are important for all types of organization and a wide range of contexts.

Planning a social marketing campaign

When planning programmes or awareness campaigns, it is important to target programmes and messages to reach and meet the needs of the intended audience. In health communications, these concepts take on the following meanings:

Product – is the knowledge, attitudes or behaviour you want the audience to adopt.

Price – can be interpreted as what the target audience must give up in order to receive the programme's benefits.

Promotion – is the means for persuading the target audience that the product is worth the price.

Place – refers to how the message is disseminated, such as through electronic or print media, or community programmes.

Stage 1 – Planning and selecting the strategy
This stage provides the foundation for the entire social marketing process. An assessment of the problem, the target audience and the available resources is conducted before moving ahead. During this planning process, the target audience should become increasingly segmented. This segmentation will aid in the development of appropriate messages. Goals and objectives for the programme will be developed at this time.

Stage 2 – Selecting channels and materials
Channels are how the message will be delivered, whether it is face to face, group, mass media, or a combination of channels. The more the channels selected, the more the target audience will be exposed to the message. Determining the channel prior to producing materials is important because different materials work better in different channels.

Material selection involves using what you have learned about your target audience to your advantage. Time and money can be saved by selecting materials that are specific to the audience you are trying to reach.

Stage 3 – Developing the materials and pre-testing
Draft the materials, pre-test them with the target audience and, if necessary, revise them. Determine if materials get the intended results, or revise them accordingly. Pre-testing adds time to the project but it can help to avoid producing materials that the target audience do not read.

Stage 4 – Implementing the programme
A method for tracking and evaluating the programme should be in place before it starts. The tracking method should help to identify those areas where changes may be needed.

Stage 5 – Assessing effectiveness
The type of evaluation conducted at this stage will depend upon several factors, including money, time, policies regarding the ability to gather information, the level of support for evaluation and the overall design of the programme.

Types of evaluation

○ *Formative evaluation* – includes pre-testing of materials, and is designed to test the strengths and weaknesses of a programme before it is ready for implementation.
○ *Process evaluation* – reviews the tasks of implementing the programme.
○ *Outcome evaluation* – is used to gather descriptive information. It gathers information about knowledge and attitude changes, expressed intentions of the target audience and the initiation of policy changes.
○ *Impact evaluation* – is the most comprehensive of the four types of evaluation. It focuses on the long-term outcomes of the programme and long-term behaviour change.

Stage 6 – Refining through feedback

If the programme is to be continued, revisions of the programme should be undertaken. If this is the end of the programme, documentation of what was learned should be made so as to assist others who may undertake a similar project in the future. An evaluation report should be prepared that could be used to secure funding to continue the programme and assist others conducting similar activities.

Integrated marketing communications

Creating an integrated marketing communications (IMC) plan is important for achieving maximum effectiveness.

Using the elements of the communications mix in a co-ordinated way so as to achieve the objectives of a promotion. Usually, a combination of marketing communications tools is used to meet specific campaign objectives. For example, advertising campaigns are often supported with sales promotions activities, or public relations or both. The role of marketing communications is to:

○ Differentiate a product/brand (to make it different to a competitor's brand or seem different through effective positioning).
○ Remind and reassure a target audience with regard to benefits (to encourage (re)purchase).
○ Inform a target audience by providing new information (e.g. of a new brand or flavour).
○ Persuade an audience to take a particular set of actions (e.g. visit a theatre, stop smoking).

The following example shows how companies see the advantages of an integrated approach.

Integrated marketing communications

Washington State University uses integrated marketing as a disciplined approach to communicating about the University to both internal and external audiences for the purpose of advancing its goals and strategic vision. In sum, the University's integrated marketing programme is the communication process for achieving WSU's strategic plan.

The integrated marketing programme is focused on four goals:

1. Increasing the enrollment of high-performing students
2. Building awareness and support among influencers
3. Increasing the enrollment of top graduate students
4. Improving organizational communications.

Now in its fourth year, the programme began with an in-depth analysis of the University's programme strengths, target markets, and communication practices, together with the identification of marketing goals critical to the University's success. A focused campaign to increase the number of high-performing students choosing to enroll at WSU led the first two years of this effort. Now ongoing and well established, that campaign continues as the core focus of the programme. It has also laid the groundwork for the integrated marketing programme to shift to the second phase of work.

In the second phase of the programme, WSU has expanded its work towards building its reputation with leaders state-wide and increasing the enrollment of top graduate students. Using the successful model of the student recruitment campaign, WSU's strategy for influencing leaders focuses on two issues simultaneously:

1. Building WSU's reputation with identified, influential audiences
2. Building relationships with those audiences to actively engage them with the University in advancing WSU's strategic priorities.

Major executions aimed at immersing these audiences in the progress of WSU include leadership tours, WSU Connections in Seattle, *World Class. Face to Face Showcase*, and work supporting the University's state and federal agenda. That work is supported by continued awareness-building through broad markets that influence these individuals, such as *Washington State Magazine*, major news media exposure, and leveraging the image advertising that supports the student recruitment campaign.

Types of marketing communications

There are many different terms used to describe the various methods used by organizations to communicate with customers and other stakeholder groups. They include personal selling and non-personal selling (advertising, sales promotion, public relations and direct marketing). Advertising is any paid form of non-personal presentation by an identified sponsor. Sales promotion is a short-term incentive to encourage the purchase or sale of a product. Public relations aims to build and sustain good relations with the organization's stakeholders and publics through favourable publicity, building up a good 'corporate image', and handling or heading off unfavourable rumours, stories and events. Direct marketing is direct communications with carefully targeted individual consumers to obtain an immediate response through the use of non-personal tools (mail, telephone, fax and e-mail).

With *push strategies*, marketers use personal selling to promote their product to retailers and wholesalers, not the end-user. They include special incentives such as discounts, promotional materials and co-operative advertising. Advertising and sales promotions are part of pull strategies, which build consumer awareness so that the consumer will ask retailers to carry the product. The strategies are not exclusive and, in fact, most companies use both to increase their promotional effectiveness. By selecting a combination of promotional mix elements, marketers attempt to achieve the organization's promotional objectives: to provide information, differentiate a product, increase demand and add to a product's value.

Personal selling

Personal selling is often the most expensive element of the marketing communications mix because it is resource-intensive, and involves high contact and customer maintenance costs. In some instances, personal sales have been replaced by direct mail, telemarketing and e-mail. Personal selling includes activities such as:

Prospecting – Gathering information in order to gain sales leads and prospective clients.

Communicating – Being the provider of information about the organization, its products, services and after-sales care.

Selling – Persuading a potential customer to adopt the product.

Market research/information gathering – Environmental scanning, competitor intelligence, customer intelligence.

Servicing of accounts – Maintaining and providing ongoing customer service, including technical support, financial contractual arrangements and logistical arrangements.

Allocating – Ensuring that the allocation of products to customers is undertaken at all times, in particular in times of production shortages.

Customer relationship building – Building and sustaining long-term customer relationships.

Evaluation of personal sales

Evaluating and measuring sales performance is based upon the sales objectives set for the organization. But the objectives set will be SMART, and therefore clearly defined and clearly linked with marketing objectives and overall corporate performance goals.

It is likely that sales performance will be measured against objectives on a regular basis, anything from weekly to quarterly. However, in most organizations sales performance against actual planned achievement is measured on a monthly basis.

It is also likely that other factors relating to sales performance will be measured, such as:

- o *Productivity* – calls per day, calls per account, total number of orders versus calls.
- o *Account development* – total of new accounts, total of existing accounts, growth of sales from existing accounts.
- o *Expenses* – expenses versus number of calls made, cost per call.

With the evolution of IT, sales measurement techniques are becoming more sophisticated and more effective, and the speed at which information becomes available is of the essence. A drastic reduction in sales performance can mean that other elements of the promotional mix might be subject to increased activity to compensate for the drop in sales. However, the drop in income often inhibits too much marketing expenditure of a contingency nature to be undertaken.

Advertising

Advertising is one of the most influential forms of communication within the promotional mix and is particularly effective at reaching large audiences with specific messages. Depending on the media used, costs of reaching individuals can be lowered compared to other forms of communications. It can be used at different stages of purchasing, or for awareness creation at the early stages of a new product launch. Its main purpose is to inform, persuade and remind customers to purchase products and services. Advertising objectives are expressed in terms of promoting products, organizations and services, or stimulating demand, increasing sales, brand and product awareness, and reminding and reinforcing perceptions of a product or service.

Measuring advertising effectiveness is important for understanding how well ads are performing and what changes need to be made to improve performance. Promotion research consists of media and message research. Media research measures audience composition and size for media vehicles as a basis for determining ratings. Audience measurement services include magazine, local radio, national radio and television. Multiple measurement methods are usually preferable to single techniques to assess advertising effectiveness. There has been a trend towards greater use of sales promotion in comparison with advertising. This shift is part of the movement from pull- to push-oriented marketing, particularly in the case of consumer-packaged goods. The factors that underpin this shift include increased brand parity, growing price sensitivity, reduced brand loyalty, the fragmentation of the mass market, reduced media effectiveness, growing short-term orientation, and favourable consumer responsiveness to sales promotions.

Sales promotions

Sales promotions often complement advertising, and may be planned and executed in parallel with associated advertising and possible public relations campaigns. They are used to encourage customers to trial products and services, and then to purchase them. The main aims and associated objectives of sales promotions are, for example, to increase brand and product awareness, attract new customers, increase trial and adoption of new and existing products, increase brand usage and to encourage trading up to the next size or the next range. Sales promotions can be a highly targeted and flexible form of communications and evaluation of their effectiveness is usually an integral part of the communication through, for instance, coupon redemption, money-off vouchers/coupons, buy one get one free, discounts, trial-sized products and so on.

Public relations

Some commonly used measures of results are:

Budget – Has the planned activity been achieved within budget and timescale?

Awareness – Established through using market research activities.

Attitude – Positivity or negativity and whether there is any change in consumer behaviour.

Media coverage and tone – Coverage in a range of media – number of column inches, key headings and the tone.

Positioning – Comparative information about the relative position of the organization and the competition.

Response generation – Enquiries or leads linked to reference codes or enquiry sources, for example a particular newspaper.

Share price – Highly publicized scandals such as Enron and WorldCom show that share prices can be manipulated, especially when exceeding a particular level is a management target, the achievement of which means that large bonuses can be earned. During the so-called 'dotcom boom', some worthless stock was also heavily promoted by brokers. A share price can also be affected by a myriad of external factors outside a company's control so, all in all, a healthy degree of scepticism is needed before relying on share price as a guide to anything.

Sales – When an organization suffers from negative perception, sales tend to drop. The challenge is to rehabilitate the image in order to increase sales.

Direct marketing activities

Direct marketing may take the form of direct mail, telemarketing, electronic marketing and online marketing. It is immediate, customizable to individual consumers or groups of consumers, and interactive. Direct e-mail marketing includes unsolicited bulk e-mail and opt-in direct e-mail. Generally, direct marketing allows for easy measurement of effectiveness. Data mining (the extraction of hidden predictive information from large databases) is used to 'drill down' into the data to any level of detail needed to identify common characteristics of high-volume users. Clusters of consumers who share specific characteristics, such as income, education and brand loyalty, can be identified as targets for marketing efforts. Direct mail is the most commonly used direct-marketing advertising medium and marketers are able to target messages to specific market segments and quickly evaluate the success of a mailshot. It also enables greater personalization compared to mass media advertising.

Evaluation of direct marketing activities is based upon the predetermined objectives of the campaign. Typical measures for successful implementation of the direct marketing campaign will include:

- o Response rate
- o Conversion rate
- o Order value
- o Repeat orders.

Often, this information will be gathered through a range of voucher and campaign response codes that will be able to distinguish the source of the direct mail or promotion. However, the cost per enquiry and per order needs to be identified. Click-through rates are a common online measurement.

Direct mail is losing its effectiveness. The response rate is high enough to make junk mail one of the most cost-effective forms of marketing. But that could be changing. The problem seems to be too many envelopes cluttering too many mail boxes. When it comes to soliciting a sale the phone produces the highest response rate, at an average of 8.6 per cent.

Some of the dodgiest marketing outfits now use the phone to tout their offers. In Britain, automatic dialling machines are used to call mobile phone numbers at random, but then to hang up after just one or two rings. Seeing a missed call, the unsuspecting recipient will usually ring back just in case it is something important, only to be greeted by a sales pitch.

Source: Adapted from *The Economist*, 24 November 2005.

Trade promotions

Good trade promotions, that is a good 'push strategy', highly incentivized, backed up by appropriate merchandising and appropriate advertising, may be advantageous. Specific methods might include, for example, allowances and discounts, free merchandise, selling and marketing assistance, co-operative advertising, merchandising allowances, market information and product training. The following case study from Toshiba demonstrates its integrated approach to marketing.

Case study

Toshiba has a long history of developing marketing programmes that are the result of direct consumer research and input.

The integrated marketing disciplines

With insight into its consumers' wants and behaviours, Toshiba can be more effective in its unified product sales, training, advertising, public relations, trade show and online teams with consistent, integrated messages and themes. Toshiba's advertising campaign promotes the brand as well as its full line of TVs and Digital Audio Video products. The new advertisements focus on Toshiba's lifestyle appeal while focusing on the overall breadth of the Toshiba line of products and their ease-of-use features, modern space saving designs and convenience.

Toshiba's public relations programme has focused on the impact of consumer electronics on consumer's lifestyles, particularly the benefits, features and overall experience. By implementing a combination of media relations, product reviews, creative mailers, product placement opportunities, media tours, trade events and more, Toshiba's public relations programme, continues evolving to communicate, educate and increase consumer awareness of Toshiba products to a larger yet targeted audience.

Toshiba's online communications redesigned website (www.tacp.toshiba.com) provides access to product information and registration, owner's manuals and service information as well as enabling consumers to purchase accessories including Portable DVD batteries and TV stands. The look and feel of the site also integrates a lifestyle theme that connects all of Toshiba's marketing disciplines. Online communications and the unveiling of www.gigabeat.com were also key for the launch of gigabeat® as Toshiba re-entered the portable digital audio category.

As part of its integrated marketing strategy, Toshiba strategically positions its Training and Dealer Support Team in metropolitan areas around the United States, in order to provide support for key retail partners. This internal team is composed of dedicated and knowledgeable product trainers (Field Support Representatives) who help the sales force make it easier for consumers when they are looking to buy their next Television or Digital Audio Video player. Toshiba understands the importance of building relationships at the store level and arming front line sales people with the tools necessary to sell Toshiba products successfully.

Toshiba has also developed a full array of product materials including catalogues and product specific collateral to meet customers' needs. Catering to different sets of needs, Toshiba offers catalogues devoted to its main TV and Digital Audio and Video lines, its Cinema Series® line, the new Integrated HD Television line, accessories and stands, and dimensional drawings which include measurements and weights and carry the telltale lifestyle images to reinforce the Toshiba brand and products. The result is an integrated marketing campaign and strong partnerships that will allow Toshiba to leverage its brand at retail in order to develop a solid presence in the crowded MP3 market.

Marketing channels

Increasingly, organizations are examining the whole demand chain that links raw material, components and manufactured goods, and how they are moved to their customers. The starting point should be the customer needs for which the organization needs to mobilize its resources. However, the term 'supply chain' is challenged because it suggests too linear a view of purchase, production and consumption. A more contemporary term is 'value network'. Philip Kotler in his book *Marketing Management* (Kotler, 2003) expresses the wish that marketers will look more widely than the customer side of the value network and participate in upstream activities. This would mean that they became network managers, not only customer and product managers.

Marketing channels are an integral part of the marketing mix, and they provide the means by which products and services are made available to end-user customers. They link manufacturers with their target markets, and are the means by which customers can access the products and services that they want. They consist of a number of different organizations each of which fulfils a particular role. Typically, a conventional channel will consist of a producer, wholesaler, retailer and end-user customer who need to collaborate and co-operate with each other. Intermediaries assume particular roles in relation to the other members of the marketing channel according to their position.

Hybrid channels

There are also 'hybrid' channels with different strategies used to reach different types of customers. For example, IBM uses its sales force for its largest accounts, telemarketing for medium-sized accounts, direct mail for small accounts, retailers to sell to even smaller accounts and the Internet for speciality items. The Internet has had a major impact on established marketing channel structures because it allows direct contact between, for example, a service provider and the customer. Low-cost airlines is an example of this. Overall, the effect of more direct selling has been to reduce the number of intermediaries.

Distribution channels

A distribution channel consists of individuals and organizations who ensure that a product or service is available to the customer at the right place and time. A channel comprises marketing intermediaries, for example transportation companies, merchants, agents, wholesalers, warehouses and retail outlets. The successful management of the supply chain depends on motivating and controlling distributors and distribution outlets. Investing in intermediaries and their activities motivates them to undertake marketing within their network, thus adding value to the customer–supplier relationship. Traditionally, manufacturers operated within the area of production and marketing of brands, and retailers focused on selling activities. Interaction between the two was often based on manufacturers acting as 'order takers' and retailers as 'sales outlets'.

The challenge of making products and services available to customers around the world when, where and how they want them is complex. Technology transfer has made product advantages difficult to maintain but distribution is seen as having the potential for achieving a competitive advantage if marketing channels can be designed to provide excellent customer service. This means that members of the channel need to work together to create added value. A competitive advantage gained through better distribution is not so easily copied and may offer more of a sustainable competitive advantage. The main objective of physical distribution is to decrease costs while increasing service to the customer. The manager will need to consider the order processing, materials handling, warehousing, inventory management and transportation issues. Managers strive for a good balance of service, costs and resources. Therefore, effective planning is paramount to ensure that this happens by determining what level of customer service is acceptable, yet realistic in terms of costs. As physical distribution affects every element of the marketing mix, it is important that the customers' needs are at the top of the list. An effective physical distribution programme should have a positive impact on customer satisfaction; for example, some companies offer guaranteed 'next day' delivery.

Wholesaler

Wholesalers buy products from the manufacturer, store them within their warehouses and sell the products on to the trade. Producers try to increase demand, and support marketing activity through various push and pull strategies. Both wholesalers and retailers want their respective customers to perceive a high level of service and value in the goods and services they purchase.

Retailer

Nowadays, retailers often have a presence on the high street and the Internet. They provide the link between the customer and the producer, and may require a lot of technical support, customer services backup, stock ordering facilities, systems underpinning the sales process, information and merchandise. Retailers provide wholesalers with sales contacts and outlets and help them by purchasing small quantities of stock on a regular basis. Retailers focus on end-user consumers and consider their buying motivations.

Distributors and dealers

Distributors and dealers stock products for manufacturers and sell them on, including after-sales service, warranties and credit facilities. Dealers often specialize in a particular brand and sell them to the end-user, making the channel shorter.

Agents, brokers and facilitators

Agents and brokers act on behalf of the manufacturer and bring buyers and sellers together.

Franchisee

A franchisee holds a contract to market and supplies a product or service that has been very strictly designed and developed by the franchiser. There are often restrictions on store design and layout, and what is sold within the retail outlet.

Merchandiser

Merchandisers are responsible for promotional displays in stores relating to different products.

Channel management

Power is not distributed evenly in most distribution channels and conflict can occur which is either horizontal, involving disagreements between channel members at the same level in the distribution chain, or vertical, occurring between channel members at different levels. Conflict in marketing channels can occur for a variety of reasons over issues such as stock levels, pricing and sales order processing. Sometimes it is because channel members have different priorities, and are focused on different business elements. A manufacturer might be focused more on products and processes, and a retailer may be focused more on customers and the processes necessary to meet their needs. Poor communication between channel members can be a cause of conflict but communication is an important co-ordinating mechanism for all members of a marketing channel. The willingness of members to share information and associated resources is an important factor because it enables an openness between parties, through which full information can be exchanged. This means that the producer must be willing to share sensitive information, and the distributor must be willing to share information about themselves, their customers and markets.

Horizontal conflict occurs among companies at the same level of the channel. For example, dealers in an area can complain about other dealers who are too aggressive in their pricing and advertising or by selling outside their assigned territories. Vertical conflict occurs between different levels of the same channels.

To overcome this, sometimes companies implement a vertical marketing system (VMS), a planned network of distribution channels designed to reduce conflict among channel members and resolve other distribution problems. This is where producers, wholesalers and retailers act as a unified system. One channel member owns the others, has contacts with them, or has so much power that they all co-operate.

The following advertisement gives an indication of the wide range of activities that a channel manager could be involved in. Take note of the wide range of people that the manager has to interact with.

Direct marketing: Channel marketing manager

Job advertisement

Seagate Technology is seeking a Programme Manager for the Direct Marketing Channel. Develop comprehensive business plans and execution for each of the critical online and direct marketing channels, including portal/distribution, affiliates, search engine marketing and other online advertising placements. Works with sales, channel marketing, and direct marketing buyers to develop and evaluate virtual merchandising and marketing programmes specific to the direct marketing channel to drive POS revenue. Work with internal departments to drive programme benefits. Recommend and develop messaging for support materials and implement on-line programme communications. Create innovative and compelling promotions that drive conversions and sales. Develop and review catalogue advertisements and collateral. Conducts audits of web properties and ensure compliance, consistency of messaging, and brand integrity. Manage direct marketers promotional calendars and develop implementation plans to execute new promotions. Collaborate with marketing team to develop merchandising opportunities within partner sites and maximize sales of specific products. Develop training materials and programmes for direct marketers out-bound sales reps to drive awareness and sales of Seagate products. Assist in managing internal/external resources to execute training activities. Monitor and track effectiveness of promotional programmes, and overall programme metrics and ROI. Budget Management.

Experience required:

At least 6–8 years of experience in marketing with 3 years marketing to consumers or online merchandising for a consumer business. Proven track record in strategy development and comprehensive business leadership. Consistent history of business-building success and passion for results. Proven experience successfully managing large online partnerships critical to overall business success. Excellent communications, relationship-building and interpersonal skills. Excellent analytical and negotiation skills. Experience making data-driven decisions, and good business acumen. Strong attention to detail, with a quality assurance focus. Ability to thrive in a fast-paced fluid environment.

Superior knowledge of Microsoft Office. Ability to drive/lead/work with many diverse personalities across multiple functional areas - matrix project management. Self-motivated and results-oriented. Proven judgement, decision-making, and execution skills. Ability to multitask and prioritize competing priorities.

Education required:

BA/BS in Marketing or Business required; MBA a plus.

The promotional mix in the marketing channel

A marketing channel is an organized network of agencies and institutions, which in combination perform all the functions required to link producers with end-customers to accomplish the marketing task. It enables goods and services to be moved from producers and providers to consumers. Within a channel, upstream trading partners for a retailer are, for example, wholesalers, manufacturers and producers. Downstream activity takes place along the distribution chain, for example, from manufacturer to retailer to customer.

Channel communications help to hold together a channel of distribution and they are important in the development of channel relationships. However, the nature of marketing communications in a marketing channel is different from communications aimed at consumers because different audiences have different information needs. For example, in comparison with consumers, distributors tend to make a smaller number of high value orders less frequently. The promotional mix in a marketing channel is aimed mainly at conveying information relating to product features and benefits. For this purpose, advertising is expensive and relatively inefficient whereas personal selling, combined with activities such as direct marketing, the Internet, exhibitions and sales literature, could provide an effective promotional mix.

Difference between consumer and business-to-business marketing communications

	Consumer-orientated markets	Business-to-business markets
Message reception	Informal	Formal
Number of decision-makers	Single or few	Many
Balance of the promotional mix	Advertising and sales promotions dominate	Personal selling dominates
Specificity and integration	Broad use of promotional mix with a move towards co-ordinated mixes	Specific use of below-the-tools but with a high level of co-ordination and integration
Message content	Greater use of emotions and imagery	Greater use of rational, logic and information-based messages although there is evidence of a move towards the use of imagery
Length of decision time	Normally short	Longer and more involved

	Consumer-orientated markets	Business-to-business markets
Negative communications	Limited to people close to the purchaser/user	Potentially an array of people in the organization and beyond
Target marketing and research	Great use of sophisticated targeting and communication approaches	Limited but increasing use to targeting and segmentation approaches
Budget allocation	Majority of budget allocated to brand management	Majority of budget allocated to sales management
Evaluation and measurement	Great variety of techniques and approaches used	Limited number of techniques and approaches

Source: Fill (2002) cited in Beamish, K. (2003) CIM Advanced Certificate Coursebook, Butterworth-Heinemann, *Marketing Communications*. Used with kind permission.

Marketing communications in the B2B sector have been transformed by technological advances (Beamish, 2003). In the B2B sector, marketing communications can fulfil a variety of specific objectives which will vary according to the circumstances:

1. To create and maintain awareness
2. To generate sales leads
3. To pre-sell sales calls
4. To contact minor members of the decision-making unit
5. To build corporate and product images
6. To communicate technical information
7. To support the promotional effort.

The CIM Advanced Certificate 2003–2004 coursebook on *Marketing Planning* (Beamish, 2003) uses the DRIP acronym to describe the use of marketing communications in a marketing channel.

Focus of the message	Potential needs
Differentiation	Downstream so that channel members understand how a particular manufacturer (or particular products) adds value and is different from its competitors and other products that they carry
	Upstream to flag attention and to secure stock, support and resources
Reinforcing	Reminding downstream members of any superior product features and support facilities that are available
	Reassuring them of the benefits of continuity and reliability
	Reminding upstream members of their needs, problems and the support that is available
	Reassuring them that the business is working hard on their behalf, that they have their interests in mind
Informing	Providing downstream members with suitable levels of customer support and upstream members with market and performance information
Persuading	Encouraging downstream members to carry extra stock, provide facilities and meet service levels
	Stimulating upstream members to allocate stock, promotional support and favourable financial arrangements

Personal selling is a major communications tool in the marketing channel because face-to-face meetings between buying and selling organizations help to develop and maintain inter-organizational relationships. The willingness of organizations to share information is important to the development of sustainable relationships.

Intranet

An intranet uses a company's internal network to publish, distribute and display information for anyone directly connected to the network. Intranets allow authorized staff to access the information they need and it can encourage the sharing of knowledge from the different parts of an organization. Different types of information, prepared by different people in different parts of the business can be integrated into a single document. Staff can have easy access to information at their computer, even photographic images and technical drawings. Information can be shared rapidly when transmitted through e-mail, either within a company or outside via the Internet.

Extranets

Extranets can be used to engage distributors and producers, and allows for fast, accurate, low cost exchange of information. It involves building bridges between the public Internet and private corporate intranets, and can be seen as part of a company's intranet that is made accessible to other companies, to the public, or comprises components that enable the collaboration with other companies. Maximizing accessibility will mean that many partners can be involved and the more the participants, the greater the rates of return from the system. Extranets can also help companies to finally realize the benefits of Just-In-Time (JIT) inventory systems.

Other uses of extranets include:

- Private newsgroups that co-operating companies use to share valuable experiences and ideas.
- Groupware collaboration in the development of new products or services.
- Training programmes that companies develop and share.
- Shared product catalogues accessible only to wholesalers or those in the trade.
- Project management and control as part of a common work project.

Value-added activities

Examples of the kinds of value-added activities that intermediaries can undertake are: analysing information such as sales data, evaluating channel activities, co-ordinating advertising, personal selling, promotions and so on, facilitating communication, maintaining relationships between manufacturer and retail outlets, and providing advice, technical support, after-sales service and warranties.

Channels perform most effectively when they co-operate, co-ordinate and integrate their activities. Vertical channel management is where two or more channel members are connected by ownership or legal obligation. Marketing mix activities are more integrated, and often more effective because of this. Horizontal channel integration is the merging of organizations at the same level of channel operation under one management, for example, through mergers and takeovers.

The following case study shows a typical working day for a marketing channel executive in a mobile phone manufacturing company.

A day in the life of a Channel Marketing Executive

Toria works for a mobile phone company as a Channel Marketing Executive. She provides channel marketing/retail support to dealers and channel members (managing and planning merchandiser programme, dealers' roadshow and events, POS fulfilment, etc.). She manages product launches and marketing collaterals' fulfilment to channel members.

9:00 a.m. – My morning begins with replying to dealers' fax and e-mail requests of the company's channel marketing/retail support. The most exciting part of my day is when we have an active discussion with channel members on how to implement activities and formulate strategies.

10:00 a.m. – Meeting with channel members to discuss new promotional activities or events. Today, we discussed the upcoming dealer roadshow.

11:00 a.m. – I am contacting dealers about any updates pertaining to the company or their shops. I work with the rest of my colleagues as a team to implement dealer events and sales training. My time is mostly spent meeting with channel members to work out dealer events. I also visit them at retail shops to ensure that there is retail support and wide exposure of the company's brand presence.

3:00 p.m. – Meeting with a dealer to discuss his roadshow.

7:00 p.m. – Time to go home. This is the usual time I leave from the office. However, when I am on site at a roadshow, I leave around 9 p.m. so that I can ensure logistic arrangements are met before the event starts.

Consumer and business-to-business marketing communications

The importance of B2B communications is underpinned by buoyant Internet-based marketing communications compared with relatively slow growth in the B2C market.

The most important difference, however, is that organizational buying decisions are taken by *groups* of people rather than individuals. A key issue is to identify the individuals who comprise the decision-making unit.

Communications in marketing channel networks

A planned, channel-orientated communications strategy should contribute to and reinforce the partnerships in the network. There are many factors that can influence channel communication strategy, for example:

- *Power* – Are some organizations more important than others?
- *Direction* – Are communications one-way or two-way?
- *Frequency* – How often should messages be sent?
- *Timing* – Should messages be sent to all members simultaneously or serially?
- *Style and content* – Should messages be formal/informal? What must be included?
- *Distortion* – Will messages be received, stored and acted upon as the originator intends?

267

Review and evaluate the effectiveness of communications activities

The apocryphal quote about half of all advertising being a waste of money but it is not clear which half serves as a reminder that measuring the success of communications activities can be difficult. However, there are techniques that can be used for different purposes.

Evaluating channel effectiveness

It is essential that having selected an appropriate distribution channel and intermediaries, their efficiency, effectiveness and performance are continually managed.

Key performance and evaluation measures include:

○ Regular reviews
○ A forum for problem review and solution
○ Monthly, quarterly and yearly sales data analysis
○ Average stock levels
○ Lead and delivery times
○ Zero defects
○ Customer service complaints
○ Marketing support – achieving marketing objectives, level of marketing activity, sales promotions, distributor incentives
○ Spot-check of distributions further down the supply chain
○ Annual performance audit.

From an Internet perspective, typical evaluation methods of marketing effectiveness might include:

○ Number of leads
○ Increased sales
○ Customer retention
○ Increased market share
○ Brand enhancement and loyalty
○ Customer service.

Many organizations measure the effectiveness of their marketing communications, and there are a range of techniques and procedures available. Increasingly, it is the synergy that derives from effective co-ordination of all activities that determines overall success. Single elements of the communications mix are not used in isolation. Different parts of a campaign can be assessed and the evaluation process can be carried out at different stages of a marketing campaign, that is, before, during and after a campaign has been launched. However, the overall impact of a co-ordinated marketing communications campaign and the degree to which the promotional objectives have been achieved are key measures that interest stakeholders.

Whilst the primary focus is upon ascertaining whether objectives have been met and the strategy has been effective – efficiency is also of interest. There should be a strong emphasis on 'efficiency', 'effectiveness' and 'value for money', which means making the best use of the available resources to achieve the best possible outcomes. However, some aspects of marketing are notoriously difficult to evaluate; for example, advertising. Whilst communications is one element of the marketing mix, the other elements should be evaluated as well.

Pre-testing is about showing unfinished advertisements, often to focus groups to gather their reactions and to understand their reasoning. Post-testing is concerned with the evaluation of a campaign once it has been released. A typical measurement is the number of enquiries or direct responses elicited by a single advertisement or campaign. Recall and recognition tests are common post-testing procedures for advertisements.

Tracking studies involve collecting data from buyers on a regular basis in order to assess their perceptions of ads. Sales promotion evaluation includes methods such as consumer audits and general sales information, retail audits including, for example, changes in stock levels, distribution, market share and so on immediately after a promotional campaign. Sales force feedback is also a common measure.

Voucher/coupon redemption – Usually coded so that the different response rates in different media can be tracked.

Calculating ROI

Obviously, the power of metrics diminishes if the information is merely distributed, and not intelligently assessed and acted upon by management. Return on Investment is the most critical measure of marketing programmes for making decisions that will help maximize company profits. Return on Investment in its simplest form is: {Net Profit (pre-marketing investment) – Net Profit (post-marketing investment)} – Investment = Return. Return/Net Profit (pre-marketing investment) = ROI.

Australia: State of Victoria Government Communication Evaluation Guidelines Key Principles

- o Evaluation involves assessment of the degree to which an activity's objectives have been met as a result of the activity.
- o Evaluation is an internal part of all communications projects, not an optional extra.
- o Evaluation should be planned at the outset of a communications project.
- o Evaluation must be properly budgeted for. As a rule of thumb, 10 per cent of a project's budget should be allocated to evaluation.
- o A good test of the usefulness of an evaluation is to ask the following questions:

    - Does it effectively identify the *success/failure* of the project?
    - Does it effectively identify *the reasons for success/failure* of the project?
    - Does it effectively identify the *cost-effectiveness* of the project?

Broadly speaking, evaluation can address:

- o *Activity* – what was done (for example, wrote, designed and produced brochures).
- o *Output* – what communication took place (for example, distributed each brochure to 1000 people).
- o *Outcome* – what was achieved in terms of knowledge, attitudes and behaviour. Outcome evaluation is far more important, useful and relevant than activity or output evaluation. All significant projects should be evaluated on their outcomes.

Evaluation tools
Methods commonly used to measure project outcomes and outputs include:

- ○ Surveys
- ○ Focus groups
- ○ Web statistics
- ○ User feedback.

The choice of method in any case depends principally on the objectives being measured against and the budget available.

---

1. *Accountability* – The evaluation should identify an individual, responsible, office holder who is accountable for the overall programme/activity.
2. *Situation analysis* – A situation analysis should provide sufficient rationale for the program purpose and objectives. It should include background to the activity, including the source of the original reason for the project.
3. *Rationale for approach* – Research/evidence should be cited in support of the approach taken, its form and extent.
4. *Aims and objectives* – The over-arching *aim* from the original project plan should be provided.
5. *Target audience/s* – Target audience should be identified, and a rationale provided for them.
6. *Communications activities* – All project communications activities should be listed and a rationale provided for the choice.
7. *Selected media* – Media used should be listed and a rationale provided for the selection.
8. *Key messages/creative* – Key messages/creative should be cited/described, and a rationale/evidence provided for their selection.
9. *Output/outcome measurement tools* – Measurement tools used as part of the evaluation should be specified and a rationale provided, if necessary.
10. *Evaluation findings* – Findings should be clearly stated, and address the objectives.
11. *Key Success Factors* – Factors critical for the success (or failure) of the activity to achieve its objectives should be identified.
12. *Recommendations* – The evaluation should make recommendations for the future, reflecting learnings gleaned from the evaluation.
13. *Budget* – Budget and expenditure figures should be provided, and a statement should be made in respect of the cost-effectiveness of the activity.

Customer service

Customer service can be interpreted as any contact, whether active or passive, between a customer and a company that influences customer perceptions. Customers make positive or negative judgements according to whether companies meet or exceed their expectations and meet their wants and needs. This involves more than the face-to-face contact or direct service that a customer receives. It includes all the elements that are part of the production and distribution of products and services.

The Institute of Customer Service describes excellent customer service as:

- ○ Delighting the customer, satisfying all their needs and giving them something extra to remember you by.
- ○ Making every customer feel special, giving them the impression that they are your No. 1 priority.
- ○ Giving every customer a memorable experience, ensuring they will be pleased to return to you next time.

o Treating every customer with respect, satisfying all their needs and exceeding their expectations.
o Putting customers first – prioritizing their needs and delivering a swift, friendly and efficient service.
o Anticipating and exceeding all customers' expectations.
o Being there for your customers – to provide a rapid, reliable and unbeatable service to them.
o Showing customers you care about them; being professional at all times.
o Adding value to their lives through your dedication, skills and professionalism in satisfying their needs and resolving any difficulties.
o Making the difference for all your customers so they will return to you through choice.
o Establishing a valuable relationship with your customers based on trust, reliability, empathy and your ability to deliver your promises every time.
o Making a commitment to your customer and keeping it.
o Being personable, precise, proactive and professional at all times and in all your dealings with customers.
o Showing you care enough to make the difference for every customer.
o Satisfying customers' needs in a way that shows you genuinely care about them as individuals.
o Welcoming and handling well a customer's enquiries or complaints so that the customer is satisfied and advocates the products and services to others.

Trends in customer service

In November 2004, The Customer Care Alliance conducted an online survey to investigate current trends and performance levels in delivering customer care in Great Britain. Following an e-mail invitation, 7000 British consumers took part in the study that examined the problems they experienced with products and services they used, what they did to address such problems and, if they contacted the organization responsible, the effectiveness of the response they received.

o 77 per cent of consumers experienced at least one problem in the past year with the products and services they consumed.
o The top five industry sectors responsible for problem experience were eating and drinking out, postal services, banking, telephone and rail travel.
o The five most frequent problem issues were product or service did not meet expectations (43 per cent), poor product or service quality (36 per cent), unsatisfactory service – unrelated to repair (31 per cent), delivery delay or non-delivery (21 per cent) and misleading information/advertising (18 per cent).
o 64 per cent were extremely or very upset over their most serious problem.
o Of those who complained, 70 per cent contacted by telephone at some time but the primary means of contact were – telephone (52 per cent), face to face (24 per cent), letter (13 per cent) and e-mail (7 per cent).
o The main reason for not complaining (35 per cent) was I did not believe anything **would** be done about my problem.
o It took an average of 4.5 contacts to resolve a problem.
o Satisfaction dropped from 31 per cent for one contact to 6 per cent if three or more were required.
o Only 10 per cent of problems were resolved within one day, 20 per cent took more than 30 days and 37 per cent of respondents felt that their problem had still not been resolved.
o 53 per cent felt they had lost time over the incident and 44 per cent were financially out of pocket over the incident.
o 83 per cent complained to the organization responsible.

- ○ 53 per cent shared their experience with friends/colleagues and 30 per cent decided never to do business with the organization again.
- ○ Satisfaction dropped from 42 per cent for immediate resolution to 12 per cent or less when it took more than 14 days.

What complainants wanted

- ○ 47 per cent wanted an apology but only 29 per cent got one.
- ○ 44 per cent wanted an explanation but only 22 per cent got one.
- ○ 32 per cent wanted an assurance that their problem would not be repeated but only 7 per cent got one.
- ○ Overall, only 10 per cent were completely satisfied with the action taken to resolve their most serious problem.
- ○ Satisfaction with action taken had a direct correlation with overall satisfaction.
- ○ Many only wanted a non-monetary remedy to their problem but 33 per cent of complainants felt they had received nothing as a result of their contact.

http://europe.customercarealliance.com/UK-Customer-Care-2005.pdf

The following case study highlights the results of a 2004 survey of senior managers with customer service responsibility. Three in four British companies say that they are not easy to do business with.

Customer dis-service built into British Business

77 per cent of businesses admit they are not easy to deal with.

71 per cent fail to gather data on their customers' total experience.

56 per cent of companies fail to incentivize managers to improve the customer experience.

When asked why they fail to understand the causes of bad customer experiences, the top two reasons given are lack of internal resource and poor cross-departmental collaboration. This is the conclusion of the 'Fast + Simple' research report from Budd, the customer service consultancy. The report paints a picture of British business systematically failing its customers, by failing to close the loop from customers' reported frustrations to actual improvements they can feel. Companies need to jettison 'silo' thinking and collaborate across business units and departmental boundaries to act quickly and systematically to interpret customer feedback. Says Peter Massey, CEO of Budd. Just 3 in 10 businesses have regular cross-department reviews and just 1 in 20 of organizations implement formal programmes to exchange learning.

The report highlights seven principles which underpin any approach to systematic excellence. By effectively linking hard and soft processes companies can close the loop between the customer and operations.

To be successful and prevent customer frustration businesses need to:

- Actively listen to the customer – rather than just hearing them
- Make the right people accountable for improvement
- Fix the things that make a difference to customers – addressing root causes not symptoms
- Measure projects and operations with the same success-indicators – so it is clear what makes a difference to customers
- Collaborate end-to-end across the business, to ensure the frontline can deliver what the customer wants
- Track what happens and make sure the customer can see the difference
- Put in a consistent process, not a one-off.

Source: http://www.insightexec.com/cgi-bin/item.cgi?id=131008.

As industries mature and companies can no longer easily differentiate themselves by attributes such as products or pricing and technological innovations are widely available, customer service becomes a critical competitive advantage. Service and support interactions are often the only direct contact the company has with the customer and the quality of those interactions has a significant impact on long-term success. Organizations are facing increased pressures to do more with less. Many are being asked to provide service to more customers and/or support a wider range of products and services as budgets are reduced or remain flat.

There is a growing emphasis on the common management of diverse customer service communications channels, which include the phone, e-mail and web. Managing the channels as separate 'silos' makes it difficult to integrate information and gain a holistic view of a customer's preferences and purchasing profile. Organizations are looking for ways to treat all incoming service requests as a single, manageable queue so they can optimize efficiency.

An integrated customer service process can reduce cost, save time and improve profitability. Linking customer service information with sales data improves business scheduling and helps target potential customers. It helps to avoid duplication of effort and presents a unified, informed image.

The benefits of good customer service

The whole of an organization is implicated in customer service although some companies have dedicated customer service departments. Customer service is a link in a chain between buyer and seller and one of a series of links between stages in a marketing channel.

Increased customer retention rates
It has been repeatedly shown that good service leads directly to increased customer retention rates but the service has to be of a high standard to genuinely keep customers.

Reduced costs of running the business
Increased customer retention rates means the resources associated with setting up the customer's details are reduced to only one over a long time period, compared to a constant stream of new customers coming in as others leave. Regular customers can be serviced more efficiently. Good service means lower complaint rates, and therefore less time and cost involved in dealing with such complaints.

Reduced marketing costs

Many studies have shown that it costs around three to five times as much to attract a new customer compared to making the same sale to an existing customer. Customers can take on part of the marketing function by making recommendations and referrals. Personal referrals are one of the strongest influences on service adoption, and hence the strongest form of marketing.

Stronger position in the competitive marketplace

Companies identified as being good service providers tend to have higher revenue growth compared with poor service competitors. Customers that stay with a company for a long time are more profitable. They are more likely to make repeat purchases of the same goods and services, more likely to purchase other products or services, and often maintain higher balances/accounts.

Improved internal communication, staff relations and morale

Employees who receive positive feedback from their interactions with customers and a reduction in the number of complaints are bound to feel more satisfied with their work than working in a hostile climate. In turn this contributes to better customer service, and a virtuous circle is set in train. Being part of a service that is recognized as poor is damaging to morale.

Customer care

The culture of the organization is the basis of good customer service because it embodies the values of the organization, including how customers and employees should be treated. Motivated and valued staff is the basis of good customer care. Customers may interact with a number of different people during any transaction. The pre-transaction, transaction and post-transaction activities are the customer's chain of experience. An organization committed to customer service should try to understand and gain feedback about the customer's chain of experience.

Developing customer service

Sometimes, customer-care training focuses on superficial issues such as 'have a nice day' and doesn't look at the underlying causes of poor service; for example, management style, lack of empowerment of customer facing staff and lack of continuous training. If you are truly a customer-centric organization, you will literally live and breathe your customers' needs. Every activity should be tuned into making profit for all stakeholders, particularly customers, by maximizing the benefits available to them throughout the delivery and post-delivery processes. That means you have to work towards improving the 'life' of the individual or organization, and this also requires a system of needs and business improvement prioritization across the supply and value chain. So, Hood explains, you first of all must undertake a needs definition analysis of both your organization and customers. The next step is to ascertain which activities are going to have a greater impact on ROI for all of your stakeholders, which activities are necessary and in what order they must be achieved according to their potential impact and benefits. So measure not just inside your company, measure the customer too. Customer-centricity has to enhance the value of the relationship to create a win-win situation otherwise it isn't customer-centricity. The question is: how are you going to become customer-centric? To be customer-centric, you need to manage your total marketing – taking a broader, holistic approach to profit and strategy-making.

Source: By Graham Jarvis, Editor, CIMTech International, editor@cimtech.org http://www. insight-exec.com/cgi-bin/item.cgi?id=131131.

Essentials of customer care

Customer audit

- Who are your current customers?
- What proportion of the business does each represent?
- Who is the 'buyer'?
- Are their needs satisfied?
- How can the service offered to them be improved?

If employees are expected to deliver high-quality customer care, their views should be canvassed for ideas about how customer service could be improved. They also need access to good quality training in areas such as dealing with telephone calls and managing customer complaints efficiently and effectively. A website can be used to give customers the services and information they want. A good database can also help with the organization and planning of customer contacts.

Implementing a customer care programme

Successful customer care means making the customer want to return and getting them to recommend products and services to others. Customer care should be about focusing staff energies on offering value, getting it right first time and continuous improvement. A formalized customer care programme with involved leadership helps to give a clear focus to roles and responsibilities.

Excellence depends on knowing customers' needs and expectations. Anticipating needs can provide a competitive advantage. A range of approaches can be used, including:

- Feedback direct from customers and staff
- Direct discussion with customers
- Analysis of customer complaints, enquiries and thank-yous
- Attitude surveys and questionnaires
- Visits to premises
- Focus-group discussions and customer audits.

Customer care involves a host of elements that contribute to genuine care and value for the customer. Focus the recruitment process on customers and ask questions at the interview stage, covering, for example:

- Candidates' experiences with customers
- Service levels and customer expectations
- The prioritization of customer needs over in-house organizational activities
- Incentives to motivate front-line staff
- Include customer care in the induction programme.

Communications need to be right and the right message needs to be conveyed to all staff in the right way. If internal communications are not working then external communications will not be successful either. Communications have to be reliable, consistent and regular so that all people receive and interpret messages in the same way.

Prompt and sympathetic handling of complaints can turn an unhappy customer into a loyal one.

All staff should be familiar and comfortable with the organization's procedure so that they are prepared to receive complaints and are able to deal with them promptly and accurately.

Let the customer air the grievance without interruption.

Acknowledge the customer's viewpoint – even if you don't agree.

Apologize – say sorry if a mistake has been made, but there's no need to overdo it.

Find a solution – establish what needs to be done to rectify the problem.

Keep the complainant informed – lack of ongoing information can exacerbate the problem.

Reach a conclusion to resolve the problem for the customer quickly – a more permanent solution may take longer to find.

Follow-up – check that promised action happens.

Monitoring and evaluating customer service

A number of issues that impact upon quality measurement are:

- o The difference in perception between employees and customers
- o The inseparability of production and consumption
- o The individuality of employees' performance and customers' perceptions.

There is a proposed formula for measuring these components:

- o *Customer expectations* – service organizations' perceptions of customer expectations
- o *Customer experience* – service organizations' perceptions of customer experience.

The following are examples of processes that can contribute to the monitoring and evaluation of the service that customers receive:

- o *Marketing research* – gather information about services, and delivery of them
- o *Observing customer* – staff interactions as the latter receive a service
- o Interviews to understand their perceptions and expectations versus their experience
- o *Customer satisfaction surveys* – questionnaires to monitor customer satisfaction
- o *Mystery consumer experience* – include a mystery person in the delivery of the service
- o *Evaluating dissatisfaction* – examine the main causes of customer dissatisfaction
- o *Monitoring image* – how is the image of the service perceived
- o *Performance appraisals* – of staff involved in the delivery of a service
- o *Employee group discussions* – internal marketing practice.

SERVQUAL

Measuring customer satisfaction is important for many organizations. The SERVQUAL Methodology was developed originally by customer satisfaction researchers Valarie Zeithaml, A. Parasuraman and Leonard Berry (*Delivering Quality Service*, Free Press: 1990). The Methodology helps organizations to better understand what customers value and how well their current organizations are meeting their needs and expectations. SERVQUAL provides a benchmark based on customer opinions of an excellent company, on your company, on the importance of ranking of key attributes, and on a comparison to what your employees believe customers feel. It provides a detailed information about: customer perceptions of service (a benchmark established by your own customers); performance levels as perceived by customers; customer comments and suggestions and impressions from employees with respect to customers' expectations and satisfaction.

GAP 1 What managers and customers see as important; GAP 2 What managers see as important and the specifications; GAP 3 The specification and the delivery; GAP 4 The delivery and the claim/promise; GAP 5 Expectations and perceptions

Examples of the kinds of questions that can be asked are:

Desired level – The excellence level of service desired. Please consider the level of service you would desire for each of the statements below. If you think a feature requires a very high level of service quality, choose number nine in the second column. If you think a feature requires a very low level of service quality, choose number one in the second column. If your requirements are less extreme, choose an appropriate number in between.

Perceived level – Your perception of the service quality that is provided (see third column). Please use the same nine-point scale to evaluate the level of service you perceive.

With regard to	My DESIRED service level is: LOW 1 2 3 4 5 6 7 8 9 HIGH	My PERCEPTION of service level is: LOW 1 2 3 4 5 6 7 8 9 10 HIGH
1. Providing services as promised		
2. Dependability in handling client's problems		
3. Performing services right at the first time		
4. Providing the service at the promised time		
5. Keeping clients informed of when something will be done		
6. Prompt service to clients		
7. Willingness to help clients		
8. Readiness to respond to clients' requests		
9. Personnel who instil confidence in their clients		
10. Making clients feel assured		
11. Personnel who are always courteous and considerate		
12. Personnel who have the expertise to look after clients' needs		
13. The individual attention that clients get		

14. Personnel who deal with clients in a caring fashion
15. Personnel who have the clients' best interest at heart
16. Personnel who understand the needs of their clients
17. The modern equipment and apparatus available
18. The visually appealing facilities
19. Convenient office hours
20. How would you rate the *overall quality of service* provided?

Case study

Monsoon is a design-led retailer operating two chains – Monsoon and Accessorise. Monsoon aims to provide its customers with an experience that is distinctively different, in terms of product offering and levels of customer service. The company recognizes that its people, and in particular its continuing ability to inspire, motivate and reward them, are critical to the achievement of this aim.

Monsoon has ten service standards to ensure that a consistently high level of service is provided in all their branches. They are:

1. Every customer should be acknowledged within two minutes of entering the branch.
2. Every branch will have a 3-hour window (customer service time).
3. If a customer is holding an item of stock, a member of staff must always approach and offer assistance.
4. When a customer is trying on an item of stock, a member of staff must always be actively working with them.
5. Every customer that an assistant is working with must be offered a secondary product.
6. The telephone should not be answered when serving a customer, except if no one else is free and staff excuse themselves first.
7. If an item is out of stock an alternative item should be found or a solution offered, for example phone another branch or mail order.
8. Every purchasing customer must have the account card mentioned to them at the till point.
9. A positive comment must be made to all customers at the till point; where possible this should be a feature or benefit.
10. Customers should always be thanked and given a smile on the completion of the sale.

Monsoon has a customer service award scheme for its staff, including an employee of the month award. Pay rises and performance related pay are also connected with superior levels of customer service.

Source: http://www2.monsoon.co.uk/.

Because Monsoon's service standards are clearly set out they can be evaluated comparatively easily through direct observation. Obviously, the methods of monitoring and evaluating customer service that are used depend on the type of business and the organizational context. Large companies are more able to introduce sophisticated monitoring systems compared to smaller organizations. Business sectors such as finance, insurance, call centres often record customer telephone calls for training purposes.

Ways to improve customer service

Personalize communications – For example, greeting a customer by name, personalize the e-mail addresses of customer-facing employees.

Create opportunities for feedback

Find out from new customers why they chose the company over the competition. Ask existing customers what could be better. Enable online feedback by putting an e-mail response form or newsgroup on the website. Encourage complaints, as only one in ten dissatisfied customers bothers to complain, usually dissatisfied customers just take their custom elsewhere. Carry out occasional customer satisfaction surveys. Contact any customer who has stopped buying and keep a record of customer feedback to help identify problem areas.

Establish a customer hotline, and make sure the number is on every piece of paper sent out.

- Monitor and analyse the contact you have with customers.
- Use software to discover which webpages are most popular.

Differentiate between different customer segments

When marketing, if appropriate, differentiate between different market segments.

- Potential customers who have not yet purchased anything. For example, someone who has made an enquiry as a result of an advertisement where the aim is to build interest in what you have to offer.
- Another segment is customers who have already made a purchase, where your aim is to increase the frequency of their buying and to sell them other products and services.
- Premium customers who already make regular purchases. Sometimes, a few large customers generate a high proportion of profits and it is important to make sure that their needs are being met. Invite key customers to special events. Try to reinforce the idea that they are valued customers but without being unduly obtrusive or obsequious. Above all, don't be like Uriah Heep who was ever so 'umble'.

Added-value schemes

A successful loyalty scheme pays for itself by encouraging more frequent purchases. The most common loyalty schemes are based on offering rewards to loyal customers. Several businesses can collaborate to support the same loyalty scheme. An accounting system may need to track the purchasing activity of each customer and recognize when discounts have been earned. The following case study is an example of service standards and also shows how customers with special needs are catered for.

Customer Management in action: Manchester United

Manchester United is a global sports/media organization with interests in retail, media and financial services. The importance of having a strong relationship with customers is even more important when the customers are also fans. The Club has an estimated 75 million supporters in 24 different business markets. It is a complex business ranging from retail with sales of shirts and memorabilia through to magazine subscriptions and credit cards and mortgages. The Club faces a significant challenge in interacting with its supporters, understanding their needs and communicating with them in order to ensure the maximum advantage for the Club's commercial interests.

The Club needed a coherent customer relationship management system and embarked on a worldwide programme. The first phase was to further develop channels in order to connect to its supporters around the world. The second phase was to convert supporters into customers and maximize the potential of the Manchester United brand directly and indirectly through its partner network. It has been pulling together information from multiple databases, including Membership, ticketing, www.manutd.com, the Manchester United Museum and financial service partners. The Club has developed a data warehouse and the next step is effective segmentation of that data. The Club is moving towards the stage of trying to predict what people would buy if they were offered products and services at the right time? Having a comprehensive view of a customer is critical to the level and nature of the service the Club can offer. The relationship with the supporters is the lifeblood of the business. The important thing is that this is being driven by the needs of the Club's business strategy.

Source: Adapted from CMC: The Customer Management Community, December 2005, http://www.insightexec.com/

Plan for introducing better customer service

1. Review other organizations with good reputations for good customer service. Look at how this compares with practices in the target organization.
2. Agree what customer service means and how it will be interpreted in the target organization.
3. Agree customer service standards and procedures.
4. All staff should participate in the process of change. Establish a working group or project team that has representation from all the parts of the organization that have an influence on customer service.
5. Review strengths and weaknesses.
6. Agree and communicate customer satisfaction performance targets.
7. Develop plans to implement changes, including an internal marketing plan.
8. A training programme aimed at everyone who has an influence on customer service should be devised or outsourced and implemented.

The following case study highlights the need to target and retain their most attractive customers and expanding their base of profitable customers. This is necessary because the cost of acquiring new customers greatly exceeds the cost of retaining existing customers.

Customer retention management

There are a number of techniques for measuring customer satisfaction linked to profitability. Established customers tend to be more profitable because:

○ They place frequent, consistent orders, and cost less to serve
○ They tend to buy more
○ Satisfied customers may sometimes pay a premium price
○ Retaining customers makes it difficult for competitors to enter a market or increase their share
○ Satisfied customers often refer new customers to the supplier at no extra cost
○ A higher retention rate implies fewer new customers need to be acquired.

Customer retention in business-to-consumer (B2C) markets

In consumer markets, customer retention schemes are focused around loyalty cards. Loyalty schemes are based on accessing information from customer databases, and making use of direct response media such as direct mail and telemarketing. Product-based sales promotion advertising is more widely used by retailers who do not use loyalty schemes.

Retaining customers in business-to-business (B2B) markets

The basic principles that a B2B market should consider in relationship development:

Technical support – providing added value to clients in industrial markets.

Technical expertise – providing expertise can be a good selling point for the organization.

Resource support – making available a range of cost-effective resources to support the relationship.

Service levels – these appear to be of growing importance and will relate in particular to time, delivery and product quality.

Reduction of risk – using exhibitions, trial use and product delivery guarantees.

Relationship marketing

Key dimensions that provide a basis for a relationship:

Reliability – ability to perform the promised service dependably and accurately.

Responsiveness – willingness to help customers and provide prompt service.

Assurance – knowledge and courtesy of employees, and their ability to inspire trust and confidence.

Empathy – caring, individualism, and attention the firm provides its customers.

Tangibles – physical facilities, equipment and appearance of personnel.

Gronroos (1994) defined relationship marketing as identifying, establishing, maintaining, enhancing and, where necessary, terminating the relationship with customers and other stakeholders, at a profit. Relationship marketing is focused on maximizing the lifetime value of desirable customers and customer segments. Strategies need to enhance relationships with key 'markets', including internal ones as well as external relationships with customers, suppliers, referral sources, influence markets and recruitment markets. A relationship marketing approach aims to bring the elements of quality, customer service and marketing into an integrated relationship. This helps marketers to focus on maintaining and enhancing customer relationships. The types of interactions that take place between buyers and sellers can be viewed on a continuum, ranging from transaction to relationship.

Transaction marketing	Relationship marketing
Focus more on single sale	Focus more on customer retention
Orientation more on product features	Orientation more on product benefits
Comparatively short timescale	Comparatively long timescale
Little emphasis on customer service	High emphasis on customer service
Limited customer commitment	Higher customer commitment
Moderate customer contact	Higher customer contact
Quality is primarily a concern of production	Quality is the concern of all

Case study

Wal-Mart Stores Inc. has been ranked number one in the USA by Fortune magazine for a second year in a row. Wal-Mart uses one-to-one relationship marketing tactics, executed by the famous Wal-Mart greeter. A greeter at the door thanks customers for coming in, assists with a shopping cart, and provides a 'goodbye thank you' upon departing the store. So why don't others adopt this simple marketing tactic? – because relationship marketing is not as simple as it seems. It takes a type of commitment different than traditional marketing.

Relationship Marketing has 4 key components:

It has to be personalized – Personalization can come in the form of a highly targeted direct mail piece, a phone call or e-mail.

It has to be targeted – Wal-Mart invests in maintaining relationships with existing customers. By targeting this group, Wal-Mart establishes long-term relationships with their most loyal shoppers.

It has to be meaningful – If the Wal-Mart greeter did not look you in the eye while saying 'hello', the greeting would not have a lasting impact.

It should be interactive – Many Wal-Mart greeters learn the names of frequent shoppers. It is important to make relationship marketing interactive so you can hear feedback. Don't forget the value of real conversations and face-to-face meetings. There is a reason why Wal-Mart employs more than 164 000 associates 55 and older to greet customers at the door.

Source: Relationship Marketing King Wal-Mart Still No. 1 by Doug Edge, 29 April 2003.

Relationship marketing and mass customization

Mass customization enables companies to focus on what customers want, rather than what the company can produce. It also allows companies to produce individually tailored products. There is a longer history of using this approach with services such as banking stockbroking rather than products. Mass customization is also more common in B2B markets and the simplest approach is to design a product that buyers can customize themselves. Dell Computers allows the buyer to design an individual computer and then track it through to delivery. Much of Dell's production, up to the point of final assembly, is outsourced which means that suppliers at every link in the chain need good timely information about what customers want, and when. Speed and good communications are essential if mass customization is to work.

Dell's business model

While other PC makers rely on resellers, retailers, and other agents to carry much of the burden of marketing and sales, Dell has to reach out to customers largely through its own efforts. And while other PC makers can run high-volume assembly lines to achieve economies of scale, Dell must tailor each order to meet customer specifications, a process that puts heavy demands on shop floor employees, suppliers, logistical systems, and information systems. Direct sales means that Dell must reach out to potential customers, either through its own sales force or through advertising and other marketing efforts. Dell's use of the direct approach provides it with detailed knowledge about its customers. The direct approach also allows Dell to identify customer trends early so it can respond with the desired products before its competitors can, in order to achieve mass customization of products. Build-to-order requires Dell to have very close co-ordination between Dell's sales and manufacturing arms and between Dell and its suppliers. It achieves this by refining its business processes, developing close relationships with a limited number of suppliers, and using IT to facilitate communication within and outside the company. The build-to-order production system is the focal point of Dell's business operations, the common contact point for sales, procurement, logistics, manufacturing, and delivery. Build-to-order production, or mass customization, should also gain footholds in more industries as companies look to differentiate their products and avoid pure price competition.

The Age of E-tail (Birch, Gerbert and Schneider (2000)) conveys the message that the future of shopping is online and the result of this will be the need for companies to offer almost everything in ways that are specifically tailored to the customer. Personalized products, such as cars and PCs, are made to individual specifications and soon all successful e-tailors will offer almost everything tailored individually to the customer. E-tailors need repeat business to achieve profitability but e-customers are fickle.

Summary

There are a variety of approaches to planning the design, implementation and evaluation of communications campaigns. Marketing communications are used to develop relationships or communicate with a range of stakeholders including the provision of support for members of a marketing channel. There are also a variety of ways to review and evaluate the effectiveness of communications activities.

Hints and tips

Integrated communications is a typical example of the task that faces the professional marketer. Not only must the right things be done but they must be done in the right sequence and at the right time.

A firm grasp of the nature of the communications issues and proposes a number of justified activities. Some innovative suggestions are made. Both 'push' and 'pull' elements are covered.

Bibliography

Beamish, K. (2003) 'Communication Strategies and planning', *Marketing Communications*, Harlow: Butterworth-Heinemann.

Birch, A., Gerbert, P. and Schneider, D. (2000) *The Age of E-tail*, 4th European edition, Milford, CT: Capstone.

Carlzon, J. (1987) *Moments of Truth*, Harper.

Kotler, P. (2003) *Marketing Management*, 11th edition, New York: Prentice Hall.

Past examination papers for the Marketing Management in Practice module can be found in Appendix 5.

appendix 1
guidance on examination preparation

Preparing for your examination

You are now nearing the final phase of your studies and it is time to start the hard work of exam preparation.

During your period of study you will have become used to absorbing large amounts of information. You will have tried to understand and apply aspects of knowledge that may have been very new to you, while some of tho information provided may have been more familiar. You may even have undertaken many of the activities that are positioned frequently throughout your Coursebook, which will have enabled you to apply your learning in practical situations. But whatever the state of your knowledge and understanding, do not allow yourself to fall into the trap of thinking that you know enough, that you understand enough, or even worse, that you can just take it as it comes on the day.

Never underestimate the pressure of the CIM examination.

The whole point of preparing this textbook for you is to ensure that you never take the examination for granted, and that you do not go to the exam unprepared for what might come your way for 3 hours at a time.

One thing is for sure: there is no quick fix, no easy route, no waving a magic wand and finding you know it all.

Whether you have studied alone, in a CIM study centre, or through distance learning, you now need to ensure that this final phase of your learning process is tightly managed, highly structured and objective.

As a candidate in the examination, your role will be to convince the Senior Examiner that you have credibility for this subject. You need to demonstrate to the examiner that you can be trusted to undertake a range of challenges in the context of marketing and that you are able to capitalize on opportunities and manage your way through threats.

You should prove to the Senior Examiner that you are able to apply knowledge, make decisions, respond to situations and solve problems.

Very shortly we are going to look at a range of revision and exam preparation techniques, and at time-management issues, and encourage you towards developing and implementing your own revision plan, but before that, let's look at the role of the Senior Examiner.

A bit about the Senior Examiners!

You might be quite shocked to read this, but while it might appear that the examiners are 'relentless question masters' they actually want you to be able to answer the questions and pass the exams! In fact, they would derive no satisfaction or benefits from failing candidates; quite the contrary, they develop the syllabus and exam papers in order that you can learn and then apply that learning effectively so as to pass your examinations. Many of the examiners have said in the past that it is indeed psychologically more difficult to fail students than pass them.

Many of the hints and tips you find within this Appendix have been suggested by the Senior Examiners and authors of the Coursebook series. Therefore, you should consider them carefully and resolve to undertake as many of the elements suggested as possible.

The Chartered Institute of Marketing has a range of processes and systems in place within the Examinations Division to ensure that fairness and consistency prevail across the team of examiners, and that the academic and vocational standards that are set and defined are indeed maintained. In doing this, CIM ensures that those who gain the CIM Professional Certificate Professional Diploma in Marketing and Professional Postgraduate Diploma in Marketing are worthy of the qualification and perceived as such in the view of employers, actual and potential.

Part of what you will need to do within the examination is be 'examiner friendly' – that means you have to make sure they get what they ask for. This will make life easier for you and for them.

Hints and tips for 'examiner friendly' actions are as follows:

- Show them that you understand the basis of the question, by answering *precisely* the question asked, and not including just about everything you can remember about the subject area.
- Read their needs – how many points is the question asking you to address?
- Respond to the question appropriately. Is the question asking you to take on a role? If so, take on the role and answer the question in respect of the role. For example, you could be positioned as follows:

'You are working as a Marketing Assistant at Nike UK' or 'You are a Marketing Manager for an Engineering Company' or 'As Marketing Manager write a report to the Managing Partner.'

These examples of role-playing requirements are taken from questions in past papers.

- Deliver the answer in the format requested. If the examiner asks for a memo, then provide a memo; likewise, if the examiner asks for a report, then write a report. If you do not do this, in some instances, you will fail to gain the necessary marks required to pass.
- Take a business-like approach to your answers. This enhances your credibility. Badly ordered work, untidy work, lack of structure, headings and subheadings can be off-putting. This would be unacceptable in the work situation, likewise it will be unacceptable in the eyes of the Senior Examiners and their marking teams.
- Ensure the examiner has something to mark: give them substance, relevance, definitions, illustrations and demonstration of your knowledge and understanding of the subject area.
- See the examiner as your potential employer or ultimate consumer/customer. The whole purpose and culture of marketing is about meeting customers' needs. Try this approach – it works wonders.

- Provide a strong sense of enthusiasm and professionalism in your answers; support it with relevant up-to-date examples and apply them where appropriate.
- Try to do something that will make your exam paper a little bit different – make it stand out in the crowd.

All of these points might seem quite logical to you, but often in the panic of the examination they 'go out of the window'. Therefore it is beneficial to remind ourselves of the importance of the examiner. He/she is the 'ultimate customer' – and we all know customers hate to be disappointed.

As we move on, some of these points will be revisited and developed further.

About the examination

In all examinations, with the exception of Marketing Management in Practice at Professional Diploma level, the paper is divided into two parts.

- Part A – Mini-case study = 50 marks
- Part B – Option choice questions (choice of two questions from four) = 50 per cent of the marks (each question attracting 25 per cent).

For the Marketing Management in Practice paper, the same approach is taken. However, all of the questions are directly related to the case study and in this instance the case material is more extensive.

Let's look at the basis of each element.

Part A: The mini-case study

This is based on a mini-case or scenario with one question, possibly subdivided into between two and four points, but totalling 50 per cent of overall marks.

In essence, you, the candidate, are placed in a problem-solving role through the medium of a short scenario. On occasions, the scenario may consist of an article from a journal in relation to a well-known organization.

Alternatively, it will be based upon a fictional company, and the examiner will have prepared it in order that the right balance of knowledge, understanding, application and skills is used.

Approaches to the mini-case study

When undertaking the mini-case study there are a number of key areas you should consider.

Structure/content

The mini-case that you will be presented with will vary slightly from paper to paper and, of course, from one examination to the other. Normally, the scenario presented will be 250–500 words long and will centre on a particular organization and its problems or may even relate to a specific industry. However, please note, for Marketing Management in Practice, the case study is more significant as all the questions are based upon the case materials.

The length of the mini-case study means that usually only a brief outline is provided of the situation, the organization and its marketing problems, and you must therefore learn to cope with analysing information and preparing your answer on the basis of a very limited amount of detail.

Time management

There are many differing views on time management and the approaches you can take to manage your time within the examination. You must find an approach to suit your way of working, but always remember, whatever you do, you must ensure that you allow enough time to complete the examination. Unfinished exams mean lost marks. A typical example of managing time is:

Your paper is designed to assess you over a three hour period. With 50 per cent of the marks being allocated to the mini-case, it means that you should dedicate somewhere around 100 minutes of your time to both read and write up the answer on this mini-case, leaving a further 80 minutes for the remaining questions. Some students, however, will prefer to allocate nearly half of their time (90 minutes) on the mini-case, so that they can read and fully absorb the case, and answer the questions in the context of it. This is also acceptable as long as you ensure that you work extremely 'SMART' for the remaining time in order to finish the examination.

Do not forget that while there is only one question within the mini-case, it can have a number of components. You must answer all the components in that question, which is where the balance of time comes into play.

Knowledge/skills tested

Throughout all the CIM papers, your knowledge, skills and ability to apply those skills will be tested. However, the mini-cases are used particularly to test application, that is your ability to take your knowledge and apply it in a structured way to a given scenario. The examiners will be looking at your decision-making ability, your analytical and communication skills and, depending on the level, your ability as a manager to solve particular marketing problems.

When the examiner is marking your paper, he or she will be looking to see how you differentiate yourself, looking at your own individual 'unique selling points'. The examiner will also want to see if you can personally apply the knowledge or whether you are only able to repeat the textbook materials.

Format of answers

On many occasions, and within all examinations, you will most likely be given a particular communication method to use. If this is the case, you must ensure that you adhere to the requirements of the examiner. This is all part of meeting customer needs.

The likely communications tools you will be expected to use are:

- Memorandum
- Memorandum/report
- Report
- Briefing notes
- Presentation
- Press release
- Advertisement
- Plan.

Make sure that you familiarize yourself with these particular communications tools and practise using them to ensure that, on the day, you will be able to respond confidently to the communication requests of the examiner. Look back at the Customer Communications text at Certificate level to familiarize yourself with the potential requirements of these methods.

By the same token, while communication methods are important, so is meeting the specific requirements of the question. This means you must understand what is meant by the precise instruction given. *Note the following terms carefully*:

o *Identify* – Select key issues, point out key learning points, establish clearly what the examiner expects you to identify.

o *Illustrate* – The examiner expects you to provide examples, scenarios and key concepts that illustrate your learning.

o *Compare and contrast* – Look at the range of similarities between the two situations, contexts or even organizations. Then compare them, that is ascertain and list how activities, features and so on agree or disagree. Contrasting means highlighting the differences between the two.

o *Discuss* – Questions that have 'discuss' in them offer a tremendous opportunity for you to debate, argue, justify your approach or understanding of the subject area – *caution* it is not an opportunity to waffle.

o *Briefly explain* – This means being succinct, structured and concise in your explanation, within the answer. Make your points clear, transparent and relevant.

o *State* – Present in a clear, brief format.

o *Interpret* – Expound the meaning of, make clear and explicit what it is you see and understand within the data provided.

o *Outline* – Provide the examiner with the main concepts and features being asked for and avoid minor technical details. Structure will be critical here, or else you could find it difficult to contain your answer.

o *Relate* – Show how different aspects of the syllabus connect together.

o *Evaluate* – Review and reflect upon an area of the syllabus, a particular practice, an article and so on, and consider its overall worth in respect of its use as a tool or a model and its overall effectiveness in the role it plays.

Source: Worsam, Mike, *How to Pass Marketing*, Croner, 1989.

Your approach to mini-cases

There is no one right way to approach and tackle a mini-case study, indeed it will be down to each individual to use their own creativity in tackling the tasks presented. You will have to use your initiative and discretion about how best to approach the mini-case. Having said this, however, there are some basic steps you can take.

o Ensure that you read through the case study at least twice before making any judgements, starting to analyse the information provided, or indeed writing the answers.

o On the third occasion read through the mini-case and, using a highlighter, start marking the essential and relevant information critical to the content and context. Then turn your attention to the question again, this time reading slowly and carefully to assess what it is you are expected to do. Note any instructions that the examiner gives you, and then start to plan how you might answer the question. Whatever the question, ensure the answer has a structure: a beginning, a structured central part and, finally, always a conclusion.

o Keep the context of the question continually in mind: that is, the specifics of the case and the role which you might be performing.

o Because there is limited material available, you will sometimes need to make assumptions. Don't be afraid to do this, it will show initiative on your part. Assumptions are an important part of dealing with case studies and can help you to be quite creative with your answer. However, do explain the basis of your assumptions within your answer so that the examiner understands the nature of them, and why you have arrived at your particular outcome. *Always ensure that your assumptions are realistic.*

○ Only now are you approaching the stage where it is time to start writing your answer to the question, tackling the problems, making decisions and recommendations on the case scenario set before you. As mentioned previously, your points will often be best set out in a report or memo type format, particularly if the examiner does not specify a communication method.

○ Ensure that your writing is succinct, avoids waffle and responds directly to the questions asked.

Part B: Option choice questions

Part B is comprised of four traditional questions, each worth 25 per cent. You will be expected to choose two of those questions, to make up the remaining 50 per cent of available marks. (Again please note that the structure is the same for Marketing Management in Practice, but that all questions are applied to the case study.)

Realistically, the same principles apply for these questions as in the case study. Communication formats, reading through the questions, structure, role-play, context and so on – everything is the same.

Part B will cover a number of broader issues from within the syllabus and will be taken from any element of it. The examiner makes the choice, and no prior direction is given to students or tutors on what that might be.

As regards time management in this area, if you used about 100 minutes for the mini-case you should have around 80 minutes left. This provides you with around 40 minutes to plan and write a question, to write, review and revise your answers. Keep practising – use a cooker timer, alarm clock or mobile phone alarm as your timer and work hard at answering questions within the time frame given.

Specimen examination papers and answers

To help you prepare and understand the nature of the paper, go to www.cim.co.uk/learningzone or to access Specimen Answers and Senior Examiner's advice for these exam questions. During your study, the author of your Coursebook may have, on occasions, asked you to refer to these papers and answer the questions. You should undertake these exercises and utilize every opportunity to practise meeting examination requirements.

Each of the Professional Diploma coursebooks has, at the end of it, some examination questions and guidance provided by the authors and Senior Examiners, where appropriate, to provide you with some insight into the types of questions asked.

The specimen answers are vital learning tools. They are not always perfect, as they are answers written by students and annotated by the Senior Examiners, but they will give you a good indication of the approaches you could take, and the examiners' annotations suggest how these answers might be improved. Please use them.

Other sources of information to support your learning through the learning zone are 'Hot Topics'. These give you scope to undertake a range of associated activities related to the syllabus and study areas, and will also be very useful to you when you are revising.

Key elements of preparation

One Senior Examiner suggests the three elements involved in preparing for your examination can be summarized thus:

1. Learning
2. Memory
3. Revision.

Let's look at each point in turn.

Learning

Quite often students find it difficult to learn properly. You can passively read books, look at some of the materials, perhaps revise a little, and regurgitate it all in the examination. In the main, however, this is rather an unsatisfactory method of learning. It is meaningless, shallow and ultimately of little use in practice.

For learning to be truly effective it must be active and applied. You must involve yourself in the learning process by thinking about what you have read, testing it against your experience by reflecting on how you use particular aspects of marketing, and how you could perhaps improve your own performance by implementing particular aspects of your learning into your everyday life. You should adopt the old adage of 'learning by doing' If you do, you will find that passive learning has no place in your study life.

Below are some suggestions that have been prepared to assist you with the learning pathway throughout your revision.

- o Always make your own notes, in words you understand, and ensure that you combine all the sources of information and activities within them.
- o Always try to relate your learning back to your own organization.
- o Make sure you define key terms concisely, wherever possible.
- o Do not try to memorize your ideas, but work on the basis of understanding and, most important, applying them.
- o Think about the relevant and topical questions that might be set – use the questions and answers in your Coursebooks to identify typical questions that might be asked in the future.
- o Attempt all of the questions within each of your Coursebooks since these are vital tests of your active learning and understanding.

Memory

If you are prepared to undertake an active learning programme then your knowledge will be considerably enhanced, as understanding and application of knowledge does tend to stay in your 'long-term' memory. It is likely that passive learning will only stay in your 'short-term' memory.

Do not try to memorize in parrot fashion; it is not helpful and, even more important, examiners are experienced in identifying various memorizing techniques and therefore will spot them as such.

Having said this, it is quite useful to memorize various acronyms such as SWOT, PEST, PESTLE, STEEPLE, or indeed various models such as Ansoff, GE Matrix, Shell Directional

Policy Matrix and so on, as in some of the questions you may be required to use illustrations of these to assist your answer.

Revision

The third and final stage to consider is 'revision', which is what we will concentrate on in detail below. Here just a few key tips are offered.

Revision should be an ongoing process rather than a panic measure that you decide to undertake just before the examination. You should be preparing notes *throughout* your course, with the view to using them as part of your revision process. Therefore, ensure that your notes are sufficiently comprehensive that you can reuse them successfully.

For each concept you learn about, you should identify, through your reading and your own personal experience, at least two or three examples that you could use; this then gives you some scope to broaden your perspective during the examination. It will, of course, help you gain some points for initiative with the examiners.

Knowledge is not something you will gain overnight – as we saw earlier, it is not a quick fix; it involves a process of learning that enables you to lay solid foundations upon which to build your long-term understanding and application. This will benefit you significantly in the future, not just in the examination.

In essence, you should ensure that you do the following in the period before the real intensive revision process begins.

o Keep your study file well organized, updated and full of newspaper and journal cuttings that may help you formulate examples in your mind for use during the examination.
o Practise defining key terms and acronyms from memory.
o Prepare topic outlines and essay answer plans.
o When you start your intensive revision, ensure it is planned and structured in the way described below. And then finally, read your concentrated notes the night before the examination.

Revision planning

You are now on a critical path – although hopefully not too critical at this time – with somewhere in the region of between 4 and 6 weeks to go to the examination. The following hints and tips will help you plan out your revision study.

o You will, as already explained, need to be very organized. Therefore, before doing anything else, put your files, examples, reading material and so on, in good order, so that you are able to work with them in the future and, of course, make sense of them.
o Ensure that you have a quiet area within which to work. It is very easy to get distracted when preparing for an examination.
o Take out your file along with your syllabus, and make a list of key topic areas that you have studied and which you now need to revise. You could use the basis of this book to do that, by taking each unit a step at a time.
o Plan the use of your time carefully. Ideally, you should start your revision at least 6 weeks prior to the exam, so therefore work out how many spare hours you could give to the revision process and then start to allocate time in your diary, and do not double-book with anything else.

o Give up your social life for a short period of time. As the saying goes 'no pain – no gain'.

o Looking at each of the subject areas in turn, identify which are your strengths and which are your weaknesses. Which areas have you grasped and understood, and which are the areas that you have really struggled with? Split your page into two and make a list on each side. For example:

Planning and control	
Strengths	**Weaknesses**
Audit – PEST, SWOT, Models	Ratio analysis
Portfolio analysis	Market sensing
	Productivity analysis
	Trend extrapolation
	Forecasting

o Break down your list again and divide the points of weakness giving priority in the first instance to your weakest areas and even prioritizing them by giving each of them a number. This will enable you to master the more difficult areas. Up to 60 per cent of your remaining revision time should be given over to that, as you may find you have to undertake a range of additional reading and also perhaps seeking tutor support, if you are studying at a CIM Accredited Study Centre.

o The rest of the time should be spent reinforcing your knowledge and understanding of the stronger areas, spending time testing yourself on how much you really know.

o Should you be taking two examinations or more at any one time, then the breakdown and managing of your time will be critical.

o Taking a subject at a time, work through your notes and start breaking them down into subsections of learning, and ultimately into key learning points, items that you can refer to time and time again, that are meaningful and that your mind will absorb. You yourself will know how best you remember the key points. Some people try to develop acronyms, flowcharts or matrices, mind maps, fishbone diagrams and so on, or various connection diagrams that help them recall certain aspects of models. You could also develop processes that enable you to remember approaches to various options. (But do remember what we said earlier about regurgitating stuff, parrot fashion.)

Figure A1.1 is just a brief example of how you could use a 'bomb-burst' diagram (which, in this case, highlights the uses of advertising) as a very helpful approach to memorizing key elements of learning.

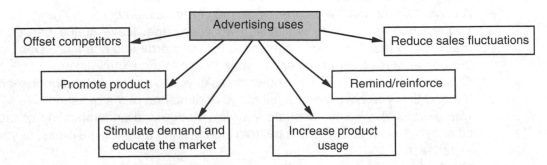

Figure A1.1 Use of a diagram to summarize key components of a concept
Source: Adapted from Dibb, Simkin, Pride and Ferrell, *Marketing Concepts and Strategies*, 4th edition, Houghton Mifflin, 2001

- Eventually you should reduce your key learning to bullet points. For example: imagine you were looking at the concept of Time Management – you could eventually reduce your key learning to a bullet list containing the following points in relation to 'Effective Prioritization'.

  - Organize
  - Take time
  - Delegate
  - Review.

- Each of these headings would then remind you of the elements you need to discuss associated with the subject area.
- Avoid getting involved in reading too many textbooks at this stage, as you may start to find that you are getting confused overall.
- Look at examination questions in previous papers, and start to observe closely the various roles and tasks they expect you to undertake, and importantly, the context in which they are set.
- *Use the specimen exam papers and specimen answers* to support your learning and see how you could actually improve upon them.
- Without exception, find an associated examination question for the areas that you have studied and revised, and undertake it (more than once, if necessary).
- Without referring to notes or books, try to draft an answer plan with the key concepts, knowledge, models and information that are needed to successfully complete the answer. Then refer to the specimen answer to see how close you are to the actual outline presented. Planning your answer, and ensuring that key components are included and that the question has a meaningful structure, is one of the most beneficial activities that you can undertake.
- Now write the answer out in full, time constrained and written by hand, not with the use of IT. (At this stage, you are still expected to be the scribe for the examination and present handwritten work. Many of us find this increasingly difficult as we spend more and more time using our computers to present information. Do your best to be neat. Difficult handwriting is often off-putting to the examiner.)
- When writing answers as part of your revision process, be sure to practise the following essential examination techniques

  - *Identify and use the communication method* – Requested by the examiner.
  - *Always have three key parts to the answer* – An introduction, a middle section that develops your answer in full, and a conclusion. Where appropriate, ensure that you have an introduction, main section, summary/conclusion and, if requested or helpful, recommendations.
  - *Always answer the question in the context or role set.*
  - *Always comply with the nature and terms of the question.*
  - *Leave white space* – Do not overcrowd your page; leave space between paragraphs, and make sure your sentences do not merge into one blur. (Don't worry – there is always plenty of paper available to use in the examination.)
  - *Count* – How many actions the question asks you to undertake and double-check at the end that you have met the full range of demands of the question.
  - *Use examples* – To demonstrate your knowledge and understanding of the particular syllabus area. These can be from journals, the Internet, the press, or your own experience.
  - *Display your vigour and enthusiasm for marketing* – Remember to think of the Senior Examiner as your Customer, or future employer, and do your best to deliver what is wanted to satisfy their needs. Impress them and show them how you are a 'cut above the rest'.
  - Review all your practice answers critically with the above points in mind.

Practical actions

The critical path is becoming even more critical now as the examination looms. The following are vital points.

- o Have you registered with CIM?
- o Do you know where you are taking your examination? CIM should let you know approximately 1 month in advance.
- o Do you know where your examination centre is? If not, find out, take a drive, time it – whatever you do don't be late!
- o Make sure you have all the tools of the examination ready. A dictionary, calculator, pens, pencils, ruler and so on. Try not to use multiple shades of pens, but at the same time make your work look professional. *Avoid using red and green as these are the colours that will be used for marking.*

Summary

Above all, you must remember that you personally have invested a tremendous amount of time, effort and money in studying for this programme and it is therefore imperative that you consider the suggestions given here as they will help to maximize your return on your investment.

Many of the hints and tips offered here are generic and will work across most of the CIM courses. We have tried to select those that will help you most In taking a sensible, planned approach to your study and revision.

The key to your success is being prepared to put in the time and effort required, planning your revision, and equally important is planning and answering your questions in a way that will ensure that you pass your examination on the day.

The advice offered here aims to guide you from a practical perspective. Guidance on syllabus content and developments associated with your learning will become clear to you as you work through this Coursebook. The authors of each Coursebook have given subject-specific guidance on the approach to the examination and on how to ensure that you meet the content requirements of the kind of question you will face. These considerations are in addition to the structuring issues we have been discussing throughout this Appendix.

Each of the authors and Senior Examiners will guide you on their preferred approach to questions and answers as they go. Therefore, where you are presented with an opportunity to be involved in some activity or undertake an examination question either during or at the end of your study units, do take it. It not only prepares you for the examination, but also helps you learn in the applied way we discussed above.

Here, then, is a last reminder:

- o Ensure you make the most of your learning process throughout.
- o Keep structured and orderly notes from which to revise.
- o Plan your revision – don't let it just happen.
- o Provide examples to enhance your answers.
- o Practise your writing skills in order that you present your work well and your writing is readable.
- o Take as many opportunities as possible to test your knowledge and measure your progress.

o   Plan and structure your answers.
o   Always do as the question asks you, especially with regard to context and communication method.
o   Do not leave it until the last minute!

The writers would like to take this opportunity to wish you every success in your endeavours to study, to revise and to pass your examinations.

Karen Beamish
Academic Development Advisor

appendix 2

assignment-based assessment

Introduction – the basis to the assignments and the integrative project

Within the CIM qualifications at both Professional Certificate and Professional Diploma there are several assessment options available. These are detailed in the outline of modules below. The purpose of an assignment is to provide another format to complete each module for students who want to apply the syllabus concepts from a module to their own or a selected organization. For either qualification there are three modules providing assessment via an assignment and one module assessed via an integrative work-based project. The module assessed via the integrative project is the summative module for each qualification.

	Entry modules	Research & analysis	Planning	Implementation	Management of Marketing
Professional Post Graduate Diploma	Entry module – Professional Post Graduate Diploma	Analysis & Evaluation	Strategic Marketing Decisions	Managing Marketing Performance	Strategic Marketing in Practice
Professional Diploma	Entry module – Professional Diploma	Marketing Research & Information	Marketing Planning	Marketing Communications	Marketing Management in Practice
Professional Certificate		Marketing Environment	Marketing Fundamentals	Customer Communications	Marketing in Practice
Introductory Certificate		Supporting marketing processes (research & analysis, planning and implementation)			

Outline of CIM 'standard' syllabus (© The Chartered Institute of Marketing, September 2003)

The use of assignments does not mean that this route is easier than an examination. Both formats are carefully evaluated to ensure that a grade B in the assessment/integrative project route is the same as a grade B in the examination. However, the use of assignments does allow a student to complete the assessment for a module over a longer period of time than a three-hour examination. This will inevitably mean work being undertaken over the time span of a module. For those used to cramming for exams, writing an assignment over several weeks which comprises a total of four separate questions will be a very different approach.

Each module within the qualification contains a different assignment written specifically for the module. These are designed to test understanding and provide the opportunity for you to demonstrate your abilities through the application of theory to practice. The format and structure of each module's assignment is identical, although the questions asked will differ and the exact type of assignment varies. The questions within an assignment will relate directly to the syllabus for that particular module, thereby giving the opportunity to demonstrate understanding and application.

The assignment structure

The assignment for each module is broken down into a range of questions. These consist of a core question and a selection of optional questions. The core question will always relate to the main aspects of each module's syllabus. Coupled with this are a range of four optional questions which will each draw from a different part of the syllabus. Students are requested to select two optional questions from the four available. When put together these form the assessment for the entire module. The overall pass mark for the module is the same as through an examination route, which is set at 50 per cent. In addition, the grade band structure is also identical to that of an examination.

Core question

This is the longest and therefore the most important section of your assignment. Covering the major components of the syllabus, the core question is designed to provide a challenging assignment which both tests the theoretical element and also permits application to a selected organization or situation. The word limit for this task will be indicated to you by the CIM and will be included in the rubric on the front of the assignment. It also outlines the regulations for including additional materials in the form of appendices. However, the appendices should be kept to a minimum. Advice here is that there should be no longer than five pages of additional pertinent information.

Optional questions

There are a total of four questions provided for Professional Certificate and Professional Diploma of the syllabus from which a student is asked to select two. Each answer is expected to provide a challenge although the actual task required varies. Again the word count for these tasks will be in the rubric on the front of the assignment.

These are designed to test areas of the syllabus not covered by the core question. As such it is possible to base all of your questions on the same organization although there is significant benefit in using more than one organization as a basis for your assignment. Some of the questions specifically require a different organization to be selected from the one used for the core question. This only occurs where the questions are requiring similar areas to be investigated and will be specified clearly on the question itself.

Within the assignment there are several types of questions that may be asked, including:

- o *A report* – The question requires a formal report to be completed, detailing an answer to the specific question set. This will often be reporting on a specific issue to an individual.
- o *A briefing paper or notes* – Preparing a briefing paper or a series of notes which may be used for a presentation.
- o *A presentation* – You may be required either to prepare the presentation only or to deliver the presentation in addition to its preparation. The audience for the presentation should be considered carefully and ICT used where possible.
- o *A discussion paper* – The question requires an academic discussion paper to be prepared. You should show a range of sources and concepts within the paper. You may also be required to present the discussion paper as part of a question.
- o *A project plan or action plan* – Some questions ask for planning techniques to be demonstrated. As such, the plan must be for the timescale given and costs shown where applicable. The use of ICT is recommended here in order to create the plan diagrammatically.
- o *Planning a research project* – Whilst market research may be required, questions have often asked for simply a research plan in a given situation. This would normally include timescales, the type(s) of research to be gathered, sampling, planned data collection and analysis.
- o *Conducting research* – Following on from a research plan, a question can require the student(s) to undertake a research gathering exercise. A research question can be either an individual or a group activity depending upon the question. This will usually result in a report of the findings of the exercise plus any recommendations arising from your findings.
- o *Gathering of information and reporting* – Within many questions information will need gathering. The request for information can form part or all of a question. This may be a background to the organization, the activities contained in the question or external market and environmental information. It is advisable to detail the types of information utilized, their sources and report on any findings. Such a question will often ask for recommendations for the organization – these should be drawn from the data and not simply personal opinion.
- o *An advisory document* – A question here will require students to evaluate a situation and present advice and recommendations drawn from findings and theory. Again, any advice should be backed up with evidence and not a personal perspective only.
- o *An exercise, either planning and/or delivering the exercise* – At both Stage One and Stage Two, exercises are offered as optional questions. These provide students with the opportunity to devise an exercise and may also require the delivery of this exercise. Such an activity should be evidenced where possible.
- o *A role-play with associated documentation* – Several questions have asked students to undertake role-plays in exercises such as team-building. These are usually videoed and documentation demonstrating the objectives of the exercise provided.

Each of these questions relate directly towards specific issues to be investigated, evaluated and answered. In addition, some of the questions asked present situations to be considered. These provide opportunities for specific answers relating directly to the question asked.

In order to aid students completing the assignment, each question is provided with an outline of marking guidance. This relates to the different categories by which each question is marked. The marker of your assignment will be provided with a detailed marking scheme constructed around the same marking guidance provided to students.

For both the core and optional questions, it is important to use referencing where sources have been utilized. This has been a weakness in the past and continues to be an issue. There have been cases of plagiarism identified during marking and moderation, together with a distinct lack of references and bibliography. This becomes more important at Stage Two where the nature of the syllabus lends itself to a more academic approach. It is highly recommended that a bibliography be included with each question and sources are cited within the text itself. The type of referencing method used is not important, only that sources are referred to.

Integrative project structure

The integrative project is designed to provide an in-company approach to assessment rather than having specified assignments. Utilized within the summative module element of each level's syllabus, this offers a student the chance to produce a piece of work which tackles a specific issue. The integrative project can only be completed after undertaking other modules as it will rely on information in each of these as guidance.

Professional Diploma Assignments – Marketing Management in Practice

How to pass the integrative assignment

The process to complete a successful assignment is given in Figure A2.1.

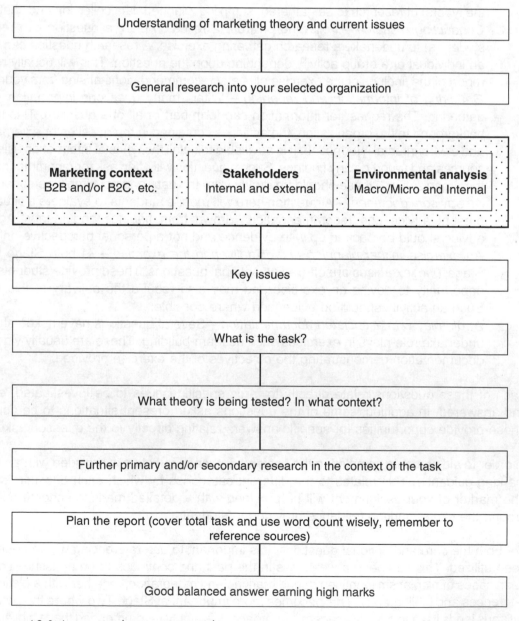

Figure A2.1 An approach to an integrated assignment

Understanding of marketing theory and current issues

This is covered on page 316 and is not repeated here.

General research into your selected organization

An important first task before you start to complete any of the detailed assignments is to prepare the ground and do some general research. However, it has its parallel in a challenge facing an engineer to build a bridge (Figure A2.2a,b). Faced with this situation the engineer does not say 'no problem just send me down 20 000 tonnes of steel and 100 000 tonnes of concrete and I will have it sorted!' There are reasons why the Sydney Harbour Bridge is different to the San Francisco Bridge in construction. Some research and planning is needed. So, it is with an integrative project.

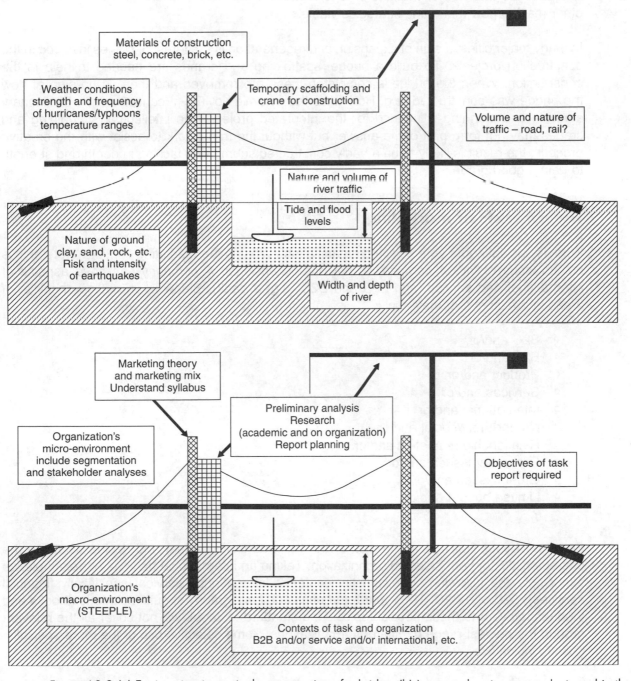

Figure A2.2 (a) Engineering issues in the construction of a bridge; (b) Integrated assignment task viewed in the context of the bridge building model

One preliminary question is: What are the characteristics of the river to be bridged? (width, depth, rate of flow, tidal and flood levels, nature and volume of river traffic, etc.). In a marketing context, what are the characteristics of the marketing problem? (Does it have elements of B2B and/or services and/or international and/or ...?).

The nature of the bridge will be affected by the ground conditions (clay, sand, rock, frequency and intensity of earthquakes, etc.) and the weather conditions (frequency of hurricanes, typhoons and temperature extremes to be expected, etc.). In the marketing task, the shape and content of the output will be affected by the macro- and micro-environment.

The way in which the bridge is built will depend on the development of building theory and materials of construction (e.g. the replacement of steel reinforced concrete with carbon-fibre composites reducing weight and reducing maintenance). This can be viewed as a parallel to the arrival of the Internet for marketers. One is making new forms of construction possible, the other making new marketing strategies viable.

In many major cities, a sign of expansion and regeneration is the forest of cranes involved in the construction projects. To build a bridge, scaffolding and cranes are needed to help in the construction. When the bridge is completed these are removed and there is no sign of how the bridge was constructed (e.g. How were the pyramids of Egypt constructed?). Preliminary analysis and planning is needed for the integrated project. The intellectual scaffolding and cranes may not form part of the answer but without the framework to assist with the creative process, the result is likely to be a badly constructed submission lacking in depth and strength to gain a good grade.

The contexts of marketing

What is special about your selected organization? What is the marketing context? Note, this is not an issue of 'or'. A company is not one-dimensional. A company can have aspects of international and service, and B2B and B2C (e.g. a bank). Below is an outline checklist of areas and factors that may apply:

- B2C and/or
- B2B and/or
- Product and/or
- Services and/or
- International and/or
- Not-for-profit/social and/or
- Relationship marketing and/or
- Consumer issues and/or
- Green issues and/or
- Limited budget and/or
- ?

So, one of your first tasks is to look at the list (add to if needed) and decide what are the characteristics of your selected organization. Taking an international bank as our example we might note the following characteristics/contexts: international, service (specifically financial services), B2B and B2C. Thus your references and bibliography should include textbooks and theories relevant to these special topics. One standard textbook will not cover all the relevant ground for the vast range of different organizations. Some selective use of the more specialist texts is indicated.

Stakeholder analysis

As part of your general research you should draw up a stakeholder analysis table. A suggested format with some indicative stakeholder types is given in Table A2.1. Stakeholder segment: it is a good exercise to analyse the internal structure of stakeholders. Some illustrative examples are given below:

- *Customers* – B2B: segmented and/or B2C: segmented. Possibly customers' customers (e.g. P&G marketing to TESCO, then to ultimate customers – Push and Pull strategy).
- *Internal* – Management, technical. Full time, part time, shift worker, and so on.
- *Media* – TV, radio, press. International, national, regional, local, and so on.
- *Political* – International (e.g. EU), national, local, and so on.

Table A2.1 Outline stakeholders for a typical organization

Stakeholder	Stakeholder agenda	Organization's objectives	Comments
Customers	Good marketing mix offering	Promotion of mix, building relationship (RM)	Full analysis need this for each key customer segment
Consumers	Good marketing mix offering	Promotion of mix, building relationship (RM)	The buyer need not be the consumer, for example gifts
Owners	Development of stakeholder value	Reassurance on how value is being built	Note not always shareholders. Private companies and charities with trustees, and so on. Note not-for-profit 'value' as well
Employees	Stakeholder value (pay, prospects, pension, etc.)	Development of commitment, attraction and retention of key staff	Note segmentation issues (e.g. management, front line, etc.). May be taken to include potential employees
Suppliers	Stakeholder value (continued profitable business)	Relationship marketing: building and maintaining supply chain partnerships	Not only raw materials but all goods and services. May segment, for example small and international
Political	Balancing competing pressures (e.g. job and green issues)	Understanding pressures and providing reassurance about corporate objectives	May segment, for example for a supermarket National: about consumer credit Local: problems with car parking at new supermarket centre
Pressure groups	Often focused agenda (e.g. green issues) with not-for-profit elements	Understanding agenda and providing reassurance and conflict resolution where possible	Need proactive rather than reactive management. Note, may also segment, for example national over packaging, local back to that car park and location of bottle bank

303

Stakeholder	Stakeholder agenda	Organization's objectives	Comments
Media	Want a story to build circulation. Some publications' significant not-for-profit issues	Develop long-term positive relationship to give out good news and manage bad news	Segments (e.g. TV, radio, press; international, national and regional, etc.)
Partners	Stakeholder value (continued profitable partnership)	Often full mix delivery requires partners (e.g. hotel and an airline collaborating on packages)	Often occurs in B2B, e.g. several companies may work collaboratively with a computer company developing an integrated range of hardware/software components

Environmental analysis

Complete a focused STEEPLE (or one of its variants) analysis. Do not leave as 'Exchange rate: £ moving up, the £1 = $2 is a possibility'. Go on: *Exchange rate: £ moving up the £1 = $2 is a possibility, Implication is trading will be – better (UK company selling USA holidays) – worse (UK manufacturer exporting to the USA)*. A Porter competition analysis should be completed. The segmentation issues should be evaluated. A value chain analysis can be useful.

Key issues

A SWOT analysis helps focus the range of issues uncovered in the above analysis. This will then indicate the key imperative that face the organization (e.g. gain new customers, introduce new products, move into international markets, etc.).

What is the task? What theory? What context?

Figure A2.3 outlines the integration of the various threads to produce a coherent submission. The organizational audit will give you the context for your organization. This will direct you into the right selection of theory (e.g. for a charity organization, specialist texts on not-for-profit marketing). The review of the organization's marketing mix again provides a foundation for the specific assignments. Over your studies, on this and the other CIM modules, you will have developed your marketing skills and kept up with the current trends in the industry by reading the marketing and business press.

Figure A2.3 Elements of integration for a MMIP assignment

The first part of the assessment is the core section, 'the role of marketing in the organization' and covers a wide spectrum of the syllabus content.

CORE SECTION – The role of marketing in the organization – 50 per cent weighting

In this you will be required to demonstrate the application of a relevant body of theory to your selected organization. This does not imply a 'sandwich cake' structure, a descriptive layer of theory, followed by a description of the company. What is required is an integrated application of the theory. Something like Smith's theory (reference) is helpful in considering this ###### aspect of ###### The implications are ######.

As an illustration of the type of approach consider the situation for a hypothetical organization that is not-for-profit and provides services to its clients. A focused introduction might be:

is a not-for-profit organisation providing a variety of services to its clients. Table #### gives the segmentation structure for the clients and the services provided. The implication of being not for profit is #### [reference] and being a service organisation is #### [reference].

ELECTIVE SECTION – 25 per cent weighting for each of TWO options

You are required to complete TWO of the four options within this section. It is most beneficial in terms of research and so on if the organization chosen for the core section is also used in the elective section. These optional questions are more focused on specific areas of marketing management than the core question. This allows you to work in an area that interests you and will allow you to improve those skills that are relevant to developing your career. Specific topic areas may vary but typical ones are : 'The management of a marketing project', 'Managing research and information needs', Delivering a communications programme', 'Customer service', 'Managing people and teams, and managing marketing projects', 'Delivering communications and customer service programmes' and 'Developing and implementing marketing plans'.

The most frequently required submission format is a 'report'. The issues for this are covered in the next section. As noted in Figure A2.3 more primary or secondary research and additional reading may be needed, once you have defined your approach. For a financial services context, some reference to specialist writing and theories, in that area, would be appropriate. Discussions with senior management may be appropriate, to understand how the processes are intended to work, in your selected organization. It is not possible to be prescriptive given the wide range of organizations and contexts that might be selected. In most cases, some additional research work will be required, once the approach and shape of the submission has become clear from your preliminary analysis.

Academic reports

The single most important format for a CIM candidate is report format. Unless otherwise stated all assignment projects should be submitted in report format. Different contexts demand different approaches styles and the general framework (Figure A2.4) given below should be adapted as required. Comments are also made about general academic reports, for the interest of candidates who might wish to proceed to a university higher degree qualification later.

Figure A2.4 General outline of a report for an academic project

1. Submission cover sheet(s) contains all the necessary information for submission of the assignment. As cover documentation, it is not part of the formal report. Full instructions are given on the CIM website. In any doubt consult your tutor.

2. Title page including title of project and date. For CIM integrative assignments the question number should be included. Lavish colour graphics are not required; presentation is no substitute for content. A good clear professional presentation is required.

3. Summary, focused and brief (150–300) words, should include key words for computer indexing of the project for more formal academic reports.

4. For acknowledgements assistance may have been given with resources (e.g. assistance with running focus groups) or other support. It is good manners to acknowledge support.

5. Contents helps people find their way around a longer project. Longer academic projects might include page numbers of main topic headings, appendices and lists of diagrams, figures, tables and illustrations. Reports should be page numbered.

6. Brief introduction gives a clear definition of the hypothesis, issue(s) or problems covered in the report. For CIM company-based assignments, a brief overview of the company context is helpful. Lengthy descriptive sections do not earn high grades and eat into the word count.

7. Body of the report with full use of headings and subheadings. In academic reports, the more formal style should be used (e.g. 'the view is advanced' rather than 'I suggest'). Typical frameworks for marketing and communications plans are given in the CIM specimen answers to case studies. For a typical academic project (e.g. a researched-based dissertation), the major section headings might be 'Literature Review', 'Primary Research', 'Discussion of Results', and 'Conclusions & Recommendations' (these are not the suggested headings for your CIM integrative assignment reports). Cut and paste submissions are in danger of a marginal fail. What is required is some critical understanding of the relevant theory with application in the light of the given question and integrated into the context of the selected organization. Two pages of précis of the textbook theory, with a few pages of unrelated description of what the selected organization does, are not sufficient.

8. Conclusion section should summarize the findings and if appropriate give recommended courses of action (e.g. in a CIM assignment how the selected organization might improve its operations in the area covered in the report).

9. References are particularly important in academic work. Failure to properly reference work quoted can leave a suspicion of plagiarism. The CIM framework expects candidates to read around the subject and keep up with developments. References provide evidence to the examiner that you have done this (in this context references are more than just good housekeeping they are part of the process building up your marks). Tables A2.2 (books), A2.3 (journals) and A2.4 (websites) give the accepted referencing system used professionally and in academic institutions. The 'Harvard' system for referencing in the body of the report is the most widely used in business and academic work. There are many good websites from various universities that give good comprehensive guidance on referencing; http://library.open.ac.uk/help/helpsheets/cite.html#eg1 is the address for The Open University's guidance site.

10. Bibliography uses the same conventions as in referencing, the sources are the same type but this is the more general material that you consulted in your overall research but have not used directly and quoted in the body of your report.

11. Appendices should be restricted to essential support material. Complete copies of annual reports, and so on are generally not required. If some primary research was conducted with a questionnaire, then an example copy of a completed questionnaire might be appropriate. If in doubt consult your tutor.

Usually a word count is taken to include the introduction, body and conclusion of a report. Greatly exceeding the word count can result in failure in academic work. You are strongly advised to consult the precise regulations covering your submission. Length is not the test of quality (one kilogramme of cold, soggy chips is not a good eating experience; quality and quantity are different issues). What is required is a focused delivery of knowledge, understanding and application of relevant theory in the light of the given question/task and in the context of the selected organization.

Table A2.2 Outline of how to reference a book (*Source*: Elsevier author guidelines with adaptation) Kopperl, D. (1965), *Manual of Document Microphotography*, Boston, Focal Press

Field	Example
Author(s) or editor's surname followed by initials	Kopperl, D.
Year of publication in brackets	(1965)
Book title in italics	*Manual of Document Microphotography*
City where published	Boston
Publisher name	Focal Press

Table A2.3 Outline of how to reference a journal (*Source*: Elsevier author guidelines with adaptation) Kopperl, D. (1965), 'Techniques of Photography', *J. Appl. Photogr. Engng*, 2, 2, 1 pp. 117–120

Field	Example
Author(s) surname and initials	Kopperl, D.
Year of publication of journal in brackets	(1965)
Paper title in inverted commas	'Techniques of Photography'
Journal title in italics (abbreviations or acronyms are acceptable here)	*J. Appl. Photogr. Engng*
Volume	2
Issue number	2
Part/section (if applicable)	1
Page numbers plus date article written if available	117–120

Table A2.4 Outline of how to reference an Internet source (*Source*: Elsevier author guidelines with adaptation) Kopperl, D. (1965), *Techniques of photography [online]*, The Online Journal of Applied Photographic Engineering www.JAPE.co.uk/Kopp/TechPhot.html (03/07/04)

Field	Example
Author(s) surname and initial	Kopperl, D.
Year the website was constructed in brackets	(1965)
Title of the document (in italics) followed by [online]	Techniques of photography [online]
Website title plus complete URL	www.marketingonline.co.uk
Date you accessed the site in round brackets	03/07/04

Characteristics of good submissions

The characteristics of good candidates' work are:

- Selection of good relevant examples to illustrate points.
- Selection of relevant aspects of theory.
- Demonstration of more than knowledge of theory but also understanding.
- Understanding of the practical aspects of implementation of theory including overcoming problems.
- Good, well-structured reports within 10 per cent of indicative word count.
- Small but relevant appendices, but only where necessary.
- Understanding of the textbook theory and evidence of reading around the subject to find latest developments.
- Appropriate referencing for sources.
- Use of an appropriate range of sources including original research articles, current textbooks, marketing and general press and appropriate use of Internet sources.
- Focus on the specific aspects demanded by the integrative project tasks.

Issues with poor submissions

The characteristics of less good submissions for integrative projects are:

○ Poor selection of examples and a failure to use them in the illustration of points.
○ Theory 'dump' of all the notes that the candidate had acquired in and around the topic area with little understanding of what was relevant demonstrated.
○ Listing of theory rather than a demonstration of depth of understanding.
○ Little understanding of problem-solving issues and the creative use and interpretation of theory.
○ Long rambling reports in excess of 10 per cent of indicative word count with little structure and focus on the key aspects.
○ Long and often numerous appendices, including printouts of websites and material such as complete brochures and annual reports. Only strictly relevant material should be appended. The inclusion of appendices without relevance just wastes candidate's time without gaining additional credit.
○ Lack of understanding of the textbook theory and little evidence of reading around the subject.
○ Referencing that is inadequate or missing. It should be noted that inclusion of material without appropriate referencing might be interpreted as plagiarism, which is an academic offence. To avoid this risk, all sources should be acknowledged. What is required is a focused expression of the candidate's critical insight. A mosaic formed by 'cutting and pasting' a selection of web research material without attribution will result in failure.
○ Restricted range of sources sometimes apparently limited to lecture notes.
○ A lack of specific focus on aspects demanded by the integrative project tasks; more of a dump of everything in the candidate's notes, apparently in their hope that enough will be relevant to gain a pass grade.

Conclusion

These integrative project assignments are created so that candidates can use their own organization or an organization of special interest. The purpose is that this should maximize the value of the learning experience in exploring aspects of the academic material that will be of direct relevance to the development of candidates' work performance as well as gaining the CIM qualification.

Take care with your selection of examples and when appropriate, seek your tutor's advice. Do not just rely on just your lecture notes or books. Do read around the subject. Do discuss your work with colleagues and fellow students (keeping due regard to any confidentiality issues). It is this additional depth of insight developed by this that yields high grades.

These assignments are marked at the CIM centre and all work is regarded as confidential. Given that the person marking these integrative assignments has not been associated with the tutorial support, it is important to provide a brief (around one page) overview of the nature of the selected organization and its marketing environment. This provides the marker with the context to understand your development of issues in your report.

It is intended that this should be one of your most interesting and valuable learning experiences. Good luck and enjoy researching and writing your project. It should help you to improve career prospects as well as gaining your CIM qualifications.

Assignment regulations

There have been a number of changes to the assignment structure compared with previous years, timed with the introduction of the new syllabi. These have been designed to provide consistency in approach for a student whether they are completing the assessment for a module by examination, assignment or integrative project. The more significant changes include:

o For the current academic year tutors at CIM centres will mark assignments. These are then moderated by CIM assessors. An integrative project is marked by CIM assessors only.

o No resubmission of assignments, as per an examination. In previous years a range of assignments were being submitted. Where a student does not achieve the 50 per cent pass mark, they were requested to re-take the assessment for the module through examination or an assignment/integrative project.

o Whichever assessment route is selected is fixed rather than having the option to change at the last minute. Past history has shown that students sometimes begin on an assignment route, change to an examination at the last minute due to not meeting the deadline and then score badly in the examination. The paths to an assignment or examination are different and therefore it is unadvisable to switch, which is the reason for the change of rule.

o In the 2002–2003 academic year word limits for questions and assignments were introduced. This was introduced due to assignments being submitted which were of a wide variety of lengths. These ranged from under 2000 words to over 25 000 words. Where a student is completing four modules by assignment this would equal over 100 000 words – the equivalent of a medium-sized textbook or novel. As such, it became impossible for two assignments to be considered together. Therefore the word limit guidance was introduced in order to provide equality for all students undertaking the assessment by assignment.

o Two sets of assignments per year as with the examination route. With this change, students are required to complete the assignment aimed at the nearest examination session. Previously students had between 3 and 9 months to complete an assignment depending upon whether it was given out in September for a June deadline or in March for the June deadline. Therefore a decision was made to follow the examination route with the intention of giving all students equal time to complete an assignment.

These summarize the key changes which have occurred due to the introduction of new syllabi with the assignment/integrative project route in order that there is parity of assessment at all levels and using all formats. Some of these changes have been significant, others minor. However, all the changes have been considered thoughtfully and with the best intentions for the students in mind.

Use of case studies

For anyone who is not working or has difficulty in accessing information on their or another organization, there are a number of case studies available which allow the completion of a module using a case-based approach rather than basing it upon an organization identified by the student. These case studies are provided on a request-only basis through your accredited CIM centre and should only be used as a last resort. Using a case study as the basis for your assignment will not mean an easier approach to the assignment. However, they do provide an opportunity to undertake assignments when no other alternative exists. Each case study comes with a certain amount of information that can be used specifically for the completion of a question. Additional information may need to be assumed or researched in order to create a comprehensive assignment.

Submission of assignments/integrative project

The following information will aid not only yourself and your tutor who marks your work but also the CIM assessor who will be moderating your work and moderating the integrative project. In addition, the flow diagram represents the process of an assignment/integrative project from start to final mark.

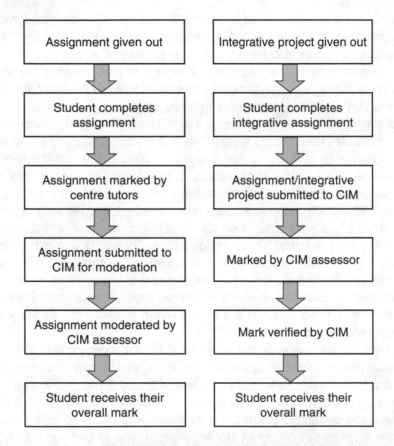

When completing and submitting assignments or the integrative project, refer to the following for guidance:

- ○ Read through each question before starting out. Particularly with the core question there will be a considerable amount of work to undertake. Choose your optional questions wisely.
- ○ Answer the question set and use the mark guidance given regarding the marking scheme.
- ○ Reference each question within the assignment and use a bibliography.
- ○ Complete all documentation thoroughly. This is designed to aid both the CIM and yourself.
- ○ Ensure that the assignment is bound as per instructions given. Currently, assignments are requested not to be submitted in plastic wallets or folders as work can become detached or lost. Following the submission instructions provided aids both the CIM administrators and the CIM assessor who will be marking (integrative project) or moderating (assignments) your work.

  o Complete the candidate declaration sheet showing that you have undertaken this work yourself. *Please note that if you wish the information contained in your assignment to remain confidential you must state this on the front of the assignment.* Whilst CIM assessors will not use any information pertaining to your or another organization, CIM may wish to use the answer to a question as an example.

An assignment will be marked by a tutor at your CIM centre followed by moderation by a CIM assessor. The integrative project will be marked by a CIM assessor as per an examination with moderation by the CIM. To ensure objectivity by CIM assessors there exists a mark-in meeting prior to any marking in order that standardization can occur. The senior assessor for each subject also undertakes further verification of both examinations and assessments to ensure parity between each type of assessment.

Based on the appendix written by David Lane, Former Senior Moderator (Advanced Certificate), February 2003 with amendments.

Further study

Most colleges keep a bank of past projects. Look at past projects to get ideas to develop your own approach. These are not only useful for style and note this may need adaptation for your CIM report). Be selective and look at projects in your selected area. These may give you useful key references. Past projects in a library are just like journals and may be used as such. Remember it is essential to reference any material you directly use.

Hints and tips

Do not rush to start to write your report. Complete the analysis of your selected organization's marketing environment and read around the relevant theory. Remember to read articles or textbooks in your selected area (e.g. if your selected organization is a bank, look at some textbooks on financial services). Draw up a project time plan to allow you to do this preliminary groundwork.

Bibliography

Anderson, J. and Poole, M. (2001) *Assignment and Thesis Writing*, 4th edition, Wiley.

Cameron, S. (2005) *The Business Students Handbook: Learning Skills for Study and Employment*, 3rd edition, FT Prentice Hall.

appendix 3
how to pass the case study exam

What your exam paper has to demonstrate

The assignment and examination routes to the Professional Diploma in Marketing are intended to ensure that candidates have attained the same set of learning outcomes. The details of this are set out by the Chartered Institute of Marketing. Summarising this into a brief format they are that: candidates have knowledge and understanding of a range of topics and theory (as given in the syllabus), have read a little around the subject to gain more insight and can apply this knowledge and understanding in an integrated way to a variety of marketing situations (e.g. FMCG, SME, B2B not-for-profit, etc.). The balance of knowledge and application changes through the various levels of the CIM qualification. Figure A3.1 gives a schematic outline of this. For the Professional Diploma in Marketing a balance of theory, application and evaluation is required. Simple knowledge of the theory without application will not gain a pass at this postgraduate level. This implies more than reading textbooks is required. To apply theory requires the development of skills (e.g. problem-solving). Skills are developed not by reading but by practising. In this section, a framework is proposed to help you develop the mix of skills and knowledge to pass this exam successfully. The outline of this process is shown in Figure A3.2.

Figure A3.1 The balance of concepts, application and evaluation to pass CIM assessments

Figure A3.2 An approach to a case study exam

Understanding marketing theory

Take great care that you understand how to use the models and marketing theories. Figure A3.3 shows a generalized version of the Boston matrix. In the box marked 'Dog', it is noted that often a product is in the decline phase; that is to say the market growth is negative, find a textbook that indicates this possibility. Relative market share to Who? What 'market' are we talking about? Aston Martin does not compete with the Ford Ka. The implication of this is that we know and understand the segmentation structure for the market situation.

Figure A3.3 Adapted Boston (BCG) Matrix

The situation is more complicated for some case studies, for a range of product/market situations the Boston matrix is of little use. The implication of the Boston matrix is that competitive advantage is correlated with market share, often true for FMCG products. However, for highly technical products in a B2B context, it may be a technological advantage that is the issue. The more flexible GE matrix may be more appropriate in this case. Know your tools (theory). Know which one to use, in what situations. Knowing how to draw the two models (Boston matrix and GE matrix) does not give you the skill to use and apply them. A sculptor does not learn how to create by reading a book alone. You only gain proficiency in the use of tools (theory) by reading and then practising their application.

Current issues

The marketing environment is turbulent. During 2005 oil and gas prices increased sharply as did many metals such as copper and gold. Such increases put cost pressures onto manufacturers. However, with severe international competition such companies may have difficulty in raising the price of their manufactured goods. When taking these professional exams, candidates are expected to have a general understanding of the international business climate. This comes from reading magazines and papers.

What is a case study?

A case study is a brief overview of a business situation. The purpose of the case study is to allow you to demonstrate your ability to analyse a marketing situation. To do this effectively, for this integrative paper, you need to know, understand and have experience of the application of the relevant theory. This is an active process not a memory exercise. So, practice on a range of case studies is essential, two are given in this coursebook. The specimen answers are available on the CIM website. However, do not be tempted to look at these too early. They are the 'winning post'. If you do not learn how to 'run the race' (analyse the case study, etc.) when you get into the exam you will not know how to win through. Simply memorizing past case studies is not a strategy to pass this exam. You need to learn analysis and problem-solving skills. This needs active practice, not just passive reading revision. On analysing the case study you may need to make realistic assumptions (in a 3-hour exam the case study has to be simplified to keep to a readable length). A wide knowledge of current marketing and business climate developments, demonstrated in the exam, will gain you marks. In any case, theory, if you have no understanding of the continuously evolving international business climate, will not gain you career success.

After the general analysis there can be a diagnosis of the situation. What are the key issues? Read the questions carefully to see just what is required. What theory is being tested? What is the context? In what format is the answer required? Plan your answer before you start writing. The whole process, shown in Figure A3.4, will allow you to develop a balanced, insightful, approach.

Read and analyse the case study

With a highlighter pen read the study. Highlight key words and make brief notes as to what are the key issues. What is the marketing context? Note this is not an issue of 'or'. A case study is not one-dimensional. A case study can be international and service, and B2B and B2C (e.g. a bank). Below is an outline of areas and factors that may apply:

- o B2C and/or
- o B2B and/or
- o Product and/or
- o Services and/or
- o International and/or
- o Not-for-profit/social and/or
- o Relationship marketing and/or
- o Consumer issues and/or
- o Green issues and/or
- o Limited budget and/or
- o ?

Stakeholders

Who are the key stakeholders? What are the issues relevant to them and the case study organization? Note: just as with customers, stakeholders can segment. Some typical examples of potential stakeholders are given below:

- o Customers (B2B: segmented and/or B2C: segmented). Possibly customers' customers (e.g. P&G marketing to TESCO, then to ultimate customers – Push and Pull strategy)
- o Suppliers
- o Distributors and agents
- o Internal (segmented, e.g. management, technical, full time, part time, shift worker, etc.)
- o Owners (note different types of ownership are possible, e.g. individual, co-operative, trustee, shareholder, etc.)
- o Industry (competitors, trade associations, etc.)
- o Media (may segment, e.g. TV, radio, press. International, national, regional, local)
- o Political (may segment, e.g. international (e.g. EU), national, local)
- o Regulatory
- o Pressure groups
- o General public.

In particular, it is necessary to identify, from the stakeholders analysis, who the communication targets might be. This is required for tasks such as 'Write a marketing plan' or 'Write a communications plan'.

Environmental analysis

Focused use of STEEPLE (or one of its variants), Porter competition and segmentation issues should be considered for the external environment. The value chain can be used if the internal issues are an important aspect of the case study scenario. As noted, with the portfolio models it is not the ability to remember STEEPLE that is required, you need to develop practice in its application.

Key issues

A SWOT analysis helps focus the range of issues uncovered in the above analysis. This will then indicate the key imperatives that face the organization (e.g. gain new customers, introduce new products, move into international markets, etc.).

What is the question?

Specimen answers to past questions are not for 'learning' in parrot fashion. They are for you to be able to compare your solution to a situation. They are an aid to practice, not another textbook. This issue is important as candidates must answer the question asked in the exam, not the specimen answer from last time. Take care to answer the question fully. In an outline context of a marketing plan, for example, is the 'product' simply 'a product', or are there elements of service? If service is an element, the service-extended marketing mix should be used.

What theory is being tested? In what context?

Question 2 of the '@ Wrap' case study (June 2005) was:

'@Medi Wrap' is a new venture for '@ Wrap'

    a. What information will the company require for the development of the market for '@Medi Wrap'? **(15 Marks)**
    b. How might this information be obtained? **(10 Marks)**

The question requires more than just a framework of theory. Candidates should demonstrate that they understand this is not just a 'normal' product but has applications in a medical/sports context. Section 'b' requires more than a statement 'Primary and secondary research should be conducted. Quantitative data could be collected with a questionnaire and qualitative information with focus groups'. This could apply to almost any marketing research situation. Context-specific development of the answer is required.

What is the format?

The two most common formats for this exam are 'report' (default format for all CIM questions unless otherwise indicated) and 'plan' (e.g. Marketing or communications). Plans should be written in report format. Outline heading structures are given below for marketing and communications plans. These basic outlines may need adaptation. Some exam issues are added as comments.

Outline structure for a marketing plan

Report heading [*very short, marks not gained here.*]

Mission aims and objectives [*very brief note of overall business mission and objectives.*]

Environmental analysis

> **STEEPLE** [*or variant*]

> **Competition** [*Porter five forces recommended*]

> **Segmentation/stakeholders** [*May not be a separate heading but some explicit under-standing of these issues should be demonstrated in the case study context.*]

SWOT [*Short and focused. A key factor in marginal fail papers is to spend far too much time on the above headings. Balance your plan and allow time to develop your strategy, mix and control sections.*]

Objectives [*Context-specific, for example, do not write 'implement SMART' objectives. Give some context-specific SMART objectives.*]

Strategy [*Needs relevant, context-specific use of strategy theory. Selective use of models such as Ansoff, Porter generic strategies, Boston matrix, GE matrix. You must be selective. Marks are not gained for remembering how to draw all the models. You must make the model used relevant and context-specific. To be able to do this quickly takes skill. Practice on past case studies.*]

Marketing mix

> **Product** [*Relevant context-specific points – not 'superior quality product', this may be true but could apply to any situation. It has not demonstrated any context-specific application of marketing theory.*]

> **Price** [*Relevant context-specific points – not 'superior value', this may be true but could apply to any situation: it has not demonstrated any context-specific application of marketing theory.*]

> **Place** [*Relevant context-specific points – not 'saturation distribution', this may be true but could apply to any situation. It has not demonstrated any context-specific application of marketing theory.*]

> **Promotion** [*Relevant context-specific points – not 'Mass TV advertising' in every case. A major mistake is to suggest 'mass TV advertising', when the organization is small. There is not enough money in the budget for it. Another error is to suggest TV advertising for a focused B2B context. Communications must be relevant to the context and the stakeholders. Know the difference between a communications plan and a marketing plan. You must demonstrate your application of relevant marketing theory to the given case study context with relevant insightful proposals.*]

People [*Is the context 'service' or containing elements of service? If so develop the service extension in a relevant context-specific way. If not just write a line, 'Product context so service extension (People, Physical evidence and Process) is not relevant'. This demonstrates to the examiner that you know the full mix and have made a positive decision to exclude its development, a correct decision in a product-only situation. However, by noting the service extension you are indicating that this was a positive decision and not that you do not know about the service extension to the marketing mix.*]

Physical evidence [Relevant context-specific points.]

Process [Relevant context-specific points.]

Budget and schedule [*Make context-specific.*]

Control and feedback [*Balance scorecard type approach is fine. Do not make too long but try to make some context-specific points, look back at your objectives.*]

Outline structure for a communications plan

The broadest structure is much the same as for a marketing plan but the business objectives are replaced with the marketing objectives. We are operating at the next level of detail. In real life there would be parallel detailed plans for product, price, place and service extension. However, much work in other marketing mix areas may be done by other parts of the organization, for example R&D (product development), finance (pricing and credit systems) and production/logistics (manufacture and physical distribution). The communications plan is very much the 'baby' of marketing and rightly gets more focus in marketing books. Not all of the elements given below may be needed. In some circumstances (e.g. an 'e' based strategy), sections may need expansion. This is a rough outline that needs to be adapted to suit the given case study circumstance.

Report heading [*very short, marks not gained here.*]

Mission aims and objectives [*Very brief, note of overall marketing mission and objectives.*]

Environmental analysis

STEEPLE [or variant. Focused on the communications issues, so builds on from that for the overall marketing plan. We are into the next level of detail.]

Competition [A note on what the competition is doing and how this affects communications planning for the organization.]

Segmentation/stakeholders/target publics/audiences [It is not possible to write a communications plan without considering with whom you are communicating.]

SWOT [*Possibly a very brief SWOT analysis focused on communications issues.*]

Objectives [*Context-specific, do not write 'implement SMART' objectives. Give some context-specific SMART objectives. Objectives should be linked to the key stakeholder/target publics. It is not possible to frame communications objective without some consideration of the communications target(s).*]

Strategy [*Needs relevant, context-specific use of strategy and theory. Selective use of concepts and models such as branding, 'Push–Pull' and AIDA, etc.*]

Communications mix [*Note this may need to be adapted for different segments and 'push and pull' elements of the communications strategy.*]

Advertising [*Relevant context-specific point. Note the comments about TV advertising in the section on marketing plans. Develop detail as appropriate. Potential headings are given below.*]

TV

Radio

Print

Newspapers [*Develop detail, such as daily/weekly, as necessary.*]

Magazines [*Develop detail as necessary.*]

Directories [*Develop detail as necessary.*]

Outdoor

Cinema

Other

PR [*Relevant context-specific points.*]

Publicity [*Relevant context-specific points. Publicity is not free. The media may be. It does have costs, PR to generate it.*]

Personal selling [*Relevant context-specific points.*]

Point of sale [*Relevant context-specific points.*]

Sales promotion [*Relevant context-specific points.*]

Direct marketing [*Relevant context-specific points.*]

E-communications (websites etc.) [*Relevant context-specific points.*]

Sponsorship [*Relevant context-specific points.*]

Exhibitions [*Relevant context-specific points.*]

Other [*Relevant context-specific points.*]

Integration [*How do the communications activities integrate with the other six elements of the service extended marketing mix? All elements of the mix can participate in communication. What contributions are being made to your plan by the other six elements, e.g. packaging.*]

Media schedule [*Make context-specific.*]

Budget [*Make context-specific.*]

Control and feedback [*Do not write 'primary and secondary research' and leave it as such. Do not make it too long but try to make some context-specific points, look back at your communications objectives.*]

Other formats

Other formats used in CIM exams include memos, letters, budgets, schedules and briefing notes.

Question plan

In the analysis of marginal fail papers against good pass papers, it was noted that marginal fail candidates tend not to question plan. Students in the upper quartile of performance tend to question plan. A UK training manual for meetings had a cartoon where the caption was: 'Before opening your mouth, put the brain in gear': before your write an answer, think and plan. This is important as in the time stress of the exam; it is easy to cover 5Ps, not 7Ps, as an example. If you have question planned, mark the Ps off as you cover them, so you shouldn't forget one.

Time

A common reaction, when looking through the above process, is that there is not enough time. There is enough time but only if you practice case studies and exam technique. Better to practice now than fail an exam and then have all the time, expense and trouble of a re-sit.

The successful exam process

Figure A3.4 gives the outline of the successful exam process.

Figure A3.4 The successful examination process

Before revision

Learn and understand the theory and content of the programme as you progress. An attempt to cram in knowledge in the last few weeks will not work. This exam requires understanding and application as well. This must be developed throughout the programme with the skills of case study analysis and answer writing. You need to set this all in the current business context so keep reading marketing magazines and business pages of newspapers during your programme, do not leave this to the revision time; this is too late. Before you start your revision, time plan to ensure you cover all the topics and practice all the skills that will be tested in the exam. Ensure that you keep a time/work/personal-life balance.

Revision and before the exam

Implement your revision plan. Make certain your plan contains active learning as well as reading (e.g. practising the application of STEEPLE). Continue with case study and exam question practice. If you have the opportunity (if offered by your tuition centre) do a mock examination. Ensure that you have your examination pack sorted (spare pens, highlighters, calculator, etc.). Know where and when the exam is to be held. Allow for problems (e.g. difficult traffic) and arrive in good time.

Examination

As given in Figure A3.4 read and analyse the case study. Read the questions, analysing what is required. Select your questions. Time plan and keep to the time plan.

For each selected question complete analysis. What theory is being tested? In what context? Keep to the required format and ensure that you make your answer context relevant (e.g. if you use an Ansoff matrix, then make certain you put some key case study material into it). End the question on time. A common cause of marginal failure is not to leave enough time for the last question.

After the exam do not have a depressing 'post-mortem'. If you have another exam, focus on what you can do in the future. If it is your last exam, you have earned some R&R!

Summary

Examination success does not depend on two weeks cramming before the exam and memorizing past case study answers. What is required is the development of knowledge, understanding and application of marketing theory into the given case study context. This requires the development of skills in analysis and problem solving to recommend appropriate marketing actions. In this section a structured approach is outlined which will allow you to develop this skill and achieve success, not only in the exam but also in your marketing career.

Further study

In this workbook there are a selection of recent exam case studies. Further case studies are available on the CIM website. The more case studies you work through the more you will develop your skills

Hints and tips

Do not 'zap through' to look at the specimen answers when working through past case studies. Work through the case study and develop your own answers. Only then compare these with the specimen answers provided and the senior examiner's comments. Discuss your approach with your tutor and other students. Only by this process you will fully develop your skills.

Bibliography

Cameron, S. (2005) *The Business Students Handbook: Learning Skills for Study and Employment*, 3rd edition, FT Prentice Hall.

appendix 4
answers and debriefings

Unit 1

Debriefing Activity 1.3

Most managers have strengths and weaknesses, and few managers are strong in all respects and an awareness of personal strengths and weaknesses is an important aspect of management. Different management styles can be effective and efficient, and views about what makes an 'effective' manager might vary depending on your role or where you 'sit' in the organization. Being popular and being effective are not the same.

Unit 2

Debriefing Activity 2.1

Were you able to answer this question easily, or did it take a long time to think about the whole range of stakeholders involved with your organization? Your list should have included internal and external people. In some organizations, the expectations of different parts of the organization will be explicit, but in others it may only be implicit. Sometimes there is a disdainful view of other parts of the organization that contribute to the overheads but whose contribution to front-line activities is not so visible – for example, what is your view of personnel/HRM? finance? – Were you able to identify your key stakeholders' expectations of your team? Who did you identify as your customers? – Do you see people internal to the organization as your customers?

Debriefing Activity 2.2

In what areas does your team work well and in what areas does it need to improve? If you identified any barriers to effectiveness, how much of this is within the power of the team to overcome? – Usually, teams can improve if one of their goals is to improve how they work together. However, this may not be spoken about even though there may be a recognition that the team does not work well.

Debriefing Activity 2.3

The use of language can be a barrier even when the same language is spoken. Unit 1 provided some examples of this but business cultures can vary a lot. Every organization manifests patterns of member behaviours and values which together may be said to form a 'culture'. Organizational effectiveness and decision-making processes are influenced by cultural expression, for example attitudes and responses of employees, styles of management and so on. Interpreting and understanding organizational culture is an important activity for managers because it affects strategic development, productivity and learning at all levels. Cultural assumptions can both enable and constrain what organizations are able to do. A key role for culture is to differentiate the organization from others and provide sense of identity for its members. A strong culture is one that is internally consistent, is widely shared, and makes it clear what it expects and how it wishes people to behave. Sometimes different disciplines or departments within organizations develop their own sub-culture which can make it difficult when there is a need for people to work together to achieve the goals of the organization. Understanding what cultural differences exist within organizations is important for achieving a common approach and managing change.

Debriefing Activity 2.4

Employee specification

Factor	Essential	Desirable
Attainments	Degree preferably in a media or marketing discipline	CAM qualifications to Diploma level
Specific professional skills	Written composition and presentation skills. Media and communications strategies	–
Experience	5 years or more in a media/PR role	Preferably in a non-profit organization or consultancy
Reasoning abilities	Capacity for strategic media analysis and event management	–
Personality	Calm, proactive, assertive, confident, representative personality. Empathy with NHS values	–
Aptitudes	Networker, promoter, persuader, win rapport with clients. Create and develop promotional material	–
Physical make-up	Professional, well-groomed image. Stamina and good health	–
Circumstances	Weekend and evening work	–

Essential – Attributes essential for adequate job performance. Job cannot be performed unless these factors are present.

Desirable – Attributes that are not essential but if present will enhance effective work performance.

Source: Adapted from http://sol.brunel.ac.uk/~jarvis/bola/jobs/mediajob/perspec.html.

Unit 3

Debriefing Activity 3.2

Were you able to identify your needs and people in the organization that could help? Will you need any assistance to be able to access this help? Is your line manager likely to be supportive or will he or she see this as a threat because they may feel it makes them look like a poor manager – or is your line manager more secure about themselves and likely to be more supportive?

Unit 4

Debriefing Activity 4.3

We all need to learn from our experience of being involved in change so that the same mistakes aren't repeated. Gathering feedback after a change has been implemented could be tried providing that the raw feelings associated with change have died down. Otherwise, there is a risk of stirring things up again.

Unit 5

Debriefing Activity 5.1

How easy was it to devise a GANTT chart? – Did you find it useful? – Can you think of examples of how you could use it at work?

Debriefing Activity 5.2

There should be a lot of examples where a project management approach may be useful in a marketing context, such as developing a communications campaign or working with external agencies, for example in market research projects.

Debriefing Activity 5.3

Examples of the key areas could be as follows:

The project timetable, with particular reference to critical event times and potential bottlenecks. There should be feedback on activity times achieved and their effect on the whole project. If network analysis is used, then it is vital that the network is reworked and updated to take into account the actual performance achieved.

The project budget; budgetary control procedures can be used as in respect of any other form of budget.

Quality and performance standards; these need to be monitored against the original project specification subject to changes agreed with stakeholders in the course of project development.

Unit 6

Debriefing Activity 6.1

These are examples of the kinds of questions that can be asked. Developing and maintaining an MkIS system can be expensive so it is important that it is fit for purpose and meets the identified needs. An MkIS system should serve the whole company not a single department and integrate data from across business functions and from many sources. Data often exists already in an organization but not in a form that is useful to marketing.

Debriefing Activity 6.3

How easy did you find it to use the model? Do you have any examples of where there is a gap between theory and practice in your own organization? Would a model like EFQM be appropriate in your situation – or, if you already use such a model, how successful is it at promoting improvements?

Debriefing Activity 6.4

Were there any gaps, that is information you would like that is not available? How could this Information be obtained from other secondary sources?

Debriefing Activity 6.5

A balance needs to be struck between breadth and depth. Usually, it is possible to find out a lot about an issue from a small sample, but not as much from a larger sample. Sometimes different approaches can be combined so that, for example, a focus group can precede or follow a larger survey to probe certain issues in more detail. However, with a large survey, it is important that there is a consistency of approach, and at least some comparative data can be gained. This means that the questioners need to ask the same questions of employers, something that wouldn't happen if in-depth interviews were being held on the shop floor, not to mention the added expense. A survey of 70 000 employers is a large survey and should enable some useful conclusions to be drawn. The use of the telephone will provide data in greater depth than could be achieved by a questionnaire.

Unit 7

Debriefing Activity 7.1

Case study 1 has rather less detail than the second, and is not organized systematically. However, the size of the organization is a lot smaller in Case study 1 and it could be argued that the type of case study is 'fit for purpose'. Case study 2 is an example of a comprehensive approach and shows how some well-known marketing models can be applied. Gathering the information to do this would have incurred an expense that the company in Case study 1 may have found difficult to emulate.

Debriefing Activity 7.2

Did you manage to construct a Gantt chart to schedule the activities? The Gantt chart should show how complex the scheduling can be and how there are bottlenecks and troughs in activity, that is sometimes everything needs doing at the same time and sometimes there is a lull in activity. The aim is to try and smooth this out as far as possible whilst still keeping to deadlines. What kind of people were there in your team?– Did you include finance and human resources – or are these line management responsibilities present in your organization?

Unit 8

Debriefing Activity 8.1

Are there any conclusions or criteria that you would draw from the campaign that you identified that could be used in other campaigns? What kind of appeal was being made through the campaign? – Was it appealing to 'the rational' or 'the emotional' you? Were you able to associate the product or service with the campaign? Often, we seem to be able to remember advertisements but cannot remember the brand that is being sold.

appendix 5

past examination papers and examiners' reports

The Chartered
Institute of Marketing

Professional Diploma
in Marketing

Marketing Management in Practice

44:	**Marketing Management in Practice**
Time:	**09.30 - 12.30**
Date:	**10th December, 2004**

3 Hours Duration

This examination is in two sections.

PART A – Is compulsory and worth 50% of total marks.

PART B – Has **FOUR** questions; select **TWO**. Each answer will be worth 25% of the total marks.

DO NOT repeat the question in your answer, but show clearly the number of the questions attempted on the appropriate pages of the answer book.

Rough workings should be included in the answer book and ruled through after use.

© The Chartered Institute of Marketing 2004

Professional Diploma in Marketing

PART A

Pinnacle Pictures

Location: Pinnacle Pictures has been in business for ten years operating from a single centre on a local regional basis.

Core business: Overnight and postal photographic processing ie developing and printing of films.

Customers leave their films at selected high street agents around the region. The films are collected by van in the late afternoon. The films are processed overnight and completed pictures are delivered early the next day for collection by the customer. Customers can also elect to post their films in prepaid envelopes and prints are returned by post (this offers better value for money to the customer but obviously takes longer).

Business profile: Pinnacle Pictures has gained regional dominance by offering a value-for-money service with quality processing and reliable deliveries. With some fifty staff the company has become profitable with a turnover of £5,000,000.

Digital photography and the changing business of photographic development mean that instant photographs are much more accessible now to the general public. The expensive to use instant Polaroid camera has been replaced by relatively cheap digital cameras. With these, images can be downloaded onto a computer, printed out on inexpensive colour printers or sent to friends via email or on disc. Pictures can also be posted on a website easily to form an online photograph album; this can be accessed by friends and family or business contacts around the world.

Digital cameras have become part of the digital technology revolution and are often regarded as a necessary computer accessory like the digital scanner or are 'bundled' with new computers by the big chains of stores. In addition, many old-style photographs and other pictures can be scanned by people, enabling them to email the images to their friends or to be stored digitally on computer or disc. Many of the highest quality photographic images are still obtained using traditional photography (eg fashion photography). However, the press and public relations (PR) companies often use the highest quality digital cameras due to the convenience and necessity for speedy transfer from sometimes remote locations.

The challenge

Pinnacle Pictures must rise to this challenge. Photographs appear to be following music down the digital path, where online downloads such as MP3 files are challenging more tangible products like CDs and the already obsolete vinyl record. 'Wet' film processing technology will increasingly be replaced with digital technologies needing new skills, new people, new production processes and new marketing strategies: a management of change situation.

Your role

You have been appointed as Marketing Manager to participate in the development of the digital business including the development of internet based business.

The management of Pinnacle Pictures have also decided that a good website is critical to the development of the business. Given that this e-commerce activity will be core to the future company strategy it has been decided to recruit a webmaster to develop and maintain the Pinnacle Pictures website. Your advice will be required.

A most important capital city international art gallery has completed a digital photography programme and now has an archive of over 2,000 major pictures in high quality digital format. Visitors to the art gallery can now have postcards and reproductions produced 'online' within minutes replacing the previous restricted range produced by traditional photography and printing. The gallery wishes to make its heritage available on a more regional basis and has approached Pinnacle Pictures with a proposal that they might license these digital images. Your input will be needed.

Appendix One

Section One: Background notes on the market for Pinnacle Pictures
The market can be segmented by a number of variables, which include:

- **Cost and quality of service:** professional photographers use expensive laboratories that are able to provide the highest standards and specialised services. At the other extreme low cost providers provide a very inexpensive service with sound basic processing and very few 'extras'. Pinnacle Pictures at present occupies a middle segment providing high quality services for the amateur enthusiast and for other more demanding customers (see appendix 2 for outline of services offered)
- **Type of photographer:** professional photographers (at present not a target for Pinnacle Pictures), serious amateur photographic enthusiasts, hobbyists such as bird watchers who take pictures as part of their hobby and general domestic customers (photographs of holidays, parties, family occasions such as birthdays etc)

- **Type of media:** film (various types and sizes), digital (various types of storage media and internet file downloads)
- **Range of services demanded:** basic prints, enlargements and special services (see appendix 2)

Competition

- **Specialist laboratories** – these dominate the top end of the market for professional photography
- **'No frills' basic providers** – these dominate the lower end of the market where cheapness is the issue
- **Other middle market players**
- **Home processing** - previously with chemical 'wet' processing, only the most dedicated amateur would set up a home laboratory / dark room. Now most PCs with a colour printer can become a home digital photograph 'laboratory'. However, the quality of low-cost colour printers is limited and with high costs of ink cartridges and photographic quality paper, home printing is an expensive process

Service Issues

- **Processing time** - a key issue with many customers wanting to see their images as soon as possible. This has led to many high street outlets building 'mini laboratories' onsite to process films within one hour. Many outlets have now also incorporated computer terminals to allow customers to download files from their digital cameras for local printing at the high street outlet or for onwards transmission to a central processing facility
- **Print quality** – home-produced prints may have a restricted life, particularly if printed on poor paper. Some of the one-hour processing equipment also produces lower quality reproduction with little account made of film type. Pinnacle Pictures printing technology gives prints with an expected life of over 100 years of good quality
- **Access -** with the increasing popularity of 'broadband' access within the domestic market giving fast internet downloads and uploads, the cost and time of transmitting large files from home to a central processing laboratory have been greatly reduced. Thus people do not need to go to a high street outlet to send their files for processing. Online business is now a clear possibility

Section two: Archive sources of high-quality digital images

Certain types of organisations have been producing digital image archives: -

- Newspapers and magazines use them to preserve and have immediate access to their library of images
- Museums and art galleries use them for research purposes and to provide international access to their collections

Appendix 2

Pinnacle Pictures: outline of existing services and products

Film processing

- Standard colour processing
- Enlargements up to 30" x 40" (762 x 1016 mm)
- Slide services
- Black and white processing

Digital Services

- Digital image processing with high quality 'professional' prints
- Traditional photographic prints to digital image files
- Media conversion (e.g. Cine film to video, video to DVD etc)
- 'On line photograph albums' (internet access to pictures for family and friends) either from digital images or by converting traditional photographs to digital format

Special Services

Restoration (eg blemishes can be remove from old prints before re-printing) photographic gifts (customers own image incorporated into the product) include:

- Baseball caps
- Ceramic mugs
- Jigsaw puzzles
- Mouse mats
- Sweatshirts etc

(Material has been taken from industry sources. Pinnacle Pictures is a fictitious company for assessment purposes only)

PART A - Compulsory

Question One

a) Outline a marketing plan to develop a profitable regional business for the art gallery opportunity (incorporated in your role). This should include partnership arrangements with local organisations such as art galleries, museums and theatres for the art images.

(30 Marks)

b) What issues and actions do Pinnacle Pictures' management need to consider in the selection, appointment and induction of a webmaster into the organisation?

(20 Marks)

(Total 50 Marks)

PART A - Compulsory

PART B – Answer **TWO** Questions Only

Question Two

The online digital business will be a radical departure for Pinnacle Pictures from its traditional overnight developing and printing business via high street agents.

a) What information will the company require for the development of the online digital business?

(15 Marks)

b) How might it be obtained?

(10 Marks)

(Total 25 Marks)

Question Three

Outline the integrated marketing communications activities required to promote the online digital image processing service.

(Total 25 Marks)

Question Four

Pinnacle Pictures will have to extend its operations to include the addition of computer-based digital processes. What are the management of change issues confronting the company and how might these be dealt with effectively?

(Total 25 Marks)

Question Five

Pinnacle's new website will be launched at a major photographic exhibition in six months time. What project management tools and actions would you recommend to ensure that all necessary activities were undertaken to ensure a trouble-free exhibition launch?

(Total 25 Marks)

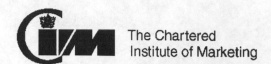

The Chartered
Institute of Marketing

Professional Diploma in Marketing

Marketing Management in Practice

44:   **Marketing Management in Practice**

SENIOR EXAMINER'S REPORT FOR DECEMBER 2004 EXAMINATION PAPER

© The Chartered Institute of Marketing, 2004

SENIOR EXAMINER'S REPORT FOR
DECEMBER 2004 EXAMINATION PAPER

MODULE NAME: MARKETING MANAGEMENT IN PRACTICE

AWARD NAME: PROFESSIONAL DIPLOMA IN MARKETING

DATE: DECEMBER 2004

1.   General Strengths and Weaknesses of Candidates

The improvement noted in the June 2005 examination has continued with the overall pass rate slightly up again. One question (question four on management of change) was relatively unpopular. A significant proportion of candidates, who attempted this question, appeared to lack an understanding of the issues involved.

General problem areas for weaker candidates continue to be the same and include:

- Generic answers with little application of the selected theory to the specific context of the case study and question. Good answers require a selection of the relevant theory (some answers just listed all the theory that might apply without selectivity) and then application and development in the given context.
- Unstructured lists of action points without any underpinning of relevant theory. Good comprehensive solutions need the theory to ensure the completed cover of the issues. Lack of knowledge and understanding of the relevant theory results in superficial answers, which will not achieve a pass grade at this level.
- Template answers from previous case study work. Each case study has distinctive aspects requiring a judged and tailored approach. A memorised template answer from a previously viewed case study will not be appropriate. The purpose of providing specimen answers to case studies is not to provide 'template' answers but to provide a benchmarking framework to which students can compare their solutions. They are intended to provide guidance and assistance in the development of skills not to provide proforma answers.
- Failure to answer the question as presented. Each question has specific contexts.
- Time management: failure to leave enough time for the last question will cause problems.
- Failure to note the developments of the syllabus and marketing theory in general. A specific area of concern was the apparent lack of knowledge and understanding of management of change.
- Failure to develop answers.
- Failure to structure answers and/or leaving gaps in the treatment of the relevant issues. It is surprising that many candidates still do not question plan. A few minutes to quickly rough out a question plan provides that vital

perspective to ensure focus on the specifics of the question and a planned cover of all the relevant issues. The danger of just rushing into the answer without planning is development can drift away from the specific focus needed and/or that key issues can be overlooked, therefore important gaps are left in the answer.

• Some candidates are still not writing in report format. Unless otherwise stated all answers are required in report format style. However lengthy introductions and title pages and contents listings for every question and sub question are not required and waste valuable time.

Good candidates demonstrated an understanding of the theory and its application to a given context in this integrative paper. Less able candidates did not demonstrate depth of understanding of the theory and as a result of this lack of understanding were unable to develop well structured, context specific, answers.

Answers need to be balanced and address all the issues. It is strongly recommended that candidates take time to pre-plan their answers before rushing on to write. This especially was an issue with question 1 (a) where many candidates spent too much time on analysis without substantive development of implementation aspects.

2. Strengths and Weaknesses by Question

Question 1a

Task: To outline a marketing plan and to develop a profitable regional business for the art gallery opportunity.

Strengths

• Most candidates had a sound knowledge of the structure for an outline marketing plan.
• In general sound points were made in the environmental analysis. However, too many students spent too much time on analysis, often repeating information from the case study and not enough time in development (e.g. proposals for an appropriate marketing mix).
• Better submissions appreciated the limited budget of the situation.

Weakness

• A significant minority of candidates did not use report format and/or did not know the appropriate framework for an outline marketing plan.
• A significant minority of candidates' answers focused almost entirely on analysis rather than implementation. Candidates should not spend too much time on analysis at the expense of demonstrating their ability to develop implementation strategies.

- Too few candidates developed tailored proposals for their marketing mix. Given that this is a service marketing context, the full service extended marketing mix was expected.
- Too often 'control' aspect was on the basis 'use balanced scorecard' with no amplification. In setting SMART objectives candidates should be considering how these can be measured. Objectives that are not measurable are not likely to be of much value in a real marketing plan.

Question 1b

Strengths

- Sound general cover of the selection process and selection criteria.
- Sound knowledge of the general issues in selection, appointment and induction of new staff.

Weakness

- Comparatively few candidates extended the selection process and criteria to suggest specific characteristics (e.g. previous web construction experience).
- Again training comments tended to be rather generic e.g. Product: 'develop knowledge of the product range' rather than 'develop product understanding, such as digital image processing...'.

Overall there was a fair level of knowledge of theory but more depth of understanding in context specific application would have been welcomed.

Question 2a

The task was to make firm context specific proposals for information to 'develop the online digital business'

Strengths

- Sound general understanding of information needs.
- Appreciation of the service and 'e' context of the situation.

Weakness

- A significant number of candidates failed to build the service implications into their reports
- Again a significant proportion of suggestions were generic rather than developed and tailored to the specific case study context.

Question 2b

The task was to make firm context specific proposals for 'How might the information be obtained?'

Strengths

- Sound general understanding of research approaches, both secondary and primary.
- Fair appreciation of the need for quantitative and qualitative data.

Weakness

- A significant number of candidates failed to build into their reports the 'e'' context.
- Yet again a significant proportion of suggestions were generic rather than developed and not tailored to the specific case study context.

Question 3

Task: To outline the integrated marketing communications activities required to promote the on-line digital processing service.

Strengths

- Some imaginative and sound suggestions were given by many candidates.
- Fair understanding of the integrated communication mix options was demonstrated in the majority of answers. This included an appreciation of the segmentation focus and the limited budget available.

Weakness

- Yet again a surprising number of answers failed to identify the relevant stakeholders. It is not possible to evaluate the effectiveness of the communications activities (as demanded in the question) unless the communications targets are identified.
- A significant minority of answers failed to demonstrate a realistic understanding of the context of a local launch e.g. proposals to use national TV. Realistic application of the theory, with some appreciation of limited budget implications, was expected for this case study.
- A significant proportion of proposals did not take account of 'e' – based opportunities.

Question 4

Task: To consider the change issues confronting the company and how they might be managed effectively. Surprisingly this was not a popular question. Marketing people are often agents of change and change management is a critical area.

Strengths

- A few candidates demonstrated an understanding of change management.
- Some general proposals were made, regrettably too often without a framework of theory

Weakness

- Many candidates attempting this question appeared to have little theoretical background, understanding or knowledge of change management.
- Too often change management was interpreted as tailoring the marketing mix, with no theory. Candidates are expected to use relevant theory to develop depth of insight in their answers.

Question 5

Task: What project management tools and actions would be recommended to ensure a trouble-free exhibition launch [for the Pinnacle Pictures' website]?

Strengths

- Fair understanding of the project management theory and tools.

Weakness

- Generic application of the concepts with little context specific development.

3.   Future Themes

The framework of understanding of theory into development of structured context specific points will be continued. Candidates are reminded that the ability to formulate plans and implement them is eminently relevant to the activities of a Marketer and this theme will continue.

Future case studies will involve a wide range of contexts that confront the practising Marketer, including Not-for-Profit, Business-to-Business and international contexts.

Candidates are expected to be aware of contemporary developments in the theory and contexts of marketing. Regrettably, too many candidates appear to be relying on tutor-prepared frameworks and did not have the skills to be able to tailor to the context specific situations given in the case study scenario. This paper demands that candidates should be able to develop theory into a given context with practical relevant answers developed structured from appropriate theory. Past case study answers are not 'templates'. Candidates need to understand the case study processes; there is no single solution to integrated case studies. What is required is an ability to understand and apply theory. Then a creative approach to problem solving is required for an innovative and original solution. Justified, self-consistent answers are required. Too often the answer to communications issues is 'mass TV advertising' demonstrating no appreciation of budget constraints or targeting specific market segments / communications publics. This is a professional exam. The criteria for success are depth of understanding and professional application. Exam 'gamesmanship' and question guessing do not give professional competence.

Candidates are reminded that such skills are not developed by simply reading lecture notes. It is necessary to work on a variety of case studies to develop the necessary depth of understanding and ability to develop appropriate answers, demonstrating problem-solving skills. Reading about best practice in current marketing journals is necessary to keep up with rapid developments in areas such as e – commerce.

The Chartered
Institute of Marketing

Professional Diploma in Marketing

Marketing Management in Practice

44:	Marketing Management in Practice
Time:	09.30 - 12.30
Date:	10 June 2005

3 Hours Duration

This examination is in **TWO** sections.

PART A - Is compulsory and worth **50%** of total marks.

PART B - Has **FOUR** questions; select **TWO**. Each answer will be worth **25%** of the total marks.

DO NOT repeat the question in your answer, but show clearly the number of the questions attempted on the appropriate pages of the answer book.

Rough workings should be included in the answer book and ruled through after use.

© The Chartered Institute of Marketing, 2005

**Professional Diploma
in Marketing**

Marketing Management in Practice

PART A

@ Wrap

An entrepreneur who perceived a market opportunity for a novel product '@ Wrap' founded the company in the UK. The product consists of high quality cling film (thin, transparent, plastic material, often used for wrapping food to keep it fresh) wound onto a cardboard core. The innovation came from the design of a plastic handle. This allows the easy application of the film, which can then be 'cut' without the use of any knife or other tools.

The product was originally developed from devices used to wrap and secure products stacked onto full-size pallets thus ensuring products remained in place in transit. The 100 mm wide '@ Wrap' product provides this type of convenience for smaller applications securing, protecting and wrapping products. The advantages are:

- Quick and easy-to-use
- Economic in use compared to other systems
- No separate knife or cutter needed (safety feature)
- No adhesive residue on packaging or merchandise
- No damage to other packaging (eg boxes)
- Retains label and merchandise visibility
- Used by major wholesalers and retailers nationwide

Consumers had perceived the value of the product when watching their goods being wrapped at the checkout and now many retailers (eg DIY and office supplies stores) now stock the product for consumer sale after frequent requests from customers. This is opening up a substantial opportunity for the company in the consumer market. A continual flow of letters and emails from satisfied customers pointed to new applications for the product.

The company has expanded rapidly from an initial small group to over 50 people. It has just moved into new premises in an industrial estate in the UK that now offers room for even further expansion. This has given some organisational problems, as the entrepreneurial owner has been used to keeping control of all activities; with increasing size and range of activities, the company is moving to a more structured approach with delegation of responsibilities.

A limited export business has started following promotion of the product at an international trade exhibition in the UK. A new agent has been recruited in a selected 'New Territory'*, and a consultant appointed to advise on product registration issues.

'New Territory'* may be taken to be any country of your own selection except the United Kingdom.

Appendix 1

'@ Wrap' product range

The versatile product is manufactured in a wide range of forms:
- Widths (100 mm, 150 mm, 200 mm and 250 mm)
- Thickness
- Roll lengths
- Colours (eg blue, black, red etc) for identification purposes
- Printed (eg with company logo or other text eg fragile)

It services a variety of applications. The starter pack contains four rolls of the product and one dispensing handle. Refill packs contain six rolls of '@ Wrap'.

Appendix 2

'@ Medi Wrap' Notes

Extract from email from the new agent in 'New Territory':

> *'Product is selling well to local retail outlets for wrapping their products.*
>
> ***Social side:*** *You know I run a local football team. We had a great game at the weekend and I found a new use for '@ Wrap'. One of the team had a small injury and the Physiotherapist decided to apply an ice pack. Guess what? '@ Wrap' is just great. It's just the right tension to keep the pack in place and when you take it off, you do not strip off all the hairs on the player's leg. Physiotherapist asked me for another few rolls to give to some his friends who work with other local teams. Gave him some blue rolls as they look more 'medical'. Feedback is fantastic – the product is just great and so easy to use.*
>
> *Never a week without us finding a new use for '@ Wrap'!'*

Extract email from consultant:

> *'I confirm that we have been able to register the '@ Wrap' product in the appropriate category as a 'medical appliance' (just like a bandage in effect) and so this will reinforce your product positioning.*
>
> *I also confirm I have been able to register ' @ Medi Wrap' as a trademark in 'New Territory'.*
>
> *In my discussions during registration it would appear that apart from the sports use there is also a market for this product in hospitals.'*

The above data has been based on a fictitious situation drawing on a variety of events and does not reflect management practices of any particular organisation.

Your role

You have been appointed in the new position of marketing manager to bring a professional approach to marketing activities and, in particular, develop new business opportunities including export markets.

Part A - Compulsory

Question 1

a. Outline a marketing plan to introduce the '@ Medi Wrap' product in 'New Territory'

(30 Marks)

b. What issues and actions do '@ Wrap' management need to consider in the selection, appointment and induction of a brand manager to develop the **export** potential of all the '@ Wrap' products including '@ Medi Wrap'?

(20 Marks)

(Total 50 marks)

PART B – Answer **TWO** Questions Only

Question 2

'@ Medi Wrap' is a new venture for '@ Wrap'

a. What information will the company require for the development of the market for '@ Medi Wrap'?

(15 Marks)

b. How might this information be obtained?

(10 Marks)

(Total 25 marks)

Question 3

Outline and justify the integrated marketing communications activities required to promote the launch of '@ Medi Wrap' in 'New Territory'.

(Total 25 marks)

Question 4

'@ Wrap' is growing at a very fast rate.

a. What change management issues confront '@ Wrap?'

(10 Marks)

b. How might '@ Wrap' address these 'management of change' issues?

(15 Marks)

(Total 25 marks)

Question 5

'@ Medi Wrap' is to be launched in 12 months time in 'New Territory'. What project management tools and actions would you recommend to ensure a trouble-free launch of this new product?

(Total 25 marks)

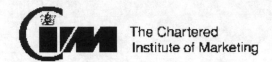

The Chartered
Institute of Marketing

Moor Hall, Cookham
Maidenhead
Berkshire, SL6 9QH, UK
Telephone: 01628 427120
Facsimile: 01628 427158
Website: http://www.cim.co.uk

The Chartered
Institute of Marketing

Professional Diploma in Marketing

Marketing Management in Practice

44: **MARKETING MANAGEMENT IN PRACTICE**

SENIOR EXAMINER'S REPORT FOR JUNE 2005 EXAMINATION PAPER

© The Chartered Institute of Marketing, 2005

SENIOR EXAMINERS REPORT FOR

JUNE 2005 EXAMINATION PAPER

MODULE NAME: MARKETING MANAGEMENT IN PRACTICE

AWARD NAME: PROFESSIONAL DIPLOMA IN MARKETING

DATE: JULY 2005

1.   General Strengths and Weaknesses of Candidates

It should be noted that the improvement in the pass rate in the 2004 examinations was maintained in the July 2005 examinations.

Common causes of poor exam performance continue to include: -
- Generic answers with little application of the selected theory to the specific context of the case study and question. Good answers require a selection of the relevant theory. Template answers (e.g. a marketing plan with generic points failing to take account of the specialised market segments - in this paper sports and medical markets) with recommendations for heavy national TV and radio advertising (without any consideration of budget implications) are likely to result in a marginal fail grade.
- Unstructured lists of action points without any underpinning of relevant theory. Good comprehensive solutions need the theory to ensure the complete cover of the issues. Lack of knowledge and understanding of the relevant theory results in superficial answers that will not achieve a pass grade at this level. This was particularly noticeable in the answers to Q1b where general points were made without reference to the necessary theory in this specific context (more discussion is given under the notes under the specific question heading).
- Reproduction of answers from previous case study work. Each case study has distinctive aspects requiring a judged and tailored approach. A memorised answer from a previously-viewed case study will not be appropriate. The purpose of providing specimen answers to case studies is not to provide 'template' answers, but to provide a benchmarking framework to which students can compare their solutions. They are intended to provide guidance and assistance in the development of skills, not to provide proforma answers.
- Failure to answer the question as presented. Each question has specific context. Care should also be taken to note when the question focused on specific elements of a broader picture. Q3 asked for consideration of 'communications activities' not a full outline communications plan. Where a full outline marketing / communications / launch plan is required this will be clearly stated in the questions (e.g. as in Q1a 'Outline a marketing plan ….')
- Time management. Time should be allocated according to the marks for a given question or sub question. Failure to leave enough time for the last question will cause problems. Two symptoms were noted in marginal papers in the June 2005 examination.
  - Failure to leave enough time for the last question
  - Failure to leave enough time in Q1a for implementation with overlong analysis covering many pages and then attempting to complete the entire implementation

and control issues in one page. A balance between analysis and implementation is required. Taking too much time over the analysis will not leave time for the development of the implementation issues.

- Failure to note the developments of the syllabus and marketing theory in general. A specific area of concern was lack of consideration of web and 'e'-communications in Q3 with weaker answers. The 'electronic' media should not be regarded as something 'special' but a commonplace addition to the marketer's range of tools.
- Failure to develop answers. This was often a symptom of insufficient time planning and management.
- Failure to structure answers (report format is required for all answers unless indicated otherwise) and/or leaving gaps in the treatment of the issues. It is vital to plan answers. Just a few minutes spent quickly roughing out a question plan will provide vital perspective to ensure focus on the specifics of the question, developing planned cover of all the relevant issues. The danger of rushing into the answer without planning is that the development can drift away from the specific focus required. Also the key issues can be overlooked. Thus important gaps are left in the answer.
- Unless otherwise stated all answers are required in report format style. However, lengthy introductions, title pages and contents listings for every question and sub question are not required. They can waste valuable time. Conversely, focused tables and context developed diagrams are welcomed.

In the next section the strengths and weakness of answers are reviewed. In some cases the same point appears in both sections. Good answers consisted of good application of the theory. Weaker submissions missed or omitted to cover some of the issues, e.g. in the present case study good answers had appropriate focus on the specific medical / sports context. Poor answers were more general and failed to move away from a 'general' FMCG type emphasis.

2.   Strengths and Weaknesses by Question

Question 1a (30 marks)

Task: 'Outline a marketing plan to introduce '@ Medi Wrap' product in New Territory'.

Strengths
- Appreciation of the specific nature of the product and identification-specific target segments.
- Development of a sound plan with balance between analysis and implementation.
- Innovative proposals for the marketing mix taking into account the specific case study context.
- Sound consideration of control issues.

Weaknesses
- Over-development of the analysis e.g. extensive consideration of portfolio analysis was not appropriate.
- Generic 'template' plans from less-able candidates with little context-specific content.
- Essay review of the issues – a structured plan was required (including control aspects). Unless otherwise stated all answers should be in report format.

Overall

Candidates who focused on the specific nature / use of the product gained good marks in this section. Generic answers with little or no context specific content did not achieve pass grades.

Question 1b (20 marks)

Task: 'What issues and actions do '@ Wrap' management need to consider in the selection, appointment and induction of a brand manager to develop the export potential of all the '@ Wrap' products including '@ Medi Wrap?'

Strengths

- Good general awareness of the selection, appointment and induction processes.

Weaknesses

- As with Q1a lack of context depth. Weaker answers give suggestions such as 'Selection on the basis of relevant experience'. This is true but generic. Answers with suggestions as to what might be relevant expedience gained higher marks.

Overall

In general, answers to the question were satisfactory, apart from the context issues discussed above.

Question 2a (15 marks)

Task: What information will the company require for the development of the market for '@ Medi Wrap'?

Strengths

- Sound context-specific points from the more able candidates (e.g. candidates focusing on the medical market made comments about needing different information for the institutional buying process when compared to the 'normal' FMCG processes).

Weaknesses

- Generic lists with little context development (e.g. 'information on size of the market etc.' with no further development).

Overall

Good answers focused on sound points to develop knowledge of specific, context-appropriate, market segments.

Question 2b (10 marks)

Task: 'How might this information be obtained?'

Strengths

- There was a tendency for candidates with good original consideration of the issues in Q2a to develop innovative and appropriate proposals for the collection of relevant information.

Weaknesses
- Poorer answers focused on a generic discussion of a MkIS system with little relevant context development.

Overall

Performance in this aspect of the question was mixed. Candidates who appreciated the nature of potential market segments produced some good answers. Less able candidates reproduced theory with little application to the case study context.

Question 3 (25 marks)

Task: 'Outline and justify the integrated marketing communications activities required to promote the launch of '@ Medi Wrap' in New Territory'.

Strengths
- Good answers: -
  - Took into account the specific target sectors
  - Proposed a range of co-ordinated activities required for a launch situation
  - Included use of web and other 'e'-based communications approaches
  - Proposed innovative and imaginative proposals

Weaknesses
- Less-able candidates produced generic communications plans.
- A surprising number of less-able candidates failed to include and web / 'e'-based components in their suggested co-ordinated communications activities.

Overall

Key to good answers here was an appreciation of the launch context.

Question 4a

Task: 'What change issues confront '@ Wrap'?'

Strengths
- This was not a popular question. Good candidates had a sound understanding of change management theory and identified the issues.

Weaknesses
- A significant proportion of the relatively few candidates that answered this question appeared to have little understanding of change management theory.

Overall

Good answers applied theory to the case study content, weaker answers contained little theory and lacked depth.

Question 4b

Task: 'How might '@ Wrap' address these ' management of change' issues?'

Strengths
- Candidates with an understanding of change management theory proposed sound approaches to the issues. Consideration of RM aspects and internal marketing were welcomed.

Weaknesses
- Candidates with little understanding of the theory produced lists with little depth or development.

Overall

In the turbulent environment confronting marketers, an understanding of change management issues is important for professionals. Weaker candidates did not demonstrate an awareness of change management theory.

Question 5

Task: "@ Medi Wrap' is to be launched in 12 months time in 'New Territory'. What project management tools and actions would you recommend to ensure a trouble-free launch of this new product?'

Strengths
- Knowledge and application of project management tools.
- Relevant context-specific proposals for action, linked to the application of the above theory.

Weaknesses
- Production of a generic chart with little discussion of other tools or application of theory to the given launch context.

Overall

Answers with the application of project management tools to the launch situation achieved good grades. Answers with generic Gantt charts with little context linkage did not gain good grades. For many candidates who attempted this question it was their last answer in the exam. Clearly many candidates who did not achieve good grades had failed to time plan and leave enough time to develop a full answer. In the stress of the exam situation, time planning is important.

3.   Future Themes

Application of knowledge requires practice, so tutors and candidates are strongly advised to practice and develop their skills on past case studies. The specimen answers are intended to be a guide to aid in the process. It is not intended that specimen answers are 'textbook' answers to be learned and reproduced in the next exam. Each exam case study has a different context and will need context specific application of marketing theory. The need is to develop skills in this process. Future themes will include B2B, consumer, service and not for profit themes. Candidates are advised to practice application of their marketing skills in various contexts, not only to gain good exam grades but also to develop their professional competence. Candidates should also read around the current marketing press and journals. Aspects of marketing such as e-commerce are fast changing and textbooks only a year old may already start to become dated in some of the fast moving areas.

appendix 6
curriculum information and reading list

Aim

The Marketing Management in Practice unit practises students in developing and implementing marketing plans at an operational level in organizations. A key part of this unit is working within a team to develop the plan and managing teams implementing the plan by undertaking marketing activities and projects. Its aim is to assist students in integrating and applying knowledge from all the units at Professional Diploma, particularly as part of a team. This unit also forms the summative assessment for the Professional Diploma.

Related statements of practice

Jc.1 Plan marketing projects and prepare budgets.
Jc.2 Manage and report on delivery against plan and objectives.
Kc.1 Define measurements appropriate to the plan or business case and ensure they are undertaken.
Kc.2 Evaluate activities and identify improvements using measurement data.
Lc.1 Manage a marketing team.
Lc.2 Maintain relationships with other functions and disciplines within the organization.
Lc.3 Encourage and help others to develop their competencies relevant to a marketing role.
Lc.4 Embrace change and modify behaviours and attitudes.

Learning outcomes

Students will be able to:

o Explain the roles and structure of the marketing function and the nature of relationships with other functions within various types of organization.
o Plan and undertake or commission marketing research for an operational marketing plan or business decision.
o Interpret qualitative and quantitative data and present appropriate and coherent recommendations that lead to effective marketing and business decisions.

- Develop marketing objectives and plans at an operational level appropriate to the organization's internal and external environments.
- Develop an effective plan for a campaign and supporting customers and members of a marketing channel.
- Use appropriate management techniques to plan and control marketing activities and projects.
- Use appropriate techniques to develop, manage and motivate a team so that it performs effectively and delivers required results.
- Define measures for, and evaluate the performance of, marketing plans, activities and projects and make recommendations for improvements.

Knowledge and skills requirements

Element 1: Managing people and teams (30 per cent)

1.1 Describe the functions, roles of marketing managers and typical marketing jobs and the nature of relationships with other functions in organizations operating in a range of different industries and contexts.

1.2 Develop and maintain effective relationships with people in other functions and disciplines within the organization.

1.3 Identify and explain the key challenges of managing marketing teams in a multi-national or multi-cultural context.

1.4 Explain how you would use the techniques available for selecting, building, developing and motivating marketing teams to improve performance.

1.5 Allocate and lead the work of marketing teams, agreeing objectives and work plans with teams and individuals.

1.6 Respond to poor performance within a marketing team by minimizing conflict, supporting team members, overcoming problems and maintaining discipline.

1.7 Explain the sources and nature of change affecting organizations and the techniques available for managing change.

1.8 Evaluate individual and team performance against objectives or targets and provide constructive feedback on their performance.

Element 2: Managing marketing projects (10 per cent)

2.1 Describe the main stages of a project and the roles of people involved at each stage.

2.2 Describe the main characteristics of successful and less-successful projects and identify the main reasons for success or failure.

2.3 Explain the importance of, and techniques for, establishing the project's scope, definition and goals.

2.4 Use the main techniques available for planning, scheduling, resourcing and controlling activities on a project.

2.5 Explain the importance of preparing budgets and techniques for controlling progress throughout a project to ensure it is completed on time and within budget.

2.6 Explain the main techniques for evaluating the effectiveness of a project on its completion.

Element 3: Managing knowledge and delivering marketing research projects (20 per cent)

3.1 Explain the concept, and give examples, of the application of information and knowledge management, highlighting the role of marketing and employees within the organization.

3.2 Design a research project aimed at providing information as part of a marketing audit or for marketing and business decisions.

3.3 Manage a marketing research project by gathering relevant information on time and within the agreed budget.

3.4 Make arrangements to record, store and, if appropriate, update information in the MkIS, a database created for the purpose or another system.

3.5 Analyse and interpret information and present, as a written report or oral presentation, appropriate conclusions or recommendations that inform the marketing and business decisions for which the research was undertaken.

3.6 Review and evaluate the effectiveness of the activities and the role of the individual and team in this process.

Element 4: Developing and implementing marketing plans (20 per cent)

4.1 Develop an operational marketing plan, selecting an appropriate marketing mix for an organization operating in any context such as FMCG, business-to-business (supply chain), large or capital project-based, services, voluntary and not-for-profit, or sales support (e.g. SMEs).

4.2 Use the main techniques available for planning, scheduling and resourcing activities within the plan.

4.3 Identify appropriate measures for evaluating and controlling the marketing plan.

4.4 Review and evaluate the effectiveness of planning activities and the role of the individual and team in this process.

Element 5: Delivering communications and customer service programmes (20 per cent)

5.1 Plan the design, development, execution and evaluation of communications campaigns by a team of marketers, including external agencies and suppliers.

5.2 Use appropriate marketing communications to develop relationships or communicate with a range of stakeholders.

5.3 Manage and monitor the provision of effective customer service.

5.4 Use marketing communications to provide support for members of a marketing channel.

5.5 Use marketing communications techniques for an internal marketing plan to support management of change within an organization.

5.6 Review and evaluate the effectiveness of communications activities and the role of the individual and team in this process.

Related key skills

Key skill	Relevance to unit knowledge and skills
Communication	Develop a research brief
	Develop a research proposal or plan
	Present research results to decision-makers
	Present and justify a marketing or communications plan
	Produce effective marketing communications
	Assess the impact of a campaign
Application of number	Determine information requirements for a business or marketing decision
	Plan a research project
	Use quantitative research methods, analysis and calculations
	Conduct a marketing audit
	Use forecasting techniques
	Set objectives
	Set and justify a budget
	Forecast likely response rates
	Measure marketing performance and communications effectiveness
Information technology	Use IT tools for research planning
	Use IT tools to acquire, store, retrieve and communicate research data
	Use IT tools for forecasting, modelling options, budgeting and measuring performance for a marketing plan or a communications campaign
Working with others	Work as part of a team in planning, undertaking, and measuring and evaluating results for a research, planning or a communications project
Improving own learning and performance	Review current capabilities
	Identify opportunities and set realistic targets for development and learning
	Plan how these targets will be met (methods, timescales, resources)
	Use a variety of methods for learning
	Seek feedback, monitor performance and modify approach
	Assess effectiveness of learning and development approach
Problem solving	Use research to establish the critical features of a business or marketing problem
	Formulate a marketing solution within defined constraints
	Select a marketing mix appropriate to a specific context
	Recommend changes to marketing processes
	Formulate a communication solution within defined constraints

Assessment

As the summative assessment at this level, the assessment will require students to demonstrate knowledge and skills in all areas covered by the four units of Professional Diploma. CIM will normally offer two forms of assessment for this unit from which study centres may choose: written examination (a 'midi' case study) and an integrative assignment. Specimen papers and guidance on the structure, format and approach of these assessments will be published separately.

CIM may also recognize, or make joint awards for, units at an equivalent level undertaken with other professional marketing bodies and educational institutions.

Recommended support materials

In addition to the texts from the other units at Professional Diploma, the following texts and resources are available to support this unit.

Core texts

Boddy, D. (2002) *Management: An Introduction*, 2nd revised edition, London: FT Prentice Hall.

Dibb, S., Simkin, L. Pride, W. and Ferrell, O. (2005). Marketing concepts and strategies 5th European edition. Boston, Houghton Mifflin.

Martin, P. (2002) *Getting Started in Project Management*, Chichester: John Wiley.

Workbooks

Williams, J. and Curtis, T. (2006) *Marketing Management in Practice*, Oxford: Butterworth-Heinemann.

BPP (2003) *Marketing Management study text*, London: BPP Publishing.

Supplementary readings

Adair, J. (2002) *Inspiring Leadership*, London: Thorogood.

Andersen, E.S. (2004) *Goal directed project management: effective techniques and strategies*, 3rd edition, London: Kogan Page.

Belbin, R.M. (1996) *Management Teams: Why they Succeed or Fail*, Oxford: Butterworth-Heinemann.

Brown, A. (1998) O*rganizational Culture*, 2nd edition, London: FT Prentice Hall.

Cameron, S. (2004) *The MBA handbook: skills for mastering management*, Harlow: FT Prentice Hall. (Particularly suitable for candidates studying via the project route)

Cameron, S. (2005) *The business student's handbook: learning skills for study and employment*, Harlow: FT Prentice Hall. (Particularly suitable for candidates studying via the project route)

Drummond, G., Ensor, J. and Ashford, R. (2003) *Strategic marketing*, 2nd edition, Oxford: Butterworth Heinemann.

Hilton, S. and Gibbons, G. (2002) *Good Business: Your World Needs You*, London: Texere.

Lancaster, G. and Reynolds, P. (2005) *Management of marketing*, Oxford: Butterworth Heinemann.

Parker, C. and Stone, B. (2002) *Developing management skills for leadership*, Harlow: FT Prentice Hall.

Trompenaars, F. (1997) *Riding the waves of culture*, 2nd edition, London: Nicholas Brealey.

BPP (2006) *Marketing management: practice and revision kit*, London: BPP Publishing.

BH (2006) *CIM Revision cards: marketing management in practice*, Oxford: BH/Elsevier.

Trompenaars, F. and Hampden–Turner, C. (1997) *Riding the Waves of Culture*, 2nd revised edition, London: Nicholas Brealey.

Woodcock, M. (1989) *Team Development Manual*, 2nd revised edition, Aldershot: Gower.

Marketing and management journals

Students can keep abreast of developments in the academic field of marketing by reference to the main marketing journals, a selection of which are listed in the Appendix to this document.

Press

Students will be expected to have access to current examples of marketing campaigns and so should be sure to keep up-to-date with the appropriate marketing and quality daily press. A selection of marketing press titles is given in the Appendix to this document.

Websites

A list of websites that tutors and students may find useful is shown in the Appendix at the end of this document.

Additional resources

There are many useful diagnostic tools for those interested in learning more about themselves and the workings of teams, a few of which are mentioned here. Permission should be obtained from the appropriate sources for use of these tools.

- o Learning styles questionnaire, Honey and Mumford
- o Team roles questionnaire, Belbin
- o Leadership style questionnaire, Hersey, Blanchard, Reddin, Blake, Mouton
- o Work Motivation Inventory, Chartwell Bratt
- o Strengths Deployment Inventory, E. Porter, S. Maloney.

Overview and rationale

The Marketing Management in Practice syllabus requires a broad and practical demonstration of marketing at an operational level and an awareness of the strategic context. It provides an opportunity for students to develop and implement an operational marketing plan, so applying, as part of a team, the theory of research, planning and marketing communications provided in the previous three units. This unit also provides the final assessment of students' ability to create an operational marketing plan. As such, it forms an important measure of the students' ability to meet organizations' requirements of an operational marketer.

From an educational standpoint, this unit seeks to integrate learning from the full Professional Diploma syllabus. As such, it is best suited to delivery after the other units of the Professional Diploma. It should be lively and fun for all involved. It rounds off the Professional Diploma and so provides a springboard for Professional PG Diploma at the next level, which goes on to develop students for a role in strategic marketing.

Approach

Marketing Management in Practice is about developing and managing teams to add value to the organization's activities and deliver effective results. Like members of other functions and disciplines within organizations, marketers work towards departmental and broader organizational objectives. They work in teams, both within the marketing function and, importantly, with people in other functions.

It is important to recognize that the context within which marketers are operating is continually changing as a result of both external and internal influences. No organization is detached from international influences, even if the organization does not have to deal with international customers. Organizations source materials from around the globe, access international markets from a desk, compete with other organizations from around the world, and imitate global behaviour. It is, therefore, appropriate in this unit to cover international issues as part of everyday marketing life in organizations.

Marketers and marketing managers must be able to work effectively themselves, for example managing time and problem solving. They must also be able to manage and motivate people and teams to produce results. Using Adair's model of leadership, effective team performance is contingent on a balance between:

- The needs of the task.
- The needs of the individuals within the team.
- The maintenance needs of the team as a whole.

Syllabus content

The syllabus for this unit uses Adair's concept. It provides underpinning theory on managing teams to help with managing individual needs and team needs to get the most from the team. It also provides basic project management techniques to help with managing the task. These two elements provide the final skills and knowledge for marketers to develop and implement marketing plans at an operational level. The remainder of the syllabus for this unit is about the development and implementation of an operational marketing plan, including the management of information, communications and human resources. In other words, students should apply within a marketing team the theory of marketing research and information, planning and communications covered in the earlier units. This should be achieved through a project.

A syllabus can contain only so much and this syllabus assumes that, on entry to the unit, students have the skills to manage themselves (defined in the key skill 'Improving own learning and performance') and the principles of motivation, leadership, power and influence relevant to the team context. If students do not have these skills, then study centres may wish to impose additional required learning or provide additional sessions and materials.

Element 1: Managing people and teams

This element provides the underpinning knowledge required for the selection, development and maintenance of effective marketing teams. It is particularly important to stress the organizational and global context within which marketing teams are operating and how different organizations adopt different approaches to marketing depending on their context and culture. In cases where this subject is taught by a HR tutor, it is important that it is set within a marketing context. This subject is developed further in the Professional PG Diploma. It is also important to use this element to build on the Key Skills 'Working with others' and 'Improving own knowledge and performance'.

Element 2: Techniques for managing marketing projects and activities

Managing the planning and performance of a marketing task by a team requires skills in planning, scheduling, directing, motivating and monitoring. The techniques of project management equip marketing managers to manage marketing activities and projects effectively. This element provides the underpinning knowledge of the techniques, which are then applied in the marketing activities that make up the rest of the syllabus for this unit.

Element 3: Managing knowledge and delivering market research projects

Knowledge management is about people. We need to motivate and enthuse the people we manage with a willingness and desire to share and exchange knowledge. We cannot do this by simply presenting them with a piece of IT equipment. It requires a cultural norm of open communication and informing and sharing knowledge and motivating and rewarding knowledge sharing that benefits the business.

This element builds on the underpinning knowledge developed in the Marketing Research and Information unit by providing students with the opportunity to plan and undertake or commission a research project as a team activity as part of a marketing audit feeding into a marketing plan or business decision.

Element 4: Developing and implementing marketing plans

This element requires effective teamwork and a good understanding of the marketing planning process and techniques to produce successful outcomes. This element builds on the underpinning knowledge developed in the Marketing Planning unit by providing students with the opportunity to develop and implement a marketing plan as a team activity. It is important that the implementation issues are explored in some depth. Apart from providing students with valuable learning, this will test the realism of the plans they have developed.

Element 5: Delivering communications and customer service programmes

This element builds on the underpinning knowledge developed in the Marketing Communications unit by providing students with the opportunity to manage campaigns or communication programmes as a team activity using appropriate techniques to develop or maintain stakeholder relationships, manage the provision of customer service, provide support for a marketing channel or deliver an internal marketing plan.

Delivery approach

This syllabus covers approximately 45 hours of tutor-directed learning, usually fifteen 3-hour sessions if delivered face-to-face. As a guide, study centres should allocate up to one third of these sessions to cover the underpinning theory on and techniques for managing teams and managing projects and any coaching required on the assessment. These can, and indeed should, be active sessions with students using these techniques rather than just lectures.

Two thirds of the sessions should be allocated to a significant practical project involving the formulation and implementation of an operational marketing plan. This should cover the management of information, communications and human resources. It is important that these sessions are of a practical nature. All the necessary theory should have been covered in the previous three units, so the emphasis in this unit should be the application of this theory within a marketing team. The nature of the project undertaken may depend on which form of assessment the students will use. A typical project will consist of:

- ○ Planning the project to be undertaken to meet the brief given.
- ○ Undertaking the task. This will involve collecting and analysing information and developing a marketing plan.
- ○ Planning, scheduling and resourcing marketing activities within the plan, identifying and overcoming problems during implementation.
- ○ Measuring and evaluating the outcomes.
- ○ Reflecting on the performance of the team and the individuals in it.

Additional resources (Syllabus – Professional Diploma In Marketing)

Introduction

Texts to support the individual units are listed in the syllabus for each unit. This Appendix shows a list of marketing journals, press and websites that tutors and students may find useful in supporting their studies at Professional Diploma.

Marketing journals

Students can keep abreast of developments in the academic field of marketing by reference to the main marketing journals.

- ○ *Corporate Reputation Review* – Henry Stewart
- ○ *European Journal of Marketing* – Emerald
- ○ *Harvard Business Review* – Harvard
- ○ *International Journal of Advertising* – WARC
- ○ *International Journal of Corporate Communications* – Emerald
- ○ *International Journal of Market Research* – WARC
- ○ *Journal of Consumer Behaviour An International Review* – Henry Stewart
- ○ *Journal of the Academy of Marketing Science* – Sage Publications
- ○ *Journal of Marketing* – American Marketing – Assoc. Pubs Group
- ○ *Journal of Marketing Communications* – Routledge
- ○ *Journal of Marketing Management* – Westburn Pubs Ltd

- o *International Journal of Market Research* – NTC Pubs
- o *Journal of Product and Brand Management* – Emerald
- o *Journal of Services Marketing* – Emerald
- o *Marketing Review* – Westburn Pubs Ltd

Press

Students will be expected to have access to current examples of marketing campaigns and so should be sure to keep up-to-date with the appropriate marketing and quality daily press, including:

- o *Campaign* – Haymarket
- o *Internet Business* – Haymarket
- o *Marketing* – Haymarket
- o *Marketing Business* – Chartered Institute of Marketing
- o *Marketing Week* – Centaur
- o *Revolution* – Haymarket

Websites

The Chartered Institute of Marketing

www.cim.co.uk	The CIM site with information and access to learning support for students
www.cim.co.uk/learningzone	Full details of all that's new in CIM's educational offer including specimen answers and Hot Topics

Publications on-line

www.revolution.haynet.com	Revolution magazine
www.marketing.haynet.com	Marketing magazine
www.FT.com	A wealth of information for cases (now charging)
www.IPA.co.uk	Need to register – communication resources
www.booksites.net	Financial Times/Prentice Hall Text websites

Sources of useful information

www.acnielsen.co.uk	AC Nielsen – excellent for research
http://advertising.utexas.edu/world/	Resources for advertising and marketing professionals, students, and tutors
www.bized.com	Case studies
www.corporateinformation.com	Worldwide sources listed by country
www.esomar.nl	European Body representing Research organizations – useful for guidelines on research ethics and approaches
www.dma.org.uk	The Direct Marketing Association
www.eiu.com	The Economist Intelligence Unit
www.euromonitor.com	Euromonitor consumer markets
www.europa.eu.int	The European Commission's extensive range of statistics and reports relating to EU and member countries
www.managementhelp.org/research/research.htm	Part of the 'Free Management Library' – explaining research methods
www.marketresearch.org.uk	The MRS site with information and access to learning support for students – useful links on ethics and code of conduct
www.mmc.gov.uk	Summaries of Competition Commission reports

www.oecd.org	OECD statistics and other information relating to member nations including main economic indicators
www.quirks.com	An American source of information on marketing research issues and projects
www.statistics.gov.uk	UK Government statistics
www.un.org	United Nations publish statistics on member nations
www.worldbank.org	World bank economic, social and natural resource indicators for over 200 countries. Includes over 600 indicators covering GNP per capita, growth, economic statistics, etc

Case sites

www.bluelagoon.co.uk	Case – SME website address
www.ebay.com	On-line auction – buyer behaviour
www.glenfiddich.com	Interesting site for case and branding
www.interflora.co.uk	e-commerce direct ordering
www.moorcroft.co.uk	Good for relationship marketing
www.ribena.co.uk	Excellent targeting and history of comms

© CIM 2005

Index